Research and Development in Intelligent Systems XXII

Max Bramer, Frans Coenen and
Tony Allen (Eds)

Research and Development in Intelligent Systems XXII

Proceedings of AI-2005, the Twenty-fifth SGAI International Conference on Innovative Techniques and Applications of Artificial Intelligence, Cambridge, UK, December 2005

 Springer

Professor Max Bramer, BSc, PhD, CEng, FBCS, FIEE, FRSA
Faculty of Technology, University of Portsmouth, Portsmouth, UK

Dr Frans Coenen, PhD
Department of Computer Science, University of Liverpool, Liverpool, UK

Dr Tony Allen, PhD
Nottingham Trent University, UK

British Library Cataloguing in Publication Data
A catalogue record for this book is available from the British Library

ISBN-10: 1-84628-225-X   Printed on acid-free paper
ISBN-13: 978-1-84628-225-6

Printed in the United Kingdom

9 8 7 6 5 4 3 2 1

Springer Science+Business Media
springer.com

TECHNICAL PROGRAMME CHAIR'S INTRODUCTION

M.A.BRAMER
University of Portsmouth, UK

This volume comprises the refereed technical papers presented at AI-2005, the Twenty-fifth SGAI International Conference on Innovative Techniques and Applications of Artificial Intelligence, held in Cambridge in December 2005. The conference was organised by SGAI, the British Computer Society Specialist Group on Artificial Intelligence.

The papers in this volume present new and innovative developments in the field, divided into sections on Information Learning, Integration and Management, AI and the World Wide Web, Networks and Biologically Motivated AI, Multi-Agent Systems, Case-Based Reasoning, Knowledge Discovery in Data and Reasoning and Decision Making.

This year's prize for the best refereed technical paper was won by a paper entitled *Reusing JessTab Rules in Protégé* by David Corsar and Derek Sleeman (University of Aberdeen, UK). SGAI gratefully acknowledges the long-term sponsorship of Hewlett-Packard Laboratories (Bristol) for this prize, which goes back to the 1980s.

This is the twenty-second volume in the *Research and Development* series. The Application Stream papers are published as a companion volume under the title *Applications and Innovations in Intelligent Systems XIII*.

On behalf of the conference organising committee I should like to thank all those who contributed to the organisation of this year's technical programme, in particular the programme committee members, the executive programme committee and our administrator Collette Jackson.

Max Bramer
Technical Programme Chair, AI-2005

ACKNOWLEDGEMENTS

AI-2005 CONFERENCE COMMITTEE

Dr Tony Allen, Nottingham Trent University	(Conference Chair)
Dr Alun Preece, University of Aberdeen	(Deputy Conference Chair, Electronic Services)
Dr Nirmalie Wiratunga, The Robert Gordon University	(Poster Session Organiser)
Professor Adrian Hopgood, Nottingham Trent University	(Workshop Organiser)
Professor Ann Macintosh, Napier University	(Application Programme Chair)
Richard Ellis, Stratum Management Ltd	(Deputy Application Programme Chair)
Professor Max Bramer, University of Portsmouth	(Technical Programme Chair)
Dr Frans Coenen, University of Liverpool	(Deputy Conference Chair, Local Arrangements and Deputy Technical Programme Chair)
Rosemary Gilligan	(Research Student Liaison)

TECHNICAL EXECUTIVE PROGRAMME COMMITTEE

Professor Max Bramer, University of Portsmouth (Chair)
Dr Frans Coenen, University of Liverpool (Vice-Chair)
Dr Tony Allen, Nottingham Trent University
Mr John Kingston, University of Edinburgh
Dr Peter Lucas, University of Nijmegen, The Netherlands
Dr Alun Preece, University of Aberdeen
Dr Nirmalie Wiratunga, The Robert Gordon University

TECHNICAL PROGRAMME COMMITTEE

Barry O'Sullivan (University College Cork)

Alun Preece (University of Aberdeen)

James Reilly (University College Dublin)

Gerrit Renker (The Robert Gordon University)

Juan Jose Rodriguez (University of Burgos)

María Dolores Rodríguez-Moreno (Universidad de Alcalá)

Fernando Sáenz Pérez (Universidad Complutense de Madrid)

Miguel A. Salido (Universidad Politécnica de Valencia)

Jon Timmis (University of York)

Kai Ming Ting (Monash University)

Andrew Tuson (City University)

M.R.C. van Dongen (University College Cork)

Marcel van Gerven (University of Nijmegen, The Netherlands)

Graham Winstanley (University of Brighton)

Nirmalie Wiratunga (The Robert Gordon University)

Fei Ling Woon (University of Greenwich)

Yi Zhang (University of Aberdeen)

CONTENTS

SESSION 5a: KNOWLEDGE DISCOVERY IN DATA

SESSION 5b: REASONING AND DECISION MAKING

Note: x indicates SGAI recognition award

TECHNICAL KEYNOTE ADDRESS

Computational Intelligence for Bioinformatics: The Knowledge Engineering Approach

Prof. Nikola Kasabov

Knowledge Engineering and Discovery Research Institute, KEDRI
Auckland University of Technology, Auckland, New Zealand
nkasabov@aut.ac.nz, **www.kedri.info**

Abstract – This presentation introduces challenging problems in Bioinformatics (BI) and then applies methods of Computational Intelligence (CI) to offer possible solutions. The main focus of the talk is on how CI can facilitate discoveries from biological data and the extraction of new knowledge.

Methods of evolving knowledge–based neural networks, hybrid neuro-evolutionary systems, kernel methods, local and personalized modeling techniques, characterized by adaptive learning, rule extraction and evolutionary optimization [1], are emphasized among the other traditional CI methods [2].

CI solutions to BI problems such as: DNA sequence analysis, microarray gene expression analysis and profiling, RNAi classification, protein structure prediction, gene regulatory network discovery, medical prognostic systems, modeling gene-neuronal relationship, and others are presented and illustrated.

Fundamental issues in CI such as: dimensionality reduction and feature extraction, model creation and model validation, model adaptation, model optimization, knowledge extraction, inductive versus transductive reasoning, global versus local models, and others are addressed and illustrated on the above BI problems. A comparative analysis of different CI methods applied to the same problems is presented in an attempt to identify generic and specific applicability of the CI methods. A comprehensive environment NeuCom (**www.theneucom.com**) is used to illustrate the CI methods.

Computational neurogenetic modeling [3,4] is introduced as a future direction for the creation of new, biologically plausible CI methods for BI and Neuroinformatics applications. These models can help discover patterns of dynamic interaction of genes and neuronal functions and diseases.

Keywords: Computational Intelligence, Adaptive knowledge-based neural networks, Evolving connectionist systems, Bionformatics, Neuroinformatics, Personalised modeling, Computational neurogenetic modeling.

References
[1] N.Kasabov, Evolving Connectionist Systems: Methods and Applications in Bioinformatics, Brain Study and Intelligent Machines, Springer Verlag, 2002 (www.springer.de)
[2] N.Kasabov, Foundations of neural networks, fuzzy systems and knowledge engineering, MIT Press, 1996 (www.mitpress.edu)

[3] N.Kasabov and L.Benuskova, Computational Neurogenetics, *Journal of Computational and Theoretical Nanoscience*, vol.1, No.1, American Scientific Publishers, 2004 (www.aspbs.com)

[4] N.Kasabov, L.Benuskova, S.Wysosky, Computational neurogenetic modelling: Gene networks within neural networks, Proc. IJCNN 2004, Budapest, 25-29 July, IEEE Press

Biodata: Professor Nikola Kasabov is the Founding Director and the Chief Scientist of the Knowledge Engineering and Discovery Research Institute KEDRI, Auckland (www.kedri.info/). He holds a Chair of Knowledge Engineering at the School of Computer and Information Sciences at Auckland University of Technology. He is a Fellow of the Royal Society of New Zealand, Fellow of the New Zealand Computer Society, a Senior Member of IEEE and a member of the T12 committee of the IFIP. He holds MSc and PhD from the Technical University of Sofia, Bulgaria. His main research interests are in the areas of: intelligent information systems, soft computing, neuro-computing, bioinformatics, brain study, speech and image processing, novel methods for data mining and knowledge discovery. He has published more than 320 publications that include 15 books, 80 journal papers, 50 book chapters, 25 patents and numerous conference papers. He has extensive academic experience at various academic and research organisations: University of Otago, New Zealand; University of Essex, UK; University of Trento, Italy; Technical University of Sofia, Bulgaria; University of California at Berkeley; RIKEN Brain Science Institute, Tokyo; University of Keiserslautern, Germany; Delft University of Technology, and others. He is one of the founding board members of the Asia Pacific Neural Network Assembly (APNNA) and was its President in 1997/98. Kasabov is on the editorial boards of 7 international journals and has been on the Program Committees of more than 50 international conferences in the last 10 years. He chaired the series of ANNES conferences (1993-2001). Kasabov is a co-founder of Pacific Edge Biotechnology Ltd (www.peblnz.com). More information of Prof. Kasabov can be found on the Web site: http://www.kedri.info. He can be contacted on: nkasabov@aut.ac.nz.

BEST TECHNICAL PAPER

Reusing JessTab Rules in Protégé

D Corsar, D Sleeman
Computing Science Department, University of Aberdeen
Aberdeen, UK
{dcorsar,sleeman}@csd.abdn.ac.uk

Abstract

Protégé provides a complete ontology and knowledge base management tool. Along with JESS, JessTab provides one method of rule based reasoning over a Protégé ontology and knowledge base. However once JessTab rules have been created for a knowledge base, they are explicitly tied to it as they name particular classes and slots, which greatly hinders their reuse with further knowledge bases. We have developed a two phase process and a supporting tool to support the reuse of JessTab rule sets. The first phase involves changing the class and slot references in the rule set into an abstract reference; the second phase involves automatically mapping between the abstract rules and further knowledge bases. Once mappings have been defined and applied for all the classes and slots in the abstract rules, the new rule set can then be run against the new knowledge base. We have satisfactorily tested our tool with several ontologies and associated rule sets; moreover, some of these tests have identified possible future improvements to the tool.

1 Introduction

Ontologies have become one of the most widely used forms of domain knowledge capture. When used effectively they provide us with an explicit definition and a common understanding of a domain and the properties, relationships and behaviours of its components that can be communicated between people and machines.

RDF and RDFS [14], DAML+OIL and OWL [1] are representational formalisms for describing ontologies. Other languages provide mechanisms for querying these representations, for example RDQL [21]. Similarly, languages such as SWRL [9] and the various RuleML projects [25] allow one to formally specify rules for reasoning with the content of an ontology. While these formalisms provide a way to capture queries, an inference engine is still required to run them. One rule engine currently growing in popularity is JESS, the Java Expert System Shell; for examples of two recent projects involving JESS see [8] and [12].

JESS was originally developed by the Sandia National Laboratories as a Java implementation of the popular C Language Integrated Production System (CLIPS) [3], although it has since evolved into a powerful Java rule engine and scripting language in its own right [7]. The rise in JESS's use may be in part due to the useful JessTab [5] plugin for the widely used Protégé[1] [24] ontology editor which allows developers to run JESS rules against an ontology created and populated in Protégé.

1.1 Ontology Tied Rules

As with CLIPS, JESS requires explicit definitions of the data types that will be used in the form of templates. Conveniently, there is a mapping command in JessTab which automatically produces these templates based on the classes and slots of a Protégé ontology. Along with the templates, JESS requires a set of facts (which are instantiations of the templates) to reason over. Again, helpfully the mapping command automatically creates facts from the corresponding instances which are defined as part of a Protégé project. When writing JessTab rules, the developer refers to these templates and facts as if they had been created as part of the main JessTab program. In doing this, the rules are explicitly tied to the ontology as they are required to name particular classes and slots.

Having the rules tied to a particular ontology in this way is unavoidable, but it greatly hinders reusing a set of JessTab rules developed for one ontology with additional ontologies/knowledge bases. This is because reuse of a set of rules requires one to carry out a manual mapping between the class and slot names in the JessTab rules and those in the second (and subsequent) ontologies/knowledge bases. Further, this would be a tedious and very error prone process.

For this reason, we have developed a plugin for Protégé, which supports the developer with this task. Given a set of JessTab rules (JessTab rules differ slightly from standard JESS rules as they need to link to the Protégé ontology) and a further ontology, our tool attempts to automatically map concept names featured in the rules to concept names in the "new" ontology. To achieve this, we make use of techniques used in the ontology mapping, merging and alignment sub-fields, namely partial and exact string comparisons and synonym look-up in a lexical database (WordNet [6]). We also provide facilities for the user to define mappings manually.

In section 2 we discuss some current ontology mapping and merging tools; in section 3 we outline two scenarios where our tool could be used; in section 4 we briefly outline our tool's functionality; in section 5 we describe experiments we have performed and report some results. In section 6 we discuss some modifications inspired by our experiments which should improve our tool's performance and section 7 concludes this report with a summary of our findings.

2 Related Work

As mentioned above, we make use of techniques originally developed in the ontology mapping, merging and alignment fields. There have been various approaches to these tasks including use of specially designed algebras [17], use of

---

[1]Protégé-2000 and its successors up to the latest version, Protégé 3.1

lexical analysis of the concept names in the two ontologies, as well as having the user manually define mappings with the aid of a specially designed user interface. Below we focus on the latter two approaches.

A popular web-based ontology management tool with the facility to assist with merging is Stanford KSL's Chimaera [15]. Chimaera provides limited support with ontology mapping, by allowing multiple ontologies to be loaded, automatically examining their concept names and providing the user with a list of similarly named concepts. The principal mapping approach used here is the detection of common substrings. This approach is very effective for pairs of concepts that have related names, but clearly is ineffective when the same concepts are expressed using synonyms, for example "person" and "individual."

Another Stanford product, PROMPT [19] provides a suit of ontology management tools, in the form of a further Protégé plugin. One of these tools, iPROMPT [18], was developed as an interactive ontology-merging tool, which assists the user by providing suggestions for merging, analyzing any resulting conflicts and suggesting relevant conflict resolution strategies. The latter two functions are concerned only with a pre-determined list of conflicts, and are triggered in response to the user selecting one of the suggested changes.

When determining its suggested mappings, iPROMPT makes use of two factors: a measure of linguistic similarity between names, combined with the internal structure of concepts and their location in the ontology. The linguistic similarity measures of iPROMPT are based solely on substring matching of the various concept names; it makes no use of a lexical database for matching synonyms, and so consequently suffers similar problems to Chimaera.

One tool which uses lexical databases is ONION [16]. The ONION algorithm was designed to address the problem of resolving semantic heterogeneity amongst ontologies. Mitra and Wiederhold implemented two methods of addressing this task: one based, like ours, around a lexical database, while the other uses domain specific corpora. Briefly ONION's algorithm evaluates two expressions for similarity and assigns them a similarity value. When the two terms being compared are not identical, ONION makes use of either a thesaurus (WordNet) or a corpus in assigning the value. If the value is above a user set threshold, then the mapping is accepted.

The results of Mitra and Wiederhold's experiments indicated that generally the corpus based mapping approach produced more accurate mappings than the thesaurus technique. However, the main difficulty with the corpus approach is generating the corpus. In their experiments Mitra and Wiederhold used the Google [10] search engine to find sources that were both relevant to the domain of the ontologies and contained some of their key concepts. Various sized corpora were used ranging from 50 to 1000 webpages. Although this approach provided the more accurate results, the initial investment of time and effort necessary to acquire such a corpus would no doubt be very large, making this an infeasible approach for supporting the mappings between many domains.

3   Example Scenarios

There are many scenarios where reuse of an existing set of rules could be beneficial. Practically any developer building a new application requiring a set of similar or identical rules to those used in a previously developed application could benefit from the use of our tool. By semi-automating the rule reuse process, the developer could benefit from, amongst other things, reduced design, implementation and testing costs.

Below we outline two examples where our tool has been used. The first example involves building simulations of two seemingly disparate areas - shopping and water treatment, while the second emphasises the reuse of a problem solving method (ruleset) in two distinct route planning applications.

3.1   Simulating Shopping and Water Treatment

Our first example involves the creation of two different simulations, which at their core use similar procedures, meaning their development could be achieved by using our approach. At a very abstract level, the day to day activity of a retail store is

1. it receives stock from some supplier(s),
2. it stores this stock either in a store room or on the shelves,
3. customers buy items reducing the stock level,
4. it orders new stock,
5. return to step 1.

In this problem, the environment (the retail store) can be easily represented by an ontology. Likewise the processes noted above can be simulated by a series of JessTab rules coded to run against that ontology.

At a similarly abstract level, water treatment plants feature similar underlying processes

1. receives water from sources,
2. stores it in treatment tanks,
3. passes the results onto desired locations,
4. signals that it can process more water,
5. return to step 1.

Again, the environment (the water treatment plant) can easily be represented by an ontology and the processes by JessTab rules. However, as the underlying processes in water treatment are in essence very similar to those of the store, our tool could be used to reconfigure the problem solver (the JessTab rules) implemented for the store to provide similar functionality for the water treatment plant.

Although it is unlikely that the second set of rules will provide all the detail required for a complete simulation of a water treatment plant, it could form the basis for such a simulation, and in so doing should reduce the development costs.

3.2 Route Planning

Our previous example illustrated reuse of the same set of rules in building simulations in two different domains. Our second example is similar and illustrates the reuse of a route planning problem solver with two distinct applications, based on two different ontologies.

A highly researched field, route planning, has many applications ranging from the classical vehicle route finding problem [4], to various tasks in robotics and artificial intelligence, to determining flow rates in IP networks [2].

Numerous algorithms have been developed over the years (for example A*, Iterative Deepening A* (IDA*) [13], and Recursive Best First Search (RBFS)) to solve, what is essentially a search problem. A typical scenario involves finding the best path from one location to another in an environment (usually represented as a graph, in which the nodes represent states and the arcs represent pathways). The notion of "best path" can mean different things in different applications, and so algorithms typically incorporate a suitably configured evaluation metric when deciding which potential path to investigate first.

Although typically a graph is used, it is possible to represent the environment as an ontology. Classes can represent locations with attributes containing details of locations reachable from it (with classes representing pathways). Given such an ontology, a route planning algorithm could then be implemented as a series of JessTab rules to perform planning based on the ontology.

For example a retail company could use an ontology to represent its warehouse, describing the items in it, and their locations relative to one another. A JessTab rule base could be used to calculate the shortest route around the warehouse when collecting items to fulfil orders. The same set of rules could later be reused with a second ontology representing a courier company's deliveries and their locations. Our tool could help tailor the original planning algorithm for use against the deliveries ontology to calculate the cheapest route for the courier to take when delivering orders.

Although the above two examples are discussed at a highly abstract level they serve to illustrate two separate uses for our tool. Both show how two tasks, which may not necessary at first appear to be related, can make use of the same underlying JessTab rules. Using our tool to achieve this reuse would simplify the process for the developer and consequentially enable him to benefit from reduced development and implementation costs for the second, and subsequent, tasks.

4 The JessTab Rule Reuse Process

We have developed a reuse process composed of two distinct phases. The first phase consists of two actions: the extraction of class names, slot names, and slot types from the relevant ontology[2]; and the generalisation of this informa-

---

[2]If the relevant ontology is not available, the class and slot names could be extracted from the rule set, however the slot data type information would be not be available.

tion to produce a set of ontology independent rules. During the second phase the independent rules are mapped to the new ontology to which they are to be applied. Figure 1 shows a representation of these processes, including the relations between the two phases. Below we discuss the two phases in more detail.

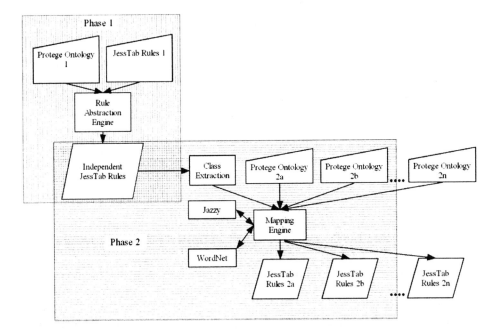

Figure 1: Illustration of the JessTab rule reuse process

4.1   Phase 1 - Rule Abstraction

The rule abstraction phase is the first stage and is identified in Figure 1 by the vertical stripe filled box in the upper left corner labelled "Phase 1." During this phase a set of JessTab rules and the corresponding ontology are passed to the Rule Abstraction Engine. Here the tool extracts from the ontology class names, and in the case of slots, both their names and their types. The JessTab rules are then rewritten replacing each class and slot name with a more general form. This removes all the references to the original ontology, making the resulting rule set more abstract and ontology-independent.

The abstract forms of both the class and slot names have a similar structure. Abstracted class names consist of a predefined prefix concatenated with the original class name. The default prefix is simply "XX_", so for example every reference to the class name "Person" in the rules is replaced by the string "XX_Person". Slots are treated similarly; however their abstracted name consists of the prefix, concatenated with the slot name, concatenated with the slot data type. For example an Integer slot with the name "age" is replaced by the string "XX_age_Integer", a slot of type String with the name "title" is replaced by "XX_title_String."

There are several reasons for transforming the names in this manner: the first is to ease the extraction of the ontological information from the rules in the second (mapping) phase; the second is to provide slot data type information to the mapping stage to enhance the automatically suggested mappings; also this naming convention is more helpful to the user than cryptic abstract names (for example "class1," "slot1," "slot2," etc.).

4.2   Phase 2 - Rule to Ontology Mapping

After successful completion of the rule abstraction phase, the independent rules contain enough information to enable the Class Extraction component of Phase 2 to build a list of the classes (and their slots). Combined with a second ontology we have enough information to attempt to map the classes (and slots) extracted from the rules to the new ontology. This phase is illustrated by the horizontal stripe filled box in the lower right corner of Figure 1 labelled "Phase 2."

The basic mapping algorithm is:

1. Extract all the classes and their associated slot information from the abstract JessTab rules and store them in a list.
2. For each class extracted from the abstract JessTab rules
   (a) Find the most suitable class in the new ontology to map to, and suggest the individual (slot and class name) mappings.
3. Update the rules to reflect suggested mappings and allow the user to complete and/or correct the mappings.

Clearly the key step is 2a - finding the most suitable mappings for the classes. We derive our suitability ratings by applying some commonly used lexical analysis techniques - namely string comparison, spell checking (provided by Jazzy [26]) and synonym lookup in a lexical database (WordNet accessed via JWord [11]). For a mapping to be suggested the calculated similarity rating for two names (either class names or slot names) must exceed a threshold set by the user. Furthermore, slot mappings are only suggested for slots with the same data type. This means that if a slot extracted from the abstract JessTab rules has type String it will only be mapped to slots in the ontology of type String and not, for example, to those of type Integer or Float. This is to ensure no data type errors occur when the rules are run against the ontology. When searching for potential mappings, our tool compares every slot of every extracted class, along with the class name, with those in the ontology. If any two slots are suitable for mapping they are given a classification based on how that mapping was achieved (the classification mechanisms are discussed below). At this level a mapping simply consists of a *from string* (the name from the abstract JessTab rules), a *to string* (the name from the new ontology) and the mapping classification. Once this process has been performed for all the classes, the mappings which have the highest values and which maintain a unique mapping between a rule-class and an ontology-class, are recommended to the user as the most likely mapping for his configuration.

We define three distinct mappings operators; these are:

1. *Direct mapping.* Direct mappings consist of two strings that are identical, or where one has been determined to be a minor variant of the other. A typical example is the mapping from "XX_age_Integer" to the Integer slot with name "age".

2. *Constituent mapping.* In constituent mappings, the constituents[3] of each string are extracted and compared. If the two strings share at least a (settable) percentage of constituents then a constituent mapping is suggested. An example is the mapping from "XX_date-of-birth_String" to a slot of type String named "birthDate" (where the threshold level is set at 60%).

3. *WordNet mapping.* In WordNet mappings the constituents of each string are extracted, and WordNet is used to find synonyms of each constituent. If the percentage of synonyms in the *from string* appearing in the constituents of the *to string* (and vice versa) is greater than the threshold percentage, a WordNet mapping is suggested. A successful WordNet mapping is from "XX_yearly-earnings_Integer" to a slot of type Integer named "annual-remuneration" (where the threshold level is set at 60%), as "yearly" maps to "annual" and "earnings" maps to "renumeration" (and of course both slots are of type Integer so data type consistency is maintained).

In principle each mapping between an extracted class and a new ontology class consists of direct, constituent and WordNet mappings. As noted earlier each of the mappings will return a value, the largest value (providing it's over a threshold) is the one which is recommended to the user. In the case of a numerical tie, the algorithm selects the mapping by applying the following precedence rule:

Direct Mappings > Constituent Mappings > WordNetMappings

Currently the tool supports mappings between each extracted class to a single class in the ontology. In a few cases this may result in some extracted classes not having a mapping. To minimise this, after the mapping algorithm has produced the list of mappings, a global optimisation algorithm is applied. This algorithm analyses the suggested mappings to determine if choosing a suboptimal mapping for one class would result in more classes being mapped. If this is the case, then this alternative mapping configuration is suggested to the user.

Suppose we have a situation where we have 3 classes in the abstracted rules, let's call them RC_1, RC_2, and RC_3 and further suppose the new ontology has 3 classes, let's call them AC_1, AC_2, and AC_3. Then suppose the best new mappings between the abstract rules and the actual classes are as shown in Figure 2.

If we optimise the local mappings we will have:

---

[3]The constituents of a string are the words that make up that string. We use the symbols '-', '_' and (in mixed case strings) upper case letter to denote the start of new words. For example the string *date-of-birth* has constituents *date*, *of* and *birth*.

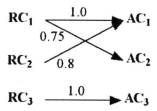

Figure 2: Sample mappings illustrating the need for the enhanced mapping algorithm.

$RC_1 \mapsto AC_1$ (1.0); $RC_3 \mapsto AC_3$ (1.0); and no mapping for RC_2 and AC_2.

This mapping set is unacceptable as some of the classes are unmapped. However, our enhanced algorithm would suggest the following mappings:

$RC_1 \mapsto AC_2$ (0.75); $RC_2 \mapsto AC_1$ (0.8); $RC_3 \mapsto AC_3$ (1.0).

In this mapping set all the classes are mapped, and if we use a simple evaluation, we would have a higher mapping score: 2 in the first case and 2.55 in the second. (It is appreciated that a more sophisticated mapping function is likely to be used.)

5 Results

To evaluate the performance of our tool, we conducted a series of experiments designed to test first the rule abstraction process and second the mapping capabilities. Each test involved the development of an initial JessTab rule set, which was based around an initial ontology. This ontology was either created by ourselves, or downloaded from the Stanford KSL OKBC server (accessed via the Protégé OBKB Tab plugin[22]). Once each set of rules had been developed to a satisfactory level, we built further ontologies with which to test the mapping functionality.

Tables 1[4] and 2 provide a selection of the results from our tests with the Document ontology from the Stanford KSL OKBC server's Ontolingua section. Table 1 gives results for the mappings of selected class names and Table 2 gives the results for the slot mappings. The columns of Table 1 detail the concept name (in the Document ontology), the abstract name it was given after Phase 1, and details of the mappings produced in tests with two separate applications, detailing the concept it was mapped to and the mapping operator selected. The columns of Table 2 are identical with the additional column stating the slot type.

These results offer a good illustration of the type of support the user can expect from our tool. The "Document" concept in Table 1 demonstrates nicely the direct mapping: in Application A the name is identical, in Application B the

---

[4]The spelling mistakes in Table 1 are intentionally left as they illustrate the minor variant checking feature of direct mappings.

Name	Abstract Name	Mapped in to			
		Application A		Application B	
		Name	Mapping Operator	Name	Mapping Operator
Document	XX_Document	Document	Direct	Docment	Direct
Book	XX_Book	Book	Direct	Volume	WordNet
Thesis	XX_Thesis	Thesis	Direct	Dissertation	WordNet
Masters-Thesis	XX_Masters-Thesis	ThesisMasters	Constituent	Masters-Dissertation	WordNet
Doctoral-Thesis	XX_Doctoral-Thesis	DoctoralThesis	Constituent	Dissertation-Doctoral	WordNet
Miscellaneous-Publication	XX_Miscellaneous-Publication	AssortedPublishing	WordNet	Miscellaneous-Publishings	WordNet
Artwork	XX_Artwork	Art	WordNet	Artistry	Manual
Technical-Manual	XX_Technical-Manual	TechnicalMnual	Direct	Manual-Technical	Constituent
Computer-Program	XX_Computer-Program	ComuterProgram	Direct	Computer-Programme	WordNet
Cartographic-Map	XX_Cartographic-Map	Cartographical-Correspondence	WordNet	Cartographical-Mapping	WordNet

Table 1: Results for mapping the classes of the Document ontology[4]

Name	Data Type	Abstract Name	Mapped in to			
			Application A		Application B	
			Name	Mapping Operator	Name	Mapping Operator
Has-Author	String	XX_Has-Author_String	Author	Direct	HasWriter	WordNet
Has-Editor	String	XX_Has-Editor_String	HasEditor	Direct	Editor-Of	Manual
Title-Of	String	XX_Title-Of_String	Title	Constituent	TitleOf	Direct
Publication-Date-Of	String	XX_Publication-Date-Of_String	IssueDate	WordNet	Date-Of-Publication	Constituent
Publisher-Of	String	XX_Publisher-Of_String	Publication-House	Manual	PublisherOf	Direct

Table 2: Results for mapping the slots of the Document ontology

minor spelling error in "Docment" is picked up by our tool and has no adverse effect on the suggested mapping. Both tables exhibit examples of constituent mappings, while the WordNet mappings also feature prominently both with one-word name examples ("Book" to "Volume") and multi-word concept names ("Cartographic-Map" and "CartographicalCorrespondance").

6 Discussion

Overall we were very pleased with the outcome of these experiments. However, they do suggest that some modifications to the tool, particularly the mapping phase, could be beneficial. One significant change would be to allow the user to specify how deep the tool searches WordNet for synonyms. This is best described by means of an illustration. Take the "Artwork" concept in Table 1 line 7. In Application B the user was required to manually map this concept to "Artistry." When suggesting a mapping, the tool looked up synonyms of artwork in WordNet, which returned "artwork," "art," "graphics" and "nontextual matter." Had the tool searched another level (i.e. looked up synonyms of art, graphics and so on), it would have found "artistry" is a synonym of "art" and suggested a mapping. However, performing deeper searching like this could dramatically increase the time taken by the automatic mapper, and so the user would have to decide how deep to search.

A second significant change involves relaxing the slot data type matching constraint. Currently, suggested slot mappings are only made between slots of the same type (to avoid run time errors). However many slot types are compatible with each other; for example, an Integer can also be considered a Float (but not, of course, the reverse). Relaxing this constraint would increase the number of slots considered during the automatic mapping but would still ensure no run time data incompatibility errors.

One relatively minor modification which might improve the accuracy of the automatic mapping, particularly when searching for constituent mappings, would be the removal of surplus words from concept names. Words such as "has," "is," and "of" often feature in concept names to help the user understand their purpose. However they have relatively little meaning for the mapping algorithm, but can often dramatically affect the similarity rating of two concept names. Consider the two concepts "Has-Author" and "Writer-Of" both used to indicate the author of a document. Currently our system would assign them a similarity rating of .50 (which, depending on the threshold level may mean a mapping is not suggested), but by removing "Has" and "Of" we increase this to 1.0 guaranteeing a mapping is suggested.

7 Summary

The experiments performed have provided favourable results, although there are some enhancements which could be made. However, by automating part of the reuse process, our tool can be of considerable use to a developer wishing to reuse a set of JessTab rules with further ontologies. In fact, we claim to have gone some way to implementing the vision, developed by John Park and Mark Musen [20] of creating ad-hoc knowledge-base systems from existing problem solving methods (here JessTab rule sets) and knowledge bases (here Protégé OKBC/OWL ontologies).

8 Acknowledgments

This work is supported under the Advanced Knowledge Technologies (AKT) IRC (EPSRC grant no. GR/N15764/01) comprising the Universities of Aberdeen, Edinburgh, Sheffield, Southampton and the Open University. See http://www.aktors.org

References

[1] Grigoris Antoniou and Frank van Harmelen. Web Ontology Language: OWL. In Staab and Studer [23], pages 67–92.

[2] Antoine B. Bagula. Hybrid traffic engineering: the least path interference algorithm. In *SAICSIT '04: Proceedings of the 2004 annual research conference of the South African institute of computer scientists and information technologists on IT research in developing countries*, pages 89–96. South African Institute for Computer Scientists and Information Technologists, 2004.

[3] NASA/Johnson Space Center. CLIPS. http://www.ghg.net/clips/CLIPS.html.

[4] Richard D. Cuthbert and Larry Peckham. APL models for operational planning of shipment routing, loading, and scheduling. In *WSC '73: Proceedings of the 6th conference on Winter simulation*, pages 622–631. ACM Press, 1973.

[5] Henrik Eriksson. The JESSTAB Approach to Protégé and JESS Integration. In *Proceedings of the IFIP 17th World Computer Congress - TC12 Stream on Intelligent Information Processing*, pages 237–248. Kluwer, B.V., 2002.

[6] Christiane Fellbaum, editor. *WordNet: An Electronic Lexical Database.* The MIT Press, Cumberland, RI, 1998.

[7] E. Friedman-Hill. *Jess In Action: Rule-Based Systems in Java.* Manning Publications Co., Greenwich, CT, 2003.

[8] Christine Golbreich. Combining Rule and Ontology Reasoners for the Semantic Web. In Grigoris Antoniou and Harold Boley (Eds.), editors, *Rules and Rule Markup Languages for the Semantic Web*, pages 6–22. RuleML, Springer-Verlag Berlin and Heidelberg, November 2004.

[9] Ian Horrocks, Peter F. Patel-Schneider, Harold Boley, Said Tabet, Benjamin Grosof, and Mike Deal. SWRL: A Semantic Web Rule Language Combining OWL and RuleML. W3C Member Submission, May 2004.

[10] Google Inc. Google. http://www.google.com.

[11] Kunal Johar and Rahul Simha. Jword 2.0. http://www.seas.gwu.edu/ simhaweb/software/jword/index.html.

[12] Joe Kopena. DAMLJessKB. http://edge.mcs.drexel.edu/assemblies/software/damljesskb/damljesskb.html.

[13] R.E. Korf. Depth-First Iterative-Deepening: An Optimal Admissible Tree Search. *Artificial Intelligence*, 27:97–109, 1985.

[14] Brian McBride. The Resource Description Framework (RDF) and its Vocabulary Description Language RDFS. In Staab and Studer [23], pages 51–66.

[15] Deborah L. McGuiness, Richard Fikes, James Rice, and Steve Wilder. An Environment for Merging and Testing Large Ontologies. In *Proceedings of the Seventh International Conference on Principles of Knowledge Representation and Reasoning (KR2000)*, pages 483–493. Morgan Kaufmann, 2000.

[16] Prasenjit Mitra and Gio Wiederhold. Resolving Terminological Heterogeneity in Ontologies. In *Proceedings of Workshop on Ontologies and Semantic Interoperability at the 15th European Conference on Artificial Intelligence (ECAI 2002)*, 2002.

[17] Prasenjit Mitra and Gio Wiederhold. An Ontology-Composition Algebra. In Staab and Studer [23], pages 93–116.

[18] Natalya F. Noy and Mark A. Musen. PROMPT: Algorithm and Tool for Automated Ontology Merging and Alignment. In *Proceedings of the Seventeenth National Conference on Artificial Intelligence (AAAI-2000)*, 2000.

[19] Natalya F. Noy and Mark A. Musen. The PROMPT suite: interactive tools for ontology merging and mapping. *International Journal of Human-Computer Studies*, 59(6):983–1024, 2003.

[20] John Park and Mark Musen. The Virtual Knowledge Constructor: A Schema for Mapping Across Ontologies in Knowledge-Based Systems. PhD Thesis Proposal. Stanford University, 1999.

[21] Andy Seaborne. RDQL: A Query Language for RDF. W3C Member Submission, January 2004.

[22] Michael Sintek. OKBC Tab Website. `http://protege.stanford.edu/plugins/okbctab/okbc_tab.html`.

[23] Steffen Staab and Rudi Studer, editors. *Handbook on Ontologies.* International Handbooks on Information Systems. Springer, 2004.

[24] Stanford Medical Informatics, Stanford University. Protégé Website. `http://protege.stanford.edu`.

[25] The Rule Markup Initiative. RuleML Homepage. `http://www.ruleml.org`.

[26] Tom White. Can't Beat Jazzy: Introducing the Java Platform's Jazzy New Spell Checker API. `http://www-106.ibm.com/developerworks/java/library/j-jazzy/`.

SESSION 1a:

INFORMATION LEARNING, INTEGRATION AND MANAGEMENT

Robot Docking Based on Omnidirectional Vision and Reinforcement Learning

David Muse, Cornelius Weber and Stefan Wermter
Hybrid Intelligent Systems, School of Computing and Technology
University of Sunderland, UK. Web: www.his.sunderland.ac.uk

Abstract

We present a system for visual robotic docking using an omnidirectional camera coupled with the actor critic reinforcement learning algorithm. The system enables a PeopleBot robot to locate and approach a table so that it can pick an object from it using the pan-tilt camera mounted on the robot. We use a staged approach to solve this problem as there are distinct sub tasks and different sensors used. Starting with random wandering of the robot until the table is located via a landmark, and then a network trained via reinforcement allows the robot to turn to and approach the table. Once at the table the robot is to pick the object from it. We argue that our approach has a lot of potential allowing the learning of robot control for navigation removing the need for internal maps of the environment. This is achieved by allowing the robot to learn couplings between motor actions and the position of a landmark.

1 Introduction

Navigation is one of the most complex tasks currently under development in mobile robotics. There are several different components to navigation and many different sensors that can be used to complete the task, from range finding sensors to graphical information from a camera. The main function of robot navigation is to enable a robot to move around its environment, whether that is following a calculated or predefined path to reach a specific location or just random wandering around the environment. Some of the components involved in robotic navigation are *(i)* localisation, *(ii)* path planning and *(iii)* obstacle avoidance. For an overview of localisation and map-based navigation see [1 & 2]. When discussing robot navigation, simultaneous localisation and map building should be included (see [3, 4 & 5] for some examples).

There has been a lot of research and systems developed for robot navigation using range finding sensors (sonar, laser range finders etc) [6, 7 & 8] but there has been less research into visual robotic navigation. There are recent developments in the field of visual navigation mainly concentrating on omnidirectional vision (see [9, 10 & 11] for examples).

Many of the navigation systems implemented for robot navigation still use hard coding which causes a problem with the lack of adaptability of the system. However, some systems have included learning (see [12 & 13] for examples). A common training method used for the learning systems are various forms of reinforcement learning, [14] provides a good overview. These learning algorithms overcome the problem of supervised learning algorithms as input output pairs are not required for each stage of training. The only thing that is required is the assignment of the reward which can be a problem for complex systems as discussed in [15]. However, for systems where there is just one goal this does not pose a problem as the reward will be administered only when the agent reaches the goal.

The focus on this paper is to extend the system developed in [16] where reinforcement learning is used to allow a PeopleBot to dock to and pick an object (an orange) from a table. In this system neural vision is used to locate the object in the image, then using trained motor actions (via the actor critic learning algorithm [17]) the aim is to get the object to the bottom centre of the image resulting in the object being between the grippers of the robot.

There are some limitations to the system which need to be overcome to improve its usefulness. For example, the docking can only work if the object is in sight from the beginning which results in the system being confined to a very small area. Also the system fails if the object is lost from the image. Finally, the angle of the robot with respect to the table is inferred from the odometry, which makes it necessary to start at a given angle. None of these are desirable and it is the aim of this work to address some of the limitations and extend the range that the robot can dock from.

The system proposed in this paper will make use of an omnidirectional camera to locate and approach a table in an office environment. The use of an omnidirectional camera allows the robot to continuously search the surrounding environment for the table rather than just ahead of the robot. Here the extended system will use the omnidirectional camera to locate the table via a landmark placed beneath it. Once located the robot is to turn and approach the table using a network trained by reinforcement.

The remainder of the paper is structured as follows; Section 2 discusses the task, the overall control of the system and what triggers the shifts between the different phases. The first phase uses an omnidirectional camera to detect any obstacles and take the necessary action to avoid them and is discussed in Section 2.1. The second phase uses the omnidirectional camera to locate the position of the landmark in relation to the robot, which it then passes to a neural network to produce the required motor action on the robot and is discussed in Section 2.2. The final phase uses a neural system with the pan tilt camera mounted on the robot to allow the robot to dock with the object on the table and pick it up; this is discussed in Section 2.3. Section 3 covers the algorithm used for the table approaching phase of the extended scenario. The experimentation of the extended scenario is then described in section 4. Finally, Sections 5 and 6 cover the discussion and summary respectively.

2 The Scenario

The overall scenario is illustrated in Figure 1. It starts with the robot being placed in the environment at a random position away from the table. The robot is then to wander around the environment until it locates the table (Phase I). This phase uses conventional image processing to detect and avoid any obstacles. Once the table is located via a landmark placed beneath it the robot is to turn and approach the table

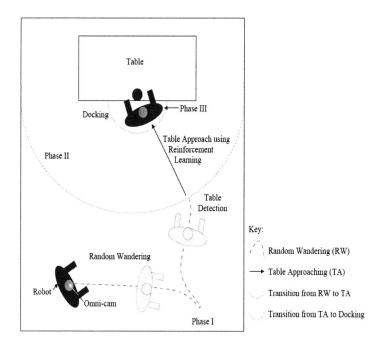

Figure 1 - Scenario

(Phase II). Then once at the table the robot is to pick the object from the table (Phase III), this system is discussed in [16]. Both Phase II & III use neural networks trained with the Actor Critic learning algorithm.

The first two phases of the system use an omnidirectional camera illustrated in Figure 2 and the final phase uses the pan tilt camera mounted on the robot.

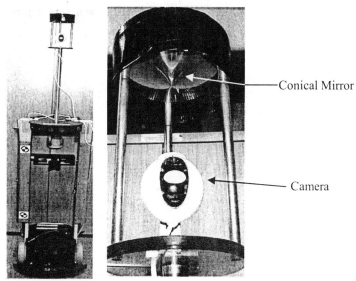

Figure 2 – (Left) PeopleBot Robot with mounted omnidirectional camera, (Right) Close up of the Omnidirectional Camera

To enable the integration of the three phases an overall control function was needed to execute the relevant phases of the system depending on the environmental conditions. Figure 3 shows the control algorithm.

```
While the robot is not at the table
        Take a picture (omnidirectional)
        Check if the landmark is in sight
        If the landmark is not in sight
                Wander
        Else the landmark is in sight
                Pass control to the actor critic and get exit status
                If exited because landmark is lost
                        Go back to Wandering
                Else exited because robot is at the table
                        Pass control to the object docking
                End if
        End if
End While
```

Figure 3 - System Algorithm

When the robot is not at the table, or the landmark is not in sight, the robot checks for the landmark at each iteration through the system. The landmark that the robot looks for is produced by a board of red LED's which is located directly beneath the table as illustrated in Figure 4.

While the robot has not located the landmark the random wandering system is executed. If the landmark has been located then control is passed to the table approaching behaviour which runs to completion. There are two possible outcomes for the table approaching which are; *(i)* Lost sight of the landmark and *(ii)* Reached the table. If the landmark has been lost then the robot starts to search for it again, otherwise it has reached the table and control is passed to the object docking which completes the task.

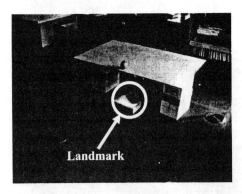

Figure 4 - Setup of the Environment: The landmark is used to identify the position of the table

2.1   Phase I – The Random Wandering

This behaviour allows the robot to move around the environment while avoiding obstacles. The system uses an omnidirectional camera (Figure 2 right) to get a view of the environment surrounding the robot. From this image the robot is able to detect obstacles and produce the required motor action to avoid them. To perform this detection the behaviour uses classical image processing to remove the background from the image and leave only perceived obstacles, as seen in Figure 5. Here the original image taken by the omnidirectional camera is in the left of the figure, with different stages of the image processing shown in the centre and right.

Figure 5 – Obstacle Detection

The centre image is the intermediate stage where just the background of the image has been removed; this is achieved by colour segmentation of the most common colour from the image. To find the most common colour in the image a histogram is produced for the RGB values of each pixel. Then the value with the largest density is found and any colour within the range of +/- 25 of the most common colour is removed. This removes the carpet from the image (assuming that the carpet is present in the majority of the image) which leaves the obstacles and some noise. Also at this stage the range of the obstacle detection is set removing any noise from the periphery of the image. Then the noise is removed by image erosion followed by dilation. The erosion strips pixels away from the edges of all objects left in the image. This removes the noise but it also reduces the size of any obstacles present. To combat this once the erosion has been performed, dilation is performed to restore the obstacles to their original size, the shape of the obstacles are slightly distorted by this process. However, the obstacles left in the final image are still suitable to produce the required motor action to avoid them. The last stage of the image processing is to use edge detection to leave only the outlines of the obstacles (Figure 5 right).

The robot always tries to move straight ahead unless an obstacle is detected in the robot's path. When this happens the robot turns the minimum safe amount allowed to avoid the obstacles. In the example provided in Figure 5, the robot cannot move straight ahead so the robot would turn to the left until it can avoid the obstacle on the right of the image. As the image is a mirrored image of the environment the objects which appear on one side of the image are physically to the other side of the robot. Once the robot has turned the required amount it would start to move straight and the obstacle detection would then be performed again.

2.2   Phase II – The Table Approaching Behaviour

This phase of the system allows the robot to approach the table (landmark) once detected. This has two exit statuses which are *(i)* the robot lost sight of the landmark or *(ii)* the robot has reached the table. If the robot looses sight of the table it goes back to the wandering phase until it locates the landmark again. This can happen if the landmark moves behind one of the supporting pillars of the conical mirror. If the robot reaches the table, control will be passed to the final stage of the system which is to dock to and pick up the object.

To allow the robot to move to the table a network was trained using the Actor Critic reinforcement learning rule [17]. The state space was the image with the goal set to where the landmark is perceived to be in front of the robot. The motor action that the network performs is to rotate the robot to the left or to the right depending on where the landmark is perceived in relation to the robot. The input to the network is the x y coordinates of the closest point of the perceived landmark. Once the landmark appears to be ahead of the robot, the robot then moves forward, checking that the landmark is still ahead of it. Once the landmark is ahead of the robot and less than the threshold distance of 1 meter the robot then moves directly forward until the table sensors located on the robot's base are broken. When this happens the robot is at the table and control is given to Phase III.

The robot only looks for the landmark in the range that the robot can detect directly ahead (as the webcam produces a rectangular image, more can be seen to the sides of the robot. The range is set to the maximum distance the image can detect ahead of the robot; this is roughly 2m). If the landmark is detected outside this range when the robot turned it would lose sight of the landmark, therefore anything outside this region is ignored. If the landmark appears in the right side of the detectable range then the robot should rotate to the left as the image is mirrored, if it appears in the left the robot should rotate to the right and if it is straight ahead of the robot then it should move forward.

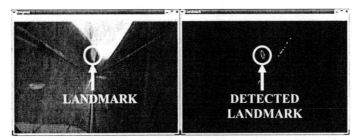

Figure 6 - Landmark Detection

To detect the landmark classical image processing is once again employed to detect the landmark as shown in Figure 6. The original image is in the left of Figure 6 with the landmark highlighted and the detected landmark is highlighted in the right of Figure 6. The first stage to the image processing is to perform colour segmentation where it segments any colour that is the designated colour of the landmark. Once this process is complete edge detection is used to leave just the edges of the remaining objects. Then it is assumed that the largest object left in the image is the landmark. The last stage of the image processing is to locate the closest point of the landmark to the robot. This point is then fed into the network to produce the required action by the robot.

2.3   Phase III – Docking

This phase allows the robot to dock to and pick an orange from the table. The functionality of the system is described in [16]. However, there is a problem with this system for the integration into the extended scenario; the odometry of the robot is set to 0 and the robot must start parallel to the table to allow the robot to dock to the orange. With the table approaching system it cannot be guaranteed that the robot will be parallel to the table and hence the robot will not know the relationship between the odometry and the angle of the table.

Before this system is integrated it is required that the angle of the table to the robot is calculated. To solve this it is planned to use image processing to detect and calculate the angel of the table in relation to the robot. Once the robot reaches the table a picture will be taken using the conventional pan tilt camera mounted on the robot. The edge of the table will then be detected using colour thresholding and edge detection.

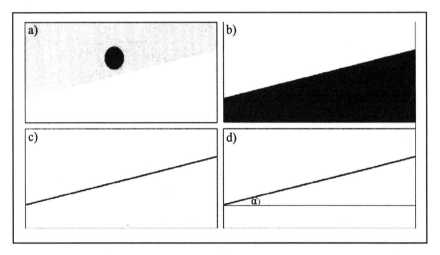

Figure 7 - Edge Detection of the Table

The thresholding will be performed in the same way as in Phase I with the most common colour being removed. It is assumed that the most common colour will either be *(i)* the colour of the table itself or *(ii)* the colour of the carpet beneath the table. In both cases the edge between the removed colour and the remaining colour will be the edge of the table. Using edge detection the coordinates of the two end points of this line can be found and from this the angle of the table calculated and used with the odometry to get the robot to dock to the orange.

Figure 7 demonstrates this image processing using the artificial image (a), here the white is thought to be the most common colour so will be removed and the remaining components of the image are changed to white (b). The next stage is to perform the edge detection (c). With this done the angle can be calculated (d) and used to alter the odometry of the robot. This is to remove the constraint that the robot must arrive parallel to the table.

3 Actor Critic Algorithm

The developed network is an extension of the actor critic model used in [17]. Here the system has been adapted to work with continuous real-world environments. We have used this algorithm in two phases of the scenario: first, the approach to the table (Phase II), and then to perform the docking at the object. In Phase II, the input to the network is the position in the omnidirectional image where the landmark appears as opposed to the location of the agent in the environment. In Phase III, the input is the perceived location of the object of interest from the standard robot camera.

For the architecture of the network developed for Phase II, it was decided that there would be two input neurons; one for the x and y coordinates respectively, 50 hidden units to cover the state space of the image and two output neurons one for each of the actions to be performed and one neuron for the critic. The architecture is illustrated in Figure 8. The hidden area covers only the detectable region of the image with each neuron covering roughly 40mm^2 of actual space. This results from the fact that the detectable range of the environment is roughly a radius of 2m from the robot. All units are fully connected to the hidden layer. Initially the critics' weights are set to 0 and are updated by Equation 4. The Actor weights (Motor Action units) are initialised randomly in the range of 0 – 1 and are updated via Equation 7. Finally, the weights connecting the input units to the network (High level vision) are set to 1 and these weights are not updated.

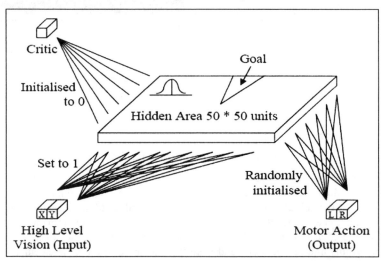

Figure 8 - Architecture of the Network. The nodes are fully connected, the input for the x, y coordinates are normalised into the range 0-50 and the output of the network generates the motor action to rotate the robot

Equation 1 describes the firing rate of the "place cells" (here the term place cell is used loosely as they encode a perceived position of a landmark in the image) to be calculated. The firing rate is defined as:

$$f_i(p) = \exp\left(-\frac{\|p - s_i\|^2}{2\sigma^2}\right) \qquad (1)$$

where p is the perceived position of the landmark, s_i is the location in the image where neuron i has maximal firing rate and σ is the radius of the Gaussian of the firing rates covering the image space of each neuron. This was set to 0.75 during the experiments. The firing rate C of the Critic is calculated using Equation 2 and has only one output neuron as seen in Figure 8. The firing rate of the critic is thus a weighted sum of all of the firing rates of the place cells.

$$C(p) = \sum_i w_i f_i(p) \qquad (2)$$

To enable training of the weights of the critic some method is needed to calculate the error generated by the possible moves to be made by the robot. This is made possible by Equation 3 and the derivation of this equation can be found in [17].

$$\delta_t = R_t + \gamma C(p_{t+1}) - C(p_t) \qquad (3)$$

However as R_t only equals 1 when the robot is at the goal location and $C(p_{t+1})$ is 0 when this occurs and vice versa they are never included in the calculation at the same time. γ is the constant discounting factor and was set to 0.7 for the experiments. With the predicted error, the weights of the critic are updated proportionally to the product of the firing rate of the active place cell and the error (Equation 4).

$$\Delta w_i \propto \delta_t f_i(p_t) \qquad (4)$$

This concludes the equations that were used for the place cells and the critic, finally there are the equations used for the actor. There were two output neurons used in this experiment, one to make the robot rotate to the left and the other to make the robot rotate to the right. The activation of these neurons is achieved by taking the weighted sum of the activations of the surrounding place cell to the current location as illustrated in Equation 5.

$$a_j(p) = \sum_i z_{ji} f_i(p) \qquad (5)$$

A probability is used to judge the direction that the robot should move in, this is illustrated in Equation 6. Here the probability that the robot will move in one direction is equal to the firing rate of that actor neuron divided by the sum of the firing rate of all the actor neurons. To enable random exploration when the system is training, a random number is generated between 0 and 1. Then the probability of each neuron is incrementally summed; when the result crosses the generated value that action is executed. As the system is trained the likelihood that the action chosen is not the trained action decreases. This is because as the network is trained the probability that the trained action will occur will approach 1.

$$P_j = \frac{\exp(2a_j)}{\sum_k \exp(2a_k)} \qquad (6)$$

Ultimately, the actor weights are trained using Equation 7 in a modified form of Hebbian learning where the weight is updated if the action is chosen and not updated if the action is not performed. This is achieved by setting $g_j(t)$ to 1 if the action is chosen or to 0 if the action is not performed. With this form of training both the actor and the critics weights can be bootstrapped and trained together.

$$\Delta z_{ji} \propto \delta_t f_i(p_t) g_j(t) \qquad (7)$$

4 Experimentation and Results

To train and test the network separate training and test data sets were produced. The training set contained 1000 randomly generated samples and the test set contained 500 randomly generated samples. These samples were stored in separate vectors and contained the following information *(i)* the normalised x coordinate of the landmark, *(ii)* the normalised y coordinate of the landmark, *(iii)* the angle of the landmark in relation to the robot and *(iv)* the distance of the landmark from the robot. During training each sample was fed into the network and it ran until the goal was achieved. Therefore, after each epoch there would be 1000 successful samples and the testing data was fed into the network without any training taking place.

The trained weights of the critic are shown in Figure 9 (d), which took 50 epochs to get the training to the level shown. It would have been impractical to train the network on the robot due to the time it would require, so a simple simulator was employed which used the training set to perform the action recommended by the network (this used the same data that would be generated from the image processing). This was achieved by calculating the next perceived position of the landmark. This greatly reduced the time needed to train the network, for the 50 epochs it took roughly 5 hours to train (including the testing after each epoch) on a Linux computer with a 2GHz processor and 1 Gigabyte of ram. Figure 9 also shows the untrained weights (a), the weights after the presentation of 1 training sample (b) and the weights after the presentation of 500 training samples (c). Here it can be seen that the weights spread from the goal location around the network during the training. There is a 'V' section of the weights that remain untrained, this relates to the goal location (see Figure 8) so no training is needed in this section of the network as the required state is reached.

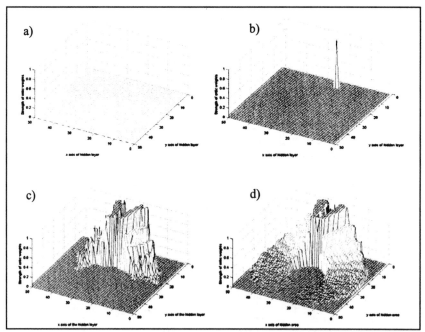

Figure 9 - Strength of Critic Weights During Training. (a) untrained weights, (b) weights after presentation of 1 sample, (c) weights after presentation of 500 samples and (d) weights after 50 epochs of training

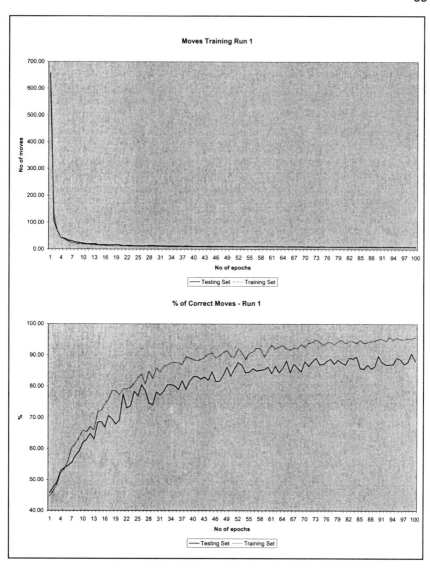

Figure 10 - Training Stats (Top) average number of steps required to reach the goal location during the testing of the network. (Bottom) percentage of correct moves made during the testing of the network.

Figure 10 shows the statistics gathered during the training of the network. After each epoch of training the network is tested both with the training data and the testing data. Here the samples are presented to the network and data gathered about *(i)* number of steps needed to reach the goal and *(ii)* the percentage of correct moves made by the network at each step. During this testing of the network training was prohibited and the relevant statistics gathered. This was done three times with all results being similar. Figure 10 (top) shows the average number of moves needed after each epoch for the goal to be reached. An average is taken for both the test and training set so the test value is averaged over the 500 test samples and the training over the 1000 training samples. Initially, with no training, it takes on average approximately 650 steps for the agent to reach the goal location. This rapidly decreases and settles to about 10 steps after roughly 30 epochs, the number of steps required for the testing and training sets are very similar and the performance is as good on the testing set as the training set.

Figure 10 (bottom) illustrates the percentage of correct moves made at each step during the testing of the network. As expected initially, as the agent moves randomly the number of correct moves is roughly 50%, as there are two actions to be performed. This steadily rises during training, however, this doesn't stabilise after 30 epochs like the number of moves does. The performance keeps improving although the rate of improvement does decrease after approximately 60 epochs. In addition, the testing set doesn't perform as well as the training set does during the testing; this doesn't affect the average number of moves required to reach the goal.

5 Discussion

The developed system has been successful in allowing the robot to approach the table from random places in the environment. Once the orange docking is linked, the scenario will be complete. Reinforcement learning has been successfully used in two of the phases of this application. This illustrates that reinforcement learning is a viable option for use in robot navigation tasks.

This poses quite an interesting question; humans can easily see distinctive differences in tasks; would we be able to train a computer to do a similar thing? Instead of the programmer splitting the state space, could the computer automatically partition the state space? This has been approached in [18 & 19]. In these papers different techniques are adopted to partition the state space. Simple portioning of the state space would not have been a viable option in our approach as one network would be needed for the entire system. However, this would result in a large state space covering in our application the visual inputs of the omnidirectional camera as well as the pan-tilt camera. Therefore we have addressed this "curse of dimensionality" problem by segmenting the task into phases resulting in two smaller manageable state spaces.

Investigation could be made into improvements in the network to enhance the percentage of correct moves made. Some possibilities could include increasing the number of samples in the training set to increase the coverage of the training, allowing more starting locations to be trained. Another possibility could be to adjust the training algorithm to allow a smoother degrade in the strength of the critics weights. As the agent move away from the goal location there are large decreases in the strength of the weights to the extent that when the landmark appears behind the agent the critic's weights are very weak so the agent may still be moving randomly in this section. A smoother decrease in the critic's weights would allow this section of the network to have stronger weight connections and thus improve the performance of the network. There is one method that could be used to improve the network instantly which would be to switch from exploration of the environment to exploitation. Here the actor unit would be chosen which would give maximum reward. This however could lead to suboptimal solutions if used too early in training.

An alternative to the developed system could be to pan and tilt the camera that is supplied with the robot to find the target from a large distance and perform the whole action based on this visual information. So instead of keeping the camera in a fixed position the camera could be moved to locate the table and object. This requires a coordinate transform to allow the calculation of the angle to the object given the odometry of the robot, the perceived position of the orange on the camera image and the pan of the camera. This is also an approach which we are currently pursuing [20] While such an approach enhances the range of an action strategy that relies on a single state space, there will remain situations in which a multi-step strategy has to be employed, such as if the target object is not visible from the starting point. Without the object visible, again one strategy is needed to get the robot close to the table and another for the docking to the object.

6 Summary

This paper has discussed the navigation system developed to allow the robot to firstly locate and dock to a table via a landmark. This greatly extended the range of docking of the system developed in [16]. Both systems (the original docking and the extended navigation) used the actor critic reinforcement technique to train the networks they used to achieve their goals. The extended navigation system trained its own network to allow the robot to move to the table, which has been demonstrated to work effectively. Once at the table the docking phase is able to complete the task. The navigation system developed has shown that reinforcement learning can successfully be applied to a real world robot navigation task. This system shows great potential for the development of a more advanced navigation system.

Acknowledgements

This is part of the MirrorBot project supported by the EU, FET-IST programme, grant IST-2001-35282, coordinated by Prof. Wermter.

References

1. Filliat, D. & Meyer, J.A. Map-based navigation in mobile robots. I. A review of localization strategies. J. of Cognitive Systems Research 2003, 4(4):243-282

2. Filliat, D. & Meyer, J.A. Map-based navigation in mobile robots. II. A review of map-learning and path-planning strategies. J. of Cognitive Systems Research 2003, 4(4):283-317

3. Dissanayake, M.W.M.G. Newman, P. Clark, S. Durrant-White, H.F. & Csorba, M. A solution to the simultaneous loacalization and map building (SLAM) problem. IEEE Transactions on Robotics and Automation 2001, 17(3):229-241

4. Tomatis, N. Nourbakhsh, I. & Siegwart, R. Hybrid simultaneous localization and map building; a natural integration of topological and metric. Robotics and Autonomous Systems 2003, 44:3-14

5. Guivant, J.E. Masson, F.R. & Nebot E.M. Simultaneous localization and map building using natural features of absolute information. Robotics and Autonomous Systems 2002, 40:79-90

6. Carelli, R. & Freire, E.O. Corridor navigation and wall-following stable control for sonar-based mobile robots. Robotics and Autonomous Systems 2003, 45:235-247

7. Maaref, H. & Barret, C. Sensor-based navigation of a mobile robot in an indoor environment. Robotics and Autonomous systems 2002, 38:1-18
8. Delgado, E. & Barreiro, A. Sonar-based robot navigation using nonlinear robust observers. Automatica 2003, 39:1195-1203
9. Menegatti, E. Zoccarato, M. Pagello, E. & Ishiguro, H. Image-based Monte Carlo localisation with omnidirectional images. Robotics and Autonomous Systems 2004, 48:17-30
10. Fiala, M. & Basu, A. Robot navigation using panoramic tracking. Pattern Recognition 2004, 37:2195-2215
11. Jogan, M. & Leonardis, A. Robust localisation using an omnidirectional appearance-based subspace model of environment. Robotics and Autonomous Systems 2003, 45:51-72
12. Gaussier, P. Joulain, C. Banquet, J.P. Lepretre, S. & Revel, A. The Visual Homing Problem: An Example of Robotics/Biology Cross Fertilization. Robotics and Autonomous Systems 2000, 30:155-180
13. Gaussier, P. Revel, A. Joulain, C. & Zrehen, S. Living in a Partially Structured Environment: How to Bypass the Limitations of Classical Reinforcement Techniques. Robotics and Autonomous Systems 1997, 20:225-250
14. Sutton, R.S. & Barto, A.G. Reinforcement Learning An Introduction. MIT Press 1998
15. Wörgötter, F. Actor-Critic models of animal control – a critique of reinforcement learning. Proceeding of Fourth International ICSC Symposium on Engineering of Intelligent Systems 2004
16. Weber, C. Wermter, S. & Zochios, A. Robot docking with neural vision and reinforcement. Knowledge Based Systems 2004, 12:165-72
17. Foster, D.J. Morris, R.G.N. & Dayan, P. A model of hippocampally dependent navigation, using the temporal learning rule. Hippocampus 2000, 10:1-16
18. Kondo, T. & Ito, K. A reinforcement learning with evolutionary state recruitment strategy for autonomous mobile robot control. Robotics and Autonomous Systems 2004, 46:11-124
19. Lee, I.S.K. & Lau, A.Y.K. Adaptive state space partitioning for reinforcement learning. Engineering Applications of Artificial Intelligence 2004, 17:577-588
20. Weber, C. Muse, D. Elshaw, M. & Wermter, S. Neural robot docking involving a camera-direction dependent visual-motor coordinate transformation. AI 2005 (submitted)

Global EM Learning of Finite Mixture Models using the Greedy Elimination Method

Zeke S. H. Chan and N. Kasabov

Knowledge Engineering and Discovery Research Insititute
(KEDRI), Auckland University of Technology, New Zealand

Abstract

The standard learning method for finite mixture models is the Expectation-Maximization (EM) algorithm, which performs hill-climbing from an initial solution to obtain the local maximum likelihood solution. However, given that the solution space is large and multimodal, EM is prone to produce inconsistent and sub-optimal solutions over multiple runs.

This paper presents a novel global greedy learning method called the Greedy Elimination Method (GEM) to alleviate these problems. GEM is simple to implement in any finite mixture model, yet effective to enhance the global optimality and the consistency of the solutions. It is also very efficient as its complexity grows only linearly with the number of data patterns. GEM is demonstrated on clustering synthetic datasets using the mixture of Gaussian model, and on clustering the shrinking spiral data set using the mixture of Factor Analyzers.

1 Introduction

Finite mixtures are flexible statistical modelling methods, useful for a wide range of applications including clustering and feature selection [1, 2]. The standard method for learning mixture models is the Expectation-Maximization (EM) algorithm [3], which performs hill-climbing from a given initial condition (usually randomized) to a local maximum likelihood (ML) estimate.

However, despite its simplicity, the standard EM algorithm suffers two well-known problems: first, the estimates are only locally optimal; and second, their qualities are sensitive to the initial conditions. To alleviate these problems, methods based on greedy learning [4-6], simulated annealing [7], and stochastic simulation (e.g. Markov Chain Monte Carlo [8] and Genetic Algorithms [9]) have been proposed. The later two methods are intrinsically computationally intensive and may not be feasible for large datasets such as microarray data. Previously proposed greedy EM methods proceed in an incremental or growing manner, i.e. they start with one component, and then add new components one-by-one until the mixture model contains the desired number of components. This type of greedy methods, which we call the Greedy Incremental (GInc) Methods, is intrinsically inefficient because its complexity grows exponentially with the number of data points. Moreover, it often involves complex heuristics that are cumbersome to implement.

This paper presents a novel global greedy learning method called the Greedy Elimination Method (GEM). In contrast to the GInc methods, GEM proceeds decrementally, starting with many components and then eliminating them one-by-one. We show that GEM is a very practical global EM learning method: it is very effective in enhancing the global optimality and the consistency of the solutions, yet it is very simple and robust to implement in any finite mixture model. Moreover, it is efficient for large datasets as its complexity grows linearly with the number of data patterns. We perform comparative analysis between the standard EM, multi-start EM [1], GInc and GEM on learning the mixture of Gaussians (MG) model for clustering synthetic data. To demonstrate that GEM is versatile even for different finite mixture models, we apply GEM on learning the Mixture of Factor Analyzers (MFA) model [10] for clustering the shrinking spiral data, in which GEM consistently outperforms the multi-start EM.

2 Methods

2.1 EM Learning of Finite Mixture Models

A finite mixture model is a probabilistic-weighted sum of k components:

$$p(\mathbf{y} \mid \boldsymbol{\theta}) = \sum_{m=1}^{k} \alpha_m p(\mathbf{y} \mid \boldsymbol{\theta}_m) \tag{1}$$

where $\mathbf{y} \in \Re^d$ is an observed d-vector, α_m is the mixing probability and $\boldsymbol{\theta}_m$ is the set of parameters characterizing the mth component for $m=[1,...,k]$. Being probabilistic, the mixing probabilities must sum up to 1. The most common finite mixture model is the MGs model for clustering, where each component $\boldsymbol{\theta}_m \equiv \{\boldsymbol{\mu}_m, \mathbf{C}_m\}$ defines a separate Gaussian distribution $N(\cdot)$ with mean $\boldsymbol{\mu}_m$ and covariance $\mathbf{C}_m$

$$p(\mathbf{y} \mid \boldsymbol{\theta}_m) \equiv N(\mathbf{y}; \boldsymbol{\mu}_m, \mathbf{C}_m) = (2\pi)^{-d/2} |\mathbf{C}_m|^{-1/2} \exp\left[-\frac{1}{2} (\mathbf{y} - \boldsymbol{\mu}_m)^T \mathbf{C}_m^{-1} (\mathbf{y} - \boldsymbol{\mu}_m) \right] \tag{2}$$

Given a collection of n observed patterns $\mathbf{Y} = \{\mathbf{y}^{(1)},...,\mathbf{y}^{(n)}\}$, the complete data log-likelihood of the finite mixture model is given by

$$L = \log p(\mathbf{Y} \mid \boldsymbol{\theta}) = \log \prod_{i=1}^{n} p(\mathbf{y}^{(i)} \mid \boldsymbol{\theta}) = \sum_{i=1}^{n} \log \sum_{m=1}^{k} \alpha_m p(\mathbf{y}^{(i)} \mid \boldsymbol{\theta}_m) \tag{3}$$

The standard method for learning the finite mixture models is the EM algorithm. Starting from some initial conditions, EM converges to a maximum likelihood solution via iterating between the E-step and M-step, which computes the conditional expectation of the complete log-likelihood given the current estimate $\hat{\boldsymbol{\theta}}(t)$ (commonly known as the Q-function), and updates the parameters to maximize the conditional expectation, respectively. However, since the initial parameters are usually randomly adopted from the training data, the EM estimates are only locally optimal and their qualities are sensitive to the initial conditions.

2.2 Greedy Elimination Method (GEM) for Finite Mixture Models

GEM was first proposed in [11] where it was successfully applied to the K-means algorithm. In this paper, we extend it to the EM learning of finite mixture models. GEM is a pruning algorithm that proceeds in a decremental manner – i.e. starting with many components, and then eliminating them one-by-one until the mixture model contains the desired number of components. This difference is illustrated in Fig. 1 with a clustering example using MG.

time →

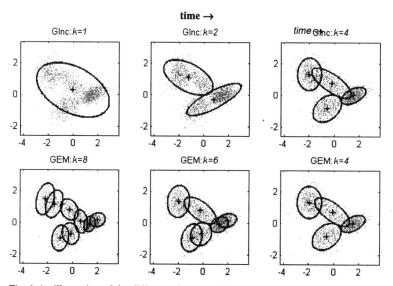

Fig. 1 An illustration of the difference between GInc and GEM in clustering a set of 2-D data into 4 clusters using the mixture of Gaussians model. k denotes the number of clusters. (Top row, left to right) GInc proceeds incrementally from 1 to 4 clusters. (Bottom row, left to right) GEM proceeds decrementally from 8 down to 4 clusters.

GEM is implemented as follows. To describe the changing number of components in a mixture model over the greedy learning process, we use k, k_{start} and $k_{desired}$ to notate the current number, the starting number, and the desired number of components in the model, respectively. First, we choose an enlargement factor $\alpha > 1$ that determines the starting number of components $k_{start} = \alpha k_{desired}$, and then train an initial model with k_{start} components using the standard EM. Based on limited trials, we find that the optimal α value is very much problem-dependent, yet $\alpha = 2$ appears to give very cost-effective solutions under general situations. Then, one-by-one, GEM (i) removes the component without which the model yields the highest *lower-bound* log likelihood (defined later), and then (ii) EM-optimizes the reduced model.

The greedy elimination process continues until $k_{desired}$ components remain in the model. Let θ_{-j} represent the model with the jth component removed. The lower-bound log likelihood of θ_{-j}, denoted by $\log p_{LB}(Y \mid \theta_{-j})$, is computed using the likelihood and the mixing coefficients of the original model as in (3), except that (a) the jth component and its mixing coefficients are not included in the inner summation, and (b) the remaining mixing coefficients are re-estimated using the standard update equation, i.e.

$$\log p_{LB}(Y \mid \theta_{-j}) = \sum_{i=1}^{n} \log \left(\sum_{m=1, m \neq j}^{k} \widehat{\alpha}_m p(y^{(i)} \mid \theta_m) \right) \tag{4}$$

where

$$\widehat{\alpha}_m = \frac{1}{n} \sum_{i=1}^{n} p(\theta_m \mid y^{(i)}) \tag{5}$$

The log likelihood of the reduced model θ_{-j} in (4) is the "lower-bound" because the model can be further EM-converged to achieve higher likelihood value. It is a very efficient means for comparing the optimality of the k different reduced models (i.e. $\theta_{-j} \forall j = [1,...,k]$), since it can be quickly computed using the conditional probabilities $p(y^{(i)} \mid \theta_m), \forall i, m$ that are available from the previous E-step. Now the optimal component to be eliminated, indexed j_e, is formally given as

$$j_e = \arg\max_j \log p_{LB}(Y \mid \theta_{-j}) \tag{6}$$

The procedures of GEM are summarized as follows:

Step 1:	Initialize with $k_{start}=\alpha k_{desired}$ ($\alpha > 1$) components.
Step 2:	Perform EM until convergence is achieved. If $k=k_{desired}$, exit; otherwise continue.
Step 3:	Eliminate the component without which the lower bound of the log likelihood (4) is maximized.

The motivation of GEM is to increase global coverage of the search space by scattering a large number of components in the initial phase of the search. GEM's unconventional greedy progression raises three significant advantages. First, GEM is very easy to implement even in different mixture models, requiring only a few lines of extra code to incorporate equations (4), (5) and (6) into the standard EM program. Unlike GInc, GEM does not require complex heuristics (discussed later). It is also very robust as it has only one control parameter – the enlargement factor α.

Second, GEM is very efficient as its complexity is only linear in the number of data points. By making use of the lower bound likelihood to direct the component elimination procedure, GEM requires only a single EM run at each transition stage of $[k_{start}, k_{start} -1,...,k_{desired}]$ components. The total number of likelihood calculations is therefore

$$\sum_{k=k_{start}}^{k_{desired}} cnk = cnk_{desired} \cdot \frac{1}{2}\left(k_{desired}(\alpha^2 -1)+\alpha -1\right) \equiv O(n\alpha^2 k_{desired}^2) \tag{7}$$

which is linear in n and polynomial in k and α. For a global clustering algorithm, GEM is very economical since typically $(n >> k)$ and $(n >> \alpha)$.

Third, we can record the model likelihood at each intermediate stage of component elimination, and apply the method of Bayesian or Akaike Information Criteria to determine the optimal number of components.

2.3 Comparative analysis between GEM, GInc and the standard EM

As a comparative analysis, we apply the standard EM, multi-start EM (which trains the model over several different random initial conditions and takes one that scores the highest likelihood), GEM, and the GInc method proposed by Verbeek [4] on learning the MGs model defined in (2) for clustering synthetic datasets. The matlab software of Verbeek's GInc method is available publicly[1]. It is more efficient than most standard GInc methods as it uses several heuristics, such as partial-EM and random covariance-splitting, to reduce the complexity to $O(gnk^2_{desired})$ where g is a constant to be defined later. For controlled testing, we generate synthetic datasets from multiple Gaussian distributions using a range of number of cluster centers (k), cluster-separability (defined by the c-separation value, c-sep) and problem-dimension (d) with maximum eccentricity of 10 [12]. Cluster-separability measures how separable the generating clusters are: low c-sep values indicate that the clusters overlap each other significantly and are therefore difficult to separate; whereas high c-sep values indicate that they overlap each other little and are therefore easy to separate. For each combination of characteristics, we generate 20 sets of data, each with 2000 training data and 5000 testing data, and use the average Kullback Leibler distance between the trained model and the generating model as the performance measure. The re-estimation formula for the mixture of Gaussians model are taken from [5].

To ensure fair comparison, the parameters of the tested algorithms are chosen such that all except for the standard EM use a similar amount of computational time (all spend roughly 20 seconds per run). Multi-start EM selects the best model over 20 runs from different random initial conditions, GEM uses an enlargement factor of α=4, and GInc uses a setting of g=30 where g is the number of data points to try in order to determine the optimal splitting positions for a component [4]. Except for GInc which initializes with the mean of the data points as the first center, the standard EM, multi-start EM and GEM use K-means for initialization. In all cases, the only stopping criterion for all EM iterations is that the complete data likelihood defined in (3) increases by less than a threshold ratio of 10^{-4}, except for (1) the partial-EM procedure of GInc and (2) the EM learning of all intermediate stages of GEM, in which a smaller threshold ratio of 10^{-3} is employed for efficiency enhancement.

Fig. 2 shows the relative performance between the tested algorithms on the synthetic datasets. It is clear that the standard EM performs worse than all other algorithms in all cases, so hereafter we will only compare between multi-start EM, GInc and GEM. At k=2 all three methods perform similarly well, but at higher

---

[1] http://staff.science.uva.nl/~jverbeek/software/.

values of k the performance differences become more apparent. The overall performance of GEM is comparable to that of GInc, and even slight better at low c-sep region ($c<0.5$), showing good global clustering property. While multi-start EM performs better than both GEM and GInc at low c-sep region, it performs badly at high c-sep region (especially at $k=16$). Given GEM's competitive performance to GInc, its consistency over the whole range of cluster separability index and dimensionality, and its ease of implementation, GEM is a very attractive alternative for global clustering.

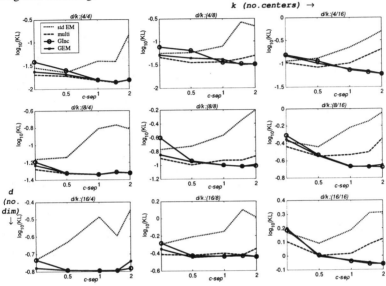

Fig. 2 Performance comparison between the standard EM, multi-start EM, GInc and GEM on clustering synthetic data generated from multiple Gaussian distributions using a range of number of centers (k), cluster-separability (c-sep) and problem-dimension (d). The overall performance of GEM is similar to that of GInc, only slight better at low c-sep region. Multi-start EM excels in the low c-sep region but performs badly at high c-sep region (c-$sep>0.5$), especially at $k=16$.

3   Experiments on Learnging Different Mixture Models

To demonstrate GEM's effectiveness on different mixture model, we apply GEM on learning the MFA model for dimensionality reduction of the well-known shrinking spiral dataset [2], and compare its performance against the multi-start EM. Details of the MFA model are as follows. The re-estimation formulas are omitted but they can be found in [10].

model/use	MFA for clustering and dimensionality reduction
model representation	$\mathbf{y} = \Lambda_m \mathbf{v} + \mathbf{n}$ where $\mathbf{v} \sim N(0,\mathbf{I})$, $\mathbf{n} \sim N(\mathbf{\mu}_m, \mathbf{\Psi}_m)$
parameters	$\theta_m = \{\Lambda_m, \mathbf{\mu}_m, \mathbf{\Psi}_m\}$
complete data likelihood	$p(\mathbf{y} \mid \theta_m) \equiv N(\mathbf{y}; \mathbf{\mu}_m, \Lambda_m \Lambda_m^T + \mathbf{\Psi})$

Factor analysis is a statistical method for modeling the covariance structure of high dimensional data using a small number of latent variables. MFA is an extension of factor analysis by using local factor models in different regions of the input space. Its objective is to model each d-vector $\mathbf{y}$ using a reduced dimensionality latent p-vector factor $\mathbf{v}$, through the so-called factor loading matrix $\Lambda_m = (d \times p)$. Given $\mathbf{v} = (p \times 1)$ is distributed with unit variance and $\mathbf{n} = (d \times 1)$ is a noise vector distributed according to $\mathbf{n} \sim N(\mathbf{\mu}_m, \mathbf{\Psi}_m)$, each component is equivalent to a Gaussian distribution with mean $\mathbf{\mu}_m$ and covariance $\Lambda_m \Lambda_m^T + \mathbf{\Psi}_m$. Experiments are performed on the "shrinking spiral" dataset, which is a benchmark dataset for testing MFA.

Again, the control parameters of multi-start EM and GEM are chosen such that both algorithms require roughly the same amount of training time. Multi-start EM selects the best model over 10 runs from different random initial conditions, and GEM uses an enlargement factor of $\alpha = 2$. The only stopping criterion is that the complete data likelihood increases by less than a threshold ratio of 10^{-4}.

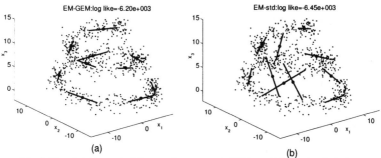

Fig. 3 The shrinking spiral data, and two sample MFA models obtained via (1) GEM and (2) the standard EM algorithm. The segments, whose ends are $(\mathbf{\mu}_m \pm \Lambda_m)$, show the location and direction of the factor components

Fig. 3 provides visualization of the datasets and two sample solutions. Experiment results are summarised in Table 1, which records the mean and the standard deviation of the log likelihood values, as well as the runtime scored by the multi-start EM and GEM. In all cases, GEM spends similar amount of computation time as the multi-start EM, yet it scores higher mean likelihood values, and in addition

44

with much lower standard deviation, suggesting higher consistency in reproducing similar clusters.

Table 1. Statistics of model likelihood values and runtime with the multi-start EM and GEM over 20 runs. Higher mean likelihood values are printed in bold.

	No. clus.	Multi-start EM			GEM		
		log like. mean	std.	time (s)	log like. mean	std.	time (s)
Shrinking Spiral data	5	-6799.11	50.4	2.6	**-6757.74**	57.8	2.1
	7	-6506.68	50.5	4.1	**-6441.05**	35.4	3.7
	9	-6324.19	51.2	5.9	**-6245.11**	8.9	5.2
	11	-6227.23	44.8	8.5	**-6162.66**	10.8	6.8
	13	-6163.46	23.3	11.1	**-6106.75**	7.5	9.1
	15	-6112.79	15.6	13.3	**-6075.75**	8.8	11.1
	17	-6090.54	16.0	15.5	**-6049.52**	5.9	15.1
	19	-6060.3	12.4	17.9	**-6032.86**	10.5	17.9

4 Conclusions

GEM is a novel greedy learning algorithm for global EM learning of finite mixture model. It is easy to implement and robust to initial conditions. Experiments on different mixture models validate its versatility and effectiveness.

Acknowledgements

This research is supported by the KEDRI postdoctoral fellow research fund and by FRST New Zealand (NERF/AUT X0201).

References

1. McLachlan, G. and D. Peel, *Finite Mixture Models*. Wiley Series in Probability and Statistics. 2000: John Wiley & Sons.
2. Figueiredo, M. and A.K. Jain, *Unsupervised Learning of Finite Mixture Models*. IEEE Transactions on Pattern Analysis and Machine Intelligence, 2002. **24**(3): p. 381-396.
3. Dempster, A.P., N.M. Larird, and D.B. Rubin, *Maximum likelihood for incomplete data via the EM algorithm*. Journal of Statistics Society, 1977. **B**(39): p. 1-38.
4. Verbeek, J., N. Vlassis, and B. Krose, *Efficient Greedy Learning of Gaussian Mixture Models*. Neural Computation, 2003. **15**: p. 469-485.
5. Vlassis, N. and A. Likas, *A greedy EM algorithm for Gaussian mixture learning*. Neural Processing Letters, 2002. **15**(1): p. 77-87.
6. Daskin, M.S., *Network and Discrete Location Models, Algorithms, and Applications*. 1995, New York: Wiley.

7. Rose, K., *Deterministic Annealing for Clustering, Compression, Classification, Regression, and Related Optimization Problems*. Proc. IEEE, 1998. **86**: p. 2210-2239.
8. Bensmail, H., et al., *Inference in Model-Based Cluster Analysis*. Statistics and Computing, 1997. **7**: p. 1-10.
9. Chan, Z.S.H. and N. Kasabov. *Gene Trajectory Clustering with a Hybrid Genetic Algorithm and Expectation Maximization Method*. in *International Joint Conference on Neural Networks*. 2004. Budapest: IEEE Press.
10. Ghahramani, Z. and G. Hinton, *The EM Algorithm for Mixtures of Factor Analyzers*. 1996, University of Toronto.
11. Chan, Z.S.H. and N. Kasabov, *Efficient global clustering using the greedy elimination method*. Electronics Letters, 2004. **40**(25): p. 1611-1612.
12. Dasgupta, S. *Learning mixtures of Gaussians*. in *IEEE Symposium on Foundations of Computer Science*. 1999. New York.

Tracking Drifting Concepts by Time Window Optimisation

Ivan Koychev[1] Robert Lothian[2]

[1] Institute of Mathematics and Informatics, Bulgarian Academy of Science,
Acad. G. Bonchev Street, bl.8, Sofia -1113, Bulgaria
ikoychev@math.bas.bg

[2] School of Computing, The Robert Gordon University
St Andrew Street, Aberdeen AB25 1HG, UK
rml@comp.rgu.ac.uk

Abstract. This paper addresses the task of learning concept descriptions from streams of data. As new data are obtained the concept description has to be updated regularly to include the new data. In this case we can face the problem that the concept changes over time. Hence the old data become irrelevant to the current concept and have to be removed from the training dataset. This problem is known in the area of machine learning as concept drift. We develop a mechanism that tracks changing concepts using an adaptive time window. The method uses a significance test to detect concept drift and then optimizes the size of the time window, aiming to maximise the classification accuracy on recent data. The method presented is general in nature and can be used with any learning algorithm. The method is tested with three standard learning algorithms (kNN, ID3 and NBC). Three datasets have been used in these experiments. The experimental results provide evidence that the suggested forgetting mechanism is able significantly to improve predictive accuracy on changing concepts.

1 Introduction

Many machine learning applications employ algorithms for learning concept descriptions. Usually, as time passes, new examples are obtained and added to the training dataset. Then the concept description is updated to take into account the new examples. These applications often face the problem that real life concepts tend to change over time, i.e. a concept description learned on all previous examples is no longer up-to-date. Hence, some of the old observations that are out-of-date have to be 'forgotten'. This problem is known as *concept drift* [16]. A prominent example of a system that should adapt to changing concepts is a system that helps users to find pieces of information in which they are likely to be interested. These systems use machine learning methods to acquire from observations a model of user's interests. However, user's interests and preferences are inclined to change over time (e.g. [7], [12] and

[13]). Such systems are usually provided with mechanisms that are able to track changing user interests.

There are two important questions that have to be addressed in case of concept drift. The first one is *how to detect a change in the concept*? If there is no background information about the process, we can use the decrease in predictive accuracy of the learned classifier as an indicator of changes in the concept. Usually the developed detection mechanism uses a predefined threshold tailored for the particular dataset (e.g. [18]). However the underlying concept can change with different speeds i.e. some times it can be *abrupt* other times it can be rather *gradual*. The detection mechanism often has difficulty in detecting both types of changes i.e. if the threshold is very sensitive it can mistake noise for concept drift or if it is not sensitive enough it can take too long to discover a gradual drift. Recently some authors suggested the use of a statistical hypothesis test to detect the changes (e.g. [4] and [9]).

The second important question is *how to adapt if a change is detected?* In some applications a fixed size time window optimised for the particular application is used (e.g. [13]). This solution is fast and easy to implement, but it requires a preliminary investigation of the domain to select the window size. Moreover if the type and frequency of the changes in the concept are unpredictable it can lead to a decrease in the classification accuracy. Other approaches use heuristics to decrease the size of the time window when changes in the concept are detected (e.g. [4] and [18]).

The next section gives a short overview of the related work. A novel mechanism that addresses both questions for dealing with the concept drift problem is presented in section 3. It uses a statistical significance test to detect concept drift. Then it employs an efficient optimisation algorithm to adapt the size of the time window. Experiments with one artificial and two real datasets are reported in section 4.

2   Related Work

Different approaches have been developed to track changing (also known as shifting, drifting or evolving) concepts. Typically it is assumed that if the concept changes, then the old examples become irrelevant to the current period. The concept descriptions are learned from a set of recent examples called a time window. For example, Mitchell et al. [13] developed a software assistant for scheduling meetings, which employs machine learning to acquire assumptions about individual habits of arranging meetings, uses a time window to adapt faster to the changing preferences of the user. Widmer and Kubat [18] developed the first approach that uses adaptive window size. The algorithm monitors the learning process and if the performance drops under a predefined threshold it uses heuristics to adapt the time window size dynamically. Maloof and Michalski [12] have developed a method for selecting training examples for a partial memory learning system. The method uses a time-based function to provide each instance with an age. Examples that are older than a certain age are removed from the partial memory. Delany et al. [3] employ a case base editing approach that removes noise cases (i.e. the cases that contribute to the classification incorrectly are removed) to deal with concept drift in a spam filtering system. The approach is very promising, but is applicable for lazy learning algorithms only. To manage the problems with gradual concept drift and noisy data, the approach in [11] suggests the use of three windows: a small (with fixed size), a medium and a large (dynamically adapted by simple heuristics). The approach presented in this paper also addresses those problems, by a carefully designed statistical test and uses an efficient optimal algorithm instead of heuristics to adapt dynamically the time window size.

The above approaches totally forget the examples that are outside the given window, or older than a certain age. The examples which remain in the partial memory are equally important for the learning algorithms. This is an abrupt forgetting of old examples, which probably does not reflect their rather gradual aging. To deal with this problem it was suggested to weight training examples in the time window according to their appearance over time [6]. These weights make recent examples more important than older ones, essentially causing the system to gradually forget old examples. This approach has been explored further in [8] and [9]. The mechanism presented in this paper is also based on the time window idea, but it seeks to improve the performance by dynamically optimising the time window size. It seems that gradual forgetting can compliment quite well the time window approach, but we choose to focus on exploring the pure approach in this paper.

Some systems use different approaches to avoid loss of useful knowledge learned from old examples. The CAP system [13] keeps old rules as long as they are competitive with the new ones. The architecture of the FLORA system [18], assumes that the learner maintains a store of concept descriptions relevant to previous contexts. When the learner suspects a context change, it will examine the potential of previously stored descriptions to provide better classification. The approach presented in [7] employs a two-level schema to deal with drifting and recurring concepts. On the first level the system learns a classifier from the most recent observations assuming that it is able to provide description of the current context. The learned classifier is accurate enough to be able to distinguish the past episodes that are relevant to the current context. Then the algorithm constructs a new training set, 'remembers' relevant examples and 'forgets' irrelevant ones. The approach presented in this paper, does not assume that old examples or models can be retrieved, because this can be very time consuming and memory intensive.

Widmer [17] assumes that the domain provides explicit clues to the current context (e.g. attributes with characteristic values). A two-level learning algorithm is presented that effectively adjusts to changing contexts by trying to detect (via meta-learning) contextual clues and using this information to focus the learning process. Another two-level learning algorithm assumes that concepts are likely to be stable for some period of time [5]. This approach uses batch learning and contextual clustering to detect stable concepts and to extract hidden context. The mechanism in this paper does not assume that the domain provides some clues that can be discovered using a meta-learning level. It rather aims to get the best performance using a single learning level.

An adaptive boosting method based on dynamic sample-weighting is presented in [9]. The approach uses statistical hypothesis testing to detect concept changes. Gama et al., [4] also use a hypothesis testing procedure, similar to that used in control charts, to detect the concept drift, calculating on all of the data so far. The mechanism gives a warning at 2 standard deviations (approximately 95%) and then takes action at 3 standard deviations (approximately 99.7%). If the action level is reached then the start of the window is reset to the point at which the warning level was reached. However, for this mechanism, it can take quite a long time to react to changes and the examples that belong to the old concept are not always completely useless, especially when the concept drift is rather gradual. The approach presented in this paper also uses a statistical test to detect concept changes, but some limitations of the plain test are addressed by a more careful selection of the test population. If a concept description is detected then the mechanism uses a fast optimisation algorithm, to find out the optimal size of the window that achieves the maximum accuracy of classification.

3 A Scheme for Tracking Drifting Concepts

Let us consider a sequence of examples. Each example is classified according to underlying criteria into one of a set of classes, which forms the training set. The task is to learn a classifier that can be used to classify the next examples in the sequence. However, the underlying criteria can subsequently change and the same example can be classified differently according to the time of its appearance, i.e. a concept drift takes place. As we discussed above to deal with this problem machine learning systems often use a time window i.e. the classifier is not learned on all examples, but only on a subset of recent examples. This section introduces an approach for learning up-to-date descriptions of drifting concept based on this idea. It addresses the two major tasks involved in dealing with drifting concepts: by suggesting an effective mechanism for detecting the concept drift and if a drift is detected optimises the size of the time window to gain maximum accuracy of prediction.

3.1 Detecting the Concept Drift

To detect concept changes the approach monitors the performance of the algorithm. For the presentation below we choose to observe the classification accuracy as a measure of the algorithm performance, but other measures, such as error rate or precision could have been used. The presented approach process the sequence of examples on small episodes (a.k.a. batches). On each step, a new classifier is learned from the current time window then the average accuracy of this classifier is calculated on the next batch of examples [13]. Then the presented approach suggests using a statistical test to check whether the accuracy of classification has significantly decreased compared with its historical level. We assume that the concept has changed if the current accuracy exceeds the appropriate test level for the normal distribution at the required confidence level. To be precise, if the average prediction accuracy of the last batch is significantly less than the average accuracy for the population of batches defined on the current time window, then a concept drift can be assumed.

As the performance level of the algorithm can vary for the different concepts and the noise level can also change over the time, we must carefully select the test population for the current time window. We can use the whole window as in [9], but the predictive accuracy at the beginning of the time window can be low because of previous concept drift. For example, you can see on Figure 2 in section Experiments, how the classification accuracy slowly increases after a concept drift. Therefore we suggest that the test is done on a sub-window that does not include the first few batches from the beginning of the time window. Clearly this mechanism will work well when the concept is shifting i.e. the accuracy is dropping abruptly. In the case where the changes in the concept are gradual the mechanism should work if the significance test is done on a relatively old population, i.e. one or a few most recent batches are not included in the test window. Such a test that uses a test population from the core of the time window will work well for both abrupt and gradual drift.

From the central limit theorem, it follows that if we want to be confident about the required test level, the test should be supplied to batches of at least 30 examples. If it appears that the current batch size is less than 30 then the algorithm can easily resize the batches to satisfy this guidance. In cases where the data set is expected to be noisier, then a larger batch size is recommended, because this will smooth changes caused by noise.

The confidence level for the significance test should be sensitive enough to discover concept drift as soon as possible, but not to mistake noise for changes in the concept. The experience from the conducted experiments shows that the "standard" confidence level of 95% works very well in all experiments. This drift detection level is rather sensitive and it assists the algorithm to detect the drift earlier. If a false concept drift alarm is triggered, it will activate the window optimising mechanism, but in practice, this only results in an insignificant decrease in the time window size.

*The presented mechanism works as follows: **If** concept drift is detected **then** the optimisation of the size of the time window is performed (see the next section) **otherwise**, the time window size is increased to include the new examples.*

3.2   Optimising the Time Window Size

In general, if the concept is stable, the bigger the training set is (the time window), the more accurately the concept description can be learned. However when the concept is changing, a big window will probably contain a lot of old examples, which will result in a decrease of the classification accuracy. Hence, the window size should be decreased to exclude the out-of-date examples and in this way to learn a more accurate classifier. But if the size of the window becomes too small, it will also lead to a decrease in accuracy. The shape of curve that demonstrates the relationship between the size of the time window and the accuracy of the classification is shown in Figure 1.

To adapt the size of the window according to current changes in the concept, Widmer and Kubat [18] pioneer the use of heuristics. However, it would be ideal if we were able to find the optimal size of the window to ensure the best classification accuracy. The approach presented in [8] tries all possible window sizes and selects the one with the smallest error rate. This brute force optimization is, of course, inefficient.

The presented mechanism suggests using the Golden Section algorithm for one-dimensional optimization [2]. The algorithm looks for an optimal solution in a closed and bounded interval $[a,b]$ - in our case the possible window sizes $X = [x_{min}, x_c]$, where x_{min} is a predefined minimum size of the window and x_c is the current size of the time window. It assumes that the function $f(x)$ is unimodal on X (i.e. there is only one max $x*$) and it is strictly increasing on $(x_{min}, x*)$ and strictly decreasing on $(x*, x_c)$, which is the shape that can be seen in Figure 1. In our case the function $f(x)$ calculates the classification accuracy of the learned model using a time window with size x.

The basic idea of this algorithm is to minimize the number of function evaluations by trapping the optimum solution in a set of nested intervals. On each step the algorithm uses the golden section ($\tau = 0.618$) to split the interval into three subintervals, as shown in Figure 1, where $l = b - \tau(b - a)$ and $r = a + \tau(b - a)$. If $f(l) > f(r)$ then the new interval chosen for the next step is $[a,r]$ else $[l,b]$. The length of the interval for the next iteration is $\tau(b - a)$. Those iterations continue until the interval containing the maximum reaches a predefined minimum size. $x*$ is taken to lie at the centre of the final interval.

The Golden Section algorithm is a very efficient way to trap the $x*$ that optimizes the function $f(x)$. After n iterations, the interval is reduced to 0.618^n times its original size. For example if $n = 10$, less than 1% of the original interval remains. Note that, due to the properties of the golden section, each iteration requires only one new function evaluation.

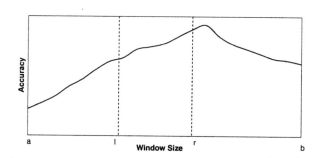

Fig. 1. A sample shape of the correlation between the window size and accuracy of the learned classifier

In conclusion, if we can assume that the classification accuracy in relation to the time window is a unimodal function then the golden section algorithm can be used as an efficient way to find the optimal size of the time window. It is possible to find datasets for which the unimodal assumption is not true – e.g. when the concept changes very often and abruptly. In such cases, we can use other optimization methods that do not assume a unimodal distribution, however they are much more expensive in time. The trade-off that we have to take into consideration is to accept that we can occasionally be trapped in a local maximum, but have a fast optimization; or find a global maximum, but have significantly slower optimization.

4 Experiments

The aim of the experiments reported in this section is to explore whether the present forgetting mechanism is able to improve the performance of different learning algorithms on drifting concepts.

All experiments were designed to follow the natural scenario of using such mechanisms [13]. For this reason the data streams were chunked on episodes/batched. The algorithm was run on this data set iteratively - on each iteration, a concept description is learned from the examples in the current time window. Then the learned classifier is tested on the next batch.

The experiments were conducted with three popular learning algorithms:

- k Nearest Neighbours (kNN) - also known as Instance Based Learning (IBL) [1]. k=3 was the default setting for the experiments reported below except for experiments with STAGGER dataset, where k=1 was chosen, because it produces a more accurate classification than k=3;
- Induction of Decision Trees (ID3) [15] (using an attribute selection criteria based on the χ^2 statistics);
- Naïve Bayesian Classifier (NBC) [14].

The first experiments were conducted with an artificial learning problem that was defined and used by Schlimmer and Granger [16] for testing STAGGER, probably the first concept drift tracking system. Much of the subsequent work dedicated to this problem used this dataset for testing purposes (e.g. [1], [4], [5], [6], [7], [12], [17] and [18]). This allows comparison of our approach with similar approaches on this data set. Those results are presented in the next subsection. Experiments also were conducted with two datasets from the UCI machine learning repository[1], which are presented in subsections 4.2 and 4.3 below.

The results from the conducted experiments are presented in Tables 1, 3, 4 and 5 below. In all these tables, rows present the used learning algorithms: kNN, ID3 and NBC. The first column shows the predictive accuracy of the algorithms using Full Memory (FM) learning – all data available up to the current moment are used for learning the concept. The second column presents the results from the experiments with Fixed-size Time Window (FTW). The third column shows the results from the experiments with the algorithms using this paper's Time Window Optimisation (TWO) mechanism. For each data set, the window size for the FTW was chosen to approximate the average time window size obtained in the experiments with the TWO

---

[1] http://www.ics.uci.edu/~mlearn/MLRepository.html

mechanism on the same dataset. This is extra help for the FTW that would not be available in a real situation where the forthcoming sequence of events is unknown. The aim here is to allow the FTW approach to show its best performance.

We used the paired t-tests with 95% confidence level to see whether the presented approach significantly changes the accuracy of learned classifiers. The pairs are formed by comparing the algorithms' accuracies on the same iteration. In the tables below, reporting the results from the experiments, the sign * denotes that the TWO approach achieves a significantly better classification accuracy than the FM and the sign ^ - that TWO is significantly better than the FTW approach.

4.1 STAGGER problem

The STAGGER problem is defined as follows: The instance space of a simple blocks world is described by three attributes: *size* = *{small, medium, large}*, *color* = *{red, green, blue}*, and *shape* = *{square, circular, triangular}*. There is a sequence of three target concepts: (1) - *size* = *small* and *color* = *red*; (2) - *color* = *green* or *shape* = *circular;* and (3) - *size* = *(medium or large)*. 120 training instances are generated randomly and classified according to the current concept. The underlying concept is forced to change after every 40 training examples in the sequence: (1)-(2)-(3). The setup of the experiments with the STAGGER dataset was done exactly in the same way us in other similar works. The retraining step is 1, however there is a test set with size 100, generated randomly and classified according to the current concept. This differs from the other experiments where the retraining step and the test set are the same - a batch.The size of the FTM is set up to 25, which approximates the average size of the optimised windows.

Memory: Algorithm:	FM	FTW	TWO
kNN	63.03	80.47	86.56*^
ID3	69.05	83.73	89.03*^
NBC	69.97	82.99	90.26*^

Table 1. The improvement of the classification accuracy when the TWO mechanism is applied to the STAGGER dataset

Table 1 shows the results from the experiments with this dataset. In this dataset we have two abrupt changes in the underlying concept and the fixed size time window is able to improve the classification accuracy significantly compared with the full memory. The TWO mechanism additionally improves the classification accuracy significantly compared to FTW.

Figure 2 shows a plot of the results from the experiments with NBC, which illustrate the behaviour of the three mechanisms. It can be seen from the chart that when the algorithm uses the TWO mechanism it adapts faster to the changes.

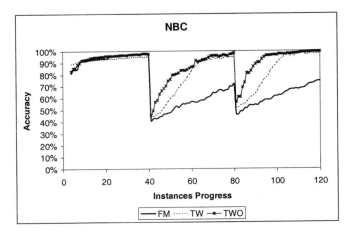

Fig. 2. Classification accuracy of the NBC using Full Memory, Time Window and Time Window Optimisation.

Figure 3 shows the average size of the time window for each step in one of the experiments with NBC-TWO. The experiments with other algorithms produce very similar graphs.

As we mentioned above the STAGGER problem was used by a number of other systems that deal with concept drift. To compare the present approach with the previous approaches, we summarised all available results from experiments using this dataset in Table 2. The first ten rows of this table present the results from experiments with other similar approaches. The last three rows present the results from the experiments with the algorithms using the Time Window Optimisation (TWO) mechanism. The results are shown in more detail to facilitate a better comparison of the systems' performance on different concepts: (1), (2) and (3), shown in separate columns. The last column shows the average performance on the whole dataset. We will look more closely at the results from the second and third concepts, where actually the systems adapt to changes in the underlying concept. The performance of the systems on this dataset depends on the basic learning algorithms, which seem to perform differently on this dataset. Therefore we will mainly be interested in comparing the systems that use the same basic learning algorithm.

The algorithms that use the present TWO mechanism (rows 11-13) significantly outperform the first three systems (rows 1 to 3). The results presented in row 4, are

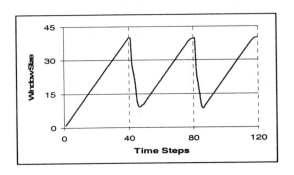

Fig. 3. The average window size for each step in the experiment with NBC-TWO

from the experiments with the COPL mechanism, using NBC as the basic learning algorithm. Therefore, we compared it with NBC-TWO, which achieves a significantly better performance for this dataset.

The FLORA systems reach significantly higher accuracy, than all other approaches on the first concept, which is actually a stable one. However, NBC-TWO and ID3-TWO significantly outperform all FLORA systems on the concepts (2)-(3), i.e. after concept drift has occurred. In general, kNN does not perform very well on this dataset, despite this kNN-TWO significantly outperforms the FLORA2 and FLORA3 algorithms on the concepts (2)-(3).

Concept: Algorithm:	(1)	(2)	(3)	(1)-(2) -(3)
1. IB2 [1]	80.4	51.9	55.6	63.9
2. AQBL [12]	89.6	57.2	55.7	67.0
3. AQPM [12]	89.7	70.5	75.1	79.9
4. COPL (NBC) [7]	91.2	78.9	85.9	85.3
5. FLORA 2 [18]	98.8	80.4	80.3	86.5
6. FLORA 3 [18]	98.7	80.7	79.5	86.0
7. FLORA 4 [18]	98.0	82.5	82.7	87.7
8. kNN – GF [6]	91.8	79.5	83.2	84.8
9. ID3 – GF [6]	93.9	78.3	89.0	87.07
10. NBC – GF [6]	92.4	83.9	88.9	88.4
11. kNN – TWO	*91.9*	*81.4*	*86.3*	*86.5*
12. ID3 – TWO	*93.1*	*84.2*	*89.8*	*89.0*
13. NBC – TWO	*93.9*	*85.4*	*91.5*	*90.3*

Table 2. Average classification accuracy of systems with embedded concept drift tracking mechanisms on the STAGGER dataset

The results reported in rows 8 to 11 are from algorithms that use the Gradual Forgetting (GF) mechanism [6]. For this dataset the GF mechanism uses a fixed-size (30) time window in which the examples are assigned gradually decreasing weights using a linear forgetting function. We are comparing TWO and GF mechanisms on pairs that use the same learning algorithm (e.g. rows 9 and 12). We can see that there is no difference in average accuracy on the first concept. There is a small, but significant improvement of the accuracy obtained by TWO for the changed concepts (2)-(3).

4.2   German Credit Dataset

This subsection presents the results from the experiments conducted with the German credit dataset, from the UCI machine learning Repository. The dataset contains 1000 Instances of bank credit data which are described by 20 attributes. The examples are classified in two classes as either "*good*" or "*bad*". To simulate hidden changes in the context the dataset was sorted by an attribute then this attribute was removed from the dataset for the experiments. Using an attribute to sort the data set and in this way simulate changing context is a commonly used approach to set up experiments to study concept drift. Two sorted datasets were created using the German credit dataset: The first one was sorted by a continuous attribute: *"age"*, which would produce a gradual drift of the *"class"* concept. The second one was sorted by the attribute *"checking_status"*, which has three discrete values. We aimed in this way to create abrupt changes of the *"class"* concept. The dataset was divided into a sequence of batches, each of them containing 10 examples. The size of the FTM is set to 200, which approximates the average size of the optimised windows.

Memory: Algorithm:	FM	FTW	TWO
kNN	68.25	72.37	77.75*^
ID3	77.00	75.50	79.00*^
NBC	78.37	75.87	78.63 ^

Table 3. The improvement of the classification accuracy when the TWO mechanism is applied to the Credit dataset (sorted by *"age"* attribute).

Table 3 shows the results from the experiments with the Credit dataset (sorted by *"age"* attribute). With all algorithms an improvement in classification accuracy was achieved when the algorithms using TWO mechanism were applied. All these improvements are significant except the comparison with NBC-FM.

Table 4 shows the results from the experiments with the Credit dataset (sorted by *"checking_status"* attribute). The results show that the TWO mechanism improves the classification accuracy of the algorithms and these improvements are significant for all algorithms.

Memory: Algorithm:	FM	FTW	TWO
kNN	64.00	71.75	77.13*^
ID3	64.87	71.75	75.25*^
NBC	74.37	74.14	77.76*^

Table 4. The improvement of the classification accuracy when the TWO mechanism is applied to the Credit dataset (sorted by *"checking_status"* attribute).

The results also show that a fixed time window does not always provide an improvement of the accuracy and can even be destructive compared to the full memory learning algorithm. The problem with it is that we do not know in advance how the concept will change and what will be the best size in the future. Even with some "cheating", by using a time window approximating the average optimal window size in the experiments with the TWO mechanism, an improvement is achieved in only half of the cases with this dataset.

4.3 Spam dataset

Experiments have also been conducted with the Spam dataset from the UCI machine learning Repository. Spam is an unsolicited email message. The dataset consists of 4601 instances, 1813 (39.4%) of which are spam messages. The dataset is represented by 54 attributes that represent the occurrence of a pre-selected set of words in each of the documents plus three attributes representing the number of capital letters in the e-mail. To simulate the changing hidden context the examples in the dataset are sorted according to the *"capital_run_length_total"*, which is the total number of capital letters in the e-mail. This attribute and the related two attributes *"capital_run_length_average"* and *"capital_run_length_longest"* are removed from the dataset, because they can provide explicit clues for the concept changes. The sorted dataset was divided into a sequence of batches with a length of 10 examples each.

Memory: Algorithm:	FM	FTW	TWO
kNN	90.12	90.10	92.48*^
ID3	87.08	86.56	89.51*^
NBC	90.61	90.78	91.56*^

Table 5. The improvement of the classification accuracy when the TWO mechanism is applied to the Spam dataset, sorted by *"capital_run_length_total"* attribute (ster 10).

Table 5 presents the results from the experiments with the Spam dataset comparing full memory learning, time window with fixed size and the time window with optimized size. For this dataset the fixed window size was set to 400 - an approximation of the average window size for this dataset used by the TWO mechanism. For this dataset for two of the algorithms (kNN and NBC) the fixed time window improves the classification accuracy, but not significantly in either case. For ID3 we can even see a slight decrease in the accuracy. An improvement of the classification accuracy for all algorithms was achieved when the TWO mechanisms were applied and all those improvements are significant compared to FM and FTW as well.

Figure 4 shows on the same diagram: the classification accuracy on the test step (the thin line) and the size of the optimised time window (the thick line) on each step. It can be seen that a drop in the accuracy normally leads to a decrease of the time widow size. However, a sudden decrease in the classification accuracy does not always indicate a concept drift, it can be caused by noise in the data stream. The presented algorithm is very robust to such noise, merely decreasing the window size insignificantly, e.g. see the arrow 1 on Figure 4. However, it remains sensitive enough to detect genuine concept drifts that decrease the accuracy by a relatively small value – e.g. see the arrow 2 on Figure 4. The detection mechanism flags both real and false concept drifts, but the window size optimizer responds very differently to the two possibilities.

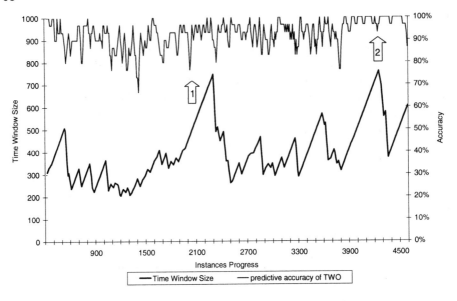

Fig. 4. The relationship between the accuracy of prediction measured on the test set and the time window size.

5 Conclusion

The paper presents a mechanism for dealing with the concept drift problem, which uses a statistical test to detect whether the current concept is changing. If a concept drift is detected, then the mechanism optimizes the time window size to achieve maximum accuracy of prediction. The algorithm is self-adapting and it can be used in many datasets without any predefined domain-dependent heuristics or parameter. Moreover, the developed mechanism is not attached to a particular learning algorithm. It is general in nature and can be added to any relevant algorithm.

The results from experiments with three learning algorithms using three datasets provide strong evidence that the mechanism is able significantly to improve the classification accuracy on drifting concepts.

Acknowledgements

We would like to thank Gerhard Widmer, and Marcus Maloof for providing data from their experiments. Thanks also to David Harper, Dietrich Wettschereck and Nirmalie Wiratunga for their very helpful comments on an early draft of the paper. This research was partially supported by EU FP6 Marie Curie grant KT-DigiCult-Bg, MTKD-CT-2004-509754.

References

1. Aha, D., Kibler, D. and Albert, M.: Instance-Based Learning Algorithms. Machine Learning 6, (1991) 37-66
2. Burghes, D. and Graham, A.: Introduction to Control Theory including Optimal Control: Ellis Horwood Series Mathematics and its Applications. John Wiley & Sons (1980)
3. Delany, SJ., Cunningham. P., Tsymbal, A. and Coyle, L.: A Case-Based Technique for Tracking Concept Drift in Spam Filtering. In: Macintosh, A., Ellis, R. & Allen T. (eds.) Applications and Innovations in Intelligent Systems XII, Proceedings of AI2004, Lecture Notes in Computer Science, Springer (2004) 3-16
4. Gama, J., Medas, P., Castillo, G. and Rodrigues, P.: Learning with Drift Detection. In: Ana, C., Bazzan, S. and Labidi (Eds.): Proceedings of the 17th Brazilian Symposium on Artificial Intelligence. Lecture Notes in Computer Science, Vol. 3171, Springer, (2004) 286-295
5. Harries, M. and Sammut, C.: Extracting Hidden Context. Machine Learning 32 (1998) 101-126
6. Koychev, I.: Gradual Forgetting for Adaptation to Concept Drift. Proceedings of ECAI 2000 Workshop on Current Issues in Spatio-Temporal Reasoning, Berlin, (2000) 101-107
7. Koychev, I.: Tracking Changing User Interests through Prior-Learning of Context. In: de Bra, P., Brusilovsky, P., Conejo, R. (eds.): Adaptive Hypermedia and Adaptive Web Based Systems. Lecture Notes in Computer Science, Vol. 2347, Springer-Verlag (2002) 223-232
8. Klinkenberg, R.: Learning Drifting Concepts: Example Selection vs. Example Weighting. In Intelligent Data Analysis, Special Issue on Incremental Learning Systems Capable of Dealing with Concept Drift, Vol. 8, No. 3, (2004) 281-300
9. Kukar, M.: Drifting Concepts as Hidden Factors in Clinical Studies. In Dojat, D., Elpida T. Keravnou, Pedro Barahona (Eds.): Proceedings of 9th Conference on Artificial Intelligence in Medicine in Europe, AIME 2003, Protaras, Cyprus, October 18-22, 2003, Lecture Notes in Computer Science, Vol. 2780, Springer-Verlag (2003) 355-364
10. Chu, F.and Zaniolo, C.: Fast and light boosting for adaptive mining of data streams. In: Proc. of the 8th Pacific-Asia Conference on Knowledge Discovery and Data Mining. Lecture Notes in Computer Science, Vol.3056, Springer-Verlag, (2004) 282-292
11. Lazarescu, M., Venkatesh, S. and Bui H. H.: Using Multiple Windows to Track Concept Drift. In the Intelligent Data Analysis Journal, Vol 8 (1), (2004) 29-59
12. Maloof, M. and Michalski, R.: Selecting examples for partial memory learning. Machine Learning 41 (2000) 27-52
13. Mitchell, T., Caruana, R., Freitag, D., McDermott, J. and Zabowski, D.: Experience with a Learning Personal Assistant. Communications of the ACM 37(7) (1994) 81-91
14. Mitchell T. Machine Learning. McGraw-Hill (1997)
15. Quinlan, R.: Induction of Decision Trees. Machine Learning 1 (1986) 81-106
16. Schlimmer, J. and Granger, R.: Incremental Learning from Noisy Data. Machine Learning 3, (1986), 317-357
17. Widmer, G.: Tracking Changes through Meta-Learning. Machine Learning 27 (1997) 256-286
18. Widmer, G. and Kubat, M.: Learning in the presence of concept drift and hidden contexts: Machine Learning 23 (1996) 69-101

Hierarchical knowledge-oriented specification for information integration

Madalina Croitoru   Ernesto Compatangelo

Department of Computing Science, University of Aberdeen
Aberdeen, UK

Abstract

We present a novel methodology for manipulating sources in a knowledge integration scenario. Firstly, we define and exploit an appropriate data model, namely Knowledge Oriented Specification, to represent and to query data sources without having to align their background knowledge. Secondly, we propose a structured knowledge representation formalism, namely Layered Conceptual Graphs, which present the data at different levels of detail. We explain how the two formalisms can be jointly used to provide a hierarchical approach to integration.

1   Introduction

Information integration is a broad notion that encompasses the combination of different kinds of distributed, heterogeneous sources such as databases and web sites. The integration process generates a 'unified' view of two or more individual sources; this view can be either virtual (if the sources remain physically distinct) or concrete (if the sources are physically merged) [24]. The user of an information integration system is then able to query the unified view resulting from the integration process, getting results that could not be retrieved from any of the individual sources if independently considered.

One of the main problems in the integration process is the semantic mismatch between sources. Approaches attempting to solve these problems can be grouped in two different categories, namely *multi-agent systems* and *global information systems* (either based on databases or based on ontologies).

- Intelligent Information Integration has been a popular application for multi-agent systems. Due to their approach to interoperability, systems based on multi-agent approaches (InfoSleuth [1], KRAFT [25] and others that use Conceptual Graphs [20]) are already performing an integration task. Despite their advantages (namely, dealing with dynamically changing environments) multi-agent systems also suffer from several drawbacks [20]. These include increased testing costs, failure due to a non-collaborative agent, and memory structuring problems. Peer-to-peer integration systems, which are also included in this category [2], face several ontology alignment challenges too.

- The architecture of global information systems features one global domain against which a number of sources are integrated. As the sources are heterogeneous (*i.e.*, they use different models to store data), the global schema must provide an appropriate abstraction for all data in all sources. The integration method differs from one approach to the other. The Local As View(LAV) approach (used in TSIMMIS [15]) describes data sources as containing answers to views over the global schema. The Global As View (GAV) approach (used in the Information Manifold [17] and in InfoMaster [11]) describes a mediated schema containing answers to views over source relations. The LAV approach allows new sources to be modularly added and removed, while the GAV approach requires source descriptions to be modified when changes occur. Query answering is thus straightforward in GAV (as the answers can be obtained by composing the query with the views), while LAV requires a more sophisticated form of query rewriting. To get the best of both worlds, the Both As View (BAV) approach, based on reversible schema transformation sequences, has been developed in the Automed project [16].

Another kind of problem that arises from current approaches to knowledge integration is the complexity of the integration process. This is often due to the choice of a 'heavyweight' knowledge model — as opposed to a 'lightweight' model — used to describe both the participating sources and their unified view. By heavyweight model, we mean a frame-based one, such as the Protégé model used in the PROMPT approach to ontology alignment and merging [14]. By lightweight model, we mean a less structured (and expressive) one, such as the graph model used in the ONION approach to ontology articulation [21].

Previous work on ontology integration based on a 'shrinkable' heavyweight model [5] suggests that early integration stages may be more effectively managed if the model becomes 'lightweight'. Unsurprisingly, more meaningful interschema mappings are identified if most 'heavyweight constraints' (e.g. cardinality constraints, attribute types) are relaxed or ignored.

We believe that independently of whether the early stage of information integration is either manual or automated, a 'minimalist' (*i.e.*, a lightweight) knowledge model could facilitate the identification of interschema mappings. Hence, in this paper we advocate the use of a knowledge model that extends and adapts conceptual graphs. We thus propose an integration approach based on a Knowledge-Oriented Specification of information (KOS for short); in our opinion, this approach will provide a new way of addressing the problem.

2   The KOS approach to knowledge integration

We are developing an integration approach that performs knowledge combination in a way which differs from any of those used in existing approaches. Rather than defining *knowledge tuples* and mapping them from the mediated view to the sources, we use a *description of knowledge*, both in the sources and in the mediated view. Only when queries are issued the corresponding mappings are introduced to retrieve the actual data tuples.

Our approach also differs from existing ones in terms of the *knowledge representation formalism* used to describe data in the sources. We use Conceptual Graphs (CGs for short), benefitting both from their expressive power and from their associated reasoning capabilities. In our opinion, Conceptual Graphs have attractive features that make them suitable for the development of an effective data integration system. Firstly, their structure allows domain experts to build domain descriptions in an visual manner. Secondly, the structure of CGs facilitates the usage of graph homomorphism techniques [6] for knowledge querying and rewriting. Methodologically, our approach does not fall into any of the LAV, GAV, or BAV categories both in terms of data representation and in terms of querying. Moreover, because of the translation rules that we use in our approach, data is first retrieved from the sources and subsequently integrated. This means that the whole data reconciliation process is performed while the query answer is being generated, which means that the process is performed at the instance level. In this way, schema alignment problems are avoided.

2.1 Representation and methodology

We use Conceptual Graphs [26] as the knowledge representation formalism upon which to base our information integration approach for the following reasons.

- Graphs are a simple and powerful visual formalism for representing knowledge. They can be syntactically expressed in a number of different ways, some of which are particularly suitable for computer processing. Graphs offer syntactic flexibility: for instance, an RDF graph can be expressed as a triple or as a serialised XML structure. In our case, this is a clear benefit w.r.t. other knowledge representations that need an additional visual rendering which is neither so simple to define nor so immediate to understand.

- Conceptual graphs introduce a clear distinction between ontological knowledge and other kinds of knowledge (*e.g.*, factual knowledge). Considering our methodology, this is another very important issue. Description logics (DLs) also explicitly introduce such distinction by declaring classes and individuals in two separate 'conceptual containers' called T-Box and A-Box respectively. However, DLs lack visual capabilities. Moreover, there is a 'reasoning power tradeoff' between reasoning mechanisms for conceptual graphs, which are based on graph homomorphism, and reasoning mechanisms for description logics, which are based on subsumption [18].

Simple conceptual graphs (i.e., conceptual graphs that cannot represent negation) correspond to a specific fragment of FOL [22]. Extensions of conceptual graphs that allow negation have been already proposed [9]; however, in this paper we will only consider simple conceptual graphs for sake of simplicity. Even in this case, we believe that choosing conceptual graphs to represent knowledge in our approach to information integration has a threefold benefit.

Our approach to the description and to the integration of distributed, heterogeneous information sources is performed according to the following steps.

1. For every new source to be integrated, the domain expert describes the source schema in terms of conceptual graphs.

2. The data source is linked to its CG representation using a wrapper [3].

3. The conceptual graph that represent the sources is integrated in the existing graph view(s).

4. An integrated schema of their disjoint union is then extracted along with a set of rules that redirects the user queries to appropriate data sources.

5. If the integrated view is not detailed enough for the user's needs, a more detailed view is produced (if the user has access rights to such detailed view, and of course, if such view exists). This translation is achieved using Layered Conceptual Graphs, a hierarchical extension of conceptual graphs.

A example showing how the above steps work in practice is presented below, while the formalism underlying the approach is introduced in the next section.

2.2 Exemplifying GC-based information integration

We introduce our integration approach using a small example. Let us consider two data sources with information about the Dada and the Surrealist artistic movements. These two sources, represented using two different formalisms, should be integrated in the context of a museum website. This would provide a unified interface of the sources, allowing them to be simultaneously queried.

A few introductory notes on Dada and surrealism follow. Dada, founded in 1918 by Tristan Tzara, is an art movement which ridiculed contemporary culture and traditional art forms. The movement was born as a consequence of the collapse, during World War I, of social and moral values of the time. Dada artists produced works which were nihilistic or reflected a cynical attitude toward social values, and, at the same time, irrational – absurd and playful, emotive and intuitive, and often cryptic. Many artists (such as Marcel Duschamp, or Max Ernst) associated with this movement later became associated with Surrealism. Surrealism, founded in 1924 by Andre Breton, produced works of anti-art that deliberately defied reason. The movement was influenced by Freudianism and dedicated to the expression of imagination as revealed in dreams, free of the conscious control of reason and free of convention.

Figure 1 depicts two data sources that contain information on Dada and Surrealism. The information contained in these data sources is presented by the domain expert as a conceptual graph called Knowledge-Oriented Specification (KOS for short) [8]. A conceptual graph consists of concept nodes (represented as rectangles) and relation nodes (represented as ovals). The concepts nodes are labelled with (i) a *type* (the concept types are ordered in a hierarchy called support) and (ii) a *marker*. The marker can either be an individual marker (constant) such as 'Andre Breton', or a generic marker (*i.e.*, a variable) such as '*'. The relation nodes are labelled by relation types which are taken from the support, where they are organised as posets.

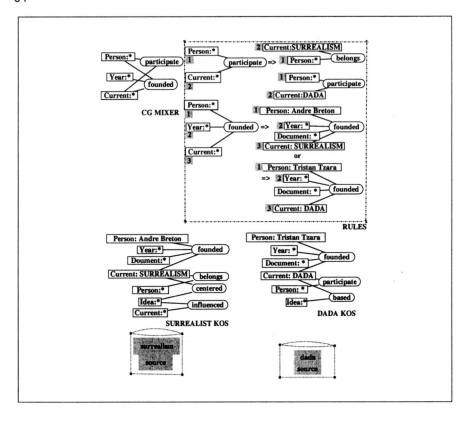

Figure 1: Integrated view on two data sources

The Knowledge-Oriented Specification of a source is a conceptual graph that represents the knowledge contained in that source. From a user viewpoint, a KOS allows to query a source in a CG-like language. Note that the KOS presents knowledge in a schematic way. This means that all concepts in the graph are either generic nodes or, in very special circumstances, constants. The data source contains all the valid instantiations of the generic concepts in the KOS graph, along with the constraints imposed by the relation nodes. A wrapper is associated to the KOS, where, for a given query, it accesses the data source and retrieves the actual information contained in the answer.

The KOS specification of the surrealism source in Figure 1 states that Andre Breton founded in a given year [1], based on a given document, the Surrealist current. The graph also depicts the fact that Surrealism is centered around certain ideas, those ideas influenced other currents, and certain people belonged to the Surrealist movement. The actual values of the concept variables will be retrieved from the source by the means the wrapper. Similarly, the Dada

---

[1]The symbol '*' is the generic marker for a concept. However, given the particular nature of this relation, the only value 'Year' can take is '1924'.

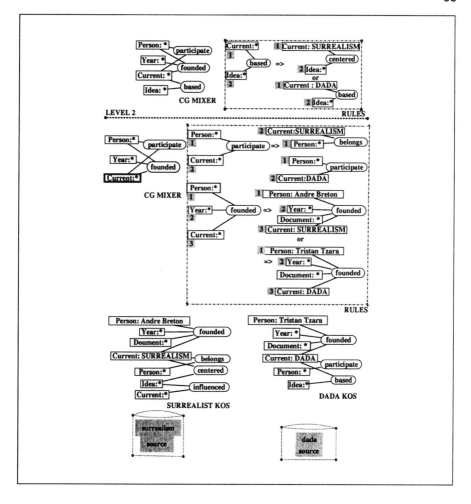

Figure 2: Hierarchical integrated view

KOS represents the fact that, according to a given document, (i) Tristan Tzara founded in a given year the Dada movement, (ii) that Dada is based on certain ideas, and that (iii) certain people joined the Dada current.

To integrate these two sources, the domain expert presents the user with an integrated view on the two conceptual graphs. This view is also a conceptual graph, and it is the the only common source description the end-user has access to. This means the user is allowed to express queries over the joined data sources just using the concepts and the relations presented to her/him. A set of rules associated to this graph translate each integrated view relation into relations of the data sources. If the information is contained in one source only, then the rule simply translates the integrated relation into the KOS relation of the source. If the information is contained in more then one source, then the rule will contain all of the relevant source KOS relations. The wrapper will retrieve the results, and then the results will be combined (using special operators like '=', '>' etc.) and presented back to the user. Note that the operators also deal with format issues (for example 1/July/2005 '=' 2005/07/01). However, this paper focuses on the formal representation and on the methodological approach used in our integration system, without addressing implementation problems. The rules also need to respect the order of the concept nodes incident to the translated relations. In Figure 1, this is done by numbering labels depicted in the greyed-out squares (the rules are represented on the right hand side of the picture, in a dotted box). An integrated view, along with an associated set of rules is called a *CG Mixer*. All the above notions (namely KOS, wrapper, rules, and CG Mixer) will be formally introduced in the next section.

As previously mentioned, the domain expert provides the user with a CG schema of the integrated sources. This shows a unified view of the combined knowledge, but the question is how much information this view should contain. If the user is only interested in people who participated in the two currents, then there is no point in presenting her/him with all the details of the current's ideologies. Therefore, the integrated view provides different levels of detail. If the user is not happy with the view s/he is provided, then s/he can ask for the next level of information. Figure 2 depicts the next level of detail, containing information about the ideas expressed in the two movements. The rules associated to this view are the same as those on the previous level for the first two relations, while a new rule is provided for the last relation.

The 'translation' between the two integrated views is done using *layered conceptual graphs*, a new hierarchical graph formalism introduced in [7]. A layered conceptual graph presents the detailed knowledge by expanding complex nodes. These nodes can either be concepts or relations, and are depicted visually as thickly bordered nodes (see 'current:*' in Figure 2). Layered Conceptual Graphs, which are a semantically sound and complete formalism, are discussedin the next section.

3   A formal model for data sources

This section formally introduces the main concepts that have been informally discussed in the previous sections, namely KOS, CG-Mixer, abd LCGs. Due to space limitations, we will not present here all the main graph theoretical notions that lead to their definition. Instead, we just introduce them informally, and provide the full mathematical definitions only for the main concepts. Full definitions (and proofs) are provided elsewhere [7, 8]. The definitions presented here back the feasibility of the approach. Indeed, formalisation not only makes concepts clear, but also explains how these notions relate to each other. In this way, future implementations will be almost straightforward.

The section is structured as follows: we introduce the notion of a support and conceptual graphs. We add semantics by using a model based interpretation. In the end of the section the notion of repository is introduced. This last definition is very important from our integration oriented point of view and is crucial for the methodology of integration. Next the KOS and the CG Mixer are introduced and their query mechanisms detailed. Finally, we present the LCG formalism that allows hierarchical depiction of the integrated view.

A **support** is a structure that provides the background knowledge about the information to be represented in the conceptual graph. It consists of *(i)* a concept type hierarchy (e.g. current, idea, year etc.), *(ii)* a relation type hierarchy (e.g. centered, founded, etc.), *(iii)* a set of individual markers that refer to specific concepts (e.g. Andre Breton) and a generic marker, denoted by * which refers to an unspecified concept. A **conceptual graph** is a structure that depicts factual information about the background knowledge contained in its support. This information is presented in a visual manner as an ordered bipartite graph, whose nodes have been labelled with elements from the support.

Definition 3.1 (Simple CGs) *A 3-tuple $SG = [S, G, \lambda]$ such that:*

- $S = (T_C, T_R, \mathcal{I}, *)$ *is a support;*

- $G = (V_C, V_R; E_G, l)$ *is an ordered bipartite graph;*

- λ *is a labelling of the nodes of G with elements from the support S, where $\forall r : r \in V_R, \ \lambda(r) \in T_R^{d_G(r)}; \forall c : c \in V_C, \ \lambda(c) \in T_C \times (\mathcal{I} \cup \{*\})$ such that if $c = N_G^i(r)$, $\lambda(r) = t_r$ and $\lambda(c) = (t_c, ref_c)$ then $t_c \leq \sigma_i(r)$.*

This definition of a conceptual graph has been initially introduced in [22].

Projection (subsumption) is a syntactic mechanism that allows for a comparison of the knowledge contained in two CGs. Subsumption checking is an NP-complete problem [23]. When the size of graph used in practice is not large, subsumption can be quickly computed [6].

Usually, CGs are given semantics by translating them to existential first order logic formulae. We propose a semantics based on model theory, adapted for our integration purposes. In order to do this we will define what the interpretation of a support is, and how to assign that interpretation to the simple conceptual graph defined on that support.

Given a data source, we need to be able to link the information (set of tuples) contained therein with the conceptual graph and its model. To do this we introduce the notion of a **repository**. A repository is a *set of tuples*, each of which makes the conceptual graph *true in a given model*. The repository is intentional (as opposed to extensional); one needs to go through the data source to be able to build it. There is no need to materialize the repository in order to use it (in the manner of materialized views for databases). A repository contains all possible interpretations for the generic concepts in the graph.

Once the data sources are defined, we need to query and integrate them with other sources. For this purpose we employ a structure called **query conceptual graphs** [10]. A query conceptual graph (QCG) allows one to represent a query over the sources in a conceptual graph like notation.

An **answer** to a QCG is the set of all data retrieved from the repository that validate the QCG. Intuitively, by taking all the instances from the repository that make the graph associated to the QCG true, one obtains its answer.

All of the above now lead to the formal definition of a **knowledge oriented specification**. This is one of the main contribution of the paper, allowing us to express our integration method in a rigorous, theoretical manner. A knowledge oriented specification of an information source is (i) a conceptual graph that visually describes that source, (ii) an interpretation for the support on which the graph is built, (iii) a repository for the graph (that contains all the data tuples) and (iv) a wrapper that ensures the communication in between the user queries and the repository.

Definition 3.2 (Knowledge Oriented Specification of an Information Source) *Let IS be an information source. A knowledge oriented specification of IS is a quadruple $KOS(IS) = (SG, \mathcal{M}, \mathcal{R}(SG, \mathcal{M}), W)$, where*
-$SG = [S, G, \lambda]$ is a CG on the support S,source support,
-$\mathcal{M} = (D, F)$ is a model for the support S,source model,
-$\mathcal{R}(SG, \mathcal{M})$ is a repository for SG in the model $\mathcal{M}$,and
-W is a wrapper, that is a software tool which, for each legal qCG $\mathbb{Q}$ for SG, returns the answer set $Ans(\mathbb{Q}, \mathcal{R}(SG, \mathcal{M}))$.

Once formally defined, the data sources can be integrated. This is the purpose of a **CG Mixer**. As shown in Figure 1, a CG Mixer depicts the integrated view, by the means of a conceptual graph, and provides the rules to allow for the translation of user queries to the appropriate data sources. The rules are defined by the relation vertices from the integrated view. As shown in Figure 1, for each relation in the integrated view, the proper translation is provided. This translation has to preserve the order of nodes in the initial relation, hence the extra labelling of concepts (depicted in greyed rectangles).

Definition 3.3 (CG Mixer) *Let $IS^1, \ldots, IS^n$ be a set of information sources, and their knowledge oriented specifications*
$KOS(IS^i) = (SG^i, \mathcal{M}^i, \mathcal{R}^i(SG^i, \mathcal{M}^i), W^i), i = 1, n$.
*A **CG Mixer** over the information sources $IS^1, \ldots, IS^n$ is a pair*
$\mathbb{M}(IS^1, \ldots, IS^n) := (SG^0, \mathbb{R})$, where
- $SG^0 = [S^0, G^0, \lambda^0]$ is a CG with $G^0 = (V_C^0, V_R^0, N_{G^0})$, and - $\mathbb{R}$ is a mapping which specifies for each $r^0 \in V_R^0$ a set $\mathbb{R}(r^0)$ of rules providing descriptions of the relation vertex r^0 in (some of) information sources. Each rule in $\mathbb{R}(r^0)$ is a triple (IS^k, A, w), where
• IS^k is an information source specified by $KOS(IS^k)$
• $A \subseteq V_R^k$ (the relation vertices set of SG^k)
• $w \in V_C^+([A]_{G^k})$ is a sequence of $d_{G^0}(r^0)$ concept vertices of the subgraph $[A]_{G^k}$ spanned in G^k by the relation vertices in A.

Rule $(IS^k, A, w) \in \mathbb{R}(r^0)$ means that the star graph $G^0[r^0]$, is translated in the source IS^k as $[A]_{G^k}$ and if $w = w^1 \ldots w^k$ $(k = d_{G^0}(r^0))$, then w^i corresponds to $N_{G^0}^i(r^0)$ $(i = 1, k)$. In other words, a rule interprets each relation vertex in the CG Mixer via a subgraph of the CG describing the appropriate local source. This is done by means of an ordered sequence of concept vertices (the relations' vertex neighbours). The CG Mixer is constructed manually by domain experts (who understand the knowledge oriented specifications of the sources). The quality of the integration system depends on the complexity of CG SG^0 and the quality of the rules. The conceptual graph SG^0 represents the visual querying interface provided to the user, in order to describe the graphical language in which (s)he can interrogate the system.

The next two definitions fully formalize the querying mechanism for our integration framework. They explain what a legal query is (the process of retrieving the actual data tuples) and how the answer to a query is built.

Definition 3.4 (Querying a CG Mixer)
Let $\mathbb{M}(IS^1, \ldots, IS^n) := (SG^0, \mathbb{R})$ *be a CG Mixer.*
*A **legal query** over* $\mathbb{M}(IS^1, \ldots, IS^n)$ *is any legal QCG for* SG^0.
Let $\mathbb{Q} = [SQ, arity, X, \lambda'_Q]$, *be a legal QCG for* SG^0, *with* $SQ = [S, Q, \lambda_Q]$, $Q = (V_C, V_R, N_Q)$, *and* $X \subseteq V_C(*)$. *Let* $V_R = \{r_1^0, \ldots, r_m^0\}$ *and* $H = [\{r_1^0, \ldots, r_m^0\}]_{G^0}$ *(the spanned subgraph of* G^0 *from which is obtained* SQ *by specialization).*

From SQ *a set* $\mathbb{R}(SQ)$ *of graphs is constructed as follows:*
- For each r_i^0 $(i = 1, m)$ *take a rule* $(IS^{k_i}, A^i, w^i) \in \mathbb{R}(r_i^0)$.
- In each graph $[A^i]_{G^{k_i}}$, *if the vertex* w_j^i *has a generic marker in* SG^{k_i} *and in* SQ *the* j-*neighbour of* r_i^0 *has been replaced by an individual marker, then the generic marker of* w_j^i *is replaced by this individual marker.*
- Consider the union of all this graphs.
- Add to the graph obtained a special set of new vertex relations in order to describe the neighborhood structure of the original graph H. *All these vertices have the special label (name)* " $=$ " *and have exactly two neighbours (with the meaning that the corresponding concept vertices represent the same object). More precisely, if* $N_H^t(r_i^0) = N_H^s(r_j^0)$ *(in* H *the* t-*neighbour of* r_i^0 *is the same concept vertex as the* s-*neighbour of* r_j^0*), then a new equality relation vertex is added to the graph already constructed, with the 1-neighbour vertex* w_t^i *of* $[A^i]_{G^{k_i}}$ *and the 2-neighbour vertex* w_s^j *of* $[A^j]_{G^{k_j}}$.

The graphs from the set $\mathbb{R}(SQ)$ *can be considered as the set of all possible query rewritings of* $\mathbb{Q}$.
Each graph $RH \in \mathbb{R}(SQ)$ *can be expressed as a disjoint union of source subgraphs, interconnected (as described above) by the equality relation vertices. Let* RH_j *be the (nonempty) subgraph of the graph* SG^j *of the source* IS^j. *For each concept vertex* w_k^j *in* $V_C(RH_j)$ *(which means that there is* r_i^0 *for which a rule* (IS^j, A^j, w^j) *has been used in the construction of* RH*), if* $N_{G^0}^k(r_i^0)$ *has a query marker, then assign a query marker to* w_k^j. *The superscripts of these new query markers can be numbered such that they will form a set* $\{1, \ldots, arity'\}$ *and also respect the meaning in* $\mathbb{Q}$ *(that is, if the two original vertices have the same query mark, then their surrogates have the same new query marks). In this way, we have obtained a legal qCG* $\mathbb{Q}_{RH}^j$ *for* SG^j.

Definition 3.5 (Answer to a qCG over a CG Mixer)
Let $M(IS^1, \ldots, IS^n) := (SG^0, \mathbb{R})$ *be a CG Mixer. Let* $\mathbb{Q} = [SQ, arity, X, \lambda_Q']$,
be a legal qCG for SG^0. *The* **answer** *to* $\mathbb{Q}$ *over* $M(IS^1, \ldots, IS^n)$ *is the set*
$Ans(\mathbb{Q}, M(IS^1, \ldots, IS^n))$ *of all tuples* $(d_1, \ldots, d_{arity}) \subseteq D^{arity}$
constructed as follows.
For each graph $RH \in \mathbb{R}(SQ)$ *consider the corresponding qCGs* $\mathbb{Q}_{RH}^j$, *find the*
sets $Ans(\mathbb{Q}^j, \mathcal{R}^j(SG^j, \mathcal{M}^j))$ *(using the wrapper* W^j*), combine the tuples from*
these sets such that the equality relation vertices of RH *to be satisfied, and the*
set of all successful combinations is $Ans(RH)$. *Finally,*

$$Ans(\mathbb{Q}, M(IS^1, \ldots, IS^n)) := \cup_{RH \in \mathbb{R}(SQ)} Ans(RH).$$

The remainder of the section will present the Layered Conceptual Graphs, a
semantically sound and complete hierarchical extension of conceptual graphs.
LCGs are used in order to be able to present the user with different detail levels
of the integrated view.

LCGs, a representation formalism evolved from CGs [27], were introduced to
addresses the inherent ontological and factual issues of hierarchical integration.
LCGs allow us to highlight a new type of rendering based on the additional
expansion of relation nodes. The idea of a detailed knowledge context can be
traced back to the definition of Simple Conceptual Graphs (SCGs) [27], to a
further development of the structures of these graphs [13], and to the definition
of the more elaborate Nested Conceptual Graphs [4].

The difference between Layered Conceptual Graphs and Nested Graphs is
due to the fact that nested graphs do not address the description of relations
between the 'zoomed' knowledge and its context. The nodes' context in nested
graphs allows transition between conceptual graphs but the overall conceptual
structure is no longer a properly defined bipartite graph. Transitional descriptions are a syntactical device which allows a successive construction of bipartite
graphs. The knowledge detailed on a level of a hierarchy is put in context by
using descriptions for both relation and concept nodes.

Definition 3.6 *Let* $SG = [S, G, \lambda]$ *be a simple conceptual graph, where* $G =$
$(V_C, V_R; E_G, l)$. *A transitional description associated to* SG *is a pair* $TD =$
$(D, (SG.d)_{d \in D \cup N_G(D)})$ *where:*

- $D \subseteq V_C$ *is a set of complex nodes.*

- *For each* $d \in D \cup N_G(D)$, $SG.d = [S.d, G.d, \lambda.d]$ *is a SCG.*

- *If* $d \in D$, *then* $SG.d$ *is the description of the complex node* d. *Distinct*
  complex nodes $d, d' \in D$ *have disjoint descriptions* $G.d \cap G.d' = G^\emptyset$.

- *If* $d \in N_G(D)$, *then either* $G.d = G^\emptyset$ *or* $G.d \neq G^\emptyset$. *In this case,* $N_G(d) - D \subseteq$
  $V_C(G.d)$ *and* $V_C(G.d) \cap V_C(G.d') \neq \emptyset$ *for each* $d' \in N_G(d) \cap D$. *Moreover,*
  $S_d \supseteq S \cup_{d' \in N_G(d)} S_{d'}$, $\lambda.d(v) = \lambda(v)$ *for* $v \in N_G(d) - D$ *and* $\lambda.d(v) = \lambda.d'(v)$
  for $v \in V_C(G.d) \cap V_C(G.d')$.

Note that if $G.d = G^{\emptyset}$ for $d \in N_G(D)$, we have no description available for relation vertex d. This either depends on a lack of information or on an inappropriate expounding. The idea traces back to the notion of context in [26] or to the more elaborate notion of nested conceptual graph [4]. However, as our approach is not just a diagrammatic representation, the bipartite graph structure is taken into account.

Definition 3.7 *Let d a nonegative integer. A layered conceptual graph (LCG) of depth d is a family* $\mathbf{LG} = \langle\ SG^0, \mathcal{TD}^0, \dots, \mathcal{TD}^{d-1}\ \rangle$ *where:*

- $SG^0 = [S^0, (V_C^0, V_R^0; E^0), \lambda^0)]$ *is a SCG,*

- $\mathcal{TD}^0$ *is a transitional description associated to SG^0,*

- *for each k, $1 \le k \le d-1$, $\mathcal{TD}^k$ is a transitional description associated to $SG^k = [S^k, (V_C^k, V_R^k; E^k), \lambda^k)] = \mathcal{TD}^{k-1}(SG^{k-1})$.*

SG^0 *is the base simple conceptual graph of the layered conceptual graph* $\mathbf{LG}$ *and $SG^k = \mathcal{TD}^{k-1}(SG^{k-1})$ $(k = 1, \dots, d)$, are its layers.*

In other words, if we have a interconnected world described by a SCG and if we can provide details about both some complex concepts and their relationships, then we can construct a second level of knowledge about this world, describing these new details as conceptual graphs and applying the corresponding substitutions. This process can be similarly performed with the last constructed level, thus obtaining a coherent set of layered representations of the initial world.

4 Conclusions

In this paper we introduce a novel knowledge-oriented specification technique for data integration. We have used this technique in the context of layered conceptual graphs in order to perform structured knowledge oriented integration. We believe that this technique can be used in different areas such as data and ontology integration, information management and retrieval or e-learning.

We also believe that a 'lightweight' knowledge model such as the one provided by conceptual graphs, which does not force schemas to look like frame-based ontologies could facilitate the identification of interschema mappings.

The contribution discussed in this paper is twofold. Firstly, we integrate in a formal way two different knowledge representation techniques, namely KOS and LCGs. Secondly, we describe the methodology of such hierarchical knowledge oriented specification for information integration.

Data sources in our approach to information integration are represented using conceptual graphs (CGs). A Knowledge Oriented Specification (KOS) for a knowledge source is a conceptual graph that syntactically describes the data. The specification does not try to exhaustively describe the sources, but it provides a description of the accessible data. These sources are linked to

72

their KOS by way of a wrapper and are encapsulated within an integrated schema. A set of rules associated with the schema directs every query to the appropriate sources during the querying process. Individual query results are then combined and provided to users. These results are presented with different detail over the integrated view of the sources, which are modelled using CGs.

No existing approaches have tackled the integration problem in the above way. Consequently, we believe that our approach offers a novel way of thinking about integration. Our approach is similar in spirit to techniques introduced by Decker and Melnik [19] and by Ehrig and Staab in the QOM approach [12].

Finally, investigating the use of natural language processing techniques for studying user queries in order to automatically define the integration hierarchies promises to be an interesting area for future research.

References

[1] R. Bayardo et al. Infosleuth: Agent-based semantic integration of information in open and dynamic environments. In *Proc. of the ACM SIGMOD Intl. Conf. on Management of Data*, volume 26/2, pages 195–206, 1997.

[2] D. Calvanese et al. Logical foundations of peer-to-peer data integration. In *Proc. of the 23rd ACM Symp. on Principles of Database Systems (PODS 2004)*, pages 241–251, 2004.

[3] B. Carbonneill and O. Haemmerle. Standardizing and interfacing relational databases using conceptual graphs. In *Conceptual Structures: Current Practices*, pages 311–330. Springer, 1994.

[4] M. Chein and M.-L. Mugnier. Positive nested conceptual graphs. *Proc. of the 5th Int'l Conf. on Conceptual Structures*, 1997.

[5] E. Compatangelo and H. Meisel. "Reasonable" support to knowledge sharing through schema analysis and articulation. *Neural Computing & Applications*, 12 (3–4):129–141, December 2003.

[6] M. Croitoru and E. Compatangelo. A combinatorial approach to conceptual graph projection checking. In *Proc. of the 24th Int'l Conf. of the Brit. Comp. Society's Spec. Group on Artif. Intell. (AI'2004)*, pages 130–143. Springer, 2004.

[7] M. Croitoru, E. Compatangelo, and C Mellish. Hierarchical knowledge integration using layered conceptual graphs. In *Proc. of the 13th Int'l Conf. on Conceptual Structures*, LNCS. Springer, 2005. To appear.

[8] M. Croitoru, E. Compatangelo, and C Mellish. Theoretical knowledge oriented specification. Technical Report AUCS/TR0506, Dept. of Computing Science, University of Aberdeen, UK, July 2005.

[9] F. Dau. Negations in simple concept graphs. In Bernhard Ganter and Guy W. Mineau, editors, *ICCS*, volume 1867 of *LNCS*, pages 263–276. Springer, 2000.

[10] F. Dau. Query graphs with cuts: Mathematical foundations. In *Proc. of the 3rd Int'l Conf. on Diagrammatic Representation and Inference*, volume 2980 of *LNAI*. Springer, 2004.

[11] O. M. Dushka and M. R Genereseth. Infomaster - an information integration tool. In *Int'l W'shop on Intelligent Information Integration*, 1997.

[12] M. Ehrig and S. Staab. Qom - quick ontology mapping. In *Proc. of the 3rd Int'l Semantic Web Conf.*, volume 3298 of *LNCS*, pages 683–697. Springer, 2004.

[13] J. Esch and R. Levinson. An implementation model for contexts and negation in conceptual graphs. In Gerard Ellis, Robert Levinson, William Rich, and John F. Sowa, editors, *ICCS*, volume 954 of *LNCS*, pages 247–262. Springer, 1995.

[14] N. Friedman Noy and M. A. Musen. PROMPT: Algorithm and Tool for Automated Ontology Merging and Alignment. In *Proc. of the 17th Nat. Conf. on Artificial Intelligence (AAAI'00)*, 2000.

[15] H. Garcia-Molina et al. The TSIMMIS approach to mediation: Data models and languages. *Jour. of Intelligent Information Systems*, 8(2):117–132, 1997.

[16] E. Jasper et al. Generating and optimising views from both as view data integration rules. *Proc. of the 6th Baltic Conf. on DB and Information Syst.*, 2004.

[17] T. Kirk, A. Y. Levy, Y. Sagiv, and D. Srivastava. The information manifold. *Information Gathering from Heterogeneous, Distributed Environments*, 1995.

[18] D. L. McGuinness and A. T. Borgida. Explaining subsumption in description logics. In *Proc. of the 14th Intl. Joint Conf. on Artificial Intelligence (IJCAI'95)*, pages 816–821, 1995.

[19] S. Melnik and S. Decker. A layered approach to information modeling and interoperability on the web. In *Proc. of the ECDL'2000 Sem. Web W'shop*, 2000.

[20] G. Mineau. A first step toward the knowledge web: Interoperability issues among conceptual graph based software agents, part I. In *Proc. of the 10th Int'l Conf. on Conceptual Structures (ICCS'2002)*, volume 2393 of *LNCS*. Springer, 2002.

[21] P. Mitra, G. Wiederhold, and M. L. Kersten. A Graph-Oriented Model for the Articulation of Ontology Interdependencies. In *Proc. of the VII Conf. on Extending DB Technology (EDBT'2000)*, LNCS, pages 86–100. Springer, 2000.

[22] M.-L. Mugnier. On generalization/specialization for conceptuals graphs. *Jour. of Experimental and Theoretical Artif. Intell.*, 1995.

[23] M.-L. Mugnier and M. Chein. Polynomial algorithms for projection and matching. In *proc. of the 7th Ann. W'shop on Conceptual Graphs*, volume 754 of *LNCS*, pages 239–251. Springer, 1992.

[24] H. S. Pinto, A. Gomez-Perez, and J. Martins. Some issues on ontology integration. In *Proc. of the IJCAI'99 W.shop on Ontology and Problem-Solving Methods (KRR5)*, pages 7.1 – 7.11, 1999.

[25] A. Preece et al. KRAFT: An agent architecture for knowledge fusion. *Intl. Jour. of Cooperative Information Systems*, 10(1 & 2):171–195, 2001.

[26] J. Sowa. *Knowledge Representation: Logical, Philosophical, and Computational Foundations*. Brooks Cole Publishing Co., 2000.

[27] John Sowa. *Conceptual Structures: Information Processing in Mind and Machine*. Addison-Wesley, 1984.

SESSION 1b:

AI AND THE WORLD WIDE WEB

The Semantic Web as a *Linguistic* Resource: Opportunities for Natural Language Generation

Chris Mellish

Department of Computing Science, University of Aberdeen
Aberdeen AB24 3UE, UK

Xiantang Sun

Department of Computing Science, University of Aberdeen
Aberdeen AB24 3UE, UK

Abstract

This paper argues that, because the documents of the semantic web are created by human beings, they are actually much more like natural language documents than theory would have us believe. We present evidence that natural language words are used extensively and in complex ways in current ontologies. This leads to a number of dangers for the semantic web, but also opens up interesting new challenges for natural language processing. This is illustrated by our own work using natural language generation to present parts of ontologies.

1   Preamble

The work described in this paper originated as part of a project to generate natural language from ontologies for the semantic web. On the face of it, this seems like a fairly straightforward application of natural language generation (NLG) research, which studies the task of generating appropriate linguistic material from originally non-linguistic inputs. Indeed, there is a growing amount of work on NLG from semantic web material, given the practical importance of presenting such material to knowledge engineers and users.

Standardly, building an NLG system requires constructing a mapping (sometimes called a lexicon) between the terms of the input representation and natural language words and phrases [11]. This mapping is always domain-dependent since, although different applications may share the same basic *syntax* for their input representations (e.g. perhaps some syntax for first order logic), nevertheless each domain has its own idiosyncratic repertoire of predicates, concepts, etc. and these map onto natural language in ways that correspond to specific language use in the domain [6].

When we started to look seriously at semantic web ontologies as the domain for NLG, it became increasingly clear that viewing human-written ontologies as just another non-linguistic form of input was missing the point in many respects. We were forced to question the traditional view of how ontologies relate to natural language and therefore what NLG from ontologies should or could be.

2   The Relation between Ontologies and Natural Language: In Theory

The semantic web relies on the representation and exchange of knowledge using agreed terms. These terms are listed and further specified in *ontologies*, logical theories specifying conceptualisations of parts of the world. These conceptualisations are simplified models of the world developed for particular purposes. In the end, successful exchange of knowledge relies on an agreement on the semantics of the terms in an ontology and in the use of these terms in ways consistent with this semantics. This is usually only possible if the intended use is similar to that envisaged when the ontology was developed.

The terms in an ontology are different in kind from natural language words, although often they appear to be related to actual words in English or some other human language [5]:

1. Terms in an ontology are given a precise formal, but shallow, description, whereas natural language word senses can only be defined informally and in a way that relies on deep human knowledge. For instance, the difference between the English words "mistake", "error", "blunder" and "slip" involves subtleties (about amount of criticism expressed and assumed accidentalness of the described event) that could not easily be stated in current ontology definition languages.

2. The whole point of ontologies is to ensure that there is exactly one meaning for each ontology term; this contrasts with the situation in natural language where there are complex word-meaning relations. For instance, the English word "leg" is ambiguous between (at least) part of a piece of furniture, part of an animal or part of a journey. Conversely, different words like "mistake" and "blunder" might be considered to have very similar meanings for some purposes.

3. Ontologies are designed to be complete and minimal for specific applications; human languages are open-ended and idiosyncratic, with gaps and duplications. For instance, Spanish has no word for the concept of "stab".

4. Terms in an ontology are carefully chosen for relevance in some domain or for some intended use. Natural language words, on the other hand, reflect the world view/culture of the language users and the historical development of this view/culture in much more complex ways.

In summary, ontologies can be regarded as a formalisation of some kind of ideal, "good practice" in natural language word use, where communication can be precise and successful every time. This is much the same as the way in which formal logic arose as an attempt to formalise "good practice" in natural language argumentation. In both cases, the formalisation captures some elements of the real world but also makes many simplifying assumptions. So it is necessary to distinguish between ontology terms and natural language words – they are very different sorts of things.

3   The Relation between Ontologies and Natural Language: In Practice

In some domains (particularly parts of Medicine) ontologies make a strict distinction between the ontology terms and natural language words that can be used to express them. In addition, ontology definition languages provide facilities (e.g. the RDFS label construct) to express natural language words separately from the ontology terms. However, in practice in many cases ontology designers choose versions of natural language phrases as their formal terms. In logical terms, it makes no difference whether a concept is labelled in a way that can be "understood" by humans, e.g. *Leg*, rather than as an arbitrary identifier, e.g. *C*40274. It is therefore natural for ontology designers to choose mnemonic names for their concepts and properties. However, there are dangers in this. Current ontology languages are extremely simple logics, with very low expressive power. So a set of axioms about the term *Leg* cannot possibly capture more than a tiny part of what (some sense of) "leg" means. The formal definition that an ontology provides for a term dramatically under-specifies what the term means. But if the ontology designer labels their concept *Leg*, unless they can turn off their in-built natural language understanding (and disambiguation) capabilities they can easily have the illusion that they have captured the exact sense that they require. Similarly a user of the ontology can easily get a false sense of security in using this concept, simply because of its name. This is an instance of the problem of "wishful mnemonics" discussed by McDermott [7]. McDermott described how inappropriate use of natural language terms for programming constructs, program modules and symbols in knowledge representation languages can mislead, in terms of the actual problem solved and the power and sophistication of the approach:

> "A good test for the disciplined programmer is to try using gensyms in key places and see if he still admires his system" [7]

And yet AI practitioners seemed to be happy to create these illusions, or unaware of what they were doing (and maybe they still are ...).

In terms of the semantic web endeavour, such problems could represent a real threat to progress. Not least, using natural language names could easily lead to an ontology designer failing to express axioms which are "obviously true" but in fact very necessary in order to make necessary distinctions for a computational agent (or a native speaker of a different language). For the purposes of this paper, however, the main conclusion to be drawn from this discussion is that the semantic web – its ontologies and knowledge bases – could actually be a lot more like natural language documents than the theory says they should be.

4 Linguistic Structures in Real Ontologies

To investigate the extent to which existing ontologies make use of natural language terms, we carried out an experiment to see what structures are present in the names used in actual ontologies available on the internet. In this experiment, we concentrated on OWL ontologies [8], filtering out ontologies (such as WordNet) that are specifically designed to represent linguistic information.

We wrote a Java program using the Google API to help us look for online ontologies coded in OWL. We did this using the keywords "owl filetype: owl", which indicates that our desired ontologies must contain the string "owl" as well as having owl as their file extension (filetype:owl indicates the file type, and every legal OWL ontology must contain the string "owl"). Using these key words, theoretically all online ontologies found by Google should be returned. Actually we obtained around five thousand links; however only some of these links were able to provide us with real ontology files, because firstly, Google limits its API not to be accessed more than one thousand times per day, and also because some of the links were not available. In total we collected 882 ontology files coded in OWL (111 Mb) as our corpus.

In analysing these ontologies, we were interested in two kinds of names, names of classes and names of properties, and wanted to know what these names consisted of. In order to detect the English words contained in these names, we used the WordNet [10] API to help us recognise English words occurring in these names. Because there are no agreed rules for how to name concepts, people use various ways of giving names, e.g., *PostgraduatePhD*, *International_Student*, *red_wine*, *Redwine*2004, *hasProducer*, *part_of* and even meaningless strings like *ABC*, *ED*009 etc. In our approach we can detect multiple English words joined together if there is any separator between them, such as a capital letter, a underline or a number. For instance, *PostgraduatePhD* will be recognised as two English words. Each name is associated with a *pattern* recording its analysis as a sequence of parts of speech. Formally, a pattern is a string in the language:

$$L = (\text{Noun}|\text{Adj}|\text{Verb}|\text{Prep}|\text{Adv}|\text{Than}|\text{Or}|\text{Un}|\text{C})^*$$

where Noun etc. name standard parts of speech (Than and Or being used for particular closed class words that appeared in the corpus), Un names an unknown word and C names a capital letter not starting a recognised word (sequences of capital letters were not further analysed). Thus, for instance, *PostgraduatePhD* is analysed as NounNoun and *ICD*10 is represented as CCUn. Patterns can be surprisingly long: for instance, the pattern

NounNounPrepNounNounPrepNounUnNoun

Pattern	Frequency	Percentage
Noun	5084	14%
NounNoun	4092	11%
UnUn	1837	5%
Un	1755	5%
AdjNoun	1528	4%
NounNounNoun	1378	4%
UnNoun	1366	4%
AdjNounNoun	681	2%
NounUn	577	2%
UnNounNoun	482	1%
...	...	...
TOTAL	37260	100%
(.)*Noun	26708	72%
Noun*	11011	30%
(C|Un)*	5266	14%

Figure 1: Frequencies of patterns in class names

is the analysis of the class name made up of the words "Muscle Layer of Secondary Duct of Left Coagulating Gland" joined by underscores. In the situation of handling a word which can be recognised as a noun and also as a verb (e.g., "work"), our system treats the word as a noun when it analyses names of classes, and treats it as a verb when analysing names of properties, because we believe that nouns have a higher possibility than verbs to occur in names of classes, while verbs have a higher possibility to occur in names of properties. In addition, our system can do simple morphological analysis including detecting plural nouns and verbs in present, past or passive tense by using two sets of linguistic rules and applying them to every input name. When the above two cases occur together (e.g., "works" may be a plural noun and also a present verb), the system gives the rules for handling plural nouns higher priority when it analyses names of classes and gives the rules for handling verbs higher priority when analysing names of properties. For instance, "works" is seen as a noun when the system analyses names of classes, but as a verb when analysing names of properties. There may be some special cases of names that our system cannot recognise, because firstly our rules may not cover all possibilities and also the WordNet API has limits on the words it can recognise. However, the analysis was enough to enable us to determine useful information about the general forms of names that people have used in defining OWL ontologies.

Figure 1 shows the frequencies of some of the patterns that applied to the 37260 different class names found. These frequencies are the frequencies that classes were *defined* in ontologies (first introduced; not the number of times they were *used*). If the same class name was used in more than one ontology,

Pattern	Frequency	Percentage
Verb	132	10%
VerbVerb	129	10%
Noun	80	6%
VerbPrep	73	5%
VerbNoun	72	5%
VerbVerbVerb	50	4%
NounPrep	36	3%
VerbVerbPrep	35	3%
Un	32	2%
VerbVerbNoun	31	2%
NounVerb	31	2%
VerbAdv	23	2%
VerbAdjVerb	23	2%
VerbUn	21	2%
VerbNounVerb	21	2%
VerbNounPrep	16	1%
. . .	. . .	. . .
TOTAL	1354	100%
Verb(.)*	885	65%
Noun(.)*	216	16%
(.)*Verb	571	42%
(.)*Prep	262	19%
(C|Un)*	43	3%

Figure 2: Frequencies of patterns in property names

it is counted several times. There were 3003 different patterns found, and the first ten are listed in order of frequency in the figure. Below are frequencies for selected meta-patterns (regular expressions over patterns). From these it can be seen that 72% of the class names ended with recognised nouns. Also 30% consisted entirely of strings of nouns (up to 7). Finally, only 14% of the class names contained no recognised word (i.e. are composed of entirely of unknown words and capital letters). So there is clearly a considerable amount of linguistic material in these names.

Figure 2 shows similar frequencies for property names. This time, for technical reasons, multiple uses of the same name in different ontologies were counted as just one occurrence. Although the numbers are smaller (and the popular patterns now include adverbs and prepositions), there are many similarities (especially when one considers that ambiguous verb/nouns will have been classed as nouns for the class names and verbs for the property names).

These figures give a striking picture of the extent of linguistic material in existing ontologies, and also of its relative complexity.

5 The Semantic Web as a Linguistic Resource

That the semantic web is partly a linguistic resource is implicitly acknowledged by applications such as ontology reconciliation [4] and ontology search [14]. Such applications assume that, in general:

1. The names of concepts and properties matter and

2. The names of concepts and properties are meaningful to a human user.

Such applications would not be able to work without making these assumptions, which basically amount to requiring that concept and property names make use of natural language words.

If the documents of the semantic web are at least partially linguistic in nature, then we can apply variations of natural language processing operations to them. Indeed, NLP techniques may be *needed* in order to fully understand what is actually stated in these documents. For instance, word sense disambiguation techniques may be required to handle concepts with unsufficiently specific defining axioms; machine translation might be required to translate ontologies into different languages. Some signs of this are beginning to be seen, for instance in work to measure the similarity between ontologies and natural language texts using an adaptation of "bag of words" models [3].

That complex NLP may be needed for significant uses of documents is disappointing news for the semantic web, but offers many interesting tasks for NLP researchers to develop existing techniques in the context of a version of semi-structured natural language.

6 Opportunities for Natural Language Generation

As we discussed in the preamble, a significant cost in developing an NLG system for a new domain is the production of a lexicon for the domain, relating concepts in the domain to natural language words that can be used to denote them. This means that NLG systems are in practice domain-dependent. Indeed, it is a significant challenge to the field to produce portable systems or even system components [9].

If semantic web documents are largely already filled with words in the desired natural language, then there is the prospect of building NLG systems very cheaply, because the lexicon comes "for free". Indeed, one can envisage domain-*independent* NLG systems for the semantic web, which have no specific domain resources but merely access to generic linguistic resources which enable them to decode the linguistic material already present in the input. NLG in such a situation avoids many of the problems of traditional NLG (specifically lexical choice) and is more like reconstituting natural language sentences from linguistic fragments – an extreme form of the kind of flexible NLG from existing phrases used in multi-document summarisation [1].

As yet, however, although many researchers have sought to produce domain-independent *frameworks* for building NLG systems for the semantic web, to our knowledge there has been no proposal to construct a single domain-independent *system* for producing language from semantic web material. Indeed, our experiment shows that some technical problems need to be addressed for this vision to become a reality:

- Concept and property names can be made from multiple words. Also abbreviations can be used. Some simple natural language analysis is necessary to handle these cases and also unknown words, which may be names.

- Morphological analysis is needed to recognise, for instance, plural nouns, present and past participles. There is also part of speech ambiguity.

- Translating from property names to appropriate realisations may be non trivial. For instance, if a concept X has the value Y for the property *contains*, does this mean that "X contains Y" or that "X is among the things that Y contains"?

It may well be possible to find appropriate engineering solutions to the above problems. But there are also dangers:

- Words may be used in unnatural technical senses, which means that referring to a concept by its name may actually mislead.

- It may not be clear which words in the NLG output are the terms of the ontology and which are informal NL words - which words are being used to explain which others?

- There may be serious consequences of cases of inaccurate analysis. E.g. a word might have a particular quite specific interpretation in this ontology, but may be used in the language as if it has another sense.

7   Our own work

Our current research is addressing the problem of presenting parts of OWL DL ontologies in natural language. This will extend existing approaches to generating from simpler DLs (e.g. [12]) by taking into account the fact that in a language like OWL DL a concept is described more by a set of constraints than by a frame-like definition. Hence information about a concept cannot be presented in a single sentence but requires an extended *text* with multiple sentences, the overall structure having to be planned so as to be coherent as a discourse. The work is also different from other work which generates text about *individuals* described using ontologies [13, 2], in that it presents the ontology *class axioms* themselves.

Following our experiments, our initial approach is to see how much can be achieved with no restrictions on the ontology (as long as it is expressed in legal

OWL DL) and only generic linguistic resources (such as WordNet). This is also motivated both because

- there is a practical need to present parts of arbitrary current ontologies (which often come with no consistent commenting or linguistic annotations) and also because

- if we can determine the main deficiencies of such an approach then we can then make informed recommendations about what kinds of extra annotations or naming conventions would be valuable in the ontologies of the future.

So we aim to maximise the use made of the existing linguistic material in an ontology, even though there could also be dangers in doing so.

The following example shows the kind of text we are currently able to generate (assuming some manual postprocessing for capitalisation and punctuation):

> *What is a MEA?*
> A MEA is a kind of Actuality which contains exactly 1 thing, which is a Cathode, an Anode and an Electrolyte. Everything a FuelCell contains is a MEA. Only something which is a FuelCell, a MEA, an Electrode or a Catalyst contains something.

Although there are no agreed principles for naming concepts and properties in ontologies, it is encouraging that a large percentage of these names include English words which can be recognised by WordNet. This gives us a chance to interpret the syntax of these names and help us produce more fluent natural language. For instance, for the constraint:

restriction(Onproperty(hasProducer)
   allValuesFrom(French))

we can say "has a producer who is French", instead of something like "has a property, hasProducer, which must have as its value, something that is in the class French". The above example gains greatly from this - in this case, WordNet is able to provide all the relevant part of speech information, except for MEA (and we have provided the information that "MEA" is a noun by hand).

Our current approach to realising an axiom in English involves a search through multiple rules matching against structural patterns in OWL axioms and attempting to exploit part of speech information about the names where this can be inferred. This search may yield several possible realisations. We currently choose between these according to how closely they come to having an "ideal" sentence length. This parameter can be set in advance according to text requirements.

In the future, we would like to find generic rules for how ontology builders name concepts and properties, and how these can be exploited in realisation, by doing further analysis of our existing corpus. The aim is to get elegant natural language without requiring domain-dependent resources.

8 Conclusions

Semantic web documents contain a surprising amount of complex linguistic material. The reliance of knowledge engineers on this leads to dangers of inadequate formalisation. It also leads to a number of interesting and challenging tasks for natural language processing. In particular, there is a prospect of building domain-independent NLG tools for presenting semantic web material.

Acknowledgments

This work is supported by EPSRC research grant GR/S62932.

References

[1] R. Barzilay, K. McKeown, and M. Elhadad. Information fusion in the context of multi-document summarization. In *Proceedings of the 37th Annual Meeting of the Association for Computational Linguistics*, pages 550–557. Association for Computational Linguistics, 1999.

[2] K. Bontcheva and Y. Wilks. Automatic report generation from ontologies: the miakt approach. In *Ninth International Conference on Applications of Natural Language to Information Systems (NLDB'2004)*, Manchester, UK, August 2004.

[3] G. Burek, M. Vargas-Vera, and E. Moreale. Indexing student essays paragraphs using lsa over an integrated ontological space. In *Proceedings of International Workshop on eLearning for Computational Linguistics and Computational Linguistics for eLearning*, Geneva, 2004.

[4] A. Hameed, A. Preece, and D. Sleeman. Ontology reconciliation. In S. Staab and R. Studer, editors, *Handbook on Ontologies in Information Systems*, pages 231–250. Springer Verlag, 2003.

[5] Graeme Hirst. Ontology and the lexicon. In S. Staab and R. Studer, editors, *Handbook on Ontologies*, pages 209–230. Springer Verlag, 2004.

[6] Richard Kittredge, Tanya Korelsky, and Owen Rambow. On the need for domain communication knowledge. *Computational Intelligence*, 7(4):305–314, 1991.

[7] D. McDermott. Artificial intelligence meets natural stupidity. In J. Haugeland, editor, *Mind Design*, pages 143–160. Bradford Books, 1981.

[8] D. L. McGuinness and F. van Harmelen. Owl web ontology language overview. http://www.w3.org/TR/owl-features/, 2004.

[9] C. Mellish, M. Reape, D. Scott, L. Cahill, R. Evans, and D. Paiva. A reference architecture for generation systems. *Natural Language Engineering*, 10(3/4):227–260, 2004.

[10] G. Miller. Wordnet: A lexical database for english. *CACM*, 38(11):39–41, 1995.

[11] Ehud Reiter and Robert Dale. *Building Natural Language Generation Systems*. Cambridge University Press, 2000.

[12] J. Wagner, J. Rogers, R. Baud, and J-R. Scherrer. Natural language generation of surgical procedures. *Medical Informatics*, 53:175–192, 1999.

[13] G. Wilcock. Talking owls: Towards an ontology verbalizer. In *Human Language Technology for the Semantic Web and Web Services, ISWC-2003*, pages 109–112, Sanibel Island, Florida, 2003.

[14] Y. Zhang, W. Vasconcelos, and D. Sleeman. Ontosearch: An ontology search engine. In *Proceedings of the Twenty-fourth SGAI International Conference on Innovative Techniques and Applications of Artificial Intelligence*. Springer Verlag, 2004.

A Distributed CBR Framework through Semantic Web Services *

Juan A. Recio-García, Belén Díaz-Agudo, Pedro González-Calero

Dep. Sistemas Informáticos y Programación

Universidad Complutense de Madrid

Madrid, Spain

email: {jareciog,belend,pedro}@sip.ucm.es

Abstract

jCOLIBRI is an Object-Oriented framework in Java that promotes software reuse for building CBR systems. It integrates the application of well proven Software Engineering techniques with a knowledge level description that separates the reasoning methods from the domain model. In this paper we present the evolution of the framework towards a Semantic Web Services (SWS) architecture where problem solving methods are represented as Web Services. In order to compose these services, our proposal uses an ontology with common CBR terminology and a Description Logic reasoner for choosing the most appropriate problem solving method.

1 Introduction

Case-Based Reasoning (CBR) is one of the most successful applied AI technologies of recent years. Commercial and industrial applications can be developed rapidly and existing corporate databases can be used as knowledge sources. Help-desks and diagnostic systems are the most common applications. CBR is based on the intuition that new problems are often similar to previously encountered problems, and therefore, that past solutions may be reused (directly or through adaptation) in the current situation. CBR systems typically apply retrieval and matching algorithms to a case base of past problem-solution pairs. Another very important feature of CBR is its coupling to learning. The driving force behind case-based methods has to a large extent come from the Machine Learning community.

Developing a CBR system is a complex task where many decisions have to be taken. The system designer has to choose how the cases will be represented, the case organization structure, which methods will solve the CBR tasks and which knowledge, besides cases, will be used by these methods. This process would greatly benefit from the reuse of previously developed CBR systems.

---

*Supported by the Spanish Committee of Science & Technology (TIC2002-01961)

Software reuse is a goal that the Software Engineering community has pursued from its very beginning [19]. From this effort a number of technologies have appeared that directly or indirectly promotes software reuse: object-oriented frameworks, component technologies, design patterns, domain analysis, software architectures, software product lines, model driven architectures, to mention just a few. Most of these technologies have been applied in those software domains where mass production is required and where reuse is a must. Unfortunately AI systems have remained for too long in the prototype arena and, in general, AI researchers do not worry too much about software engineering concerns. The most significant and long term effort within the AI community to attain effective software reuse is the KADS methodology and its descendants: CommonKADS[6] and UPML[14]. The KADS approach for building knowledge based systems proposes the reuse of abstract models consisting of reusable components, containing artificial Problem Solving Methods(PSMs), and ontologies of domain models. Nevertheless, the main emphasis in KADS is the definition of formal specification languages for the components, a formal approach to Software Engineering that departs from the mainstream results in this area.

During the last few years we have developed jCOLIBRI[1], a framework for developing CBR systems [11][12][4]. jCOLIBRI promotes software reuse for building CBR systems, and tries to integrate the best of both worlds: the application of well proven Software Engineering techniques with the KADS key idea of separating the reasoning process (using PSMs) from the domain model.

In this paper we envision the evolution of this framework into an open distributed framework where PSMs are represented as web services. This allows users to search and compose the components of their CBR applications using third party developed PSMs that are published in Internet. This way, different method families can be selected, configured and executed remotely without downloading them to a local machine. Another feature is the remote case base access as developers can publish their case bases avoiding the local installation. Section 2 describes the main ideas lying behind jCOLIBRI and its current architecture pointing out PSMs descriptions. Section 3 studies current Semantic Web Services (SWS) architectures and Section 4 describes our framework transformation into a SWS platform focusing the reasoning process using Description Logics (DL) for locating and composing web services. Finally, Section 5 concludes and explains future work.

2 jCOLIBRI

jCOLIBRI is an evolution of the COLIBRI architecture [11], consisted of a library of problem solving methods (PSMs) for solving the tasks of a knowledge-intensive CBR system along with an ontology, CBROnto[12]. The tasks and

[1]http://sourceforge.net/projects/jcolibri-cbr/

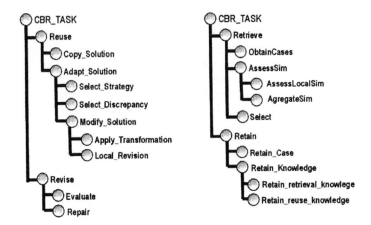

Figure 1: jCOLIBRI Task Structure

methods library is a knowledge level description [21] that guides the framework design, determines possible extensions and supports the framework instantiation process. Tasks and methods are described in terms of domain-independent CBR terminology which is mapped into the classes of the framework. This terminology is defined in CBROnto, separating the domain knowledge and the tasks and methods terminology.

CBROnto includes a task decomposition structure that is influenced by the Components of Expertise Methodology [24]. At the highest level of generality, they describe the general CBR cycle in terms of four tasks (4 Rs): *Retrieve* the most similar case/s, *Reuse* it/their knowledge to solve the problem, *Revise* the proposed solution and *Retain* the experience. Each one of the four CBR tasks involves a number of more specific sub-tasks. There are methods to solve tasks either by decomposing a task in subtasks or by solving it directly.

Figure 1 depicts the task decomposition structure we use in our framework. Besides this task structure, jCOLIBRI includes the library of PSMs to solve these tasks. It describes CBR PSMs by relating them within CBROnto concepts representing the tasks and domain characteristics. Each PSM must resolve a task, so tasks can be view as the main PSM applicability precondition.

2.1 Framework components

jCOLIBRI is organized around the following elements:

- Storage Layer: Contains the case base stored in a data base, plain text file, XML file or Description Logics ontology. The framework provides several connectors for loading cases from these sources.

- Core: Contains the configuration and execution engine.

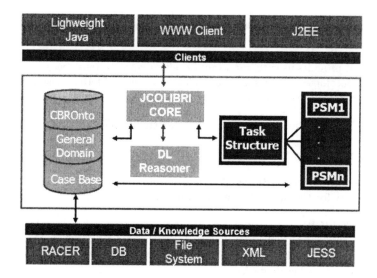

Figure 2: jCOLIBRI Framework Structure

- Tasks and Methods: Libraries with available tasks and methods for creating CBR applications.

- CBROnto, General Domain Knowledge, Case Base: Knowledge managed by the framework and generated CBR applications.

- Description Logics Reasoner. This parts enables reasoning for CBR application configuration. It allows PSM selection and composition, similarity functions applicability, etc.

- Clients: Provide the user interface. Currently, jCOLIBRI only supports standalone java user interfaces.

This structure is depicted in Figure 2. Framework instantiation is aided by several tools that allow task and method definitions, PSM composition, case description and case base connector configuration. These tools have been described in [16].

Regarding methods, most approaches consider that a PSM consists of three related parts. The *competence* is a declarative description of *what* can be achieved. The *operational specification* describes the reasoning process, i.e. *how* the method delivers the specified competence if the required knowledge is provided. And the *requirements* describe the knowledge needed by the PSM to achieve its competence [15].

Our approach to the specification of PSM competence and requirements makes use of ontologies and provides two main advantages. First, it allows formal specifications that add a precise meaning and enables reasoning support. Second, it provides us with important benefits regarding reuse because task and method ontologies can be shared by different systems. Method descriptions are stored in a XML file that includes the following elements:

Name The fully qualified name of the class that implements the method.

Description A textual description of the method.

ContextInputPrecondition A formal description of the applicability requirements for the method, including input requirements.

Type jCOLIBRI manages two types of methods: execution (or resolution) and decomposition. Execution methods are those that directly solve the task, for which has been assigned to, while decomposition methods divide the task into other subtasks.

Parameters Method configuration parameters. Parameterizes PSMs for specific instantiations.

Competencies The task (or tasks) that this method is able to solve.

Subtasks In decomposition methods this element provides the list of tasks that result from dividing the original task.

ContextOutputPostcondition Output data information obtained from the method execution. This information is used, among other things, to compose different PSMs checking which method can take as input the output of the previous one.

Using this method description, users can create a CBR application following an iterative process: First they decompose the CBR cycle into a task structure as explained in the introduction of this section. Then, while the system is not complete, they select one of the tasks without a method assigned and choose a method that resolves it.

jCOLIBRI has a tool that aids users to realize this process. It reasons about applicable methods for each task, using the method description detailed above. First, it uses the list of tasks contained in the *competencies* field to obtain only the methods that resolve the task and later computes applicable methods reasoning with, the pre/post condition data stored in the *ContextInputPrecondition* and *ContextOutputPostcondition* fields. This reasoning is done using the DL reasoner.

Following sections describe our proposal for transforming this framework based on PSMs into a distributed framework where methods are defined as services using modern Semantic Web languages.

3 jCOLIBRI as a Semantic Web Services Architecture

Nowadays, jCOLIBRI is managed using *sourceforge*[2], a software development website that provides a version control system (CVS). Users check out the source code of the framework and use its library of PSMs. They also can extend or create new methods. Our goal with jCOLIBRI has been to provide with a reference framework for CBR development that would grow with contributions from the community. But problems arise just there. If a user wants to share a new method he must send it to the developers and wait until they check that it is suitable and include it in a new framework release.

To avoid these problems we need a distributed framework where everybody can share their contributions by publishing them in Internet. Here comes our idea of translating our PSMs into Semantic Web Services.

First, we are going to introduce a brief state of the art in Web Services technologies and later we are going to present how can be applied to our framework.

3.1 Semantic Web Services Overview

Actually there are three main Semantic Web Services (SWS) architectures: OWL-S based architectures [26][25] (boosted by W3C[3]), WSMX [9] and IRS [8][13]. These platforms are composed by an architectural proposal that defines the system components and a language proposal for defining Web Services.

W3C systems have not a clearly defined components architecture, although they focus in the language: OWL-S. This standard is an evolution of OWL, a widely applied ontologies representation language. IRS platform is based on PSM descriptions founded on UPML[14] and OCML[20]. Last one, WSMX, has its own architecture and a services description language: WSML. Also, there are some initiatives that are trying to update IRS into the WSMX platform [10][13]. As result, OWL-S and WSML are the most important initiatives for describing Web Services.

Anyway, it is possible to extract common features from these platforms that must be took into account when building a Web Services system [7][26][18]:

- Shared terminology represented through ontologies.

- Information exchange protocols. SOAP is the most used protocol.

- Directory that allows services discovery. UDDI is the main protocol.

- A parser and a reasoner that understands the language used for describing services.

- Matchmaking system between goals and services.

[2]http://sourceforge.net/projects/jcolibri-cbr
[3]http://www.w3.org/

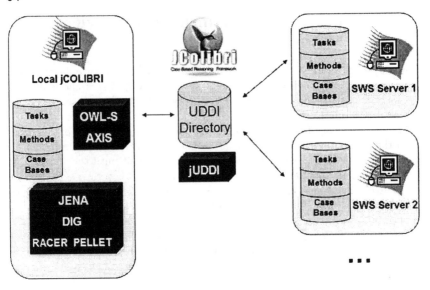

Figure 3: jCOLIBRI Semantic Web Services architecture

- Control flow primitives that organizes services composition.

- Mediators between services and data.

- Storage capabilities.

- Security capabilities.

- A coordination platform between different systems.

Our proposal for a Semantic Web evolution of jCOLIBRI uses these common features as a design guide for defining the new architecture.

After studying the available platforms we have chosen the OWL-S architecture. Main two reasons are:

- It is an OWL evolution, the most important ontology description language that is supported by several tools and platforms like PROTEGÉ.

- The another option, WSMX fixes a rigid software components architecture that can be hardly applied to our current framework design.

Once we have chosen the proper platform we must transform the framework looking at two axis: the software components and technologies, and the language description and reasoning features.

3.2 Software Components and Technologies

Our new architecture is going to maintain the current GUI for composing PSMs using task decomposition. The main difference consists on it is going to look for methods both in the local library as well as Internet. For service discovering we need a central directory where Web Services can be published. It can be easily implemented using jUDDI, an UDDI protocol implementation. This central directory can be seen as the new automatic *sourceforge* replacement where users are going to publish and discover methods.

From users point of view, they are going to have a client that allows PSM composition because it reasons with the method descriptions, and a server that facilitates PSM publishing. As it was said before, the client is going to be based on the current jCOLIBRI GUI although adding Web Services discovery capabilities using an OWL reasoner (this feature is discussed in the next section). For Web Services publishing we are using Apache AXIS [4], a SOAP and WSDL implementation, together with its OWL-S Plugin [5] that allows OWL-S publishing and discovering. Figure 3 illustrates this new architecture.

As next section describes, we need to provide ontologies management capabilities that allows reasoning over services descriptions. This is implemented using JENA[6], a Java framework for writing Semantic Web applications that can intercommunicate with different reasoners like Racer[17] or Pellet[23] using the standard DIG interface (see [3]).

3.3 Service description and reasoning capabilities

As we have already mentioned, OWL-S is an OWL ontology designed for describing Semantic Web Services and is divided into three main components:

Service Profile Defines "what the service does", in a way that is suitable for a service-seeking agent to determine whether the service meets its needs. This is the part that we are interested in this paper, as it describes services pre/post conditions.

Service Model The service model tells a client how to use the service, by detailing the semantic content of requests, the conditions under which particular outcomes will occur, and, where necessary, the step by step processes leading to those outcomes. That is, it describes how to ask for the service and what happens when the service is carried out.

Grounding Specifies the details of how an agent can access a service. Typically a grounding will specify a communication protocol, message formats, etc. Usually, applied protocols are SOAP and WSDL protocols, existing several implementations being AXIS the most popular.

---

[4]http://ws.apache.org/axis/
[5]http://ivs.tu-berlin.de/Projekte/owlsplugin/
[6]http://www.hpl.hp.com/semweb/jena2.htm

Service profile defines the method Inputs, Outputs, Preconditions and Effects (called IOPEs). Therefore, our current method description schema using XML that was introduced in Section 2.1 must be translated into this new approach. As OWL-S does not bind to any specific language for conditions representation, we have choosen an OWL subset defined as OWL-DL for representing our PSMs features because of its correspondence with DLs reasoning capabilities.

Fist of all, we must explain how methods are composed in the current framework. PSMs interchange data using a blackboard mechanism that contains the *Context* at each execution step. This context contains all the information and parameters that methods need: query, cases, intermediate calculated results, etc. Accordingly, when translating this approach into OWL-S we are going to use the inputs and outputs definitions of the service profile for interchanging this context.

Our proposal consists on representing the *ContextInputPrecondition* and the *Competencies* list as an OWL-DL description stored in the *Preconditions* attribute of the OWL-S profile. Respectively, the *ContextOutputPostcondition* is stored in the *Effects* attribute.

When composing services, we use a *context* instance C_i for representing the actual state of the CBR cycle. This context is also represented as an OWL-DL expression. Each PSM contains a context precondition concept and returns a context postcondition instance. So, if we want to compose two PSMs PSM_i and PSM_{i+1} our framework must compute if the context instance C_i returned by PSM_i can be classified as an instance of the precondition concept of PSM_{i+1}.

jCOLIBRI tasks and methods composition mechanism is going to use this schema to guide the user when assigning a method that resolves a task. The selection and composition algorithm of this new approach follows these steps: (1) Asks the services directory for published methods. (2) Looks for the current task into their *Competencies* list and selects the methods that contain the task. (3) Computes the reasoning explained in the previous paragraph for choosing the applicable methods for the current context and offers them to the user. (4) Finally, the user chooses the method that solves the current task.

Figure 4 describes the CBROnto subset (formalized in OWL) for representing jCOLIBRI contexts. A context instance is going to be composed by a case base description (size and structure), query structure, case structure and features, data types contained by cases (as they restrict applicable methods), etc. This figure only shows the *is-a* relations although the *context* object is related with the remaining concepts using several properties.

Classified below the *context* concept we have defined several contexts. Each one of these contexts represent the precondition of a PSM of our library. For example, the methods developed in the textual extension of jCOLIBRI[22] need to define a context that uses a small or medium size case base with linear organization and contains textual cases with solution. Textual cases are defined as containing at least a *Text* typed attribute. This definition can be created

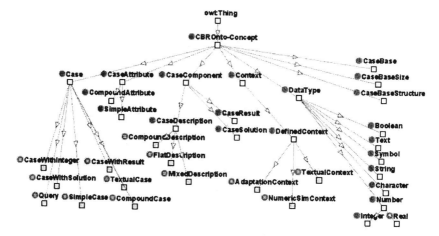

Figure 4: Context definition subset of CBROnto

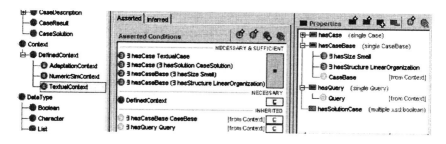

Figure 5: Defining contexts using PROTEGE

using PROTEGÉ or coded directly in OWL. Figure 5 shows the PROTEGÉ definition of these requirements.

As described before, the DL reasoner uses the services preconditions that contains contexts definitions to compute which methods are suitable for any context. Continuing with the example, we have defined a context instance that is returned by a method. It is shown in Figure 6 where concepts are drawn as circles and instances as diamonds. Our example is composed by a context instance *context1* that has case base *casebase1* that is small *small1* and has a linear organization *linearorganization1*. Case structure *case1* contains a Text data type *text1* and has a solution *solution1*. Note that several details, like case or solution structure definition has been removed for clarity reasons.

Using the reasoner we can classify the *context1* instance and infer if it is a

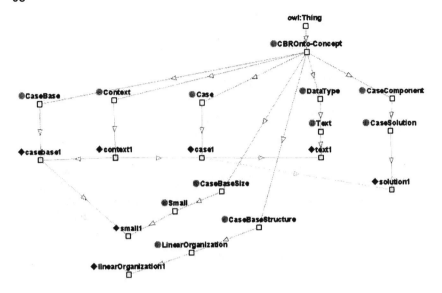

Figure 6: A context instance definition

TextualContext instance. Figure 7 shows PROTEGÉ answer when classifying *context1* into CBROnto. As result, we can know if a method is suitable for a specific context at each execution step. As we are using the Jena package for ontologies management, we can use several reasoners like Racer or Pellet, supporting the DIG reasoners interface that allows a transparent reasoner communication.

4   Conclusions

In this paper we have described the evolution of the jCOLIBRI framework towards a distributed architecture based on Semantic Web Services.

jCOLIBRI provides a battery of PSMs, and the programmer searches for the most useful for his purpose. Separating PSMs from the main core by using Web Services get us closer to the concept of software components technology, bringing its possibilities to jCOLIBRI.

Our (ambitious) goal is to provide a reference framework for CBR development that would grow with contributions from the community. This reference would serve for pedagogical purposes and for prototyping CBR systems and comparing different CBR approaches to a given problem reusing PSMs. This idea is so mature in the community that several efforts are pursuing it at time of writing: CAT-CBR [2], a component-based platform for developing CBR systems; JavaCREEK the Java implementation of the CREEK architecture for

99

Figure 7: PROTEGÉ answer when classifying a context instance

knowledge-intensive CBR systems [1]; IUCBRF [5] a Java framework developed at Indiana University, to mention just a few.

In this paper we focus on one of the key aspects of our approach: the use of a CBR ontology, CBROnto, to describe and formalize the CBR PSMs. We have made an special point of the representation of the method knowledge requirements, and have described how DLs mechanisms allow reasoning with PSM descriptions to check their applicability regarding an external context formed by the domain knowledge and the cases. Besides, DLs mechanisms make it possible to explain why the method does not fit the situation and what additional knowledge would be needed to apply the method.

References

[1] A. Aamodt. Knowledge-Intensive Case-Based Reasoning in CREEK. In *ECCBR*, pages 1–15, 2004.

[2] C. Abásolo, E. Plaza, and J.-L. Arcos. Components for Case-Based Reasoning Systems. *Lecture Notes in Computer Science*, 2504, 2002.

[3] S. Bechhofer, R. Möller, and P. Crowther. The DIG Description Logic Interface. In D. Calvanese, G. D. Giacomo, and E. Franconi, editors, *Description Logics*, volume 81 of *CEUR Workshop Proceedings*. CEUR-WS.org, 2003.

[4] J. J. Bello-Tomás, P. A. González-Calero, and B. Díaz-Agudo. JColibri: An Object-Oriented Framework for Building CBR Systems. In P. Funk and P. A. González-Calero, editors, *ECCBR*, volume 3155 of *Lecture Notes in Computer Science*, pages 32–46. Springer, 2004.

[5] S. Bogaerts and D. Leake. *IUCBRF: A Framework For Rapid And Modular Case-Based Reasoning System Development.* http://www.cs.indiana.edu/ sbogaert/CBR/IUCBRF.pdf.

[6] J. A. Breuker and W. Van de Velde. *CommonKADS Library for Expertise Modelling: Reusable Problem Solving Components.* 1994.

[7] C. Bussler, E. Cimpian, A. Mocan, M. Moran, and M. Zaremba. WSMX: An Execution Environment for Semantic Web Services. *Position paper at W3C Workshop on Frameworks for Semantics in Web Services*, 2005.

[8] M. Crubézy, W. Lu, E. Motta, and M. A. Musen. Configuring Online Problem-Solving Resources with the Internet Reasoning Service. In *Proceedings of the IFIP 17th World Computer Congress - TC12 Stream on Intelligent Information Processing*, pages 91–102, Deventer, The Netherlands, The Netherlands, 2002. Kluwer, B.V.

[9] J. de Bruijn, H. Lausen, R. Krummenacher, A. Polleres, L. Predoiu, M. Kifer, and D. Fensel. The Web Service Modeling Language WSML (final draft). http://www.wsmo.org/TR/d16/d16.1/v0.2/, March 2005.

[10] J. de Bruijn, R. Lara, S. Arroyo, J. M. Gomez, H. Sung-Kook, and D. Fensel. A Unified Semantic Web Services Architecture based on WSMF and UPML. *International Journal on Web Engineering Technology, special issue on Semantic Web*, 2005.

[11] B. Díaz-Agudo and P. A. González-Calero. An architecture for knowledge intensive CBR systems. In E. Blanzieri and L. Portinale, editors, *Advances in Case-Based Reasoning - (EWCBR'00)*. Springer-Verlag, Berlin Heidelberg New York, 2000.

[12] B. Díaz-Agudo and P. A. González-Calero. CBROnto: a task/method ontology for CBR. In S. Haller and G. Simmons, editors, *Procs. of the 15th International FLAIRS'02 Conference*. AAAI Press, 2002.

[13] J. Domingue, L. Cabral, F. Hakimpour, D. Sell, and M. E. IRS-III: A Platform and Infrastructure for Creating WSMO-based Semantic Web Services. In *Proceedings of the Workshop on WSMO Implementations (WIW)*, 2004.

[14] D. Fensel, E. Motta, F. van Harmelen, V. R. Benjamins, M. Crubézy, S. Decker, M. Gaspari, R. Groenboom, W. E. Grosso, M. A. Musen, E. Plaza, G. Schreiber, R. Studer, and B. J. Wielinga. The Unified Problem-Solving Method Development Language UPML. *Knowl. Inf. Syst.*, 5(1):83–131, 2003.

[15] A. Gómez-Pérez. Knowledge sharing and reuse. In Liebowitz, editor, *The handbook on Applied Expert Systems*. CRC Press, 1998.

[16] P. A. González-Calero, B. Díaz-Agudo, J. A. Recio-García, and J. J. Bello-Tomás. Authoring Tools in JColibri. In B. Lees, editor, *Proceedings of the 9th UK Workshop on Case-Based Reasoning*, pages 1–11, December 2004.

[17] V. Haarslev and R. Möller. Racer: A core inference engine for the semantic web. In Y. Sure and Ó. Corcho, editors, *EON*, volume 87 of *CEUR Workshop Proceedings*. CEUR-WS.org, 2003.

[18] F. Leymann. Web services: Distributed applications without limits. In G. Weikum, H. Schöning, and E. Rahm, editors, *BTW*, volume 26 of *LNI*, pages 2–23. GI, 2003.

[19] M. D. McIlroy. Mass produced software components. In *Proc. Nato Software Eng. Conf.*, pages 138–155, Garmisch, Germany, 1968.

[20] E. Motta. An Overview of the OCML Modelling Language. In *Proceddings of the 8th Workshop on Knowledge Engineering Methods and Languages (KEML)*, 1998.

[21] A. Newel. The knowledge level. *Artificial Intelligence*, 18:87–127, 1982.

[22] J. A. Recio-Garía, B. Díaz-Agudo, M. A. Gómez-Martín, and N. Wiratunga. Extending jCOLIBRI for Textual CBR. In *Proceedings of the Sixth edition of the International Conference on Case-Based Reasoning*, 2005.

[23] E. Sirin and B. Parsia. Pellet: An OWL DL Reasoner. In V. Haarslev and R. Möller, editors, *Description Logics*, volume 104 of *CEUR Workshop Proceedings*. CEUR-WS.org, 2004.

[24] L. Steels. Components of expertise. *AI Magazine*, 11(2):29–49, 1990.

[25] The OWL Services Coalition. OWL-S: Semantic Markup for Web Services. http://www.daml.org/services/owl-s/1.1/overview/.

[26] World Wide Web Consortium (W3C). Web services architecture. http://www.w3.org/TR/ws-arch/, December 2004.

Using simple ontologies to build personal Webs of knowledge

Konstantinos Kotis[*]

Department of Information and Communications Systems Engineering
University of the Aegean
Samos, Karlovassi, 83200 Greece
kkot@aegean.gr

Abstract

Current AI and Semantic Web research is striving towards solving the problem of retrieving precise knowledge from the Knowledge Web. Still, thousands of retrieved documents (most of them irrelevant) are flooding Web users who are unable to control and validate them against their queries. Although structuring Web documents is currently the most acceptable solution to the problem, it seems that the problems of a) "thousands of documents returned for a query" and b) neglecting the unstructured repositories, still remain. In this paper, we present our approach to these problems, which does not necessarily require the transformation of the current Web. We show how structured and unstructured documents could be conjunctively queried using simple ontologies built-up by the queries. More importantly, we show how personal collections of Web documents can be built and queried, so that retrieval within such structures can result in precise knowledge.

Keywords: Semantic Web, Knowledge Web, Search Engines, Web Queries

1.   Introduction

Knowledge is distributed over unstructured (HTML) and structured (RDF, OWL) Web documents. Web information is changing into a kind of information that machines can process. This machine-processable information integrates metadata to add meaning (semantics) to existing information. This way, humans' queries are able to retrieve available information, and extract knowledge from heterogeneous and distributed sources.

The need for moving from traditional web documents to semantic documents (Semantic Web) came out from the failure of keyword-based Web search engines

---

[*] Corresponding author: Tel: 0030 22730 82000, Fax: 0030 22730 82009, E-mail: kkot@aegean.gr

102

to retrieve precise information. Current keyword-based search engines are still a monopoly in retrieving information for Web users, however with only fairly acceptable precision percentages. Natural language processing and AI techniques have been put into the game in order to overcome the problem, but they have not achieved significant improvements [1].

Although there is still space to improve the precision of retrieval methods, most importantly, there is also a need to retrieve knowledge from newly built-up Semantic Web repositories such as SWOOGLE [2]. Semantic Web research efforts are tackling the problem of querying semantically annotated documents; however, in the real world of WWW users the most popular search engines are still keyword-based. Even semantic search engines such as SWOOGLE, perform a term-based search in their repository, in order to retrieve Web ontology documents which contain concepts lexicalized by the query-term(s) [2].

Furthermore, existing search engines return a large amount of results for a simple query, and more importantly, in most of the cases, this query has been repeatedly placed by the same user. For instance, let us think of a Web user who travels a lot in several different places. She queries the Web for a specific destination each time she is about to travel. The "bookmarked" Web pages are an easy way to overcome the repetition; however, this method leaves out new information added in newly created Web pages. So, the traveler must place "her personal query" every time she is about to travel, resulting in vast amounts of thousands of documents, most of them irrelevant to "what" she is seeking, and thus making her unable to control and validate every single source of information.

To tackle the problems discussed above, we propose a new framework for organizing and querying Web information, based on current technologies and the Knowledge Web. Our aim is to improve the precision of the returned information and speed up the process of validation and exploitation of the desired content. Towards this aim, the key objectives of our approach can be outlined in the following points:

a) In this new era of Semantic Web, we must not neglect valuable knowledge that unstructured documents may contain.

b) Knowledge contained within unstructured and structured documents must be somehow integrated and presented in a uniform manner to the end-users.

c) The vast amount of returned documents returned by queries must be somehow controlled, reducing their number drastically, in order to speed up the validation and exploitation process.

d) The precision of "everyday queries" must be increased in order to effectively serve the millions of Web users that depend the success of their daily knowledge-intensive tasks on the exploitation of the Web information they have gathered.

e) To accomplish their day-to-day knowledge intensive tasks, users could place simple "everyday queries" faster and more accurately, using small custom personal Webs, instead of the whole Knowledge Web.

In this paper, we discuss the above issues and propose a new framework, based also on our previous experiences concerning concept ontology concepts disambiguation and ontology alignment [3] [4] and on our vision about the future of the Knowledge Web. In section 2 we outline relative technologies and methods from the areas of Semantic Web and Information Retrieval. In Section 3 we describe our approach of querying personal Webs, and finally we conclude the paper in Section 4, commenting on our first results and future work.

2. Related Work

Current literature covers issues concerning either querying traditional Web documents or querying Semantic Web documents. Although the need for structured queries and repositories is currently accentuated, it unfortunately places the already large amount of unstructured information aside, and do not tackle the important problem of the amount of results returned for a simple query.

Several efforts are trying to improve precision in either direction (traditional Web or Semantic Web). However, there is no effort that considers queries in a unified Knowledge Web. Google (http://www.google.com) is a widely-used search engine which provides human directed search or search automated by agents/bots/crawlers that visit documents and count links ("Page relevance" algorithm). Its keyword-based search method results in thousands of documents, most of them irrelevant to the users' interest. Yahoo (http://www.yahoo.com) is another keyword-based search engine that uses hierarchies which constrain results according to semantics that humans specify. However this case is restrictive by the existence of categories of the current hierarchy implementation, and does not solve the problem of "thousands of documents returned for a query". Moreover, "intelligent" search engines like AskJeeves (http://www.ask.com) perform a semantically-based search by trying to "understand" a query placed in natural language. Strong NLP methods are applied with good results, but still, because of the vast amount of returned documents, results cannot be checked and validated against the users' intended meanings of the query-terms.

On the other hand, the Semantic Web research initiatives have already realized the significance of placing structured queries on structured documents (RDF, OWL), developing querying languages such as RQL [5] and OWL-QL [6] for queering documents in local repositories. For querying distributed structured documents, some first initiatives have been already started using either reference ontologies or P2P mappings [7] [8]. Although these initiatives address, in the correct direction, the problem of querying knowledge from distributed and heterogeneous sources, they assume that only structured documents reside in the WWW repositories.

To the best of our knowledge, there are currently two research efforts that try to apply semantic search on unstructured documents. In the Tap project [1], traditional search results (HTML documents) are augmented with relevant data pulled out from the Semantic Web [9]. A technique for disambiguating query-terms, similar to the one that we propose in this paper, is used in their approach. A lightweight query language needs to be used to place queries. Moreover, pre-existence of related Semantic Web documents is required in order to refine the results from the traditional searching methods. RDF documents have to be build out of semantic data pulled from HTML documents, a time/effort-consuming and error-prone method. The other approach of semantic querying is based on LSI

---

[1] http://tap.stanford.edu/

(Latent Semantic Indexing) [10]. In this approach HTML documents returned from a traditional searching method are indexed and re-ordered using LSI [1]. Although both approaches seem a lot promising, they are much dependant on keyword-based query results of "traditional" search engines (with their known limitations) such as Google.

To conclude, existing efforts do not solve adequately the problem of precision and controllable results of simple queries, and more importantly they do not provide a solution for a unified querying system of the Knowledge Web. Our approach borrows from these technologies towards visualizing new knowledge structures in the Web. These new structures will be addressed to users that:

a) Do not need to be familiar with a structured querying language.
b) Do not need to validate thousands of results before they exploit them.
c) Do not need to repeat queries that they (or other users) have recently and successfully used to retrieve knowledge from the Web.

The proposed approach could be viewed as a two-step process: 1) the step of building "personal Web(s)", and 2) the step of placing "everyday queries" (Figure 1). The rest of the paper is focused on the detailed description of step 1.

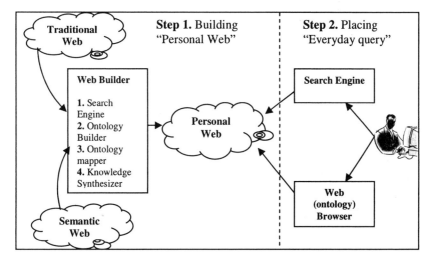

Figure 1. The two-step process of the proposed new knowledge structure approach in the Knowledge Web

3. The approach

"Everyday queries" are queries that are repeatedly placed from members of a Web community of interest, seeking knowledge related to their specific personal domain interests. The retrieved knowledge of such queries has, most of the times, been already retrieved in the past. The already retrieved knowledge can be proved sufficient to Web users in order to create their personal Webs of knowledge. This personal Web is a collection of URIs referring to Web documents which physically exist in WWW repositories. The personal Web is organized in a schema of URIs (let us call them "myURIs"). A myURI is a URI that has been selected by the Web users to be diachronically related to their personal interests. This schema can be viewed as a personal domain ontology, classifying URIs under its concepts. A myURI can be either a link to an interesting HTML document or a link to a domain concept in an interesting Web ontology document. We call this personal Web "myGnosiWeb" ("Gnosi" means "knowledge" in Greek). Provided with a collection of myGnosiWebs, a Web user can place semantic queries (utilizing their ontologies) to a much smaller amount of information, and more importantly to information that is shaped according to their personal everyday interests. Large amounts of irrelevant information are excluded, thus maximizing the precision of their queries.

To improve precision of queries placed in the Knowledge Web, bearing always in mind the personal character of "everyday queries", we propose a new querying method. The method improves precision percentages of traditional queries by querying only a small fraction of Web documents that have been pre-selected by users. The final query placed is a structured one, guided by an ontology, which can be used to retrieve knowledge from distributed personal knowledge repositories such as a collection of myGnosiWeb(s).

In the following paragraphs, we show how a myGnosiWeb can be built, and how it can reduce significantly the large amount of irrelevant documents returned by queries in the Knowledge Web, improving the precision of the returned URIs. Moreover, we show how our approach implements the querying of both structured and unstructured Web documents.

3.1   Reformulation of simple queries

One of the innovative techniques that we have experimented within the myGnosiWeb approach is outlined in this paragraph. This technique is used to disambiguate and enrich queries towards improving the precision of keyword-based search engines, as well as of the new semantic search engines that search in repositories of RDF/OWL documents. We call this technique X-query since eXtra information is added to the query prior to its execution. X-query is partially implemented and evaluated using Google's API (http://www.google.com/apis/). Its design was based on the following facts:

1. 91% of Web users try searching differently at a search engine if the initial search failed to bring up a good match in the first three pages of results [11]. The idea is that search users believe that it's more their mistake than the search engine's. In other words, instead of trying the same search elsewhere -- which might actually bring up a better result -- they may feel they've simply not come up with the right query. Web users (26%) will be satisfied with a maximum of 2 pages (20 documents) of results (the 23% said they would review only the first few matches on the first page, and the 19% percent said they would review only the entire first page of results).

2. Search engines returns a large amount of results, many of them irrelevant, for simple queries. For example, Google will return 17.300.000 links about a "book flight" query. The users may be satisfied with the first 10 ranked documents. However, Google also returns (in May 2005) a document about a "book" which talks about "flight" dynamics (in rank 9),

and a document about an archive story which talks about someone that has been instructed on how to "book" a "flight" (in rank 6). Users know what they want to look for in the Web, but they usually express it in ambiguous ways. In the previous example, an alternative query such as "reserve flight" would have eliminated ambiguous results such as documents concerning "books about flights".

In order to disambiguate users' queries, we are using the WordNet lexicon and the LSI (Latent Semantic Indexing) technique as applied in [3]. The terms that the mapped WordNet sense contains are processed and added to the query in the place of the disambiguated term. An example that shows the steps followed by the related algorithm is presented below:

1. The query "book flight" was placed in X-query.
2. The algorithm suggested the disambiguation of the first query-term, e.g. "book", by assigning to it automatically a WordNet (ver. 1.7.1) sense. If the sense assigned by the algorithm is not the intended one, Web users can select the sense that is closer to their intentions. In our example, since the automated assignment was not the intended one (due to lack of semantic information around term "book", a theory which is extensively explained in [3]), the user selected WordNet sense number 2 of the verb senses i.e. *"reserve, hold, book -- (arrange for and reserve (something for someone else) in advance; "reserve me a seat on a flight"; "The agent booked tickets to the show for the whole family"; "please hold a table at Maxim's")"*. The same process was repeated for term "flight". The assigned sense was noun sense number 9 i.e. *"flight -- (a scheduled trip by plane between designated airports; "I took the noon flight to Chicago")"*.
3. The algorithm then processed the senses mapped to each query-term, and computed the most important terms (terms that occur within the sense more times than a threshold number of times) of the sense. In our example, for the sense mapped to the query-term "book", sense-term "reserve" occurred 3 times, sense-term "hold" 2 times, and sense-term "book(ed)" 2 times. For this particular implementation, the threshold was 2, thus only the sense-term "reserve" was returned as the important term within the mapped sense. In other tested implementations (threshold = 1), sense-terms "book" and "hold" where also considered as important, thus the overall value for the execution of the query were increased, increasing the precision of the results as we will conjecture later on in the paper. For the query-term "flight" no important words have found.
4. The sense-terms that have been extracted from the mapped WordNet sense, replace the query-term that was disambiguated i.e. the term "book". Thus, the query is reformulated, and in our example it becomes "reserve flight".
5. After reformulating the query, a simple domain ontology is created on-the-fly. The ontology (called q-ontology) consists of the terms used in the initial and the reformulated query, introducing "synonym" and "is-a" (classification) relations. For instance, using the example of "book flight" (and its reformulation "reserve flight"), the ontology that will be constructed looks like Figure 2. The disambiguated query-term "book" is classified under the term "action" since the mapped WordNet sense was found in the lexicon's verb senses. More importantly, term "book" is

automatically classified under its (immediate) hypernym term that WordNet 1.7.1 has for this term. This enrichment of the ontology strengthens its semantics and increases precision when queries are mapped against this particular ontology or against the virtual network consisting of collections of such ontologies. The same happens also with term "flight"; it is classified under its immediate hypernym term "trip" since its mapping in WordNet was on a noun synset[2]. Furthermore, "book" is also related to term "reserve" via a "synonym" relation since term "reserve" was extracted by the WordNet synset (synonym set) for that particular term. Term "book" is also related to term "flight" somehow, thus an "other relation" relation is also introduced automatically. This kind of relation the user's mind can be translated in any literal that connects these two query-terms (e.g. "a", "about", "in", "for"), but this is of no interest to our implementation. In our approach, we are only interested in the connection between these two query-terms such as the classification of their union, i.e. the query "book flight" being placed under term "book", to inherit semantics of both terms.

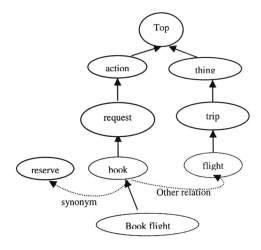

Figure 2. A q-ontology for "book flight" query. "Book" means "reserve" here.

In order to support the importance of creating this simple domain ontology based on the query, let us describe another scenario where the same example query results in a completely different ontology, since the user-intended meaning of the query-terms were completely different. Following the same steps that we have presented previously:

1. Place the initial query e.g. "book flight".
2. User selects WordNet sense number 1 of the noun senses for query-term "book" i.e. "book -- (a copy of a written work or composition that has been published (printed on pages bound together); "I am reading a good book

---

[2] A synset in WordNet is the set of synonyms that are assigned to a term

on economics")". The same process is repeated for term "flight". The assigned sense for query-term "flight" is noun sense number 7 i.e. "trajectory, flight -- (the path followed by an object moving through space)".

3. For the query-terms "book" and "flight" no important words have been found this time (threshold = 1).

4. No replacement of terms of the initial query occurred, thus the query is not reformulated. However, to increase the precision of their query, users can manually add important semantic distinctions (hypernyms) discovered in step 5, and re-start from step 1.

5. A simple ontology is created on-the-fly (see Figure 3) such as: The disambiguated query- term "book" is classified under the term "thing" since the mapped WordNet sense was found in the lexicon's noun synset. More importantly, query-term "book" is now classified under its (immediate) hypernym term "publication". Query-term "flight" is now classified under its immediate hypernym term "mechanical phenomenon". Query-term "book" is again related to term "flight". "Book flight" query is now classified under different semantics than in first scenario.

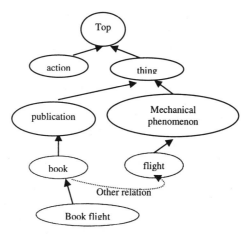

Figure 3. An example q-ontology for "book flight" query. "Book" means "publication" here.

A mapping between these two simple q-ontologies will show that although the lexicalization of both queries in both scenarios is the same, since their semantics are different, they are two completely different queries, and that is how they must be treated by an effective search engine. In the following paragraphs we will show how search engines can be enhanced with this particular technique of simple queries enrichment, and how this enhancement is used to build a personal collection of Web documents; a myGnosiWeb.

Work similar to X-query has been carried out in Tap project [12], with quite impressive precision results. However, a major difference to our approach is that in the Tap project the disambiguation process is performed on the already returned results of a traditional searching method. This method, although it will eventually re-order results and bring the "intended" ones on higher rank, suffers form the drawback that its precision is heavily based on the precision of the keyword-based searching method applied in the first place. Furthermore, changes on the indexing of Web documents are required prior to a query, in order to extract (and attach on it) each document's "sketch", i.e. a fragment of logical description (semantics) of a query-term, implied by the words of a Web document. We could think of using the re-ordering approach of Tap's project (or the one that uses LSI [1]) in conjunction to our approach i.e. after the execution of X-query.

3.2   The construction of myGnosiWeb

Up to this point, we have described how a simple unstructured (natural language) query is enriched and reformulated in a new structured query. One could argue that we have tackled one of the major research issues for the Semantic Web, i.e. building and using structured queries for the Semantic Web documents without using a specific structured query language. Furthermore, one can also argue that what we have achieved is to let "traditional" querying engines stay into the "game", since no re-design is needed for placing queries to the Web.

However this is not the major aim of our vision for the future of the Web. Indeed, we have proposed and implemented a technique such as X-query not only as a way to reformulate unstructured queries but also as a step towards building personal Web repositories. As already mentioned, the Knowledge Web must be considered to contain two different types of documents, the unstructured and the structured ones. So, in the future, querying about "book flight" should retrieve documents that provide the information on booking a flight in HTML, but also OWL documents which provide (in a structured manner) related knowledge.

The X-query provides input for 2 different processes: a) the process of using the enriched query string with Google API in order to find the first 10 ranked related documents, and b) the process of mapping the q-ontology to the ontologies encoded by OWL documents in Semantic Web repositories such as SWOOGLE. The resulted links from both processes can be considered as instances classified under the concept lexicalized by the query string term, e.g. under "book flight" for our example. What we really propose here is that every document fetched from the Knowledge Web using the new enriched and structured query, can be associated with this particular query i.e. with the particular q-ontology.

The specific collection of documents that is classified under the q-ontology is the knowledge that a specific user at a specific time and for a specific domain of interest has actually created (Figure 4). This structure of knowledge is what we call myGnosiWeb. Any Web user can create his own myGnosiWeb(s), at any time and for any domain of interest, save it in his personal working environment, update it with new URIs from time-to-time, refine the q-ontology or delete URIs of no current interest. This will eventually result in a number of personal myGnosiWeb(s) that can provide the necessary required knowledge for the user's "everyday queries". We must not forget that in everyday knowledge intensive tasks, the need to acquire the same (or similar) knowledge arises very often. Time and precision are really the motivations for using our approach instead of "traditional" search engines crawling the whole Knowledge Web. Although this idea is not new, e.g. see the effort from Yahoo under the name "My Web" (http://my.yahoo.com/), no other effort is using a conceptual model built-up from the query in order to classify the retrieved documents and provide clear semantics for the particular knowledge structure. More importantly other efforts depend on the fact that the documents retrieved and saved by their URLs are only unstructured documents.

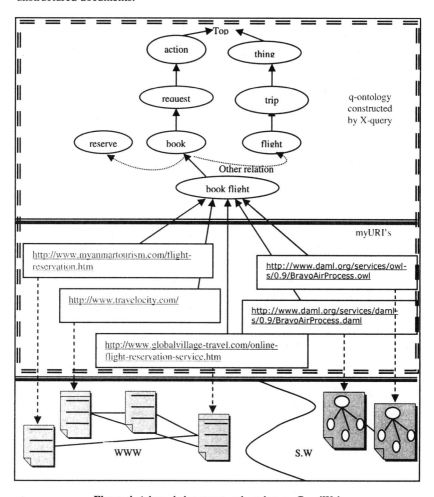

Figure 4. A knowledge structure based on myGnosiWeb

Up to this point we have described how personal knowledge can be collected from any kind of Web documents, and organized in a new knowledge structure that we call myGnosiWeb. The architecture of a system that we have designed and partially implemented to support our approach is described in Figure 5.

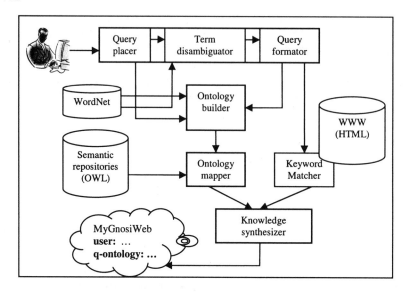

Figure 5. The processes used to construct a myGnosiWeb

The system modules are described as follows:

1. A "query-placer" which accepts an initial natural language query, takes out any stop words, and provides a list of terms in the output.
2. A "term-disambiguator" which provides (semi)-automatic assignment of WordNet senses to each query-term.
3. A "query-formator", which reformulates the initial query using the most important terms of the mapped WordNet sense.
4. An "ontology-builder" which dynamically builds a rough simple ontology (q-ontology), using each term of the initial and the reformulated query as well as WordNet semantic information about each term.
5. A "keyword-matcher" which actually does exactly what a keyword-based search engine do, retrieving however only the first 10 documents of the resulting document rank.
6. An "ontology-mapper" which maps the q-ontology to a Semantic Web repository (e.g. SWOOGLE). Most relevant (number of concepts mapped) Web ontology documents (written in OWL) will be retrieved.
7. A "knowledge-synthesizer" which combines structured (Swoogle) and unstructured (Google) documents, and classifies them in the q-ontology. The result of this process is an ontology with:
   a) A terminology consisting of concepts that are lexicalized by terms of the initial and reformulated query as well as of semantics (hypernyms, synonyms) extracted from WordNet
   b) Instances consisting of URIs that show the location of Web documents.

4. First results and future work

Our vision towards new knowledge structures of today's Knowledge Web has been shaped in the idea of building personal Web document collections of particular domains of interest. This idea is partially implemented and evaluated.

Id	Query	Intended meaning	Re-formed with X-Query
Q1	"book flight"	reserve a flight	"flight reserve"
Q2	"auto organisation"	company builds cars	"organization car business"
Q3	"place investement"	make an investment	"investment put money"
Q4	"train instructions"	how to excersize	"coach instructions"

	Google		Yahoo		X-query (using Google API)	
Id	Total	Precision*	Total	Precision	Total	Precision
Q1	17.300.000	* 100%	21.700.000	80%	837.000	100%
Q2	8.500.000	30%	4.540.000	50%	2.710.000	60%
Q3	32.000.000	40%	26.900.000	10%	2.320.000	90%
Q4	4.410.000	20%	3.490.000	30%	172.000	80%

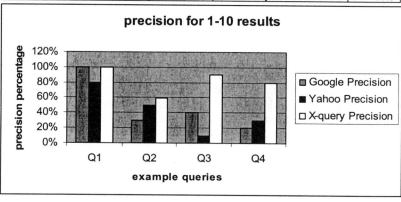

Figure 6. Measuring precision and total amount of documents for sample queries. (Note: The results presented have been gathered in early June 2005).

The enrichment and structure of natural language queries has shown that precision percentage is moving up and the amount of documents returned by search engines is reduced drastically. Experimental queries we have run using the X-query technique with Google API have resulted in high precision (100% in the best case, and 60% in the worst) for the first 10 ranked returned documents (note that also in related work, as in the PIPER project [13], the first 10 documents were used to evaluate the precision). More importantly, the amount of documents returned, compared with the amount returned by traditional searching engines such as Google and Yahoo (most popular engines according to iProspect survey [11]) was significantly reduced as depicted in the experimental cases of Figure 6.

Recall percentage is however an important parameter that we may need to consider, although we conjecture (based on surveys [11]) that in such a framework, Web users (26%) will be satisfied with a maximum of 2 pages (20 documents) of results (the 23% said they'd review only the first few matches on the first page, and the 19% percent who said they'd review only the entire first page of results). Another limitation of our approach is the dependence on the WordNet lexicon; however we do not consider WordNet as the only technology that can be used to solve the disambiguation problem. Furthermore, the on-the-fly construction of the q-ontology must be evaluated as well as the need for trust mechanisms between users. As far as the mapping between q-ontology and OWL documents is concerned, several existing (our HCONE-merge is one of them) and on-going works can be used to implement it [3].

For the evaluation of a fully implemented system (please visit http://www.icsd.aegean.gr/Postgraduates/kkot/Xquery.jpg for screenshot) towards new knowledge structures of the Knowledge Web, large scale experiments must be run in different domains and for several communities of interest. The usability of such an approach must be assessed in overall. Experiments with alternative lexicons instead of WordNet must be run.

5. Conclusions

Today's querying engines search the entire Web for knowledge within unstructured documents. Traditional keyword-based engines fail to retrieve precise knowledge. At the same time, the need for users to control and validate thousands or millions of returned documents is real. Although the Semantic Web research effort promises a solution around these problems by structuring Web documents, still important problems remain to be tackled: a) What happens with the existing unstructured documents? b) How knowledge within both types of documents can be integrated? c) How the vast amount of queries' returned documents can be controlled (reduced and validated)? d) How can we increase the precision of "everyday queries"? e) Do users really need access to the whole Knowledge Web for their day-to-day knowledge intensive tasks, or they can better answer their queries using custom personal Webs?

Trying to answer most of these questions, we have presented in this paper our approach towards a new structure of the Knowledge Web. We have proposed the structuring of the Knowledge Web into small contextualized Webs belonging to communities with specific domain interests. Placing queries to such structures can be proved not only a solution to the problem of precise retrieved information but also an effective mechanism to control the increased distributed and heterogeneous information sources. Major emphasis has been given on re-formulating simple queries by disambiguating terms in order to query, more precisely, unstructured documents. Emphasis has also been given on building simple ontologies on-the-fly in order to query structured Web documents. The idea of building "personal Webs" using such ontologies and a small set of returned documents has been also presented. "Everyday queries" can then be realized as a browsing or searching task over a selection of "personal Webs".

Our conjecture that this vision of the new Knowledge Web can be realized in the near future is based on early experiments and on our previous experiences concerning collaborative ontology engineering and ontology mapping techniques. Further work is needed to be carried out in order to be able to answer all the questions that we have placed towards this research direction.

References

1. Alesso P. Semantic Search Technology. AIS SIGSEMIS Bulletin 2004, 1(3), 86-98
2. Alesso P. Swoogle: A Semantic Web Search Engine. AIS SIGSEMIS Bulletin 2005, 2(1), 68-72
3. Kotis K., Vouros G. A., Stergiou K. Capturing Semantics towards Automatic Coordination of Domain Ontologies. Artificial Intelligence: Methodology, Systems, and Applications. Proceedings, Series: Lecture Notes in Computer Science, Subseries: Lecture Notes in Artificial Intelligence, Vol. 3192, Bussler, Christoph; Fensel, Dieter (Eds.) 2004, Springer-Verlag
4. Kotis K., Vouros G. A., Alonso J. P. HCOME: tool-supported methodology for collaboratively devising living ontologies. Book Chapter in Revised Selected Papers, Series: Lecture Notes in Computer Science, Vol. 3372, Bussler, Christoph; Tannen, Val; Fundulaki, Irini (Eds.) 2005, Springer-Verlag
5. Karvounarakis G. The RDF query language (RQL). Technical report, Institute of Computer Science, Foundation of Research Technology, 2003
6. Fikes R., P. Hayes, and Horrocks I. OWL-QL - a language for deductive query answering on the semantic web. Technical Report 2003, Knowledge Systems Laboratory, Stanford, CA
7. Bouquet P., Kuper G. M., Scoz M., Zanobini S. Asking and Answering Semantic Queries. Workshop on Meaning Coordination and Negotiation Workshop (MCN-04) in conjunction with the 3rd International Semantic Web Conference (ISWC-04), Hiroshima Japan, 2004
8. Calvanese D., Giacomo G., Lembo D., Lenzerini M., and Rosati R. What to Ask to a Peer: Ontology-based Query reformulation. In Proceedings of 9th Int. Conf. On Principles of Knowledge Representation and Reasoning, 2004
9. Guha R., McCool R., Miller E. Semantic search. Proceedings of the 12th international conference on World Wide Web, Budapest, Hungary, 2003
10. Deerwester S, Dumais TS, Furnas WG, Landauer KT, Harshman R. Indexing by Latent Semantic Analysis. Journal of the American Society of Information Science 1990, 41(6):391—407.
11. iProspect.com. iProspect's Search Engine User Attitudes Survey Results. www.iProspect.com, Inc. 2004
12. Guha R. & Garg A. Disambiguating People in Search. Proceedings of the 13th international conference on World Wide Web, New York, USA, 2004
13. Nasios Y., Korinthios G., Despotopoulos Y. Evaluation of Search Engines. Deliverable D12.3, PIPER project, SU 1112 (AD), EU, 1998 (http://piper.ntua.gr/reports/searcheng/docframe.html)

Modeling Navigation Patterns of Visitors of Unstructured Websites

K. Balog   P. Hofgesang   W. Kowalczyk
Department of Computer Science
Free University Amsterdam
De Boelelaan 1081A, 1081HV Amsterdam
The Netherlands
{balog, hpi, wojtek}@few.vu.nl

Abstract

In this paper we describe a practical approach for modeling navigation patterns of visitors of unstructured websites. These patterns are derived from web logs that are enriched with 3 sorts of information: (1) content type of visited pages, (2) visitor type, and (3) location of the visitor. We developed an intelligent Text Mining system, iTM, which supports the process of classifying web pages into a number of pre-defined categories. With help of this system we were able to reduce the labeling effort by a factor 10-20 without affecting the accuracy of the final result too much. Another feature of our approach is the use of a new technique for modeling navigation patterns: navigation trees. They provide a very informative graphical representation of most frequent sequences of categories of visited pages.

1.   Introduction

Nowadays almost every company "or organization" has its own website that plays an important role as a source of information about the company itself, its products, services, etc. Websites, due to their accessibility that is fueled by powerful search engines and by the global nature of the Internet, are often used as an important marketing instrument or as yet another communication channel through which companies exchange information with their (potential) clients. Not surprisingly, some companies put a lot of effort in making their websites attractive, well organized, efficient – sites that meet (or exceed) visitors' needs and expectations.

Development of such successful sites is usually an iterative process during which the developers get some feedback from users of the current version of the site: which pages are visited most frequently? by whom? when? what is the typical order in which pages are visited? which sequences led to an action (such as placing an order, request for an offer or information)? Etc.

A popular way of getting feedback from visitors is the analysis of log files that are generated by web servers. Unfortunately, log files contain only very elementary data: the IP-address of the visitor, the date and time of the page request, its URL and the status of the request, to mention the most important ones. Therefore, whenever possible, log files are enriched by additional data like content information of visited pages, personal information about visitors, or the visitors' "externally measured" behavior (like taking a loan after several visits to the bank's website). Some organizations use special mechanisms to collect such additional data. For example, URLs of pages from a web-shop may contain codes that refer to specific products or product categories; an e-bank may impose a login procedure for their clients, etc.

The situation is quite different when the site has no clear structure, for example, when various types of documents are allowed or when there are (almost) no restrictions imposed on topics that are presented on pages. For example, a website of a university may contain thousands of pages that are maintained by staff members, students, administration, and last but not least, by designated webmasters. These pages may contain some general information about the organization of the university, various research and educational materials, but they may also contain information about students' hobbies, favorite restaurants, travel-logs, photo albums, etc.

In this paper we address the problem of modeling navigation patterns on such highly unstructured websites. Our approach involves two steps.

First, we semi-automatically label all pages of the given website into a predefined number of categories. To minimize the human labeling effort we developed an interactive text mining tool, *iTM*, which combines several methods of active learning and text mining algorithms. With help of this system it is possible to reduce the labeling effort by a factor 10-20 without affecting the accuracy of the final result too much. For example, using the iTM system we were able to categorize about 13.000 pages of our faculty website within a few hours, labeling manually only 500 documents.

The second step involves developing graphical models, that we call *navigation trees*, for various groups of users. A navigation tree is a graphical representation of typical sessions and their statistical properties: nodes correspond to types of visited pages, links correspond to transitions from one page type to another, and weights that are assigned to links reflect conditional probabilities of such transitions.

Our approach is illustrated by two cases. In the first case we analyze navigation patterns of various groups of visitors of our faculty site: www.cs.vu.nl. The second case concerns analyzing visiting behavior of clients of an investment bank. Clients of this bank were grouped into different categories, depending on their investment strategies, age, status, etc. Using our approach it was possible to establish some relations between different groups of clients and their visiting behavior.

2.   Related Work

The modeling of behavior of web users is often labeled as Web Usage Mining, which, together with Web Content Mining and Web Structure Mining forms a new, dynamic field of research called Web Mining; see the survey of Kosala and Blockeel, [12].

A general framework for the whole web usage mining task, WEBMINER, is presented in [14].

Several models that are based on page access frequency analysis and modified association rules are presented in [1, 17, 22]. Xing and Shen [21] proposed two algorithms (UAM and PNT) for predicting user navigational preferences, both based on page visits frequency and page viewing time. Nanopoulos and Manolopoulos [15] present a graph-based model for finding traversal patterns on web page access sequences. They introduce one level-wise and two non-level wise algorithms for large paths exploiting graph structure.

While most of the models work on global "session levels", an increasing number of researches show that the exploration of user groups or clusters is essential for better characterization: Hay et al. [9] suggest Sequence Alignment Method (SAM) for measuring the distance between sessions. The proposed distance measure represents the number of edit operations (insertion, deletion, replacement) that are required to transform one session into another. SAM distance-based clusters form the basis of further examinations. Chevalier et al. [6] suggest rich navigation patterns consisting of frequent page set groups and web user groups based on demographical patterns. They show the correlation between the two types of data.

Other researchers point far beyond frequency based models: for example, Cadez et al. [5] propose a finite mixture of Markov models for modeling sequences of URL categories that are traversed by users.

There are numerous commercial software packages for deriving statistical patterns from web logs, [20]. They focus mostly on highlighting log data statistics and frequent navigation patterns but in most cases do not explore relationships among relevant features.

Pei et al. [17] propose a data structure called the web access pattern tree (WAP-tree) for efficient mining of access patterns from web logs. WAP-trees store all the frequent candidate sequences that have a support higher than a preset threshold. The information that is stored in a WAP-tree includes labels and frequency counts for nodes. In order to mine useful patterns in WAP-trees they present a WAP-mine algorithm that applies conditional search for finding frequent events. The WAP-tree structure and the WAP-mine algorithm together offer an alternative for apriori-like algorithms.

Jenamani et al. [11] use a semi-Markov process model for understanding e-customer behavior. Their method uses two matrices: a transition probability matrix P and a matrix M that holds the mean time between transitions. In this way this probabilistic model is able to model the time elapsed between transitions.

Some papers present methods based on content assumptions. Baglioni et al. [3] use URL syntax to determine page categories and to explore the relation between users' sex and navigational behavior. Cadez et al. [5] experiment on categorized data from Msnbc.com.

Visualization of frequent navigation patterns makes human perception easier. Cadez et al. [5] present a tool, WebCanvas, for visualizing Markov chain clusters. This tool represents all user navigational paths for each cluster, color-coded by page categories.

A good survey of automated text categorization techniques can be found in [18]. Boosting performance of text classifiers with help of unlabeled data is presented in Nigam at al. [16], while [2] describes some strategies for active sample selection in the context of text mining.

Two approaches for automatic classification of web pages are presented in [8] and [13]. Both are based on the idea of using public web directories (e.g., provided by Yahoo!, www.yahoo.com, or LookSmart, www.looksmart.com) as labeled collections of training documents and applying some text mining algorithms for developing classification procedures.

3.   Web Mining Process

The whole process of extracting patterns from web related data involves several steps that are depicted in Figure 1.

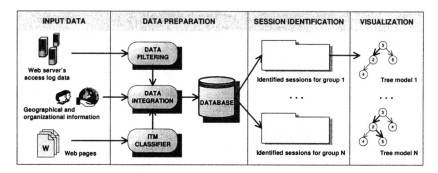

Figure 1. An overall scheme of the web mining process

The input data consists of three types of data sets: (1) access log files, (2) a collection of all pages from a website, and (3) tables that link selected IP-addresses to user types or their locations.

The first step of data preparation involves cleaning, filtering and pre-processing access logs. This step, although quite tedious is well described in the literature, see e.g., [14]. In the second step the iTM system is used to effectively categorize all pages from the given website. As a result we obtain a conversion table with URLs of site's pages and their categories. We combine this information and load them into a database together with the extra information about the users.

Session identification results in a collection of raw sessions: sequences of visited pages. By *session* we mean here a *sequence of types of pages* that were visited by the same user without breaks longer than a pre-specified time interval. Moreover, sessions can be grouped by the type of corresponding users (e.g., students, staff members) or their locations.

As a last step we visualize the sessions extracted for different groups by the means of the navigation tree models.

4. Categorization of Web Pages

When modeling navigation patterns on an unstructured website we are more interested in *types* of visited pages rather than in specific pages themselves. For example, we would like to put all pages that contain some teaching material into one category, while home pages of university staff members could form another category. In some situations, when the site is not too big, one could assign categories manually. However, in the case of sites with thousands of pages such an approach would not be feasible. Instead of labeling all the pages, one could label only a relatively small but representative sample, use that sample as a training set for building a classification model and apply that model to the remaining pages. This approach can be further improved by applying various techniques that would minimize the size of the training set (and therefore also the manual labeling effort) without adversely affecting the accuracy of the final model. There are two prominent methods of reducing the size of the training set: active learning, [2], and clever use of unlabeled data in the training process, [16].

The essence of active learning is a dynamic selection of cases for labeling: at each step the current model (or a collection of models) is applied at all unlabeled cases to identify those that are most difficult to classify; a supervisor is then asked for their (true) labels.

Unlabeled documents can be used to improve the quality of statistical estimates of model parameters. This is achieved by combining the (supervised) Naïve Bayes classification procedure with the (unsupervised) Expectation Maximization algorithm.

In this section we present an interactive document labeling and categorization system, iTM that combines several machine learning and text mining techniques to minimize the human effort that is needed to build a high quality text classifier. Using this system we were able to categorize about 13.000 pages of our university site into 13 categories just in a matter of a few hours by manually labeling only 500 pages that were selected by the system.

The iTM system supports the process of building text classifiers from unlabeled collections of documents by providing the user with a number of tools and options to minimize his/her time spent on labeling selected documents. It operates in three steps:

1) Initial sample selection. Here a small collection of documents is presented to the user, the documents are labeled and an initial classifier is constructed.

2) Active learning. The system iteratively selects a few unlabeled documents that are "most difficult" for the current classifier; after labeling them by the user, a new classifier is constructed.

3) Boosting model accuracy with help of unlabeled data. The collection of documents that were already labeled is used together with some remaining (unlabeled) documents for building the final model.

Now we will briefly describe some details.

3.1. Initial Sample Selection

The iTM system supports three methods of selecting the initial sample: manual, random, and with help of the k-means clustering.

The first two methods are straightforward: either the user selects, for each category, a few representative pages or pages are selected at random. The third method works as follows: the clustering algorithm finds k clusters of similar documents and from each cluster a document that is closest to its center is selected. In this way k documents that are relatively far away from each other are selected. The similarity between two documents is measured here by the inner product of their normalized vector representations, where every vector component (word) is weighted by the TFIDF factor, see [18].

3.2. Active Learning

Given an initial collection of labeled documents a classifier is constructed and applied to all unlabeled documents. The classifier, when applied to a document, returns, for each category, a value that represents confidence (or likelihood) that the document belongs to the category. Therefore, documents are classified with varying level of confidence. The essence of active learning is to focus on documents for which the classifier is least confident: these documents should be labeled by a "teacher", the classifier should be retrained, and the whole process of selecting most difficult cases repeated.

To define a "difficulty measure" we need some notation. Suppose that we work with C categories: 1, ..., C. Then the classifier can be used to rank all unlabeled documents with respect to each category, so for each document a rank vector $r=[r_1, ..., r_C]$ can be determined, where r_i denotes the rank of a given document with respect to class i. (The smaller the rank the more likely the document belongs to the given category.)

Now we can define, for every document, the variance of ranks v as the variance of the vector r:

$$v = \sum_{i=1}^{C} (\bar{r} - r_i)^2 \ .$$

Clearly, the smaller the variance the more difficult it is to decide on document's category.

Another strategy for selecting the most difficult documents is to develop two classifiers using different algorithms and then measure, for every document, the degree of disagreement between them:

$$v = \sum_{i=1}^{C} (r_{1,i} - r_{2,i})^2 \ ,$$

where r_1 and r_2 are normalized document rank vectors that correspond to the two classifiers. This time, the bigger the value of v the more difficult the document is. The current version of iTM uses two classification algorithms: Naïve Bayes, [16], and Boostexter, [17].

Several other strategies for selecting the "hardest" document are proposed in [2], where at each stage an ensemble of classifiers is developed and the degree of disagreement is determined by voting.

3.3. Use of Unlabeled Data

Most algorithms for supervised learning operate on training sets with all cases labeled. However, as it is shown in [19], unlabeled data can significantly improve the accuracy of the final model.

We have implemented two strategies for incorporating unlabeled data in the training process. Both are based on the same principle: given a classifier, all unlabeled documents are scored and those that are "easiest to classify" are labeled (by the classifier) and added to the new training set. We use the same measures of document "easiness" as in case of active learning: the variance of ranks and the degree of disagreement. Additionally, a threshold that determines a required level of document "easiness" has to be provided by the user.

3.4. The iTM System

The iTM system has been implemented in Java and can be obtained under the GNU public license from `http://balog.hu/itm/`. It is equipped with a powerful graphical user interface and in addition to the functionalities that were described above it offers some other features: several document conversion schemes, tools for selecting words (and their weights) that form a vocabulary, document and model browser, etc. Finally, the system can be used in a non-interactive mode. This is especially useful when one wants to experiment with various learning strategies. A more detailed description of the iTM system can be found in [4].

5. Tree Representation of Navigation Patterns

In our approach we model navigation patterns by a tree that represents sessions from a selected group of users. The root of the tree is a special node that represents the (abstract) starting point of each session. Remaining nodes are labeled by categories of visited pages (one category per node) together with their frequencies. Links correspond to transitions from one page category to another. In other words, every session is embedded in the tree: types of visited pages are mapped into nodes and every visited page increments the count variable that is stored by the corresponding node. Thus, if there are C possible categories the branching factor of the tree is at most C. The height of the tree is the same as the length of the longest session. The following pseudo-code describes the construction of navigation trees:

```
Input:
a collection of sessions
(sequences over the set of categories {1, ..., C})

Initialization:
root.count=0;
root.children=[];

Main loop:
for each session s
    root.count++;
    current_node = root;
    for i = 1..length(s)
        if exists(current_node.children[s[i]])
            current_node = current_node.children[s[i]];
            current_node.count++;
        else
            current_node.children[s[i]] =new node;
            current_node = current_node.children[s[i]];
            current_node.count =1;
        end
    end
end
```

Let us notice that the algorithm has linear time complexity (in the size of the input set).

A complete navigation tree is usually very big and contains branches that correspond to some isolated sessions. Therefore, to capture typical (frequent) patterns the tree should be pruned. This can be achieved by removing all nodes with counts smaller than a pre-specified threshold.

It is very informative to visualize (pruned) navigation trees. We have implemented several visualization procedures that plot trees using the following conventions:

1) nodes are labeled with page categories; additionally, different colors are used to represent different categories,

2) links represent transitions between categories; their thickness reflect the percentage of sessions that pass through them,

3) links leaving the same node are plotted with different shades of the black color to reflect the distribution of the corresponding sessions.

Additionally, various textual data can be attached to nodes and links, e.g., absolute counts, relative percentages, short category names, etc. Three examples of visualizations of navigation trees are shown in Figure 2, 3 and 4.

Finally, let us notice that to get an insight into various groups of users several trees should be generated and analyzed: groups determine subsets of sessions and for each subset a tree can be constructed and analyzed, possibly with various values of the pruning threshold.

6. Case Study

In the following we present two experiments. In the first case study we applied the techniques that were described in the previous sections to analyze navigation patterns of visitors of the website of our department: www.cs.vu.nl. We present a real life application of the navigation tree model in the second experiment. We visualize the frequent navigation paths of the clients of a bank.

6.1 Analysis of www.cs.vu.nl

Three sorts of data were used: access log data that were collected over a period of one month (in total about 7 million records with the total size of 1.5GB), a collection of 13.000 pages that were classified with help of iTM into 13 categories (see Table 2), and data about geographical location and organizational membership (student, staff) of visitors. The geographical locations were obtained from session IP-addresses by mapping them to the corresponding top level domains (country codes). Similarly, using some internal information about the structure of IP-addresses of computers used at the university, we could label some visitors as students or staff members.

The log files were transformed into user sessions, and page URLs were replaced by the corresponding page categories. Table 1 contains some characteristics of the 4 main groups of visitors: staff, students, domestic, and foreign.

Finally, we produced a number of navigation tree models for various groups of users using different values of the pruning parameter s. Figure 2 presents a navigation tree that was constructed for the group of all visitors.

We can see that the most important pattern is that the visitors (29.2%) start at a home page of a faculty member and then (7.8%) go to a (probably the same person's) publication page. Many visitors start directly at publication pages, likely following links provided by a search engine. The big proportion of visits to student pages was most likely generated by students of our department.

Group name	Number of sessions	Session length		
		avg	max	std. deviation
All	165 778	2.7	2 299	9.2
Location:				
Domestic	39 671	3.39	275	7.29
Foreign	79 750	2.4	352	4.74
Organization:				
Staff	2 795	5.5	193	11.41
Students	3 123	4.47	134	6.36

Table 1. Distribution of sessions for main groups of visitors

Category	Description
photo	negligible quantity of textual information with one or more images
miscellaneous	pages with absent or insufficient content. (e.g., framesets, empty files, file lists, etc.)
E/reference	e-books or manual pages for different systems or programs
E/department	department pages in English
E/project	research projects of the computer science department
E/person/faculty	pages of the faculty members (fields of research, professional background, research projects)
E/person/student	student pages (contain personal information like hobby, lyrics, etc.)
E/person/faculty publication	publications of faculty members comprising at least the abstracts
D/course	course pages in Dutch
D/person/student	student pages (contain personal information like hobby, lyrics, etc.)
other_language	pages written in other languages than English or Dutch
documents	documents in PDF or PS format (scientific papers, publications, e-books, etc.)
other documents	documents in doc, ppt, xls, rtf, txt format (administrative papers, forms, course materials etc.)

Table 2. Content categories of web pages
(E=English; D=Dutch)

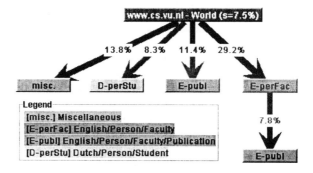

Figure 2. Navigation tree of all visits from all places

A navigation tree for visits initiated from the Netherlands is shown in Figure 3. It shows that pages in Dutch were most frequently visited by members of this group. The relatively large number of student and course pages suggests that students visiting from home are highly represented within this group.

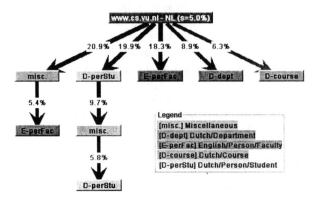

Figure 3. Navigation tree of all domestic visits

The analysis of other navigation trees (not shown in this paper) showed that the most significant pattern was a visit to a faculty member's home page followed by her/his publication page. This pattern was represented in all groups, but it was most pronounced within the "foreign" group, most likely formed by researchers from abroad. A more detailed presentation of our findings can be found in [10].

6.2   Visualizing client behavior of a bank

We applied the navigation tree model to the web data of an investment bank. The clients of the bank are classified into several categories based on their investment profiles. The marketers of the bank were interested in how the clients in the different categories behave on the website.

Since the website is well structured and the clients are required to log in, the data pre-processing was straightforward. Here we only present the visualization results.

Figure 4 presents a navigation tree model of the sessions of one of the client groups for a given period. The tree is a compact representation of 272683 sessions with 2% of support threshold. It shows that there were two popular starting pages: 62.1% of the clients started at the home page and 34.5% of them started at the login page. The navigation tree immediately shows, following the thick, black arrows, that the most frequently visited path started at the home page and was followed by the log in process and then contained a visit to the home page again, the personal home page, the portfolio overview and finally to an overview of the transaction history.

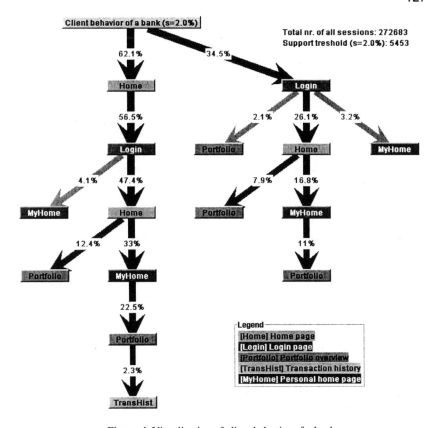

Figure 4. Visualization of client behavior of a bank

7. Conclusions

We described a practical approach for modeling navigation patterns of different groups of visitors of unstructured websites. To enrich access log data with content type of visited pages we developed an interactive text mining tool, iTM. Additionally, we proposed a simple method of visualizing frequent paths with the help of navigation trees. Using this approach we were able to analyze the behavior of several groups of visitors of our department's site. It turned out that with help of iTM we could categorize a large collection of pages from our site with a relatively small effort–a few hours of work were sufficient to manually label 500 pages (from the total collection of 13.000).

Our framework is also suitable for modeling changes in visitors' behavior over time. The changes in website organization or content can be easily handled with iTM: with a relatively small effort one can create a new labeling of all pages. The remaining tasks of data preparation, construction of navigation trees and their visualization are already fully automated.

References

1. Agrawal, R., Imielinski, T., and Swami, A. (1993), Mining association rules between sets of items in large databases. In Proceedings of the ACM SIGMOD Conference on Management of Data, pages 207–216.

2. Argamon-Engelson, S. and Dagan, I. (1999). Commitee-based sample selection for probabilistic classifiers. Journal of Artificial Intelligence Research, (11):335-360, 1999.

3. Baglioni, M., Ferrara, U., Romei, A., Ruggieri, S., and Turini, F. (2003), Preprocessing and Mining Web Log Data for Web Personalization. 8th Italian Conf. on Artificial Intelligence vol. 2829 of LNCS, p.237-249.

4. Balog, K., (2004). An Intelligent Support System for Developing Text Classifiers. MSc. Thesis, Vrije Universiteit Amsterdam, The Netherlands.

5. Cadez, I. V., Heckerman, D., Meek, C., Smyth, P., and White, S. (2003), Model-Based Clustering and Visualization of Navigation Patterns on a Web Site. Data Mining and Knowledge Discovery, vol.7 n.4, p.399-424.

6. Chevalier, K., Bothorel, C., and Corruble, V. (2003), Discovering rich navigation patterns on a web site. Proceedings of the 6th International Conference on Discovery Science Hokkaido University Conference Hall, Sapporo, Japan.

7. Cooley, R., Mobasher, B., Srivastava, J. (1999), Data Preparation for Mining World Wide Web Browsing Patterns. In Knowledge and Information System, vol.1(1), pages 5-32.

8. Dumais, S.T., and H. Chen (2000). Hierarchical classification of web content. Proceedings of the 23rd Annual International ACM SIGIR Conference on Research and Development in Information Retrieval (SIGIR'00), August 2000, pages 256-263.

9. Hay B., Wets, G., and Vanhoof K. (2003), Segmentation of visiting patterns on websites using a sequence alignment method. Journal of Retailing and Consumer Services vol.10, p.145–153.

10. Hofgesang, P.I., (2004). Web usage mining. Structuring semantically enriched clickstream data. MSc. Thesis, Vrije Universiteit Amsterdam, The Netherlands.

11. Jenamani, M., Mohapatra, P.K.J., and Ghose, S. (2003), A stochastic model of e-customer behaviour. Electronic Commerce Research and Applications vol.2, p.81–94.

12. Kosala, R., and Blockeel, H. (2000). Web mining research: A survey, SIGKDD Explorations. Newsletter of the ACM Special Interest Group on Knowledge Discovery and Data Mining 2 (1), pp. 1-15, July, 2000.

13. Mladenic, D. (1998). Turning Yahoo to Automatic Web-Page Classifier. In H. Prade, editor, Proceedings of the 13th European Conference on Artificial Intelligence (ECAI-98), pages 473-474.

14. Mobasher, B., Jain, N., Han, E., and Srivastava, J. (1996), Web Mining: Pattern discovery from World Wide Web transactions. Technical Report TR 96-050, University of Minnesota, Dept. of Computer Science, Minneapolis.

15. Nanopoulos A., Manolopoulos Y. (2001), Mining patterns from graph traversals. Data and Knowledge Engineering No. 37, pages 243-266.

16. Nigam, K., McCallum, A.K., Thrun, S., and Mitchell, T. (2000). Text classification from labeled and unlabeled documents using EM. Machine Learning, Kluwer Acedemic Press, 39(2/3),pages 103-134.

17. Pei, J., Han, J., Mortazavi-asl, B., and Zhu, H. (2000), Mining Access Patterns Efficiently from Web Logs. Proceedings of the 4th Pacific-Asia Conference on Knowledge Discovery and Data Mining, pages 396-407.

18. Sebastiani, F. (2002), Machine learning in automated text categorization. ACM Computing Surveys, 34(1), pages 1-47.

19. Schapire, R.E. and Singer, Y. (2000). Boostexter: A boosting-based system for text categorization. Machine Learning, 39(2/3), pages 135-168.

20. Web Mining and Web Usage Mining Software, http://www.kdnuggets.com/software/web.html

21. Xing, D., and Shen, J. (2004), Efficient data mining for web navigation patterns. Information and Software Technology vol.46, pages 55–63.

22. Yang, Q., Li T.I., and Wang K. (2003), Web-log Cleaning for Constructing Sequential Classifiers. Applied Artificial Intelligence vol. 17, issue 5-6, pages 431-441.

SESSION 2:

NETWORKS AND BIOLOGICALLY MOTIVATED AI

Exploring the Noisy Threshold Function in Designing Bayesian Networks*

Rasa Jurgelenaite, Peter Lucas and Tom Heskes

Radboud University Nijmegen, Nijmegen, The Netherlands

E-mail: {rasa, peterl, tomh}@cs.ru.nl

Abstract

Causal independence modelling is a well-known method both for reducing the size of probability tables and for explaining the underlying mechanisms in Bayesian networks. Many Bayesian network models incorporate causal independence assumptions; however, only the noisy OR and noisy AND, two examples of causal independence models, are used in practice. Their underlying assumption that either at least one cause, or all causes together, give rise to an effect, however, seems unnecessarily restrictive. In the present paper a new, more flexible, causal independence model is proposed, based on the Boolean threshold function. A connection is established between conditional probability distributions based on the noisy threshold model and Poisson binomial distributions, and the basic properties of this probability distribution are studied in some depth. The successful application of the noisy threshold model in the refinement of a Bayesian network for the diagnosis and treatment of ventilator-associated pneumonia demonstrates the practical value of the presented theory.

1   Introduction

Bayesian networks offer an appealing language for building models of domains with inherent uncertainty. However, the assessment of a probability distribution in Bayesian networks is a challenging task, even if its topology is sparse. This task becomes even more complex if the model has to integrate expert knowledge. While learning algorithms can be forced to take into account an expert's view, for the best possible results the experts must be willing to reconsider their ideas in light of the model's 'discovered' structure. This requires a clear understanding of the model by the domain expert. Causal independence models can both limit the number of conditional probabilities to be assessed and provide the ability for models to be understood by domain experts in the field. The concept of *causal independence* refers to a situation where multiple causes independently influence a common effect.

Many actual Bayesian network models use causal independence assumptions. However, only the logical OR and AND operators are used in practice in defining the interaction among causes; their underlying assumption is that the presence of either at least one cause or all causes at the same time give

---

*This research was supported by the Netherlands Organization for Scientific Research (NWO).

rise to the effect. The resulting probabilistic submodels are called *noisy OR* and *noisy AND*, respectively. Our feeling is that in building Bayesian-network models, the expressiveness of the noisy OR and noisy AND is too restrictive. In this paper, we discuss a way to expand the space of causal independence models using symmetric Boolean functions. It is known that any symmetric Boolean function can be decomposed into threshold functions [15]. Thus, threshold functions offer a natural basis for the analysis of causal independence models. Causal independence models with the threshold interaction function are the main topic of this paper. They will be referred to as the *noisy threshold models*.

The remainder of this paper is organised as follows. In the following section, the basic properties of Bayesian networks are reviewed. Causal independence models and Boolean functions are introduced in Section 3 as is the noisy threshold model. In Section 4, we establish a connection between the noisy threshold model and Poisson binomial distribution, and provide an interpretation of the relevant properties of this distribution. Section 6 offers results on the application of the presented theory to the refinement of an existing medical Bayesian network model. Finally, in Section 7, we summarise what has been achieved by this research.

2 Review of Bayesian Networks

A *Bayesian network* $\mathcal{B} = (G, \mathrm{Pr})$ represents a factorised joint probability distribution on a set of random variables $\mathbf{V}$. It consists of two parts: (1) a qualitative part, represented as an acyclic directed graph (ADG) $G = (\mathbf{V}(G), \mathbf{A}(G))$, where there is a 1–1 correspondence between the vertices $\mathbf{V}(G)$ and the random variables in $\mathbf{V}$, and arcs $\mathbf{A}(G)$ represent the conditional (in)dependencies between the variables; (2) a quantitative part Pr consisting of local probability distributions $\mathrm{Pr}(V \mid \pi(V))$, for each variable $V \in \mathbf{V}$ given the parents $\pi(V)$ of the corresponding vertex (interpreted as variables). The joint probability distribution Pr is factorised according to the structure of the graph, as follows:

$$\mathrm{Pr}(\mathbf{V}) = \prod_{V \in \mathbf{V}} \mathrm{Pr}(V \mid \pi(V)).$$

Each variable $V \in \mathbf{V}$ has a finite set of mutually exclusive states. In this paper, we assume all variables to be binary; as an abbreviation, we will often use v to denote $V = \top$ (true) and $\bar{v}$ to denote $V = \bot$ (false). Variables V can either act as free variables, in which case their binding is arbitrary, or they can act as bound variables, where bindings are established by associated operators. Furthermore, an expression such as

$$\sum_{\psi(I_1,\ldots,I_n)=e} g(I_1,\ldots,I_n)$$

stands for summing over all possible values of $g(I_1, \ldots, I_n)$ for all possible values of the variables I_k for which the constraint $\psi(I_1, \ldots, I_n) = e$ holds.

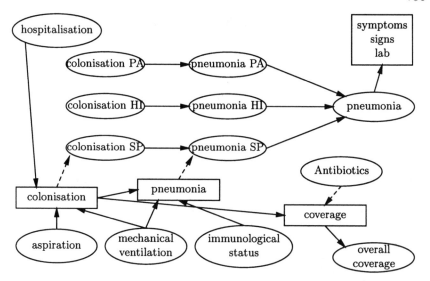

Figure 1: Detailed structure of part of the VAP model. Only three of the seven bacteria included in the model are shown. Boxes stand for collections of similar vertices. Solid arcs stand for atemporal stochastic influences, whereas dashed arcs indicate temporal influences. Abbreviations of names of bacteria: PA = Pseudomonas aeruginosa, HI = Haemophilus influenzae, SP = Streptococcus pneumoniae.

Consider the Bayesian network, shown in Figure 1, that provides motivation for the methods developed in this paper. *Ventilator-associated pneumonia*, or VAP for short, is a low-prevalence disease occurring in mechanically-ventilated patients in critical care and involves infection of the lower respiratory tract. VAP is associated with signs and symptoms such as fever, sputum production, abnormal chest X-ray and high numbers of white blood cells. As diagnosing and treating a disorder in medicine involves reasoning with uncertainty, a Bayesian network was constructed as the primary tool for building a decision-support system to support clinicians in the diagnosis and treatment of VAP [11]. The Bayesian network models the temporal process of colonisation of the mechanically ventilated patient by bacteria during stay in the critical care unit, which may, but need not, give rise to VAP with its associated signs and symptoms. This process is represented in the left part of the network. In addition, the effects of particular antimicrobial drugs, represented by the vertex 'antibiotics', is modelled in the network in terms of coverage of the bacteria by these antibiotics (each bacterium is only susceptible to some antibiotics and not too all). If a particular antibiotic covers many bacteria it is said to have a *broad spectrum*; otherwise, its spectrum is *narrow*. Prescription of broad spectrum antibiotics promotes the creation of resistance of bacteria to antibiotics, and should therefore be avoided if possible. Thus, the problem for the clinician is to ensure that the spectrum of antibiotic treatment is as narrow as possible, in

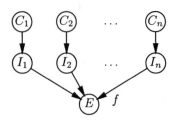

Figure 2: Causal independence model.

order to prevent the occurrence of resistance, while still covering as many of the bacteria as possible.

The Bayesian network model shown in Figure 1 includes two vertices where probabilistic information has been expressed in terms of logical operators; the conditional probability distribution defined for the variable 'pneumonia' was defined in terms of a logical OR, whereas the distribution for the variable 'coverage' was defined in terms of the logical AND. We will return to the meaning of these definitions below.

3 Causal Modelling and Boolean Functions

3.1 Causal independence

Causal independence (also known as independence of causal influence) [6, 16] is a popular way to specify interactions among cause variables. The global structure of a causal independence model is shown in Figure 2; it expresses the idea that causes $C_1, \ldots, C_n$ influence a given common effect E through intermediate variables $I_1, \ldots, I_n$ and a deterministic function f, called the *interaction function*. The impact of each cause C_l on the common effect E is independent of each other cause $C_j, j \neq l$. The intermediate variable I_l is considered to be a contribution of the cause variable C_l to the common effect E. The function f represents in which way the intermediate effects I_l, and indirectly also the causes C_l, interact to yield the final effect E. Hence, the function f is defined in such a way that when a relationship, as modelled by the function f, between $I_l, l = 1, \ldots, n$, and $E = \top$ is satisfied, then it holds that $e = f(I_1, \ldots, I_n)$. It is assumed that $\Pr(e \mid I_1, \ldots, I_n) = 1$ if $f(I_1, \ldots, I_n) = e$, and $\Pr(e \mid I_1, \ldots, I_n) = 0$ if $f(I_1, \ldots, I_n) = \bar{e}$. The smallest possible causal independence model has two cause variables.

A causal independence model is defined in terms of the causal parameters $\Pr(I_l \mid C_l)$, for $l = 1, \ldots, n$. An assumption underlying the causal independence models introduced in [12] is that absent causes do not contribute to the effect. In terms of probability theory this implies that it holds that $\Pr(i_l \mid \bar{c}_l) = 0$. As a consequence, it holds that $\Pr(\bar{i}_l \mid \bar{c}_l) = 1$. In this paper we make the same assumption.

The conditional probability of the occurrence of the effect E given the causes $C_1, \ldots, C_n$, i.e., $\Pr(e \mid C_1, \ldots, C_n)$, can be obtained from the causal parameters

$\Pr(I_l \mid C_l)$ as follows [12, 16]:

$$\Pr(e \mid C_1, \ldots, C_n) = \sum_{f(I_1, \ldots, I_n) = e} \prod_{l=1}^{n} \Pr(I_l \mid C_l). \tag{1}$$

In this paper we assume that the function f in Equation (1) is a Boolean function. Systematic analyses of the global probabilistic patterns in causal independence models based on restricted Boolean functions was presented in [12] and [8]. However, there are 2^{2^n} different n-ary Boolean functions [4, 15]; thus, the potential number of causal interaction models is huge. However, if we assume that the order of the cause variables does not matter, the Boolean functions become *symmetric* [15] and the number reduces to 2^{n+1}.

An important symmetric Boolean function is the *exact* Boolean function ϵ_l, which has function value true, i.e. $\epsilon_l(I_1, \ldots, I_n) = \top$, if $\sum_{j=1}^{n} \nu(I_j) = l$ with $\nu(I_j)$ equal to 1, if I_j is equal to true and 0 otherwise. Symmetric Boolean function can be decomposed in terms of the exact functions ϵ_l as follows [15]:

$$f(I_1, \ldots, I_n) = \bigvee_{l=0}^{n} \epsilon_l(I_1, \ldots, I_n) \wedge \gamma_l \tag{2}$$

where γ_l are Boolean constants only dependent on the function f. For example, for the Boolean function defined in terms of the OR operator we have $\gamma_0 = \bot$ and $\gamma_1 = \ldots = \gamma_n = \top$.

Another useful symmetric Boolean function is the *threshold* function τ_k, which simply checks whether there are at least k trues among the arguments, i.e. $\tau_k(I_1, \ldots, I_n) = \top$, if $\sum_{j=1}^{n} \nu(I_j) \geq k$ with $\nu(I_j)$ equal to 1, if I_j is equal to true and 0 otherwise. To express it in the Boolean constants we have: $\gamma_0 = \cdots = \gamma_{k-1} = \bot$ and $\gamma_k = \cdots = \gamma_n = \top$. Obviously, any exact function can be written as the subtraction of two threshold functions and thus any symmetric Boolean function can be decomposed into threshold functions.

The interaction among variables modelled by the pneumonia and coverage variables, as shown in Figure 1, was modelled by assuming f to be an OR and an AND, respectively. This corresponds to threshold functions τ_k with $k = 1$ for the OR, and $k = n$ for the AND. Hence, these two Boolean functions can be taken as two extremes of a spectrum of Boolean functions based on the threshold function. As by definition a patient has pneumonia independent of the specific bacterium causing pneumonia, the logical OR appeared to be the right way to model the interactions between the pneumonia variables. However, as argued before, clinicians need to be careful in the prescription of antibiotics as they have a tendency to prescribe antibiotics with a spectrum that is too broad. This casts doubts about the appropriateness of the logical AND for the modelling of interactions concerning coverage of bacteria by antibiotics. Using the threshold function τ_k with $k \neq 1, n$, may result in a better model. In the following we therefore investigate properties of the threshold function, and subsequently study its use in improving the Bayesian network model shown in Figure 1.

3.2 The noisy threshold model

Using the property of Equation (2) of the symmetric Boolean functions, the conditional probability of the occurrence of the effect E given the causes $C_1, \ldots, C_n$ can be decomposed in terms of probabilities that exactly l intermediate variables $I_1, \ldots, I_n$ are true, as follows:

$$\Pr(e \mid C_1, \ldots, C_n) = \sum_{\substack{0 \leq l \leq n \\ \gamma_l}} \sum_{\epsilon_l(I_1, \ldots, I_n)} \prod_{i=1}^n \Pr(I_i \mid C_i). \tag{3}$$

Thus, Equation (3) yields a general formula to compute the probability of the effect in terms of exact functions in any causal independence model where an interaction function f is a symmetric Boolean function.

Let us denote a conditional probability of the effect E given causes $C_1, \ldots, C_n$ in a noisy threshold model with interaction function τ_k as $\Pr_{\tau_k}(e \mid C_1, \ldots, C_n)$. Then, from Equation (3) it follows that:

$$\Pr_{\tau_k}(e \mid C_1, \ldots, C_n) = \sum_{k \leq l \leq n} \sum_{\epsilon_l(I_1, \ldots, I_n)} \prod_{i=1}^n \Pr(I_i \mid C_i). \tag{4}$$

4 The Poisson Binomial Distribution

It turns out that causal independence models defined in terms of the Boolean threshold function, as discussed above, are closely connected to the so-called Poisson binomial distribution known from statistics. After establishing this connection, we review some its relevant properties and discuss what these properties mean.

4.1 Its definition and relationship to the noisy threshold model

Let l denote the number of successes in n independent trials, where p_i is a probability of success in the ith trial, $i = 1, \ldots, n$; let $\mathbf{p} = (p_1, \ldots, p_n)$. The trials are then called *Poisson trials* [5], and $B(l; \mathbf{p})$ denotes the *Poisson binomial distribution* [3, 10]:

$$B(l; \mathbf{p}) = \left\{ \prod_{i=1}^n (1 - p_i) \right\} \sum_{1 \leq j_1 < \ldots < j_l \leq n} \prod_{z=1}^l \frac{p_{j_z}}{1 - p_{j_z}} \tag{5}$$

The Poisson trials have mean, defined as $\mu = \frac{1}{n} \sum_{i=1}^n p_i$, and variance, defined as $\sigma^2 = \frac{1}{n} \sum_{i=1}^n (p_i - \mu)^2$. When the variance $\sigma^2 = 0$, i.e., the success probability p_i is a constant p, the trials are called Bernoulli trials and $B(l; \mathbf{p})$ reduces to the binomial distribution: $B(l; p) = \binom{n}{l} p^l (1 - p)^{n-l}$.

As it was assumed that absent causes do not contribute to the effect it follows that the conditional probabilities $\Pr_{\tau_k}(e \mid C_1, \ldots, C_n)$ depend only on the 'active' causes, i.e., causes C_l that are equal to $\top$. Let $L = \{l \mid C_l = \top, l = 1, \ldots, n\}$, and let r be a bijective renumbering function, $r : L \leftrightarrow \{1, \ldots, |L|\}$, that respects the total order $<$ on the natural numbers, i.e., if $l < l'$, $l, l' \in L$, then $r(l) < r(l')$. Then, $\mathbf{p}(C_1, \ldots, C_n) = \{P(i_l \mid c_l) \mid l \in L\} = \{p_1, \ldots, p_{|L|}\}$, where $\Pr(i_l \mid c_l) = p_{r(l)}$, for each $l \in L$.

Then, the connection between the Poisson binomial distribution and the causal independence model using the noisy threshold function is as follows.

Proposition 1 *It holds that:*

$$\Pr_{\tau_k}(e \mid C_1, \ldots, C_n) = \sum_{k \leq l \leq |\mathbf{p}(C_1, \ldots, C_n)|} B(l; \mathbf{p}(C_1, \ldots, C_n)) \tag{6}$$

Proof: Note that in Section 3.2 $\sum_{\epsilon_l(I_1, \ldots, I_n)} \prod_{i=1}^n \Pr(I_i \mid C_i)$ was defined as the probability that exactly l intermediate variables $I_1, \ldots, I_n$ are true. An intermediate variable I_l can be seen as an independent trial which has a probability of success $p_l = \Pr(i_l \mid C_l)$, which is equal to 0 if $C_l = \bot$, and otherwise equal to $\Pr(i_l \mid c_l)$. Thus, in order to find the probability that exactly l intermediate variables are true it is enough to look only at those intermediate variables that have a corresponding active cause. The set of the probabilities of such intermediate variables has been defined as $\mathbf{p}(C_1, \ldots, C_n)$. Considering the definition of the Poisson binomial distribution in Equation (5), Equation (4) yields what is stated in the premise of this proposition. $\qquad\square$

If the number of active cause variables is smaller than the threshold k the conditional probability of the effect equals zero as it is shown in the following corollary.

Corollary 1 *Let* $|\mathbf{p}(C_1, \ldots, C_n)| < k, 1 \leq k \leq n$, *then* $\Pr_{\tau_k}(e \mid C_1, \ldots, C_n) = 0$.

Proof: This follows directly from Equation (6). $\qquad\square$

From Proposition 1 it follows that in a noisy threshold model with interaction function τ_k and n cause variables, $\sum_{i=0}^{k-1} \binom{n}{i}$ of the probabilities $\Pr_{\tau_k}(e \mid C_1, \ldots, C_n)$ are set to 0, while the other $\sum_{i=k}^n \binom{n}{i}$ conditional probabilities of the effect such that $|\mathbf{p}(C_1, \ldots, C_n)| \geq k$ are computed from the corresponding Poisson binomial distributions.

In comparison, the noisy AND model has only one conditional probability of the effect that is computed, i.e. $\Pr(e \mid C_1, \ldots, C_n)$ with $|\mathbf{p}(C_1, \ldots, C_n)| = n$, while the other conditional probabilities are set 0. In the noisy OR model only the conditional probability $\Pr(e \mid C_1, \ldots, C_n)$ with $|\mathbf{p}(C_1, \ldots, C_n)| = 0$ is set to 0 and the other conditional probabilities in the model are computed.

In the remainder of the paper, we review some probabilistic results for the Poisson binomial distribution. We also present examples illustrating the discussed properties. We use both n and $\rho = |\mathbf{p}(C_1, \ldots, C_n)|$ to define the cardinality of the set $\mathbf{p}$: n is used while discussing the properties of the Poisson binomial distribution and ρ is employed to analyse these properties in the context of noisy threshold models.

4.2 Statistical characterisation

4.2.1 Mean and variance

The *mean* $\mu_{\mathbf{p}}$ of the distribution $B(i; \mathbf{p})$ is by definition equal to

$$\mu_{\mathbf{p}} = \sum_{i=0}^{n} i\, B(i; \mathbf{p}),$$

and the *variance* $\sigma_{\mathbf{p}}^2$ is equal to

$$\sigma_{\mathbf{p}}^2 = \sum_{i=0}^{n} (i - \mu_{\mathbf{p}})^2 B(i; \mathbf{p}).$$

By means of some algebraic manipulation it can be shown that the mean $\mu_{\mathbf{p}}$ and variance $\sigma_{\mathbf{p}}^2$ obey the following equations: $\mu_{\mathbf{p}} = n\mu$ and $\sigma_{\mathbf{p}}^2 = n\mu(1 - \mu) - n\sigma^2$ [5]. In words: the mean of the Poisson binomial distribution $\mu_{\mathbf{p}}$ is equal to the sum of the probabilities $p_1, \ldots, p_n$. The variance $\sigma_{\mathbf{p}}^2$ increases as the set of probabilities $(p_1, \ldots, p_n)$ tends to be more and more homogeneous and attains its maximum as they become identical. Therefore, in the noisy threshold models a larger difference between the conditional probabilities $\Pr(i_l \mid C_l)$ causes a smaller variability of the success probability $B(l; \mathbf{p})$.

4.2.2 Mode

The *mode* $m_{\mathbf{p}}$ of the Poisson binomial distribution $B(l; \mathbf{p})$ is defined as a local maximum. Darroch has shown that [2]:

$$m_{\mathbf{p}} = \begin{cases} l & \text{if } l \leq \mu_{\mathbf{p}} < l + \frac{1}{l+2} \\ l \text{ or } l+1 \text{ or both} & \text{if } l + \frac{1}{l+2} \leq \mu_{\mathbf{p}} \leq l+1 - \frac{1}{n-l+1} \\ l+1 & \text{if } l+1 - \frac{1}{n-l+1} < \mu_{\mathbf{p}} \leq l+1 \end{cases} \tag{7}$$

where $0 \leq l \leq n$. Thus, the most probable number of successes $m_{\mathbf{p}}$ differs from the mean $\mu_{\mathbf{p}}$ by less than 1.

4.2.3 Shape of the Poisson binomial distribution

The Poisson binomial distribution is 'bell-shaped' [2]:

- the probabilities $B(-1; \mathbf{p}), B(0; \mathbf{p}), B(1; \mathbf{p}), \ldots, B(n; \mathbf{p}), B(n+1; \mathbf{p})$ strictly increase and then strictly decrease, except that there may be at most two equal maxima;

- the probabilities $B(-2; \mathbf{p}), B(-1; \mathbf{p}), B(0; \mathbf{p}), \ldots, B(n; \mathbf{p}), B(n+1; \mathbf{p}), B(n+2; \mathbf{p})$ first increase convexly and then concavely, and then decrease concavely and then convexly.

The largest probabilities $B(l; \mathbf{p})$ are concentrated around the mode $m_{\mathbf{p}}$ of the Poisson binomial distribution and the probabilities $B(l; \mathbf{p})$ decline in the right and left tails. From this property it follows that combined knowledge of the mode of the Poisson binomial distribution and the Boolean constants $\gamma_0, \ldots, \gamma_\rho$ can give some insight into the conditional probabilities of the effect E in the noisy threshold models.

5 Approximations of the Poisson Binomial Distribution

Since the Poisson binomial distribution has a complicated structure it is often approximated by other distributions that have well-known properties.

5.1 Poisson approximation

Let

$$P(l; \mu_\mathbf{p}) = \frac{e^{-\mu_\mathbf{p}} \mu_\mathbf{p}^l}{l!}$$

denote the Poisson distribution. The following bound on the total variation distance between the Poisson binomial distribution and the Poisson distribution was established in [10]:

$$\sum_{l=0}^{\infty} |B(l; \mathbf{p}) - P(l; \mu_\mathbf{p})| < 2 \sum_{i=1}^{n} p_i^2. \tag{8}$$

Thus, the Poisson approximation will be accurate whenever the probabilities $p_1, \ldots, p_n$ are small.

We used the Kullback-Leibler divergence [9],

$$K(B, P) = \sum_{i=0}^{n} B(i; \mathbf{p}) \lg \frac{B(i; \mathbf{p})}{P(i; \mu_\mathbf{p})}, \tag{9}$$

to measure the distance between the Poisson binomial distribution and the Poisson approximation. Figure 3 plots the Kullback-Leibler divergence between the Poisson binomial distribution with mean $\mu_\mathbf{p} = 0.1, 0.2, 0.3, 0.4, 0.5$ and the Poisson approximation. It is not surprising that the approximation becomes more accurate as the number of probabilities n increases, i.e., the value of $\mu = \frac{\mu_\mathbf{p}}{n}$ decreases.

Figure 4 illustrates how accurate the Poisson approximation is for the Poisson binomial distribution $B(l; \mathbf{p})$ when probabilities are small: $\mathbf{p} = (0.01, \ 0.06, \ 0.09, \ 0.11, \ 0.14, \ 0.19)$.

5.2 Normal approximation

Another approximation for the Poisson binomial distribution found in the probabilistic literature is the approximation by the standard normal distribution [1, 13]. Let

$$\phi(x) = \frac{1}{\sqrt{2\pi}} e^{-\frac{1}{2}x^2} \tag{10}$$

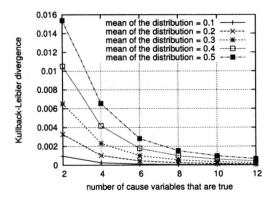

Figure 3: Kullback-Leibler divergence between the Poisson binomial distribution and the Poisson approximation.

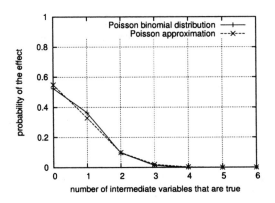

Figure 4: Poisson binomial distribution approximated by the Poisson distribution.

denote the normal density function, and let

$$\Phi(z) = \int_{-\infty}^{z} \phi(x)\mathrm{d}x. \tag{11}$$

Then for every Poisson binomial distribution B with mean $\mu_{\mathbf{p}}$, variance $\sigma_{\mathbf{p}}^2$,

$$\max_{0 \leq l \leq n} \left| \sum_{i=0}^{l} \mathrm{B}(i;\mathbf{p}) - \Phi\left(\frac{l - \mu_{\mathbf{p}}}{\sigma_{\mathbf{p}}}\right) \right| < \frac{0.7975}{\sigma_{\mathbf{p}}}. \tag{12}$$

Thus, we see that the normal approximation is accurate when the standard deviation of the Poisson binomial distribution

$$\sigma_{\mathbf{p}} = \sqrt{n\left(\mu(1 - \mu) - \sigma^2\right)}$$

is large, i.e., when $n \to \infty$.

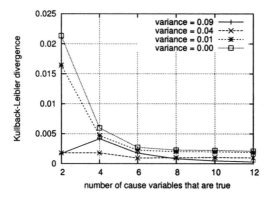

Figure 5: Kullback-Leibler divergence between the Poisson binomial distribution and the normal approximation.

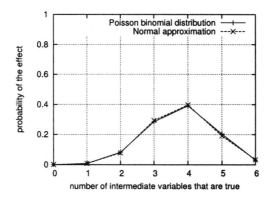

Figure 6: Poisson binomial distribution approximated by the normal distribution.

Let

$$N(i; \mu_{\mathbf{p}}; \sigma_{\mathbf{p}}) = \Phi\left(\frac{i - \frac{1}{2} - \mu_{\mathbf{p}}}{\sigma_{\mathbf{p}}}\right) - \Phi\left(\frac{i + \frac{1}{2} - \mu_{\mathbf{p}}}{\sigma_{\mathbf{p}}}\right)$$

be an approximation of $B(i; \mathbf{p})$. We use the Kullback-Leibler divergence $K(B, N)$ to measure the distance between the Poisson binomial distribution and the normal approximation.

Figure 5 shows a plot of the Kullback-Leibler divergence between the Poisson binomial distribution and the normal approximation for the probabilities $(p_1, \ldots, p_n)$ that have the same mean $\mu = 0.6$ but differ in variance σ^2 and number of probabilities n. We can see that the accuracy of the approximation improves when either the variance σ^2 or the number of probabilities n increases.

Figure 6 shows the accuracy of the normal approximation for the Poisson binomial distribution by an example: $\mathbf{p} = (0.2, \ 0.4, \ 0.6, \ 0.8, \ 0.8, \ 0.99)$, i.e.

the standard deviation of the distribution is high $\sigma_{\mathbf{p}} = 0.985$.

The Poisson binomial distribution can also be approximated by the binomial distribution [14]. The binomial approximation is accurate whenever the variance σ^2 is small.

6   Experimental Results

In Section 2, we have described a Bayesian network, shown in Figure 1, that is aimed at assisting clinicians in the diagnosis and treatment of patient with VAP in the critical-care unit. It was noted that a limitation of the present Bayesian network model is that it attempts to cover every possible bacterium by which the patient is being colonised, even if it is normally unlikely that VAP is caused by every possible bacterium included in the model at the same time. Such behaviour was accomplished by defining the interaction between the individual coverage vertices, each of them with an incoming arc from a colonisation vertex and the antibiotic vertex, by means of a logical AND. This results in the prescription of antibiotic treatment with a spectrum that is very often too broad. The hypothesis we investigated was, therefore, whether any noisy threshold model with function τ_k, where $1 < k < 7$, would yield a performance superior to that of the noisy AND model.

Initial experimentation with various Bayesian networks obtained by replacing the noisy AND by a noisy threshold model showed that for $k = 1, 2, \ldots, 7$ the noisy threshold model yielded posterior probability distributions where for $k = 1, 2$ the antibiotics prescribed were always very narrow, even when the patient was assumed to have an infection caused by 5 different bacteria. For $k = 5, 6$ the antibiotics prescribed were always broad-spectrum antibiotics.

Further experimental results were obtained by applying Bayesian networks with the noisy AND and noisy threshold model for $k = 3$ and $k = 4$ to the time-series data of 6 different patients. At each time point, each of the these Bayesian networks was used to compute the spectrum of the antibiotics considered optimal. The results are summarised in Table 1. On average, the results obtained by the noisy threshold model with $k = 4$ are best, as it never prescribed broad-spectrum antibiotics; in addition, it did not prescribe antibiotics with very narrow spectrum if the infection was caused by 2 or 3 bacteria. In conclusion, replacing the noisy AND model by a noisy threshold model did give rise to performance improvement of the Bayesian network.

7   Discussion

In this paper, we expanded the space of possible causal independence models by introducing new models based on the Boolean threshold function, which we have called noisy threshold models. It was shown that there is a close connection between the probability distribution of noisy threshold models and the Poisson binomial distribution from statistics. We have investigated what the well-studied properties of the Poisson binomial distribution mean in the

Table 1: Results of the prescription ⸱f antibiotics to 6 patients with VAP caused by 1, 2 or 3 bacteria using various causal independence models, in comparison to the clinician. Abbreviations of antibiotic spectrum: v: very narrow; n: narrow; i: intermediate; b: broad. As some of the patients were colonised by different bacteria at different days, there are 10 cases of the prescription of antibiotics.

Model \ #Bacteria	1	2	3
Clinician	3n2i	1i3n	1i
Noisy threshold ($k = 3$)	5v	4v	1v
Noisy threshold ($k = 4$)	3v2n	4n	1n
Noisy AND	1i4b	1b3i	1i

context of these newly introduced models. The noisy threshold models can be looked upon as spanning a spectrum of causal independence models with the noisy OR and noisy AND as extremes.

Even though this paper has focused on the conditional probability distributions of noisy threshold models, most of the presented theory can be exploited as a basis for the assessment of probability distributions of causal independence model where the interaction function is defined in terms of symmetric Boolean functions. This is a consequence of the fact that any symmetric Boolean function can be decomposed into a disjunction of Boolean exact functions in conjunction with Boolean constants. This basic property indicates that the theory developed in this paper has an even wider application, which, however, still needs to be explored.

Finally, it was shown that the noisy threshold model is also useful from a practical point of view by using it as a basis for the refinement of an existing real-world Bayesian network.

Acknowledgments

The authors are grateful to Stefan Visscher for his contribution to the experimental results.

References

[1] P. van Beek, *An application of Fourier methods to the problem of sharpening the Berry-Essen inequality.* Z. Wahrscheinlichkeitstheorie verw. Gebiete, 23:187-196, 1972.

[2] J. Darroch, *On the distribution of the number of successes in independent trials.* The Annals of Mathematical Statistics, 35:1317-1321, 1964.

[3] A.W.P. Edwards, *The Meaning of Binomial Distribution.* Nature 186, 1074, 1960.

[4] H.B. Enderton, *A Mathematical Introduction to Logic*. Academic Press, San Diego, 1972.

[5] W. Feller, *An Introduction to Probability Theory and Its Applications*. John Wiley, 1968.

[6] D. Heckerman, *Causal independence for knowledge acquisition and inference*. Proceedings of the Ninth Conference on Uncertainty in Artificial Intelligence, 122-127, 1993.

[7] K. Jogdeo and S.M. Samuels, *Monotone convergence of binomial probabilities and a generalization of Ramanujan's equation*. The Annals of Mathematical Statistics, 39:1191-1195, 1968.

[8] R. Jurgelenaite and P.J.F. Lucas, *Exploiting causal independence in large Bayesian networks*. Knowledge-Based Systems Journal, 18:153-162, 2005.

[9] S. Kullback and R.A. Leibler, *On information and sufficiency*. The Annals of Mathematical Statistics, 22:79-86, 1951.

[10] L. Le Cam, *An approximation theorem for the Poisson binomial distribution*. Pacific Journal of Mathematics, 10: 1181-1197, 1960.

[11] P.J.F. Lucas, N.C. de Bruijn, K. Schurink and I.M. Hoepelman, *A probabilistic and decision-theoretic approach to the management of infectious disease at the ICU*. Artificial Intelligence in Medicine, 19:251-279, 2000.

[12] P.J.F. Lucas, *Bayesian network modelling through qualitative patterns*. Artificial Intelligence, 163: 233-263, 2005.

[13] J. Pitman, *Probabilistic bounds on the coefficients of polynomials with only real zeros*. Journal of Combinatorial Theory, Series A, 77:279-303, 1997.

[14] B. Roos, *Binomial approximation to the Poisson binomial distribution: the Krawtchouk expansion*. Theory of Probability and Its Applications, 45:258-272, 2001.

[15] I. Wegener, *The Complexity of Boolean Functions*. John Wiley & Sons, New York, 1987.

[16] N.L. Zhang and D. Poole, *Exploiting causal independence in Bayesian networks inference*. Journal of Artificial Intelligence Research, 5:301-328, 1996.

A biologically motivated neural network architecture for the avoidance of catastrophic interference

J F Dale Addison, Garen Z Arevian, John MacIntyre
University of Sunderland, School of Computing and Technology, St Peters
Campus, St Peters Way, Sunderland, England, SR6 0DE
dale.addison@sunderland.ac.uk
http://welcome.sunderland.ac.uk/

Abstract

This paper describes a neural network architecture which has been developed specifically to investigate and alleviate the effects of catastrophic interference. This is the tendency of certain types of feed forward network to forget what they have learned when required to learn a second pattern set which overlaps significantly in content with the first. This work considers a neural network architecture which performs a pattern separated representation of the inputs and develops an attractor dynamic representation, which is subsequently associated with the original pattern. The paper then describes an excitatory and inhibitory function which ensures only the top firing neurons are retained. The paper considers the biological plausibility of this network and reports a series of experiments designed to evaluate the neural networks ability to recall patterns after learning a second data set, as well as the time to relearn the original data set.

1. Introduction

Catastrophic Interference can be summarised as the failure of a neural network to recall a previously learned pattern **X** when required to learn a new pattern **Y**. The problem was first illustrated by McCloskey and Cohen [1] who attempted to train a back propagation network to learn the AB-AC list learning task, where a set of words **A**, can be associated with alternative words **B** and **C**. This finding inspired a large amount of subsequent research [2,3,4,5,6,7,8,9]. The main conclusion of this research was that interference results from the continual use of the same units and weights to learn different associations. After learning a particular association with a given set of weights, any attempt to learn a new association, with its subsequent weight changes will undo the previous learning. This will occur every time shared weights are sequentially used to learn different, incompatible associations. There are effectively two ways of alleviating this problem. The first allows different units to represent different associations. The second uses slow *interleaved* learning to allow the network to shape the weights over many repeated presentations of the different associations in a manner, which accommodates their differences.

Both perspectives involve a compromise between using parameters resulting in overlapping distributed representations but also induce catastrophic interference. Alternatively the modeller could use a set of parameters which provide the model with sparser, separated representations by activating less units which reduces interference from new patterns but also loses the benefits of overlapping, distributed representations. Initial attempts to solve catastrophic interference addressed the deficiencies of the back propagation of error architecture [2,3]. In recent year the focus has moved towards the design and development of neural network architectures and algorithms which reproduce aspects of biologically motivated systems found within the mammalian cortex.

Areas such as the hippocampus have been extensively studied and documented by researchers. This work continues a body of research into catastrophic interference avoidance which argues that a biologically motivated solution based upon certain aspects of the brain which are devoted to memory offers a solution to the problem of catastrophic interference avoidance. Section 2 provides details of the hippocampus and why it does not suffer from catastrophic interference (or catastrophic forgetting) Section 3 considers previous hippocampally inspired neural network architectures, sections 4 and 5 discuss pattern separation and its implementation in this model respectively. Section 6 introduces the association matrix used for pattern recall. Section 7 provides a brief discussion of pattern completion which is the principle means of retrieving information from this network. Section 8 details the data sets employed, whilst section 9 discusses the experiments performed. Section 10 concludes the paper with observations on the results and future work to be carried out.

2.   The hippocampus

Since the pioneering work of Ramon and Cajal [11] the hippocampus has become one of the most intensely studied regions of the brain. This is possible because the structure of the hippocampus is extremely well structured and therefore easier to ascertain than other areas of the brain. In addition, the importance of the hippocampus in memory formation has been demonstrated by the effects certain diseases and traumas have upon this area. The famous case of patient H.M [12] who underwent surgery to remove parts of the hippocampus as a means of controlling severe epilepsy being a case in point. Although the operation cured his epilepsy patient H.M was left with severe anterograde amnesia (inability to recall recent memories).

A large body of literature has been produced in recent years concerning the hippocampus. From this certain general conclusions can be drawn.

- Damage to the hippocampus results in an inability to form new memories

- All memories acquired prior to the damage are still accessible.

- Although damage to the hippocampus results in the inability to form new, episodic memories, the patient is still capable of forming procedural memories.

- The hippocampus is responsible for forming certain types of memory not a storage area for memory. The hippocampus is understood to receive information from several sources to form memories concerned with specific events or facts [13]

2.1 Hippocampal internal structure

In this section a brief outline of the cellular structure of the hippocampus is provided before a model of the hippocampus and its interactions is presented later. Of particular relevance for the author's model are the following regions.

2.1.1 The Entorhinal Cortex (EC)

The entorhinal cortex is the main connection point for information transmitted via the Parahippocampal assembly, and the neo cortex. In this authors model the EC is represented as having both an input from information collected from the outside world and an output which is an exact replica of the data being input to the EC. The input aspect of the EC is responsible for transferring information to the following processing areas.

2.1.2 The Dentate Gyrus (DG)

The output from this region is carried to the CA3 region by mossy fibre cells in region CA3. The ratio of mossy fibre connections to CA3 cells is approximately 1 mossy fibre for every fifteen CA3 cells. There are approximately 300,000 CA3 pyramidal cells each of which receives about 50 mossy fibre inputs. This means the probability of the output from a particular DG cell reaching a specific CA3 cell is very low.

2.1.3 CA3 Region

Output from the CA3 cells is known to branch in two ways. The first branch forms a set of recurrent connections which synapse back to the dendrites of other CA3 cells. The others (termed Schaffer collaterals) carry the output from CA3 to region CA1. Approximately seventy five percent of the synapses onto each CA3 pyramidal cell are recurrent collateral axons from the CA3 cells themselves. This suggests that the CA3 structure could be almost entirely devoted to recurrent excitatory connections.

3. A hippocampally inspired neural network model.

The model used for the authors work on catastrophic interference is loosely based on what has been referred to the "Hebb-Marr" model of hippocampal function [14,15,16] From this model the two most important computational mechanisms are the feed forward pathway from the EC to the CA3 region via the DG, which is required for the encoding of new memories, and the recurrent connections within the CA3 which is needed to recall previously stored memories. In the next section two competing principles are discussed which are hippocampally inspired and form the fundamental computational processing aspects of this model; namely Pattern separation and pattern completion.

4. Pattern separation

Pattern separation has been suggested as one possible mechanism for the formation of different and relatively non over-lapping representations in the hippocampus. As a solution to catastrophic interference it is ideal in that it allows for different subsets of units to encode different memories. As a result there is little or no interference as different sets of weights are involved. High neuron activation thresholds lead to a conjunctive representation because only those units having the closest alignment of their weight patterns with the current input activity pattern will receive enough excitation to become activated. Accordingly the activation a unit receives is a relatively high proportion of the total number of input units that are active; meaning a specific combination of those inputs which are responsible for driving the units.

5. Pattern separation implementation

This author uses a point neuron activation function that provides a crude but effective approximation to the neural dynamics that sum all of the inputs into a particular neuron. A point neuron activation function requires an explicit separation between inputs which are excitatory or inhibitory. Abstract neuron representations simply add together inputs with both positive and negative weights. Such a state ignores the biological constraint that all inputs produced by a given sending neuron are either all excitatory or all inhibitory. The two inputs are, the level of excitation coming into the neuron from other neurons and the amount of inhibition which in a biological neural network would be provided by specialised inhibitory neurons in the cortex, but is simulated here by an inhibitory function which will be discussed in more detail later. The net input to the neuron is described as a time averaged activation function of the format.

$$\langle x_i w_{ij} \rangle_k = \frac{1}{n} \sum_i x_i w_{ij} \qquad [1]$$

where k represents the synaptic conductances. These are subsequently averaged together. The 1/n factor is usually equal to the number of connections a unit has within a given projection. The amount of excitatory conductance for a given projection g_{e_k} is an average of the individual inputs multiplied by a normalising factor which is based upon the expected activity level of the sending projection. This is represented by the variable α_k

$$g_{e_k} = \frac{1}{\alpha_k} \left\langle x_i w_{ij} \right\rangle_k \qquad [2]$$

The normalising factor enforces a constraint upon the system that each projection has roughly the same level of influence. At this stage the total level of excitatory conductance g_{e_t} is expressed as the average of the projections conductance's plus a normalised bias.

$$g_e(t) = (\frac{1}{n_p} \sum_k \frac{1}{\alpha_k} \left\langle x_i w_{ij} \right\rangle_k + \frac{\beta}{N}) \qquad [3]$$

In this formalisation n_p is the number of projections. The bias term is regarded as another projection, which would generate a disproportionate influence on the systems if it were not scaled correctly. This is achieved by dividing by the total number of input connections, N which ensures the bias weight has approximately the same importance as one normal synaptic input. Once the input conductances are calculated the membrane potential update equation is applied. The weighted average form of this equation is.

$$V_m = \frac{g_e E_e + g_i E_i g_l E_l}{g_e + g_i + g_l} \qquad [4]$$

where V_m is the membrane potential, g_e, g_i and g_l are the levels of excitatory, inhibitory and leak conductance and E_c, E_i and E_l are the driving membrane potentials for excitation, inhibition and leak. This equation is used directly within the model, but the parameter values range between 0-1 based upon normalised biologically based values.

In this model, pattern separation is achieved as follows. An initially randomly generated normally distributed weight matrix of mean 0 and standard deviation 1 is created. The weight matrix is multiplied by the number of input patterns (X) and a normalised bias term is added to the product (normalising the bias term is a method for representing the long distance which sometimes occur between synapses and neurons). The result is then presented to the neuron activation function described above and the most excited neuron is located. All activations below the maximum are set to zero. Those neurons whose activations are the highest are set to 1. The most activated neurons, and a group of neurons which are nearest to it (approximately 20% of the neurons) location (which corresponds to the row of the weight matrix) is found for each of the patterns. All elements on the row which match the pattern set are increased upwards or downwards (towards 1 or 0) depending upon whether the element is 1 or 0. A simple self organisation algorithm is used of the form;

$$\text{If } X(s,i) > 0$$

$$W(\text{Winners }(r),s) = W(\text{Winners}(r),s) + lc*(1\text{-winners}(r),s)$$

$$\text{else}$$

$$W(\text{Winners}(r),s) = W(\text{Winners}(r),s) - (lc * W(\text{Winners}(r),s))$$

Where s is the number of rows of input data, i is the number of columns of input data, X is the data matrix containing the input patterns, W is the entire weight matrix, *Winners* is a matrix which stores the winning neuron positions corresponding to the rows of the weight matrix to be updated, and lc is a learning constant. The winning row of neurons is updated until it matches the respective input pattern.

5.1   Auto associative layer

The second layer of the network receives pattern separated input directly from the first layer of the network. The neurons are recurrently connected to each other, which allow this layer to perform an auto associative function. Since there are a large number of recurrent connections within the CA3 region it has been postulated that this area could act as an auto associative memory capacity. If a new event was to be memorised it would be represented as a firing pattern of CA3 pyramidal cells which would subsequently be stored using associatively modifiable synapses on the recurrent connections. The autoassociator reproduces at the output stage the same pattern it was presented with at input. It is similar to the Hebbian rule type pattern associator, and is capable not only of storing independent memories using the same set of connections, but can also remove incomplete and noisy inputs. An autoassociator consists of a set or processing units, each with a dendrite and an output line. The external input to the autoassociator comes from an earlier stage of processing. The transformed signal is passed on by the output lines to the next processing stage.

The total input to an autoassociative network unit i consists of an external input and an internal input generated from the feed back from other units within the autoassociator. The internal input is calculated as the sum of the products of the activity of each unit connected to i and the strength of the connection between them

$$netinput_i = extinput_i + \sum_j a_j w_{ij} \qquad [5]$$

where aj is the activity of unit j which j indexes all units in the auto-associator except I wij is the strength of the connection between the recurrent input from unit j and the dendrite of unit i. Input to the autoassociator is represented by a clamped pattern of stimulation (the external input to the network) onto the dendrites. In this example the external input represent the pattern separated representation of the input pattern. A sigmoid activation function receives the external input, and the activity produced weighted by the strength of the appropriate connection produces an internal input to the other units.

The net input to any particular unit is now the sum of external and internal inputs. This results in a new level of activity in the unit, which is fed back to all other units resulting in a change in both their net input, and their activity level. The auto-associator runs for a number of cycles until it reaches a steady state where there is no further change in the internal input. The chosen method of auto-association requires the second layer to perform in a manner similar to that of the Hopfield neural network [17]. The second layer now consists of a single layer recurrent network with a symmetric weight matrix whose diagonal elements are all zero. Networks of this type store n-number of patterns as fixed point attractors. The locations of the attractors are determined by the weight matrix. The stored patterns can be specified either by direct computation via the Hebbian learning rule, or a gradient descent method such as the delta rule.

The difference between the internal and external inputs is calculated, and the strength of the weight connections is then adjusted to ensure the difference is reduced. If the internal input to a given unit is less than the external input then the connection weights are increased, whilst those carrying a negative input are reduced. The weight change rule $\Delta w_{ij} = \varepsilon \delta_i a_j$ where ε is a constant which determines the weight change for an individual trial δi, is the error on unit i and aj is the activity of unit j.

6.   Third layer architecture

The final stage of learning in this architecture is to associate each pattern separated item of data with its original pattern. This is achieved by use of a matrix structure similar to Bart Kosoko's architecture for an associative network architecture using a crossbar structure [18]. This is a matrix solution to association memory between two sets of data items. Such memory is not trained as most neural network architecture are but is the result of multiplication and summation.

Each vector A is associated with a vector B. Three correlation matrices are produced by multiplying the vectors using the equation.

$$M_1 = A_1 B_1^T \qquad [6]$$

These three matrices are then added together to produce a master weight matrix.

$$M = \sum_1^n m_n \qquad [7]$$

154

The weight matrix produced as a result of equation [12] can now be used to obtain the vector associated with any input vector. Since the resulting vector is limited to the range [1 -1] a function called signum is used which takes the form.

$$sign\,(x) = \begin{cases} -1 \text{ when } x\ <0, \\ 0 \ \text{ when } x\ =0, \\ 1 \text{ when } x\ >0. \end{cases}$$

7 Pattern completion

The purpose of pattern separation is to ensure that a smaller, more compact representation of the original pattern can be stored for use as a cue to assist in recall. The recall of the original pattern is termed pattern completion. An episodic memory system requires random sets of concurrent activities to be associated quickly and stored as one event which can be retrieved via a partial cue consisting of a sub component of the memory.

Pattern retrieval is achieved by submitting some part of it to the network. From studies of long term potentiation it has been observed that Hebbian synaptic modification operates over a time frame of approximately 1 second. As Hebbian learning is known to participate in both memory formation and other areas of the brain (LTP) it is theorised that the hippocampus would be capable of functioning sufficiently quickly to create snapshots of episodes, but with there being insufficient time to reorganise the information, each event would be stored as a simple association between different cortical inputs. An obvious issue with pattern completion concerns the ability of patterns which are subsets of previously learned patterns. Some researchers have suggested that the key influence in avoiding premature pattern completion is the activity level, generated by inhibition functions which ensure that weakly excited units do not become active.

In addition the hippocampus is also thought to play a significant role in recollecting specific studied details [19] whilst at the same time being highly context sensitive This last aspect is important from a pattern completion perspective as it provides a means of explaining how pattern completion is triggered by the use of sparse representations designed to represent the original patterns. Recall the learning sequence for the network described above.

- Input patterns are presented to the transfer layer
- Pattern separation takes place at the next layer
- Binding of patterns occurs at the auto associative layer

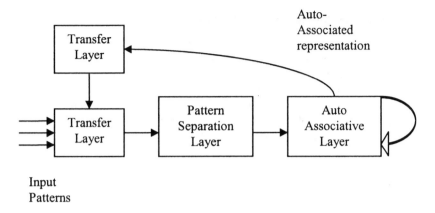

Figure 1: The basic architecture for the proposed solution. Input patterns are fed into the transfer layer from outside the architecture. The transfer layer operates in a linear fashion to move the patterns to the pattern separation layer, where excitatory and inhibitory neurons ensure a reduced, orthogonal input set is produced for the next layer. This is then subject to auto association to produce a stable attractor dynamic. Each auto-associated representation is associated with the original pattern via a connectivity matrix, which can be accessed later to reproduce the correct pattern.

8. Data sets used

For the following experiments, two data sets were used to test the architectures ability to function under a variety of catastrophic interference avoidance scenarios. The congressional voting records and edible and poisonous mushroom sets can be located at the UCI database repository [20]. Both sets were used in a similar scenario by French [6].

8.1 Congressional Voting Records

This data set includes votes for each of the U.S.A House of Representatives congressmen on 16 key votes identified by the congressional quarterly almanac (CQA). The CQA lists nine different types of votes: voted for, paired for, and announced for (these three simplified to "yea"), voted against, paired against, and announced against (these three simplified to "nay"), voted present, voted present to avoid conflict of interest, and did not vote or otherwise make a position known (these three simplified to an unknown disposition). There are 17 input attributes and 435 instances. The training and test sets are selected at random.

256

8.2   Edible and poisonous mushrooms

This data set includes descriptions of hypothetical samples corresponding to 23 species of gilled mushrooms in the Agaricus and Lepiota Family. Each species is identified as a) definitely edible, b) definitely poisonous, or of c) unknown edibility and not recommended. This latter class was combined with the poisonous one. There are twenty two attributes, and 8124 instances. The combination of 17 poisonous and three edible, and vice versa are selected to enforce the quasi-contradictory aspect of the experiments described in more detail.

9.   Experiments performed

The performance of this author's network is evaluated against standard back propagation of error using two criteria. The ability to recall previously learned patterns, and the time taken to relearn a previous data set following retraining.

9.1   Sequential learning experiment.

The data set used in this experiment is taken from the congressional voting records set at the UCI repository. Twenty patterns are selected at random from the data set corresponding to ten congressman from each of the republican and democrat parties. Each is presented sequentially to the network. The order of presentation was randomised during each run and the results averaged over fifty runs. After the twenty patterns are serially learned, the network is tested to see how many of these items it remembers. The criteria used being "how near is the networks output to 0.2 of the required output"[6]. After serial learning of the items, the network is tested on its ability to recall each item. Figure 1 shows that the biologically motivated model is below the 0.2 convergence criteria for 6 items (item numbers 15-20) and is within 0.05 of this requirement for a further 4 patterns (item numbers 10-14)

Standard back propagation of error is only able to produce two items which are within the 0.2 threshold criteria (item numbers 19 and 20) In addition table 1 demonstrates that the amount of forgetting between the final item and its immediate predecessor is considerably larger for a back propagation network than for the biologically motivated model.

Architecture	Difference
MLP/BP	0.15
Biologically motivated model	0.08

Table 1: Error difference between the final items learned and its immediate predecessor

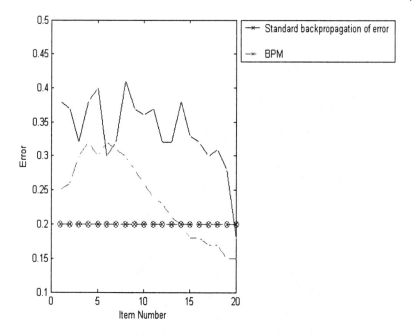

Figure 1: Amount of error for each of the 20 items learned sequentially after the final item has been learned to criteria (0.2 thresholds, indicated by the flat line as per the experimental method cited in [6]

9.2 Performance on real world data

This experiment uses the mushroom data set from the UCI data repository. Catastrophic interference can be eliminated if the network has been pre trained on a random sample of data taken from the domain in which it is expected to operate. However this only applies if the random sample captures the regularities of the operating states domain [5]. However if the new set to be learned does not share the regularities of the pre training set, the neural network must be capable of generalising from one data set, that a new data set is in fact similar to it, even though it is not identical. In this experiment two "quasi contradictory" sets of mushrooms form the UCI mushroom database were selected. The criteria for quasi contradictory being that the mushroom pairs differ by no more than three of the 22 attributes. There are 70 pairs of closely paired edible/poisonous mushrooms in this set. Twenty pairs of mushrooms are selected for the original training set, and another twenty for the quasi contradictory set. The original set consists of 17 edible mushrooms and 3 poisonous. The second mushroom set consists of mushrooms which are very similar to the original data ("contradictory set") contains 17 poisonous and 3 edible mushrooms.

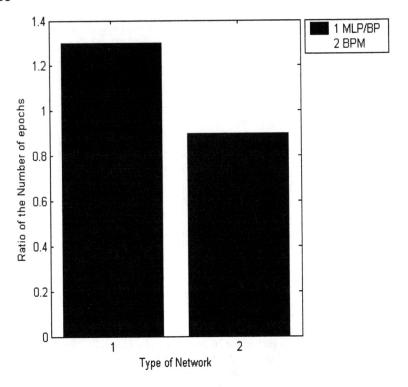

Figure 2: The ratio of the number of epochs necessary for relearning the original patterns, to the number of epochs initially required to learn these patterns (after the disruptive pattern set has been learned) as determined by the number of epochs of training time required for each run.

Figure 2 shows that relearning rates for standard back propagation of error are considerable longer than for this author's biologically motivated mode neural network. This author's biologically motivated model is capable of retaining a sufficient level of memory to allow the network to be retrained quicker than a back propagation neural network.

10. Observations

This paper has considered a biologically motivated strategy for the alleviation of catastrophic interference, based upon one possible model of memory. The architecture utilises pattern separation to reduce the dimensionality of the original input pattern which is subsequently auto associated to produce a stable attractor dynamic representation of the pattern set. This is subsequently associated with the original pattern set. In recall mode the separated representation activates the correct attractor dynamic representation which is used to activate the correct pattern. This author has compared and contrasted the performance of this model against standard back propagation of error. Using two real world data sets the biologically motivated architecture shows superior performance to feed forward neural networks using back propagation of error in both its ability to recall previously learned information, and the time to relearn a data set.

The findings from this study confirm earlier work by French [3,6] that back propagation is highly susceptible to weight disruption caused by new, overlapping pattern learning. In addition these experiments though tentative confirm that a pattern separation approach to catastrophic interference can result in significant alleviation of catastrophic interference. These experiments support the hypothesis that neural networks based upon certain neuro-scientific principles can provide an effective remedy to catastrophic interference. Although certain aspects of the model could be challenged as lacking a degree of biological plausibility the architecture is still capable of remembering the majority of previously learned information. If the second pattern set is substantially smaller than the original set this reduces the effectiveness of the biologically motivated model significantly, which is caused by the use of auto associative architectures such as the Hopfield network. In addition the architecture has to date only been tested upon binary data sets. However this caveat aside the architecture performs extremely well. Future work in this are will include a comparison of the author's model to a variety of other architectures which have been proffered as solutions to this problem.

References

1. McCloskey M, and Cohen N Catastrophic Interference in Connectionist Networks. The Sequential learning problem, In G H Bower (ed), The Psychology and Learning of Motivation, Vol 24, 109-164, NY: Academic Press. 1989
2. Kortge, C. A, Episodic memory in connectionist networks, 1993,Proceedings of the Cognitive Science Society, pp 764-771, Hillsdale, NJ,Erlbaum.
3. French, R.M Semi distributed representations and catastrophic forgetting in connectionist networks, 1992,Connection Science, 4, 365-377
4. Sloman, S.A & Rummelhart D E, Reducing interference in distributed memories through episodic gating, In Healy. A, Kosslyn. S & Shiffrin. R (eds) Essays in honour of W.K Estes, Hillsdale, NJ:Erlbaum 1992
5. McRae, K & Hetherington, P.A. Catastrophic Interference is eliminated in pretrained networks, 1993,Proceedings of the Fifteenth Annual Conference of the Cognitive Society, 723-728, Hillsdale,NJ,Erlbaum,
6. French, R.M, Pseudo Recurrent Connectionist Networks: An approach to the "sensitivity-stability" dilemma, Connection Science, 1997, 9(4), 353-379,
7. Kanerva, P Sparse distributed memory, Cambridge, MA:Bradford books, 1989
8. Kruschke, J. ALCOVE: An exemplar based model of category learning, 1992, Psychology Review, 9, 22-44
9. Ans B, Rousset S, French. R M, & Musca, S Preventing Catastrophic Interference in multiple sequence learning using coupled reverberating Elman

Networks, 2002,Proceedings of the 24th Annual Conference of the Cognitive Science Society, NJ:LEA

10. Kortge, C A Episodic memory in connectionist networks, 1993, In proceedings of the 12th Annual meeting of the Cognitive Science Society, 764-771,

11. Ramon y Cajal, Histology, 10th edition, Baltimore Wood, 1937

12 Scoville, W B & Milner B, Loss of recent memory after bilateral hippocampal lesions, Journal of Neuro Chemistry, 1957,Feb 20(1):11-21.

13. Macleod P, Plunkett P, Rolls E Introduction to connectionist modelling of cognitive processes, Oxford University Press, 1998.

14. Hebb, D The Organisation of Behaviour, Wiley & Sons, New York, 1949

15. Marr, D A theory of Cerebellar Cortex, Journal Physiology, 1969,202,437-470

16. McNaughton, B L & Morris, R G M Hippocampal synaptic enhancement and information storage within a distributed memory system, Trends in neurosciences, 1987,10(10), 408-415,

17. Hopfield J J, Neurons with graded responses have collective computational properties like those of two state neurons, Proceedings of the National academy of sciences, 81, 3088-3092, 1984

18. Kosko, B Hidden patterns in combined adaptive knowledge neural networks, 1988,International journal of approximate reasoning, 2, 337-393,

19. Yonelinas, A P The nature of recollection and familiarity: A review of 30 years of research, 2002,Journal of memory and language, 46, 441-517,

20. Blake, C L & Merz, C J, UCI Repository pf machine learning databases [http:www.ics.uci.edu/~mlearn/mlrepository.html], Irvine, CA University of California, Department of information and computer science, 1998

Fast Estimation of Distribution Algorithm (EDA) via Constrained Multi-Parent Recombination

Zeke S. H. Chan and N. Kasabov

Knowledge Engineering Discovery and Research Institute(KEDRI) ,
Auckland University of Technology (AUT), New Zealand
shchan@aut.ac.nz

Abstract

This paper proposes a new evolutionary operator called *Constrained Multi-parent Recombination* (CMR) that performs Estimation of Distribution Algorithm (EDA) for continuous optimization problems without evaluating any explicit probabilistic model. The operator linearly combines subsets of the parent population with random coefficients that are subject to constraints to produce the offspring population, so that it is distributed according to Normal distribution with mean and variance equal to that of the parent population. Moreover, the population convergence rate can be controlled with a variance-scaling factor. CMR is a simple, yet robust and efficient operator. It eliminates the requirement for evaluating an explicit probabilistic model and thus the associated errors and computation. It implicitly models the full set of $d(d-1)/2$ interdependencies between components, yet its computation complexity is only $O(d)$ per solution (d denotes the problem dimension). Theoretical proofs are provided to support its underlying principle. Preliminary experiment involves comparing the performance of CMR, four other EDA approaches and Evolutionary Strategies over three benchmark test functions. Results show that CMR performs more consistently than other approaches.

1 Introduction

Estimation of Distribution Algorithm (EDA) belongs to the class of Evolutionary Algorithms that uses probabilistic model of promising solutions to guide further exploration of the search space [1]. It is implemented in two steps: first, estimating the model parameters of the selected population, and second, sampling the new population from the estimated model. In applications to continuous optimization problem, the probabilistic model is often assumed to describe Normal distribution [2, 3]. The parameters are therefore, the population mean and variance, or their alternative representation such as that in Gaussian networks.

However, the evaluation of the probabilistic model raises two problems. First, the modelling of the full set of interdependencies includes $d(d-1)/2$ parameters (d is the problem dimension), which requires severe computational intensity and memory. This leads to the second problem, that approximation techniques are often required to reduce the number of parameters. The problem now involves selecting the model that yields the optimal trade-off between efficiency and accuracy.

The paper proposes a new multi-parent recombination operator called *Constrained Multi-Parent Recombination* (CMR) that alleviates the above problems through implementing continuous EDA without evaluating an explicit probabilistic model. CMR is a form of multi-parent recombination. To generate each offspring, CMR linearly combines a random subset of parent population with a set of random coefficients that are subject to constraints, such that the offspring is distributed according to Normal distribution with mean and variance equal to that of the parent population. CMR implicitly models the full set of $d(d-1)/2$ interdependencies between components, yet it only requires computation of $O(d)$ per solution and thus runs very fast. Moreover, the offspring variance size can be controlled by a scaling factor, which is very useful for adjusting the population convergence rate. Detailed proof of the mechanism of CMR is described. Experiments include comparing the performance of CMR, Evolutionary Strategies (ES) and four other EDA techniques of UMDA, MIMIC, EBNA and EBNA over optimizing three benchmark functions that are commonly used for evaluating Evolutionary Algorithms. Results show that CMR is more consistent than all other methods in finding the global optimum.

The rest of this paper is organized as follows. In Section 2, we overview EDA and related approaches and discuss their differences and similarities with CMR. Section 3 provides a detail description on CMR, which includes its principle, implementation and theoretical validation. Some empirical observations and remarks on the performance of CMR are also described. The experiments and results are reported in section 4. Finally, conclusions are drawn in section 5.

2 Background and Problem Definition of EDA

In the literature, most continuous EDA approaches assume that the population distribution is Normal, and all approaches require using a probabilistic model of either multivariate Normal distribution or Gaussian Network to estimate of the selected population distribution [1-3]. Although the later model is more comprehensible, the two are functionally equivalent. The parameters of one model can be transformed to the parameters of the other [4]. The full set of parameters comprises d elements for representing the mean, d elements for representing the variance and $d(d-1)/2$ elements for representing the interdependencies between components. Since the representation of the full interdependencies is of $O(d^2)$, approximation techniques are required to reduce the number of parameters for large d. This leads to the classification of EDA approaches into three groups according to the number of interdependencies considered, which are approaches that model no interdependency, pairwise interdependencies and multivariate interdependencies models. See [1-3] for a comprehensive review of these approaches. In general, the more interdependencies modelled, the better the approximation is at the cost of higher computational intensity.

Therefore, the implementation of EDA using an explicit probabilistic model requires three tasks: first, selecting the model that considers the optimal number of interdependencies, second, estimating the model parameters and third, sampling the new population from the estimate. Each task induces certain approximation or computational error and computational complexity that may accumulate and lead to an overall performance degradation. CMR, which involves only multi-parent recombination, eliminates these tasks and related problems through performing EDA without evaluating any intermediate probabilistic model. Such direct implementation also saves computational time and memory.

It is worth mentioning two other approaches that are closely related to EDA and CMR: correlated mutation by Schwefel [5-7] and Eigensystem transformed Gene Pool Recombination (GPR) [8]. Both approaches consider the full set of $d(d-1)/2$ interdependencies to achieve *rotational-invariance*. Rotational-invariance describes the property that an algorithm is unaffected by the geometrical rotation of the search space that causes linear inseparability between components. This is an important property as linear inseparability significantly degrades performance of Evolutionary Algorithms [9]. In correlated mutation, each individual is assigned its own set of mutation variances and interdependencies that are expressed in rotational angles. Mutation noise is generated through sampling a random vector from Normal distribution with mean zero and corresponding variances, and then rotating the random vector by the rotational angles. In Hansen's derandomization approach [10-12] to correlated mutation, the variance and interdependencies are learnt as a variance-covariance matrix. The purpose of representing interdependencies as rotational angles instead of correlation coefficients is to eliminate the occurrence of ill-conditioned variance-covariance matrices. Voigt's Eigensystem GPR obtains the eigenvectors of the parent population and uses them to transform the solutions to remove the interdependences between components.

Thus both correlated mutation and Eigensystem GPR require eigensystem computation to achieve rotational-invariance, which may be prohibitive for large d ($d>1000$). In addition, the memory required for storing the interdependencies is of $O(d^2)$. CMR, which uses only multi-parent recombination, requires only $O(d)$ per solution computation and no memory.

2.1 Notations

To facilitate further discussions on CMR, some notations are defined here. In general, we write matrices and vectors in bold upper- and lowercase symbols respectively to distinguish them from scalar variables. $N(\mu_x, \Sigma_x)$ denotes the multivariate Normal distribution with mean μ_x and variance-covariance Σ_x. The subscript indicates the variables from which the mean and variance are computed. For Evolutionary Algorithm, each individual solution is a vector in the real d-dimensional space. The selected population, called the *parent* population, comprises of Se individuals is denoted by $X=\{x_1, x_2, ..., x_{Se}\}$, while the newly generated population, called the *offspring* population, comprises of N individuals is denoted by $Y=\{y_1, y_2, ..., y_N\}$. $X_i \subseteq X$ denotes the ith subset of the population. To distinguish between the arithmetic value and expected value, we use $<x>$ and $Var(x)$ to represent the arithmetic average and variance respectively, and $\bar{x} = E[\langle x \rangle]$ and $\bar{\Sigma} = E[Var(x)]$ to represent the corresponding expected value.

3 Constrained Recombination

3.1 Principle

The objective of CMR is to generate offspring $Y=\{y_1, y_2, ..., y_N\}$ that is distributed according to the Normal approximation of the parent distribution (the true distribution of the parent population is unknown), i.e.

$$y_i \sim N(\mu_x, \Sigma_x) \qquad \forall i \qquad (1)$$

where μ_x and Σ_x denote the mean and the covariance of the parent $X=\{x_1, x_2, ..., x_{Se}\}$. The most straightforward method is to compute μ_x and Σ_x and then sample from $N(\mu_x, \Sigma_x)$. However, as shown in section 2, sampling from the model often requires computation of the eigensystem. CMR avoids it by using a specially designed multi-parent recombination to generate each offspring, thus eliminating evaluation of any explicit probabilistic model. The overall complexity is only $O(d)$. Detailed implementation is as follows.

3.2 Implementation

For each offspring y_i, a random subset of Γ individuals $X_i = \{x_{i,1}, x_{i,2}, ..., x_{i,\Gamma}\}$ called the *recombinants* is sampled from the selected population X. Γ is an integer chosen between 3 and Se. The recombinants are then multiplied by a set of Γ independent, identically distributed (iid) random coefficients $a_i=\{a_{i,1}, a_{i,2}, ..., a_{i,\Gamma}\}$ and summed together to generate the noise vector z_i

$$\mathbf{z}_i = \sum_{\gamma=1}^{\Gamma} a_{i,\gamma} \mathbf{x}_{i,\gamma} \qquad (2)$$

We call the linear combination in (2 *constrained linear combination* because the coefficients $\{a_{i,\gamma}\}$ are subject to the following constraints:

$$E\left[\sum_{\gamma=1}^{\Gamma} a_{i,\gamma}\right] = 0 \qquad (3)$$

$$E\left[\sum_{\gamma=1}^{\Gamma} a_{i,\gamma}^2\right] = K^2\left(\frac{N}{N-1}\right) \approx K^2 \quad \text{for large } N \qquad (4)$$

To satisfy (3 and (4, it is easily derived that $\{a_{i,\gamma}\}$ must be sampled from a probability distribution of mean $\mu_a=0$ and variance $\sigma_a^2=K^2/(N-1)$, which we have chosen to be the Gaussian distribution in this work. Constrained linear combination is the most critical procedure of CMR. It achieves three objectives:

1. Constraint (3 forces the mean of $\mathbf{z}_i$ to be zero, i.e. $<\mathbf{z}>=0$

2. Constraint (4 forces the covariance of $\mathbf{z}_i$ to be $K^2\Sigma_x$, i.e. $Var(\mathbf{z}) = K^2\Sigma_x$

3. The sum of Γ iid terms in (2 causes the distribution of $\mathbf{z}_i$ to be Normal.

As a result, $\mathbf{z}_i$ is Normal distributed with mean zero and covariance $K^2\Sigma_x$, i.e.

$$\mathbf{z}_i \sim N(0, K^2\Sigma_x) \qquad \forall i$$

Proofs are given in the next section. The final step is to compute the parent population mean μ_x as:

$$\mu_x = \langle \mathbf{x} \rangle = \frac{1}{Se}\sum_{s=1}^{Se} \mathbf{x}_s \qquad (5)$$

and add it to $\mathbf{z}_i$ to create an offspring $\mathbf{y}_i$:

$$\mathbf{y}_i = \langle \mathbf{x} \rangle + \mathbf{z}_i \qquad (6)$$

The vector addition shifts the offspring mean from zero to μ_x. Now $\mathbf{y}_i$ is distributed according to Normal distribution with mean μ_x and variance Σ_x, i.e.

$$\mathbf{y}_i \sim N(\mu_x, \Sigma_x) \qquad \forall i \qquad (7)$$

which is the same as (1 at $K^2=1$, thus we have achieved the objective of EDA. The process is repeated until N offspring are sampled. The scaling factor K^2 allows control over the relative covariance size. The computational complexity of CMR, which mainly involves $(d\times\Gamma)$ multiplications and $(d\times\Gamma)$ additions for performing linear constrained combination in Eq. 2, is of $O(d)$ per solution. The implementation of CMR is summarized in Fig. 1.

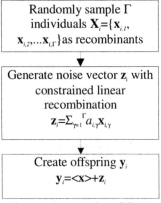

Fig. 1 Implementation of CMR.

3.3 Proofs

The most critical step of CMR is the generation of the noise vector z_i that is distributed according to Normal distribution with mean zero and covariance $K^2\Sigma_x$. This section provides the proof of these properties. The proof follows the methodology in [13]. For simplicity, we consider only one component from the parent and offspring vector for brevity, thus replacing the original symbols with $x=x$, $y=y$ and $z=z$ and the corresponding covariances $\Sigma_x = \sigma_x$, $\Sigma_y = \sigma_y$ and $\Sigma_z = \sigma_z$. The proof requires using the following expected values and products of $\{a_{i,\gamma}\}$ and $\{x_{i,\gamma}\}$:

$$E[a_{i,\gamma} a_{j,\eta}] = \begin{cases} a_{i,\gamma}^2 & \forall (i=j) \wedge (\gamma = \eta) \\ 0 & otherwise \end{cases} \tag{8}$$

since $\{a_{i,\gamma}\}$ are iid random coefficients, and also

$$E[x_{i,\gamma}] = \bar{x} \tag{9}$$

$$E[x_{i,\gamma} x_{j,\eta}] = \begin{cases} \overline{x^2} & \forall (i=j) \wedge (\gamma = \eta) \\ \bar{x}^2 & otherwise \end{cases} \tag{10}$$

since the parents $x_{i,\gamma}$ are randomly sampled from the population and are hence iid. $\bar{x}$ and $\overline{x^2}$ are the first and second moments respectively.

Theorem 1. The expected mean of the noise vector z_i, is zero, i.e. $\bar{z} = E[\langle z \rangle] = 0$. The noise average $\langle z \rangle$ is calculated by:

$$\langle z \rangle = \frac{1}{N}\sum_{j=1}^{N}\left(\sum_{\gamma=1}^{\Gamma} a_{j,\gamma} x_{j,\gamma}\right) \tag{11}$$

Applying the expectation operator to (11 and substituting in (3 and (9, we get

$$\bar{z} = E[\langle z \rangle] = \frac{1}{N}\sum_{j=1}^{N}\left(\sum_{\gamma=1}^{\Gamma} E[a_{j,\gamma}]E[x_{j,\gamma}]\right) = 0 \tag{12}$$

Q.E.D.

Theorem 2. The expected variance of the noise vector z_i equals to that of the selected population covariance scaled by K^2, i.e. $\overline{\sigma_z^2} = E[Var(z)] = K^2 \sigma_x^2$. The expected noise variance is given by $\overline{\sigma_z^2} = E[Var(z)] = E\left[\left(z_i - \langle z \rangle\right)^2\right]$. First we expand the expression $(z_i - \langle z \rangle)^2$ through substituting (2

$$\begin{aligned}(z_i - \langle z \rangle)^2 &= \left[\sum_{\gamma=1}^{\Gamma} a_{i,\gamma} x_{i,\gamma} - \frac{1}{Se}\sum_{j=1}^{Se}\left(\sum_{\gamma=1}^{\Gamma} a_{j,\gamma} x_{j,\gamma}\right)\right]^2 = \left[\left(1 - \frac{1}{Se}\right)\sum_{\gamma=1}^{\Gamma} a_{i,\gamma} x_{i,\gamma} - \frac{1}{Se}\sum_{j \neq i}^{Se}\left(\sum_{\gamma=1}^{\Gamma} a_{j,\gamma} x_{j,\gamma}\right)\right]^2 \\ &= \left(1 - \frac{1}{Se}\right)^2\left(\sum_{\gamma=1}^{\Gamma} a_{i,\gamma} x_{i,\gamma}\right)^2 + \left(\frac{1}{Se}\right)^2\left(\sum_{j \neq i}^{Se}\left(\sum_{\gamma=1}^{\Gamma} a_{j,\gamma} x_{j,\gamma}\right)\right)^2 - 2\left(1 - \frac{1}{Se}\right)\left(\frac{1}{Se}\right)\left(\sum_{\gamma=1}^{\Gamma} a_{i,\gamma} x_{i,\gamma}\right)\left(\sum_{j \neq i}^{Se}\left(\sum_{\gamma=1}^{\Gamma} a_{j,\gamma} x_{j,\gamma}\right)\right)\end{aligned} \tag{13}$$

Next, we apply the expectation operator $E[\cdot]$

$$\begin{aligned}E\left[(z_i - \langle z \rangle)^2\right] &= E\left[\left(1 - \frac{1}{Se}\right)^2\left(\sum_{\gamma=1}^{\Gamma} a_{i,\gamma} x_{i,\gamma}\right)^2\right] + E\left[\left(\frac{1}{Se}\right)^2\left(\sum_{j \neq i}^{Se}\left(\sum_{\gamma=1}^{\Gamma} a_{j,\gamma} x_{j,\gamma}\right)\right)^2\right] \\ &- E\left[2\left(1 - \frac{1}{Se}\right)\left(\frac{1}{Se}\right)\left(\sum_{\gamma=1}^{\Gamma} a_{i,\gamma} x_{i,\gamma}\right)\left(\sum_{j \neq i}^{Se}\left(\sum_{\gamma=1}^{\Gamma} a_{j,\gamma} x_{j,\gamma}\right)\right)\right]\end{aligned} \tag{14}$$

To facilitate evaluation of (14, we derive the following expected product

$$E\left[\left(\sum_{\gamma=1}^{\Gamma} a_{i,\gamma} x_{i,\gamma}\right)\left(\sum_{\gamma=1}^{\Gamma} a_{j,\gamma} x_{j,\gamma}\right)\right] = \begin{cases} K^2\left(\dfrac{Se}{Se-1}\right)(\overline{x^2} - \bar{x}^2) & i = j \\ 0 & otherwise \end{cases} \tag{15}$$

The calculation is straightforward but lengthy and is hence described in appendix A. This result allows evaluation of (14, since each term on the right of (14 contains one such product. Through substitution, we obtain the first term as

$$E\left[\left(1 - \frac{1}{Se}\right)^2\left(\sum_{\gamma=1}^{\Gamma} a_{i,\gamma} x_{i,\gamma}\right)^2\right] = \left(1 - \frac{1}{Se}\right)^2 K^2\left(\frac{Se}{Se-1}\right)(\overline{x^2} - \bar{x}^2) \tag{16}$$

The second term is given by

$$E\left[\left(\frac{1}{Se}\right)^2\left(\sum_{j \neq i}^{Se}\left(\sum_{\gamma=1}^{\Gamma} a_{j,\gamma} x_{j,\gamma}\right)\right)^2\right] = \left(\frac{1}{Se}\right)^2 (Se-1)K^2\left(\frac{Se}{Se-1}\right)(\overline{x^2} - \bar{x}^2) \tag{17}$$

And the third term is given by

$$E\left[-2\left(1-\frac{1}{Se}\right)\left(\frac{1}{Se}\sum_{\gamma=1}^{\Gamma}a_{i,\gamma}x_{i,\gamma}\right)\left(\sum_{j\neq i}^{Se}\left(\sum_{\gamma=1}^{\Gamma}a_{j,\gamma}x_{j,\gamma}\right)\right)\right]=0 \tag{18}$$

Summing the three terms together yields the remarkably simple result:

$$E\left[(z_i-\langle z\rangle)^2\right]=\left(1-\frac{1}{Se}\right)^2 K^2\left(\frac{Se}{Se-1}\right)\overline{(x^2-\bar{x}^2)}+\left(\frac{1}{Se}\right)^2(Se-1)K^2\left(\frac{Se}{Se-1}\right)\overline{(x^2-\bar{x}^2)}+0 \tag{19}$$

$$=K^2\overline{(x^2-\bar{x}^2)}$$

By definition, the expected variance of x is simply $\overline{\sigma_x^2}=\overline{(x^2-\bar{x}^2)}$. Thus finally, we obtain

$$\overline{\sigma_z^2}=E\left[(z_i-\langle z\rangle)^2\right]=K^2\overline{(x^2-\bar{x}^2)}=K^2\overline{\sigma_x^2} \tag{20}$$

It is straightforward to show that (20 can be generalized to multi-dimension, i.e. $\overline{\Sigma_z^2}=K^2\overline{\Sigma_x^2}$. This results is significant as it shows that the entire variance-covariance matrix that contains $d(d+1)/2$ unique parameters is implicitly learnt through simple multi-parent recombination that requires only computation of $O(d)$. Q.E.D

Theorem 3. The distribution of z_i tends to Normal as the number of recombinants Γ tends to infinity. Since both the random coefficients and parent individuals are uncorrelated iid, their product is also iid. According to the Central Limit Theorem, the constrained linear combination in (2, which consists of the sum over Γ of such products, tends towards Normal as Γ tends towards infinity (This intuition can also be explained by the fact that Normal random variables can be obtained by the sum of 12 uniform random variables [14]).
Q.E.D.

3.4 Empirical Observations

Here the empirical behaviour of CMR is observed with a two dimensional example. We sample a parent population of $Se=1000$ individuals from the uniform distribution with mean 0 and boundaries $x_1\in[-1, 1]$ and $x_2\in[-0.2, 0.2]$, and then rotate the population by $\pi/4$ and shift its mean to [2,2]. Next, we apply CMR to the population with scaling factor $K^2=1$ and number of recombinants $\Gamma=Se$ to generate $N=Se$ offspring. The population distribution and the frequency plot along the horizontal axis are shown in Fig. 2.

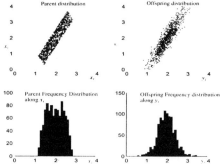

Fig. 2 The population distribution and the frequency plot along the horizontal axis of the
parent and offspring population.

From Fig. 2, we visualize that the offspring distribution is Normal and has the same mean (2,2) and rotation angle as the parent distribution. It demonstrates two important properties of CMR. First, the offspring distribution is Normal even if the parent distribution is non-Normal such as uniform in this case. Second, CMR is rotational-invariance. This is achieved by the implicit learning of the full variance-covariance matrix through constrained linear combination. In this example, the covariance of the parent and offspring are, respectively,

$$\Sigma_x = Var(\mathbf{X}) = \begin{bmatrix} .178 & .327 \\ .327 & .700 \end{bmatrix} \qquad \Sigma_y = Var(\mathbf{Y}) = \begin{bmatrix} .180 & .329 \\ .329 & .700 \end{bmatrix}$$

and are very close.

3.5 Selection of the Control Parameters K^2 and Γ

CMR has only two control parameters: scaling factor K^2 and number of recombinants Γ. The scaling factor K^2 is an important parameter that determines the ratio of the offspring variance to the parent variance and allows control over the population convergence rate. At K^2 equals unity, the offspring variance equals to the parent variance, which is is the case for general EDA approaches. However, for objective functions such as multi-modal functions that require more thorough exploration in the search space, we can set K^2 to larger values and vice-versa. Fig. 3 illustrates the effect of varying K^2 on the offspring distribution.

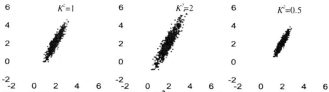

Fig. 3 The effect of varying K^2 on the offspring distribution.

Empirically, we find that the number of recombinants Γ, which ranges between 3 and Se, has little effect on the performance of CMR as long as Se is sufficiently large to approximate the Normal distribution (>40) and to provide diversity to the population. More detail on the choice of Se is discussed later. One may be concerned that for large Γ (consider the extreme case of $\Gamma=Se$), subsets of recombinants will contain overlapping individuals that affect the statistical independency of the noise vectors $\mathbf{z}_i$ and thus of the offspring $\mathbf{y}_i$. However, as shown in the proofs in section 3.3, as long as the random coefficients $\mathbf{a}_i = \{a_{i,\gamma}\}_{\gamma=1}^{\Gamma}$ are zero-mean iid variates, the noise vector $\mathbf{z}_i$, given by the sum of products of $\mathbf{a}_i$ and $\mathbf{X}_i$, is also iid.

3.6 Remarks

The proofs in section 3.3 show that CMR is functionally equivalent to continuous EDA, yet it does not require evaluating any probabilistic model. This innovation raises the following advantages:
1. CMR is very simple to implement.
2. CMR is fast and requires computation of $O(d)$.
3. The scaling factor K^2 allows control over the population convergence rate.
4. CMR avoids problems associated with learning and sampling of an explicit probabilistic model, for example, occurrence of ill-conditioned variance-covariance matrices. It is therefore robust against different objective functions.

CMR also has several limitations and these are as follows:
1. CMR can only approximate a single Normal distribution, which is also the case for most EDA approaches.
2. Since CMR does not evaluate any probabilistic model, behaviour of the search cannot be controlled through manipulating the model parameters as in the case of some EDA approaches like Population-Based Incremental Learning (PBIL) [15].
3. CMR considers the full variance-covariance matrix intrinsically, therefore population size of $O(d^2)$ is required for reliable performance. This is also the case for correlated mutation and Eigensystem GPR.

Because of these limitations, CMR is recommended only i) when a large population size of $O(d^2)$ is used and ii) when manipulation of the probabilistic model of the objective function is not required.

4 Experiments

As a preliminary experiment, we apply CMR to the suite of three benchmark functions that was used in [2, 3] for evaluating the performance of different EDA approaches. The suite is described in Table 1.

Table 1 Description of the test functions used for evaluating CMR.

Test function		Obj.	Opt.
$F_{SumCan}(\mathbf{x}) = 1 \Big/ \left(10^{-5} + \sum_{i=1}^{d} |y_i| \right)$	- $0.16 \leq x_i \leq 0.16$, $y_1 = x_1,\ y_i = x_i + y_i\text{-}1,\ i=2,...,d.$	max.	100,000
$F_{Schwefel}(\mathbf{x}) = \sum_{i=1}^{d} \left[\begin{array}{c}(x_1 - x_i^2)^2 \\ + (x_i - 1)^2 \end{array} \right]$	$-10 \leq x_i \leq 10$	min.	0
$F_{Griewangk}(\mathbf{x}) = 1 + \sum_{i=1}^{d} \dfrac{x_i^2}{4000}$ $- \prod_{i=1}^{d} \cos\left(\dfrac{x_i}{\sqrt{i}} \right)$	$-600 \leq x_i \leq 600$	min.	0

Detail description of their properties is found in [2, 3]. Performance of CMR is compared with four EDA approaches and Evolutionary Strategies (ES) and a detail description of these algorithms is found in [2]. The four EDA approaches are: Univariate Marginal Distribution Algorithm (UMDA$_c^G$: the subscript c denotes continuous function and the superscript G denotes Gaussian), Mutual Information Maximization for Input Clustering (MIMIC$_c^G$), Estimation of Bayesian Networks Algorithm (EBNA) with edge exclusive test (EBNA$_{ee}$) and with Bayesian Dirichlet equivalent metric (EBNA$_{BDe}$).

To ensure fair comparison the experiment adopts the same setting for the Evolutionary Algorithm as that in Larranaga's experiments. The problem dimension d is set to 10. The offspring population sizes for F$_{SumCan}$, F$_{Schwefel}$ and F$_{Griewangk}$ are 2000, 2000 and 750 respectively and the parent population sizes are fixed at 50% of them. For all test functions, the truncation method, complemented with keeping the best fit individual in the population, is used as the selection scheme. The maximum number of function evaluation is 300,000.

For CMR, we set the number of recombinants Γ to be 30% of the parent population size. The random coefficients $\{a\}$ are generated with the method described in appendix A. The scaling factor K^2 is unity for all test functions except F$_{Schwefel}$, which we set to 1.1. It is because the optimization of F$_{Schwefel}$ requires descending a long and windy valley and an Evolutionary Algorithm with fast population shrinkage may result in premature convergence. Therefore, K^2 is slightly raised above unity to moderate population shrinkage.

All experiments are averaged over 100 runs. The best fitness value found and the number of evaluations at which it occurs are recorded and are listed in Table 2.

Table 2 Results of the experiment averaged over 100 runs.

		CMR	UMDA$_c^G$	MIMIC$_c^G$	EBNA$_{ee}$	EBNA$_{BDe}$	ES
F$_{SumCan}$	m.value	100,000	53,460	58,775	100,000	100,000	5,910
(max.)	m.eval.	299,800	300,000	300,000	94,980	188,868	300,000
F$_{Schwefel}$	m.value	0.00041847	0.13754	0.13397	0.09914	0.0250	0
(min.)	m.eval.	298,700	131,795	132,714	128,256	126,357	232,514
F$_{Griewangk}$	m.value	0	0.011076	0.007794	0.008175	0.012605	0.034477
(min.)	m.eval.	84,570	227,751	227,019	223,820	238,728	215,431

We measure the performance mainly by the mean fitness value. The results in Table 2 show that over all three functions, CMR succeeds in finding the global optimum, outperforming all four EDA approaches. It also outperforms ES over F$_{SumCan}$ and F$_{Griewangk}$ and is only slightly slower in exploiting F$_{Schwefel}$. Clearly, CMR performs more consistently than all other methods under comparison in this test suite.

5 Conclusions

This paper introduces a new evolutionary operator called *Constrained Multi-parent Recombination* (CMR) that performs continuous Estimation of Distribution Algorithm (EDA) without evaluating any explicit probabilistic model. CMR linearly combines subsets of parent population with random coefficients that are subject to constraints to perform continuous EDA. To illustrate the its relationship with existing EDA approaches, we briefly review the principle of continuous EDA and two related approaches, which are correlated mutation by Schwefel and Eigensystem Gene Pool Recombination by Voigt. We show that the problem of continuous EDA is to an offspring population distributed according to the Normal approximation of the parent distribution, and that using probabilistic model that considers $d(d-1)/2$ interdependencies between components usually requires eigen computation. While CMR considers $d(d-1)/2$ interdependencies implicitly, being a form of multi-parent recombination, its computation complexity is only $O(d)$ per solution. Moreover, it can control the population convergence rate with a variance-scaling factor. The underlying principle and theoretical background of CMR, as well as some empirical observations of its performance are provided. While it has many advantages, its application is limited by its requirement for large population size of $O(d^2)$. Empirical experiment involves comparing the performance of CMR with four EDA approaches and Evolutionary Strategies (ES) over four benchmark test functions, in which CMR emerges as the most consistent optimizer. We conclude that CMR is a useful alternative for performing continuous EDA.

Future works include exploiting the speed and implicit covariance-learning capability of CMR to optimize nonlinear models such as Fuzzy Neural Network models, Evolving Connectionist Systems [16] and Gene Regulatory networks [17].

Acknowledgments

We thank Dr Thomas Yee of the Statistical Department of the University of Auckland for many helpful discussions. This research is supported by the KEDRI postdoctoral fellow research fund.

References

1. Pelikan, M., D. Goldberg, and F. Lobo, *A Survey of Optimization by Building and Using Probabilistic Model.* 1999, IlliGAL.
2. Larrañaga, P., et al., *Optimization by learning and simulation of Bayesian and Gaussian networks.* 1999, University of the Basque Country.
3. Larrañaga, P., et al. *Optimization in continuous domains by learning and simulation of Gaussian networks.* in *Workshop in Optimization by Building and using Probabilistic Models, 201-204. A Workshop within the 2000 Genetic and Evolutionary Computation Conference, GECCO 2000.* 2000. Las Vegas, Nevada, USA.
4. Heckerman, D., D. Geiger, and D.M. Chickering, *Learning Bayesian Networks: The Combination of Knowledge and Statistical Data.* KDD Workshop. 1994.
5. Schwefel, H.-P., *Numerische Optimierung von Computer-Modellen mittels der Evolutionsstrategie.* Interdisciplinary Systems Research. Vol. 26. 1977, Basel, Germany: Birkhauser.
6. Baeck, T., D.B. Fogel, and Z. Michalewicz, *Evolutionary Computation I. Basic algorithm and operators.* Vol. 1. 2000, Bristol: Institute of Physics Publishing.
7. Baeck, T., D.B. Fogel, and Z. Michalewicz, *Evolutionary Computataion II. Advanced algorithm and operators.* Vol. 2. 2000, Bristol: Institute of Physics Pub.
8. Voigt, H.-M. and H. Muhlenbein. *Gene Pool Recombination and Utilization of Covariances for the Breeder Genetic Algorithm.* in *the Second IEEE International Conference on Evolutionary Computation.* 1995. New York: IEEE Press.
9. Salomon, *Re-evaluating Genetic Algorithm Performance Under Coordinate Rotation of Benchmark Functions.* BioSystems, 1996. **39**: p. 263-278.
10. Hansen, N. *Invariance, Self-Adaptation and Correlated Mutations and Evolution Strategies.* in *the Sixth International Conference on Parallel Problem Solving from Nature.* 2000.
11. Hansen, N. and A. Ostermeier. *On the adaptation of arbitrary normal mutation distributions in evolution strategies: the generating set adaptation.* in *the Sixth International Conference on Genetic Algorithms.* 1995. Pittsburgh: Morgan Kaufmann.

12. Hansen, N. and A. Ostermeier. *Adapting Arbitrary Normal Mutation Distributions in Evolution Strategies: The Covariance Matrix Adaptation*. in *IEEE International Conference on Evolutionary Computation*. 1996. Nagoya, Japan.

13. Beyer, H.-G., *On self-adaptive features in real-parameter evolutionary algorithms*. IEEE Transactions on Evolutionary Computation, 2001. **5**(3): p. 250-270.

14. Ripley, B.D., *Stochastic Simulation*. 1987, New York: John Wiley & Sons.

15. Baluja, S., *Population -Based Incremental Learning: A Method for Integrating Genetic Search Based Function Optimization and Competitive Learning*. 1994, Carnegie Mellon Report.

16. Kasabov, N., *Evolving connectionist systems - methods and applications in bioinformatics, brain study and intelligent machines*. 2002, London-New York: Springer Verlag.

17. de Jong, H., *Modeling and Simulation of Genetic Regulatory Systems: A Literature Review*. Journal of Computational Biology, 2002. **9**(1): p. 67-103.

Appendix A

Our objective is to calculate the expected product

$$E\left[\left(\sum_{\gamma=1}^{\Gamma} a_{i,\gamma} x_{i,\gamma}\right)\left(\sum_{\gamma=1}^{\Gamma} a_{j,\gamma} x_{j,\gamma}\right)\right] \quad \text{for both } i=j \text{ and } i \neq j \tag{21}$$

First, for $i=j$, making use of the expected values in (8 to (10, we get

$$E\left[\left(\sum_{\gamma=1}^{\Gamma} a_{i,\gamma} x_{i,\gamma}\right)\left(\sum_{\gamma=1}^{\Gamma} a_{i,\gamma} x_{i,\gamma}\right)\right] = E\begin{bmatrix} a_{i,1}^2 x_{i,1}^2 + \cdots + a_{i,\Gamma}^2 x_{i,\Gamma}^2 \\ + a_{i,1} x_{i,1}(a_{i,2} x_{i,2} + \cdots + a_{i,\Gamma} x_{i,\Gamma}) + \\ \cdots \\ + a_{i,\Gamma} x_{i,\Gamma}(a_{i,1} x_{i,1} + \cdots + a_{i,\Gamma-1} x_{i,\Gamma-1}) \end{bmatrix}$$

$$= E\begin{bmatrix} (a_{i,1}^2 + a_{i,2}^2 + \cdots + a_{i,\Gamma}^2)\overline{x^2} \\ + a_{i,1}\overline{x}^2(a_{i,2} + \cdots + a_{i,\Gamma}) + \\ \cdots \\ + a_{i,\Gamma}\overline{x}^2(a_{i,1} + \cdots + a_{i,\Gamma-1}) \end{bmatrix} \tag{22}$$

Substituting the expectations (3 and (4 into (22 yields

$$E\left[\left(\sum_{\gamma=1}^{\Gamma} a_{i,\gamma} x_{i,\gamma}\right)\left(\sum_{\gamma=1}^{\Gamma} a_{i,\gamma} x_{i,\gamma}\right)\right] = E\begin{bmatrix} (a_{i,1}^2 + a_{i,2}^2 + \cdots + a_{i,\Gamma}^2)\overline{x^2} \\ + a_{i,1}\overline{x}^2(-a_{i,1}) + \cdots + a_{i,\Gamma}\overline{x}^2(-a_{i,\Gamma}) \end{bmatrix}$$

$$= E\left[(a_{i,1}^2 + a_{i,2}^2 + \cdots + a_{i,\Gamma}^2)\right]\left(\overline{x^2} - \overline{x}^2\right)$$

$$= K^2\left(\frac{Se}{Se-1}\right)\left(\overline{x^2} - \overline{x}^2\right) \tag{23}$$

Now we evaluate (21, for $i \neq j$. After multiplying out the two sums in (21, every term includes the product $(a_{i,\gamma} a_{j,\eta}, i \neq j)$ which has the expected value of zero by (8. Thus

$$E\left[\left(\sum_{\gamma=1}^{\Gamma} a_{i,\gamma} x_{i,\gamma}\right)\left(\sum_{\gamma=1}^{\Gamma} a_{j,\gamma} x_{j,\gamma}\right)\right] = 0 \qquad i \neq j \tag{24}$$

SESSION 3:

MULTI-AGENT SYSTEMS

A Trading Agent for a Multi-Issue Clearing House

John Debenham

Faculty of IT, University of Technology, Sydney, NSW, Australia,
debenham@it.uts.edu.au,
WWW home page: http://www-staff.it.uts.edu.au/~debenham/

Abstract. The potential size of the electronic business market offers great incentives to trading agents that can bargain, bid in auctions and trade in exchanges. Much of business negotiation is multi-issue. A generic 'information-based' agent is proposed for multi-issue negotiation. Successful negotiation depends on shrewd strategies driven by the right information. This agent has machinery to value information and to manage its integrity. A multi-issue, many-to-many clearing house, and an agent to trade in it, are proposed.

1 Introduction

Exchanges are institutions that cater to many potential buyers and sellers. Exchange mechanisms are known as *double auction mechanisms* [1]. These mechanisms either clear continuously or at discrete time steps. Continuous double auctions are used in many commodity markets and stock exchanges — they rely on high liquidity. Institutions that use discrete double auctions are sometimes known as *clearing houses* or *call markets*. In addition to capital markets, exchanges are applied to creative applications such as trading risk, generating predictions and making decisions [2].

As a means of generating predictions, exchanges have exhibited extraordinary accuracy. [3] analyzes this phenomenon and suggests that marginal traders who are motivated primarily to make a profit submit limit orders, close to the trading price. Exchanges act as an "intelligence lens" that focusses the best information that the traders have on the clearing price. For example, [4] describes the predictions by the Iowa Electronic Markets of the winner of the 1988 US presidential election that were within 0.2% of what occurred.

Put the other way, the clearing price is determined by the best information available — *the information is what matters*. So if an agent is to benefit from trading on an exchange other than by good fortune then he must have information that differs from other agents. The uniqueness of an agent's information is achieved in three ways: first, an agent may simply know something that others do not, second, an agent may attach levels of belief to its information that differ from the levels determined by others, and third, an agent may rate the importance, or relevance, of its information in a way that differs from others.

The potential size of the electronic business market and the comparatively small amount of automated negotiation presently deployed provides a major incentive for research in the area. An inherent difficulty in e-business negotiation — including e-procurement — is that it is generally multi-issue. Even a simple trade, such as a quantity of steel, may involve: delivery date, settlement terms, as well as price and the quality of the steel. Most of the work on multi-issue negotiation has focussed on one-to-one bargaining — for example [5], [6]. There has been rather less interest in one-to-many, multi-issue auctions — [7] analyzes some possibilities — despite the size of the e-procurement market which typically attempts to extend single-issue, reverse auctions to the multi-issue case by post-auction haggling. There has been even less interest in many-to-many, multi-issue exchanges. This paper addresses that issue, and proposes an exchange trading agent architecture.

The generic architecture of an "information-based" agent is presented in Sec. 2 — this enables us in Sec. 2.1 to key the work presented here to previous work in bargaining [8], and auctions [7]. The integrity of the agent's information is in a permanent state of decay, Sec. 3 describes the agent's machinery for managing this decay leading to a characterization of the "value" of information. Sec. 4 describes metrics that bring order and structure to the agent's information with the aim of supporting its management. A version of the discrete, multi-issue double auction is proposed in Sec. 5. An agent is described in Sec. 6 that is based on the material in the previous sections, and is designed to trade using that mechanism. Sec. 7 concludes.

2 Information-Based Agent Architecture

The essence of "information-based agency" is described following. An agent observes events in its environment including what other agents actually do. It chooses to represent some of those observations in its world model as beliefs. As time passes, an agent may not be prepared to accept such beliefs as being "true", and qualifies those representations with epistemic probabilities. Those qualified representations of prior observations are the agent's *information*. This information is primitive — it is the agent's representation of its beliefs about prior events in the environment and about the other agents prior actions. It is independent of what the agent is trying to achieve, or what the agent believes the other agents are trying to achieve. Given this information, an agent may then choose to adopt goals and strategies. Those strategies may be based on game theory, for example. To enable the agent's strategies to make good use of its information, tools from information theory are applied to summarize and process that information. Such an agent is called *information-based*.

A generic information-based agent architecture is described so as to link this work on exchange agents together with related work on bargaining agents [8] and auction agents [7]. Following the description of the generic architecture, the "particularization" of it for bargaining, auctions and exchanges is given in Sec. 2.1.

An agent called Π is the subject of this discussion. Π engages in multi-issue negotiation with a set of other agents: $\{\Omega_1, \cdots, \Omega_o\}$. The foundation for Π's operation is the information that is generated both by and because of its negotiation exchanges. Any message from one agent to another reveals information about the sender. Π also acquires information from the environment — including general information sources — to support its actions. Π uses ideas from information theory to process and summarize its information. Π's aim may not be "utility optimization" — it may not be aware of a utility function. If Π *does* know its utility function *and* if it aims to optimize its utility

Fig. 1. Basic architecture of agent Π

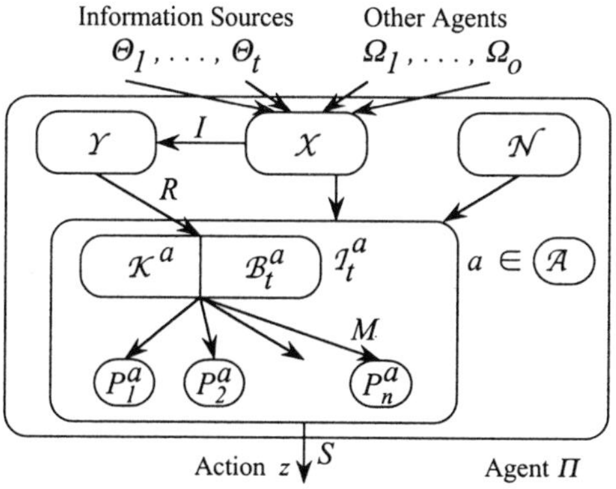

$then$ Π may apply the principles of game theory to achieve its aim. The information-based approach does not to reject utility optimization — in general, the selection of a goal and strategy is secondary to the processing and summarizing of the information.

In addition to the information derived from its opponents, Π has access to a set of information sources $\{\Theta_1, \cdots, \Theta_t\}$ that may include the marketplace in which trading takes place, and general information sources such as news-feeds accessed via the Internet. Together, Π, $\{\Omega_1, \cdots, \Omega_o\}$ and $\{\Theta_1, \cdots, \Theta_t\}$ make up a multiagent system. The integrity of Π's information, including information extracted from the Internet, will decay in time. The way in which this decay occurs will depend on the type of information, and on the source from which it was drawn. Little appears to be known about how the integrity of real information, such as news-feeds, decays, although its validity can often be checked — "Is company X taking over company Y?" — by proactive action given a cooperative information source Θ_j. So Π has to consider how and when to refresh its decaying information.

Π has two languages: C and $\mathcal{L}$. C is an illocutionary-based language for communication. $\mathcal{L}$ is a first-order language for internal representation — precisely it is a first-order language with sentence probabilities optionally attached to each sentence representing Π's epistemic belief in the truth of that sentence. Fig. 1 shows a high-level view of how Π operates. Messages expressed in C from $\{\Theta_i\}$ and $\{\Omega_i\}$ are received, time-stamped, source-stamped and placed in an *in-box* $\mathcal{X}$. The messages in $\mathcal{X}$ are then translated using an *import function* I into sentences expressed in $\mathcal{L}$ that have integrity decay functions (usually of time) attached to each sentence, they are stored in a *repository* $\mathcal{Y}$. And that is all that happens until Π triggers a goal.

Π triggers a goal in two ways: first in response to a message received from an opponent $\{\Omega_i\}$ "I'd like to purchase an apple from you", and second in response to some need, $\mathcal{N}$, "goodness, we've run out of coffee". Π's goals could be short-term such as obtaining some information "what is the time?", medium-term such as striking a deal with one of its opponents, or, rather longer-term such as building a (business) relationship with one of its opponents. For each goal that Π commits to, it has a mechanism for selecting a plan to achieve it. Π's plans reside in a plan library $\mathcal{A}$. Once a plan, a, has been activated, it extracts those sentences from the repository $\mathcal{Y}$ that are relevant to it, instantiates each of those sentences' integrity decay functions to the current time t, and selects a consistent sub-set of these sentences using its belief revision[1] function R. Those instantiated sentences that have no decay function are placed into the *knowledge base* $\mathcal{K}^a$, and those that have decay functions are placed along with their sentence probabilities into the *belief set* $\mathcal{B}_t^a$. $\mathcal{K}^a \cup \mathcal{B}_t^a = \mathcal{I}_t^a$ is the *information base* created by plan a at time t. Plan a then uses tools from information theory, including maximum entropy inference, M, to derive a set of probability distributions, $\{P_1^a, \cdots, P_n^a\}$, from $\mathcal{I}_t^a$. The way in which these derivations are performed are described in Sec. 2.2 following. Plan a implements some strategy S that uses the $\{P_1^a, \cdots, P_n^a\}$ to determine Π's action $z \in \mathcal{Z}$.

2.1 Π's Languages

The Internal Language $\mathcal{L}$. We describe three different applications of the generic architecture described above in Sec. 2. Each has its own internal language $\mathcal{L}$. For brevity we only describe the predicates in the distributions $\{P_i\}$.

[8] describes a multi-issue, bilateral bargaining agent Π, with just one opponent Ω, whose strategies are all based on the three distributions: $\mathbb{P}(\text{Acc}(\Pi, \Omega, \delta))$ for all deals δ [ie: the probability that Π should accept deal δ from agent Ω], $\mathbb{P}(\text{Acc}(\Omega, \Pi, \delta))$ for all deals δ [ie: Π's estimate of the probability that Ω would accept deal δ from agent Π], and $p_{b,\Omega}$ [ie: the probability of breakdown — the probability that Ω will "walk away" in the next negotiation round]. These three complete probability distributions are derived only from information in the signals received.

[7] describes multi-issue auctions where, for protocols with a truth telling dominant strategy, Π only constructs $\mathbb{P}(\text{Acc}(\Pi, \delta))$ [ie: the probability that Π should bid deal δ]. For protocols with equilibrium solutions that are expressed in terms of the number of bidders, Π also requires a probability distribution over the various possible number of bidders. From the auctioneer's point of view, the distribution $\mathbb{P}(\text{WinningBid}(\delta))$ [ie: the probability that δ will be the winning bid] is expressed analytically in terms of the number of bidders, and the size of the domain chosen to represent the various possible deals.

Here Π is trading in an exchange. As long as the exchange is liquid, the number of other agents engaged in buying or selling is not relevant, and Π effectively deals with just one "opponent" — the exchange. Π constructs probability distributions for the three predicates: $\Pi\text{Acc}(\delta)$ [Π believes that δ is a fair deal], $\Omega\text{Acc}(\delta)$ [Π believes that proposing deal δ to the exchange will be successful when it clears] and $\text{Panic}(\cdot)$ [Π believes that when the exchange next clears there will be a significant discontinuity in the settlement terms from previous terms].

The Communication Language $\mathcal{C}$. The communication language $\mathcal{C}$ contains the illocution particle set: $\iota = \{\text{Offer}, \text{Clear}, \text{Withdraw}\}$ with the following syntax and informal meaning (for brevity the particles for communicating with the $\{\Theta_i\}$ are not described):

---

[1] This belief revision — consistency checking — exercise is non-trivial, and is not described here. For sake of illustration only, the strategy "discard the old in favor of the new" is sufficient.

- Offer(Π, δ) Agent Π offers to trade deal $\delta = (\pi, \omega)$ with action commitments π for Π and ω for anyone accepting the trade through the exchange.
- Clear(Ω, Π, δ) Π's previously offered deal δ has cleared against a deal offered by agent Ω through the exchange.
- Withdraw(Π, δ) Agent Π withdraws the previously offered deal δ from the exchange.

2.2 Π's Reasoning

Once Π has selected a plan $a \in \mathcal{A}$ it uses maximum entropy inference to derive the $\{P_i^a\}_{i=1}^n$ [see Fig. 1] and minimum relative entropy inference to update those distributions as new data becomes available. *Entropy*, $\mathbb{H}$, is a measure of uncertainty [9] in a probability distribution for a discrete random variable X: $\mathbb{H}(X) \triangleq -\sum_i p(x_i) \log p(x_i)$ where $p(x_i) = \mathbb{P}(X = x_i)$. Maximum entropy inference is used to derive sentence probabilities for that which is not known by constructing the "maximally noncommittal" [10] probability distribution, and is chosen for its ability to generate complete distributions from sparse data.

Let $\mathcal{G}$ be the set of all positive ground literals that can be constructed using Π's language $\mathcal{L}$. A *possible world*, v, is a valuation function: $\mathcal{G} \rightarrow \{\top, \bot\}$. $\mathcal{V}|\mathcal{K}^a = \{v_i\}$ is the set of all possible worlds that are consistent with Π's knowledge base $\mathcal{K}^a$ that contains statements which Π believes are true. A *random world* for $\mathcal{K}^a$, $W|\mathcal{K}^a = \{p_i\}$ is a probability distribution over $\mathcal{V}|\mathcal{K}^a = \{v_i\}$, where p_i expresses Π's degree of belief that each of the possible worlds, v_i, is the actual world. The *derived sentence probability* of any $\sigma \in \mathcal{L}$, *with respect to* a random world $W|\mathcal{K}^a$ is:

$$(\forall \sigma \in \mathcal{L})\mathbb{P}_{\{W|\mathcal{K}^a\}}(\sigma) \triangleq \sum_n \{ p_n : \sigma \text{ is } \top \text{ in } v_n \} \tag{1}$$

The agent's *belief set* $\mathcal{B}_t^a = \{\beta_j\}_{j=1}^M$ contains statements to which Π attaches a *given sentence probability* $\mathbb{B}(.)$. A random world $W|\mathcal{K}^a$ is *consistent* with $\mathcal{B}_t^a$ if: $(\forall \beta \in \mathcal{B}_t^a)(\mathbb{B}(\beta) = \mathbb{P}_{\{W|\mathcal{K}^a\}}(\beta))$. Let $\{p_i\} = \{\overline{W}|\mathcal{K}^a, \mathcal{B}_t^a\}$ be the "maximum entropy probability distribution over $\mathcal{V}|\mathcal{K}^a$ that is consistent with $\mathcal{B}_t^a$". Given an agent with $\mathcal{K}^a$ and $\mathcal{B}_t^a$, *maximum entropy inference* states that the *derived sentence probability* for any sentence, $\sigma \in \mathcal{L}$, is:

$$(\forall \sigma \in \mathcal{L})\mathbb{P}_{\{\overline{W}|\mathcal{K}^a, \mathcal{B}_t^a\}}(\sigma) \triangleq \sum_n \{ p_n : \sigma \text{ is } \top \text{ in } v_n \} \tag{2}$$

From Eqn. 2, each belief imposes a linear constraint on the $\{p_i\}$.

Given a prior probability distribution $\underline{q} = (q_i)_{i=1}^n$ and a set of constraints C, the *principle of minimum relative entropy* chooses the posterior probability distribution $\underline{p} = (p_i)_{i=1}^n$ that has the least *relative entropy*[2] with respect to $\underline{q}$:

$$\{\underline{W}|\underline{q}, C\} \triangleq \arg\min_{\underline{p}} D(\{p_i\} \| \{q_i\}) = \arg\min_{\underline{p}} \sum_{i=1}^n p_i \log \frac{p_i}{q_i}$$

---

[2] Otherwise called *cross entropy* or the *Kullback-Leibler* distance between the two probability distributions.

182

and that satisfies the constraints. This may be found by introducing Lagrange multipliers as above. Given a prior distribution q over $\{v_i\}$ — the set of all possible worlds, and a set of constraints C (that could have been derived as above from a set of new beliefs) *minimum relative entropy inference* states that the derived sentence probability for any sentence, $\sigma \in \mathcal{L}$, is:

$$(\forall \sigma \in \mathcal{L})\mathbb{P}_{\{\underline{W}|q,C\}}(\sigma) \triangleq \sum_n \{\, p_n \, : \, \sigma \text{ is } \top \text{ in } v_n \,\} \qquad (3)$$

where $\{p_i\} = \{\underline{W}|q, C\}$. The principle of minimum relative entropy is a generalization of the principle of maximum entropy. If the prior distribution q is uniform, then the relative entropy of p with respect to q, $p\|q$, differs from $-\mathbb{H}(p)$ only by a constant. So the principle of maximum entropy is equivalent to the principle of minimum relative entropy with a uniform prior distribution.

3 Managing Information Integrity

Exchanges and clearing houses themselves generate large amounts of information although the identity of traders is at least partially concealed in the majority of stock exchanges. These institutions, particularly the continuously-clearing exchanges, rely on the availability of substantial liquidity — ie: they only survive if there are sufficient numbers of buyers and sellers to make them work. An agent trading on an exchange can expect to find itself in a dynamic, information-rich environment. The way in which Π manages its information in such an environment is now discussed.

Π's information base $\mathcal{I}_t^a$ contains sentences in first-order logic each with a sentence probability, $\mathbb{B}(\cdot)$, representing the agent's strength of belief in the truth of that statement. Maintaining the integrity of $\mathcal{I}_t^a$ is not just a matter of looking up information. Information may be temporarily unavailable, acquiring it may cost money, the information may be inherently unreliable, and its availability may be beyond the control of the agent. For example, if a chunk of information represents the action of another agent then that information can only be refreshed when the other agent acts. In a stock exchange, information such as current clearing price of stocks is likely to be available constantly and accurately. Information such as who will pay how much for what is unlikely to be available unless a trade is observed. Corporate information is generally only released spasmodically in official announcements[3].

3.1 Updating the probability distributions

Π's plans are partly driven by the probability distributions $\{P_1^a, \cdots, P_n^a\}$ in Fig. 1. These distributions are derived from the information in the repository $\mathcal{Y}$. The integrity of the information in $\mathcal{Y}$ will decay in accordance with the decay functions — unless it is refreshed. As the integrity decays, the entropy of the distributions $\{P_1^a, \cdots, P_n^a\}$ increases.

---

[3] For example, the ASX — the Australian Stock Exchange — places requirements on corporations to release (potentially) market sensitive information which is then propagated to subscribers through its "Signal G" distribution channels.

Suppose that $\mathcal{L}$ contains a unary predicate, $A(\cdot)$, whose domain is represented by the finite set of logical constants $\{c_i\}_{i=1}^d$. At time t let $p_i^t = \mathbb{B}\left(A(c_i)\right)$ for $i = 1, \cdots, d$. As time t increases *either* no information is received and the entropy of (p_i^t) should increase, *or* information is received and the distribution (p_i^t) should be refreshed. If no information is received, a geometric decay to (maximum entropy) ignorance is achieved by:

$$p_i^{t+1} = \rho \cdot p_i^t + (1-\rho) \cdot \frac{1}{d} \tag{4}$$

for a decay factor $\rho \in [0,1]$ whose value depends on the meaning of $A(\cdot)$.

Now suppose that at time t, Π receives a message from source Θ that asserts the truth of $A(c_k)$, and suppose that Π decides to attach the given sentence probability $g(\Theta)$ to $\mathbb{B}(A(c_k))$, where the value $g(\Theta)$ is Π's confidence in Θ's advice. Then the updated distribution is calculated by applying *minimum relative entropy inference*:

$$\left(p_j^t\right)_{j=1}^d = \arg\min_{\underline{b}} \sum_{i=1}^d b_i \log \frac{b_i}{p_i^{t-1}}$$

satisfying the constraint: $p_k^t = g(\Theta)$, and where $\underline{b} = (b_j)_{j=1}^d$. That is, the new distribution is the closest[4] to the previous one that satisfies the constraint. But, this depends on Π knowing $g(\Theta)$, ie: the strength of belief that Π allocates to Θ's information. The issue here is not, for example, forecasting the clearing price of a stock, it is estimating the confidence that Π has in the integrity of Θ's information. If Π can confirm the validity of Θ's advice *ex post* then a very simple way of estimating $g(\Theta)$ is by:

$$g_{\text{new}}(\Theta) = \begin{cases} \nu \cdot g_{\text{old}}(\Theta) + (1-\nu) & \text{each time } \Theta \text{ is proved correct} \\ \nu \cdot g_{\text{old}}(\Theta) & \text{each time } \Theta \text{ is proved incorrect} \end{cases}$$

for a learning rate $\nu \in [0,1]$.

3.2 Valuing Information

A chunk of information is valued only by the way that it enables Π to do something[5]. So information is valued in relation to the plans that Π is executing. A plan, a, is designed in the context of a particular representation, or environment, e. One way in which a chunk of information assists Π is by altering one of a's distributions $\{P_i^a\}$ — see Fig. 1. As a chunk of information could be "good" for one distribution and "bad" for another, the appropriate way to value information is by its effect on each distribution. For a plan a, the *value* to a of a message received at time t is the resulting decrease in entropy in a's distributions $\{P_i^a\}$ in Fig. 1. In general, suppose that a set of stamped messages $X = \{x_i\}$ is imported by plan a to the information base $\mathcal{I}_t^a$ where they are represented as the set of statements $D = \{d_i\} = R(I(X))$, where I is the import

---

[4] Precisely, it is the distribution that minimizes the Kullback-Leibler distance from the prior distribution, (p_i^{t-1}), whilst satisfying the given constraint.

[5] That is we do not try to attach any intrinsic value to information.

function and R the belief revision function. The *information* in D at time t with respect to a particular P_i^a, plan a and environment e is:

$$\mathbb{I}(D \mid P_i^a(\mathcal{I}_t^a), a, e) \triangleq \mathbb{H}(P_i^a(\mathcal{I}_t^a)) - \mathbb{H}(P_i^a(\mathcal{I}_t^a \cup D)) \quad \text{for } i = 1, \cdots, n$$

where the argument of the $P_i^a(\cdot)$ is the state of Π's information base from which P_i^a was derived. And we define the information in the set of messages X (at time t with respect to a particular P_i^a, a and e) to be the information in $D = R(I(X))$. It is reasonable to aggregate the information in D over the distributions used by a. That is, the information in D at time t with respect to plan a and environment e is:

$$\mathbb{I}(D \mid a, e) \triangleq \sum_i \mathbb{I}(D \mid P_i^a(\mathcal{I}_t^a), a, e)$$

and to aggregate again over all plans to obtain the (potential) information in a statement. That is, the *potential information* in D with respect to environment e is:

$$\mathbb{I}(D \mid e) \triangleq \sum_{a \in A} \mathbb{I}(D \mid a, e) \tag{5}$$

4 Structure of the Information Base $\mathcal{I}_t^a$

A structure is overlaid on $\mathcal{I}_t^a$. This structure aims to provide the basis for the proactive acquisition of information. As the belief that the agent holds in a chunk of information tends away from "true" or "false" towards the maximum entropy value, the integrity of that chunk should be refreshed. This structure enables Π to "survey" its information base and to identify areas that require attention.

$\mathcal{I}_t^a$ consists of sentences in first-order typed predicate logic together with sentence probabilities. Here we assume that these sentences are all Horn clauses. Using the usual notation and terminology for Horn clauses, given a clause c and a set of substitutions J, let $c(S_J(\cdot))$ denote the result of applying J to the variables in c. Then c subsumes $c(S_J(\cdot))$, and c is "equivalent to, or more general than" or "no less general than" $c(S_J(\cdot))$. The substitution operation S defines a partial ordering, $\geq_S$, on the set of all clauses.

4.1 Structure of Unit Clauses in $\mathcal{I}_t^a$

Without loss of generality we assume that the unit clauses in $\mathcal{I}_t^a$ are all positive literals — a "false" clause will then have a sentence probability of 0. Given two positive unit clauses, c_1 and c_2, both with the same predicate symbol, denote the unification of those two literals by $c_1 \cap c_2$, and the anti-unification[6] by $c_1 \cup c_2$. Given a set C of positive literals that is closed with respect to unification and anti-unification, C is a non-modular lattice where unification and anti-unification are the meet and join respectively. Given an isotone valuation v on the vertices of a lattice, the function:

$$d_1(c_1, c_2) = v[c_1] - v[c_2]$$

---

[6] The anti-unification of two positive literals is the unique literal that subsumes both of them and of all such literals is minimal with respect to the partial order $\geq_S$.

is a measure of how much "more general" c_1 is compared with c_2. The function:

$$d_2(c_1, c_2) = \begin{cases} 0 & \text{if } c_1 \text{ or } c_2 = c_1 \cap c_2 \\ v[c_1 \cup c_2] - v[c_1 \cap c_2] & \text{otherwise} \end{cases}$$

is a measure of the "distance" between c_1 and c_2. The function:

$$d_3(c_1, c_2) = v[c_1 \cup c_2] - v[c_2]$$

is a measure of how much more "novel" c_1 is compared with c_2. Another possibility is $v[c_1] - v[c_1 \cap c_2]$ but that is not so useful when the intersection is likely to be empty — ie: at the "bottom" of the lattice — if $c_2 \geq_S c_1$ then $d_3(c_1, c_2) = 0$. Suppose that B is any subset of the set of vertices, given a vertex c, then: $d_i(c, B) = \min_{s \in B} d_i(c, s)$ for $i = 1, 2, 3$, are generalizations of the three measures above.

Π may use the "more general than", "distance from" and "more novel than" measures described above to manage its unit clauses as long as it has a suitable isotone valuation. Two such valuations are now described.

An information-based valuation. Given a statement $d \in \mathcal{I}_t^a$, $d = (\mathbb{B}(c) = g)$ where c is a unit clause. The function $v[c] = \mathbb{I}(\{d\} \mid e)$ is an isotone valuation on the lattice of unit clauses. This valuation function enables Π to strategically refresh the integrity of potentially valuable chunks of information. This may then enable Π to "discover" opportunities.

A resolution-based valuation. Another isotone valuation is defined is defined in terms of the Herbrand Universe. Let H_e be the Herbrand Universe for a given environment e — the Herbrand Universe is determined by the representation e. Suppose c is a unit clause expressed in terms of the variables and constants in e. Let c/H_e be the set of ground unit clauses obtained by instantiating a unit clause c in all possible ways (subject to the type constraints of the logic) over H_e. The ground unit clauses in the set c/H_e are all unifiable with the clause c. Then define $\lambda_e(c) = $ "the number of clauses in c/H_e". λ_e is also an isotone valuation.[7]

4.2   Structure of Non-Unit Clauses in $\mathcal{I}_t^a$

The definition of potential information given in Eqn. 5 applies to *any* set of statements $D \in \mathcal{I}_t^a$. The basis for a view of the structure of non-unit clauses is to consider such a clause simply as a way of deriving the sentence probability for instantiations of its head literal given that sentence probabilities for instantiations of its body literals are known — which they always are as, even in the total absence of information, the sentence probability for a ground instance of any literal is assumed to be its maximum entropy value. In this way, a structure for non-unit Horn clauses is defined by the head literal alone,

---

[7] If the environment e contains function symbols then the Herbrand Universe is unbounded. If H_e is restricted to some fixed artificial function nesting depth then the size of c/H_e will be finite over that restricted Universe, and λ_e will be finite.

by using the information-based valuation function, and the three functions, $\{d_i(\cdot)\}_{i=1}^3$, described in Sec. 4.1.

As a simple illustration of how all this works, consider a simple rule for pairs trading[8] that states "*if* the market has not dropped *and* stock X has gained less that 5%, *and* stock Y has gained more than 10% *then* stock X will gain more than 5% (all gains being in some time period)". Suppose that the environment, e, contains the following set of four logical constants to represent "gain": $\{(-\infty, 0), [0, 5], (5, 10], (10, \infty)\}$[9]. Then this rule becomes:

$$\text{XWillGain}(y) \leftarrow \text{MarketHasGained}(m), \text{XHasGained}(x), \text{YHasGained}((10, \infty)),$$
$$m \neq (-\infty, 0), x = (-\infty, 0) \text{ or } [0, 5], y = (5, 10] \text{ or } (10, \infty)$$

where all quantities are per cent. This sentence is represented as a belief in $\mathcal{B}_t^a$ with a sentence probability of, say, 0.8. This belief becomes a constraint on the set of possible worlds, and $\{\overline{W} | \{\mathcal{K}^a, \mathcal{B}_t^a\}$ will be consistent with it. Then Eqn. 2 is used to derive values for the probability distribution $\mathbb{P}(\text{XWillGain}(\cdot))$ using maximum entropy inference. And then that probability distribution may trigger an attempt by Π to trade in stock X.

5 Discrete Double Auctions

In a discrete-time institution all traders move in a single step from initial allocation to final allocation — in a continuous-time institution exchange is permitted at any moment during a trading period [1]. [11] discusses preference elicitation in a combinatorial [multi-item] exchange with a single-issue.

An exchange mechanism has to do two things: first to match buyers and sellers and second to determine the terms for settlement — in a conventional single-issue exchange those terms are the clearing price. A good mechanism will also do this in a way that optimizes the outcome in some sense. There are two general frameworks: first when the exchange clears at a uniform, non-discriminatory price, and second when traders are paired up, perhaps in an attempt to achieve Pareto optimality, and each pays a different price. We use the standard method of dispensing with lot size by assuming that all lots are of unit size — a trader wishing to trade in amounts greater than unity simply submits multiple bids, and so may have to be content with a partially fulfilled order.

In the single-issue, uniform case there is little choice in matching buyers with sellers. If all bids and asks are arranged together in an ascending sequence, $s_{(1)}, s_{(2)}, \cdots$, then any clearing price in the interval $[s_{(m)}, s_{(m+1)}]$ will do where m is the number of bids[10]. But selecting the clearing price in this way means that a utility optimizing agent will play strategically, although this behavior tends to truth-telling as the number

---

[8] The trading tactic "pairs trading" considers two stocks with similar backgrounds — the idea being that if the two stocks are similar then the movement of their clearing prices should be similar.

[9] The choice of intervals to represent a continuous variable is made so as to respect Watt's Assumption — see [7] for a discussion.

[10] If the supply and demand functions cross then they will do so between $s_{(m)}$ and $s_{(m+1)}$.

Fig. 2. Examples showing that a discriminatory mechanism can not satisfy all of the four basic properties in general. An 'x' denotes a bid, and an 'o' denotes an ask,

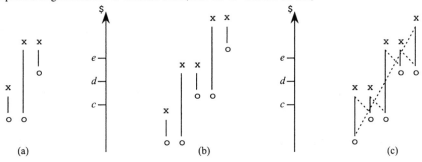

of traders increases [12]. If the clearing price is the mean of the marginal bid and the marginal ask then the mechanisms is known as a *half double auction*. [13] describes a truth-telling, dominant strategy, single-issue, uniform-price mechanism that, somewhat reminiscent of the Vickrey auction, determines the clearing price as the mean of the lowest unsuccessful ask and highest unsuccessful bid. However that mechanism is not Pareto efficient, and trade can be lost, again, this defect becomes less significant as the number of traders increases. There is no perfect mechanism.

The result in [12] is for single issue exchanges, and assumes that the buyers' and sellers' preferences are complementary — ie: what is preferred by one is not preferred by the other. This assumption is reasonable when the single issue is money. [11] approaches the problem of clearing multi-item, combinatorial exchanges using preference elicitation. Here we are interested in multi-issue exchanges for which the preferences are complementary for each individual issue[11], but agents may differ in the relative importance that they place on the issues. So an agent may conclude: "with my situation as it is, in today's market I will aim for a deal with high x and y, and low z — but tomorrow it could all be different".

In a multi-issue exchange, the mechanism will necessarily in general be discriminatory. Desirable properties that a discriminatory exchange mechanism may have are:

1. the matching is Pareto efficient;
2. the matching for any subset of bids and asks satisfies the property that it is not possible to interchange the pairing in two of the matched pairs in the subset so that the length of the "longest" link in the subset is shortened;
3. the mechanism is budget balancing, and
4. the settlement terms for two identical bids or asks are the same.

The first two properties concern the matching, and the last two the settlement. Unfortunately, it is impossible to satisfy all of these four properties in general. Figure 2 shows three single-issue examples to illustrate this.

---

[11] This assumption is particularly useful for issues with a total preference ordering because the number of possible worlds is then a linear function of the domain size. Without such an ordering it is an exponential function.

The matching in Figure 2(a) is the only Pareto efficient matching — it also satisfies the second property. But it can not also satisfy both the third and fourth. If the two lowest asks clear at $c, the highest ask at $e, the two highest bids at $e, and the lowest bid at $c, with the exchange pocketing the difference, $(e - c)$, for the central matching, then this satisfies property 4 but violates property 3. The standard non-discriminatory, half-double-auction mechanism will only clear the two highest bids with the two lowest asks at price $d. So Figure 2(a) shows that it is impossible for a mechanism to satisfy properties 1, 3 and 4. Figure 2(b) is constructed by duplicating the structure in Figure 2(a). It illustrates the same point but this time the exchange will pocket the difference on two of the trades if the fourth property is to be satisfied.

The solid line matching in Figure 2(c) is the only matching that satisfies the first two properties. This example illustrates the conflict between the second and the fourth properties. The broken line matching illustrates the folly in an over-zealous attempt to satisfy the fourth property by matching identical pair with identical pair. This then leads to a violation of the second property. In case (c) the standard non-discriminatory mechanism will only clear the three highest bids with the three lowest asks at price $d. Following the results for single-issue, non-discriminatory mechanisms ([12], [13]) we do not attempt to achieve a truth-telling dominant strategy mechanism — capturing the notion of "lowest unsuccessful ask" and "highest unsuccessful bid" will at best be obscure. The examples in Figure 2 show that property 4 is a nuisance. So we abandon property 4, and aim for a Pareto efficient, "close" matching that is budget balancing.

Suppose that a deal, δ, contains s issues $(\delta_1, \cdots, \delta_s)$. If a trader's preferences are for lower values of each of these parameters individually then he is a *buyer*, and for higher values a *seller*. A seller submits an ask $\underline{a} = (a_0, \cdots, a_s)$ and a buyer submits a bid $\underline{b} = (b_0, \cdots, b_s)$. Ask $\underline{a}$ and bid $\underline{b}$ are *compatible*, $C(\underline{a}, \underline{b})$, if $\forall i(a_i \leq b_i)$. To satisfy property 2 the mechanism requires a distance measure between a pair of bids and asks. This can be achieved by the exchange publishing a utility function, $u(\cdot)$, and defining $|a - b| \triangleq u(b) - u(a)$. No single function will satisfy everybody, but it is in the exchange's interest to appear to do the best it can. To construct the solution we start with any Pareto matching, and repeatedly interchange pairings in line with the statement of property 2 (a non-trivial exercise as property 2 is recursive), and then define the settlement terms for each match to be simply the ask — and so property 4 is satisfied for asks but not for bids. But this may not work, because although each bid and ask defines a hyper-cube of potential matches in s-space they may "miss" each other. This is addressed by traders to submitting "clouds" of bids or asks, where a *cloud* is a set from which one only may be chosen by the matching mechanism. This further increases the complexity of the matching problem.

6 An Exchange Agent

Each time the multi-issue call market described above clears the traders will see the settlement terms $(x_1, \cdots, x_s)$ for each match. This data can be expected to be moderately sparse in s-space. Π uses this, and other, data to do two separate things — the following description is from the point of view of Π acting as a buyer. First, for each possible bid, $\underline{b} = (b_1, \cdots, b_s)$ Π estimates the probability $\mathbb{P}(\Omega\mathrm{Acc}(\underline{b}))$ that $\underline{b}$ will clear in the exchange. Second, Π estimates the probability $\mathbb{P}(\Pi\mathrm{Acc}(\underline{b}))$ that Π will be prepared to place a bid $\underline{b}$. The first of these is expected to rise as each b_i increases and the second to fall — conversely if Π is a seller. Π then plays these two distributions against each other in deciding what to do.

The calculation of this apparently massive quantity of probabilities from sparse data of decaying integrity is simplified by three things. First, Π is based on logic in which a multi-issue bid or ask is simply another logical constant. Second, the agent employs maximum entropy inference that neatly "fills in the gaps" in the data with the "maximally non-committal" model. Third, the assumption of complete and complementary preference orderings for each separate issue reduces the complexity of the calculations considerably.

The estimation of $\mathbb{P}(\Omega\mathrm{Acc}(\underline{b}))$ involves forecasting trends in the exchange. This problem is addressed by time-series forecasting [14], and indeed by common sense following the occurrence of unexpected events — captured by applying unstructured data mining to news feeds — thus increasing $\mathbb{P}(\mathrm{Panic}(\cdot))$. Setting these issues aside, in a liquid exchange when the unexpected does not occur, the clearance data, with sentence probabilities discounted in time towards their maximum entropy value, should give reasonable estimates of $\mathbb{P}(\Omega\mathrm{Acc}(\underline{b}))$. When instantiated at any particular time a chunk of data is a point in s-space together with a sentence probability. Each of these forms a single constraint on the distribution which is found by applying maximum entropy inference using Eqn. 2. The arrival of new data can then *either* be accommodated by recalculating $\mathbb{P}(\Omega\mathrm{Acc}(\underline{b}))$ all over again using Eqn. 2, *or* by updating the distribution using minimum relative entropy inference and Eqn. 3.

The estimation of $\mathbb{P}(\Pi\mathrm{Acc}(\underline{b}))$ is Π's version of a utility function. Although here Π is asking "how confident am I in the supporting evidence to do such-and-such". That is, Π is *not* necessarily asking "what is the utility of such-and-such a deal". The estimation of $\mathbb{P}(\Pi\mathrm{Acc}(\underline{b}))$ depends in particular on what Π is attempting to trade. The criteria that Π applies to a bid for "10 tons of grade C steel to be delivered by Friday-week" may not be the same as for "100 cases of Chateau Kangaroo red wine" — in the latter case the integrity of information concerning the quality of the cellaring may be crucial. An approach to estimating $\mathbb{P}(\Pi\mathrm{Acc}(\cdot))$ based on a Bayesian net is described in [8], and a method using maximum entropy inference in [7].

How Π proposes a cloud of deals will depend on its strategy, S. However Π has three powerful probability distributions for S to use. $\mathbb{P}(\mathrm{Panic}(\cdot))$ estimates the probability of discontinuities. Given some confidence value α, solving $\mathbb{P}(\Pi\mathrm{Acc}(\underline{b})) \approx \alpha$ for $\underline{b}$ gives a hyper-plane of "acceptable" deals to confidence α. Similarly, $\mathbb{P}(\Omega\mathrm{Acc}(\underline{b})) \approx \beta$[12] gives a hyper-plane of deals that should succeed with expectation β. A simple strategy is to select values for α and β, then if the intersection of these two hyper-planes is non-empty this gives a cloud of bids.

---

[12] The distribution $\mathbb{P}(\Omega\mathrm{Acc}(\underline{b}))$ as described above is the probability of a single trade. If an agent wish to place an order for n multiple items then it may either construct the distribution $\mathbb{P}(\Omega\mathrm{Acc}(n, \underline{b}))$, meaning the probability of n successful trades at offered terms $\underline{b}$, or represent n as one of the issues. Further if an agent's requirements are even more intricate, such as conditional trades, then a suitable variant of $\mathbb{P}(\Omega\mathrm{Acc}(\cdot))$ is required.

190

7 Discussion

A multi-issue discrete exchange, and an agent that can trade in it, have been proposed. This proposal is based on the assumption that the preferences of all agents over the individual issues are known, and that they divide the agents into two sets, buyers and sellers, where buyers and sellers have strictly complementary preferences. The business of clearing the exchange is computationally complex, and relies on the exchange publishing an acceptable distance measure between an ask and a bid. All of this does not appear to be infeasible. Future work will address the computational complexity of the proposed solution, and will evaluate the system empirically. However this begs the question: is there a need for such an exchange? With the inherently multi-issue nature of business negotiation, including e-procurement, the answer may be "yes".

References

1. Friedman, D.: The double auction market institution: A survey. In Friedman, D., Rust, J., eds.: The Double Auction Market: Institutions, Theories and Evidence. Addison-Wesley, Reading, MA (1993) 3 – 26
2. Kambil, A., Heck, E.V.: Making Markets: How Firms Can Design and Profit from Online Auctions and Exchanges. Harvard Business School Press (2002)
3. Forsythe, R., Rietz, T., Ross, T.: Wishes, expectations and actions: A survey on price formation in election stock markets. The Journal of Economic Behavior and Organization **39** (1999) 83 – 110
4. Varian, H.: Effect of the internet on financial markets. (1998)
5. Faratin, P., Sierra, C., Jennings, N.: Using similarity criteria to make issue trade-offs in automated negotiation. Journal of Artificial Intelligence **142** (2003) 205–237
6. Fatima, S., Wooldridge, M., Jennings, N.R.: An agenda-based framework for multi-issue negotiation. Artificial Intelligence **152** (2004) 1 – 45
7. Debenham, J.: Auctions and bidding with information. In Faratin, P., Rodriguez-Aguilar, J., eds.: Proceedings Agent-Mediated Electronic Commerce VI: AMEC. (2004) 15 – 28
8. Debenham, J.: Bargaining with information. In Jennings, N., Sierra, C., Sonenberg, L., Tambe, M., eds.: Proceedings Third International Conference on Autonomous Agents and Multi Agent Systems AAMAS-2004, ACM (2004) 664 – 671
9. MacKay, D.: Information Theory, Inference and Learning Algorithms. Cambridge University Press (2003)
10. Jaynes, E.: Probability Theory — The Logic of Science. Cambridge University Press (2003)
11. Smith, T., Sandholm, T., Simmons, R.: Constructing and clearing combinatorial exchanges using preference elicitation. In: proceedings AAAI Workshop on Preferences in AI and CP: Symbolic Approaches, AAAI (2002) 87 – 93
12. Rustichini, A., Satterthwaite, M., Williams, S.: Convergence to efficiency in a simple market with incomplete information. Econometrica **62** (1994) 1041 – 1063
13. Preston McAfee, R.: A dominant strategy double auction. Journal of Economic Theory **56** (1992) 266 – 293
14. Chatfield, C.: The Analysis of Time Series. 6th edn. Chapman and Hall (2003)

An Agent-Based Approach to ANN Training

Ireneusz Czarnowski and Piotr Jędrzejowicz

Department of Information Systems, Gdynia Maritime University

Morska 83, 81-225 Gdynia, Poland

E-mail: {irek, pj}@am.gdynia.pl

Abstract

In this paper a team of agents applied to train a feed-forward artificial neural networks is proposed, implemented and experimentally evaluated. The approach is based on a new variant of the A-Team architecture. Each agent member of the team is executing its own simple training procedure and it is expected that the whole team demonstrates complex collective behavior. The paper includes a description of the proposed approach and presents the results of the experiment involving benchmark datasets. The results show that the approach could be considered as a competitive training tool.

1 Introduction

Artificial neural networks (ANN) are, nowadays, being used for solving a wide variety of real-life problems like, for example, pattern recognition, prediction, control, combinatorial optimization or classification. Main advantages of the approach include ability to tolerate imprecision and uncertainty and still achieving tractability, robustness, and low cost in practical applications. Since training a neural network for practical application is often very time consuming, an extensive research work is being carried in order to accelerate this process. Another problem with ANN training methods is danger of being caught in a local optimum. Hence, researchers look not only for algorithms that train neural networks quickly but rather for quick algorithms that are not likely, or less likely, to get trapped in a local optimum [1, 7, 13, 14].

Recently, the authors have proposed to apply to the ANN training the parallel population learning algorithm denoted as PLANN [2, 3, 4]. It has proven to be a successful tool for many benchmark instances producing high quality classifiers in a reasonable time.

In this paper we propose an extension of the PLANN-based approach, extending it into an agent based architecture with a view to further improve ANN training process in both critical dimensions - training time and a classifier performance. The paper is organized as follows. Section 2 contains formulation of the artificial neural network training problem. The following section includes main assumptions and a description of the proposed team of agents architecture, designed to train feed-forward artificial neural networks. Section 4 presents the results of the computational experiment carried to validate the approach. Finally, in the last section some conclusions are drawn and directions for further research are suggested.

2   ANN Training Problem

ANN training involves finding a set of weights of links between neurons such that the network generates a desired output signals. Training process is considered as adjusting values of these weights using a set of training patterns showing the desired ANN behaviour. In other words, given a set of training patterns consisting of input-output pairs $\{(u_1, d_1), (u_2, d_2), \ldots, (u_n, d_n)\}$ and an error function $e = (W, U, D)$, training process aims at minimizing learning error $E(W)$:

$$E(W) = \min_W \sum_{i=1}^{n} e(W, u_i, d_i), \tag{1}$$

where W is a set of the respective weights, U - is a set of inputs and D - a set of outputs.

One of the commonly used measures (error functions) is the squared-error function in which $e(W, u_i, d_i) = (d_i - f(u_i, W))^2$, where $f(u_i, W)$ represents an ANN response for input u_i, and weights W [15].

A quality of the ANN training algorithm or method can be assessed through evaluation of errors produced by the trained ANN on a given set of test patterns. In this paper the error rate calculated using the 10-cross-validation approach is used as a metric for such an evaluation.

Finding an optimal set of weights of links between neurons corresponds to solving a non-linear numerical optimisation problem. More precisely, the problem at hand can to be considered as the unconstrained non-linear minimization problem with the objective function defined by (1) and with the search space defined by the domain of the weights. Such problems, in general, are computationally hard and a chance of finding the optimum solution, especially when using gradient-based techniques, is minimal [1]. Since neural networks are applied to solving many real-life, non-trivial problems, including classification and image recognition, therefore searching for a more effective global minimization algorithms that may improve ANN performance is an important and lively research field.

3   PLANN-Team for the ANN Training

3.1   PLANN-Team Architecture and Functions

Recently, a number of agent-based approaches have been proposed to solve different types of optimization problems [12]. One of the successful approaches to agent-based optimization is the concept of A-Teams. An A-Team is composed of simple agents that demonstrate complex collective behavior.

The A-Team architecture was originally developed by Talukdar [16]. A-Teams have proven to be successful in addressing hard optimization problems where no dominant algorithm exists. Within the A-Team multiple agents achieve an implicit cooperation by sharing a population of solutions. The design of the A-Team architecture was motivated by other architectures used for optimization including blackboard systems and genetic algorithms. In fact, the A-Team infrastructure could be used to implement most aspects of these other architectures. The advantage of the A-Team architecture is that it combines a population of solutions with domain specific algorithms and limited agent interaction.

According to [16] an A-Team is a problem solving architecture in which the agents are autonomous and co-operate by modifying one another's trial solutions. These solutions circulate continually. An A-Team can be also defined as a set of agents and a set of memories, forming a network in which every agent is in a closed loop.

An asynchronous team (A-Team) is a strongly cyclic computational network. Results are circulated through this network by software agents. The number of agents can be arbitrarily large and the agents may be distributed over an arbitrarily wide area. Agents cooperate by working on one another's results. Each agent is completely autonomous (it decides which results it is going to work on and when). Results that are not being worked on accumulate in common memories to form populations. Randomization (the effects of chance) and destruction (the elimination of weak results) play key roles in determining what happens to the populations.

A-Team architecture allows a lot of freedom with respect to designing procedures for communication between agents and shared memories and as well as creation and removal of individuals (solution) from common memories. In this paper an approach to constructing a dedicated team of agents denoted as a PLANN-Team is proposed and validated. The approach makes use of the idea which has been conceived for the population learning algorithm [3, 8]. An effective search for solution of the computationally hard problems requires a cocktail of methods applied to a population of solutions, with more advanced procedures being applied only to a more promising population members. Designing and implementing a PLANN-Team is seen as an extension of the range of the available ANN training tools.

The proposed approach differs from a swarm intelligence based solutions which have been also applied to the ANN training (see for example [17]). Agents within a swarm intelligence system co-operate to construct or find a solution. A single agent might not, however, be capable of constructing it, while a typical agent - member of the A-Team, is a complete optimization procedure able to find at least a local optimum solution.

The proposed PLANN-Team includes a set of agents and a shared memory of the blackboard type. This memory is supervised by a *supervisory agent* whose tasks include taking care of communication within the PLANN-Team using some communication protocol, like for example PVM. Architecture of the system is shown in Figure 1.

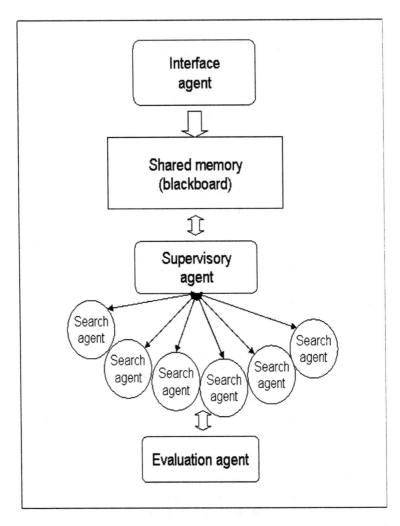

Figure 1: PLANN-Team architecture

Shared memory of the PLANN-Team is used to store a population of solutions to the ANN training problem. These solutions are called individuals. A solution is a vector of real numbers representing weights of connections between neurons of the network under training.

To initialize the PLANN-Team a number of randomly generated individuals known as the initial population should be stored in the shared memory. The initial population size is a parameter set by the user through the *interface agent*. Its role is to generate the initial population assuring feasibility of each individual as well as its conformity with the user requirements as to the population size, lower and upper bounds on value of weights and a number of vector elements.

Once the initial population has been generated and stored in the shared memory the supervisory agent can trigger the process of ANN training. This is the task of parallel, independent and autonomous agents called *search agents*. The proposed team of search agents consists of a number of autonomous and asynchronous agents of n kinds, where n is a number of learning and improvement procedures employed. A number of agents of each kind is not limited and depends on the availability of computational resources. There is, however an identical number of search agents of each kind within a population of agents. Each search agent acts independently executing a sequence of computation steps. A single computation step for a search agent includes the following:

- Sending a request to the supervisory agent who replies by sending a single, randomly chosen, individual from the shared memory.

- Executing the improvement procedure upon thus drawn individual.

- Returning the improved individual to the supervisory agent.

While executing their improvement procedures, search agents are using services of the *evaluation agent* whose solely task is to calculate the value of the quality metric, that is the error rate for the given vector of weights. Supervisory agent, upon receiving an improved individual from the search agent, replaces the worst individual from the shared memory with the received one providing it is better then the worst one.

Computation length is controlled by the user through allocating to each search agent a number of requests it is allowed to send to the supervisory agent. Computation stop when all agents have used all the allowed requests. Within the proposed approach main idea of the PLA, which is using more computationally complex improvement procedures as a number of individuals within the population of solutions decreases is, indirectly, preserved. Search agents executing more computationally complex improvement procedures would be getting rights to send a smaller number of requests then agents executing less complex procedures.

After all agents have submitted all their requests the best solution in the shared memory is considered as a final one.

3.2 PLANN-Team Search Agents

The PLANN-Team employs 5 kinds of the search agent:

- standard mutation [11],

- local search,

- non-uniform mutation [11],

- gradient mutation,

- gradient adjustment operator.

The standard mutation agent modifies an individual by generating new values of two randomly selected elements in an individual. If the fitness function value has improved then the change is accepted.

The local search agent exchanges values between two randomly selected elements within an individual. If the fitness function value of an individual has improved, then the change is accepted.

The non-uniform mutation agent acts through modifying an individual by repeatedly adjusting value of the randomly selected element (in this case a real number) until the fitness function value has improved or until nine consecutive improvements have been attempted unsuccessfully. The value of the adjustment is calculated as:

$$\Delta(t, y) = y \left(1 - r^{\left(1 - \frac{t}{T}\right) \cdot r}\right), \tag{2}$$

where r is the uniformly distributed real number from $(0, 1]$, T is equal to the length of the vector representing an individual and t is a current number of adjustment.

The gradient mutation agent modifies two randomly selected elements within an individual by incrementing or decrementing their values. Direction of change (increment/decrement) is random and has identical probability equal to 0.5. The value of change is proportional to the gradient of an individual. If the fitness function value of an individual has improved then the change is accepted.

The gradient adjustment operator agent adjusts the value of each element of the individual by a constant value Δ proportional to its gradient. Delta is calculated as $\Delta = \alpha * \xi$, where α is the factor determining a size of the step in direction of ξ, known as a momentum. α has value from $(0, 1]$. In the proposed algorithm its value iterates starting from 1 with the step equal to 0.02. ξ is a vector determining a direction of search and is equal to the gradient of an individual.

3.3 Extended PLANN-Team

The extended team has been constructed by adding two more kinds of the search agent:

- simple one-point crossover search agent,

- arithmetic crossover search agent [11].

In both cases additional agents work in two modes - the first is to produce offspring out of the two randomly selected individuals from the shared memory. The second mode involves producing offspring by a crossover between the current best solution and all the remaining solutions from the shared memory. If any offspring is better then the current worst individual in the shared memory it replaces the current worst.

4 Computational Experiment Results

To validate the proposed approach a computational experiment has been carried on the cluster of PC's with P4 processors under PVM operating system. In case of the PLANN-Team there have been 5 search agents and in case of the E-PLANN-Team 7 search agents - in both cases one of each kind. The above described environment has been used to train neural networks applied to the three popular benchmarking classification problems - Cleveland heart disease (303 instances, 13 attributes, 2 classes), Credit approval (690, 15, 2) and Wisconsin breast cancer (699, 9, 2) [9]. All datasets have been obtained from the UCI Machine Learning Repository [10].

Each benchmarking problem has been solved 20 times and the reported values of the quality measures have been averaged over all runs. The quality measure in all cases was the correct classification ratio for the 10-cross-validation approach.

All the algorithms under comparison assume a sigmoid activation function with $\beta = 1$. The cascade-PLANN generated results with 18 ± 11 hidden neurons for the Credit problem and 10 ± 2 hidden neurons for the Heart problem. The remaining algorithms used identical the network structures with (15, 15, 1) neurons in layers 1, 2 and 3 for the Credit problem, (13, 13, 1) - for the Heart problem and (9, 9, 1) - for the Cancer problem. In the shared memory 200 individuals has been stored. Each agent has been allocated 500 requests.

In Table 1 these results are compared with other results obtained using neural networks trained by the following training tools: PLANN, parallel-PLANN and cascade-PLA (for details see [2, 3, 4, 5]).

In Table 2 correct classification rates obtained using the extended PLANN-Team are compared with the results reported in the literature.

In Figure 2 accuracy of classification using the extended PLANN-Team as a training tool versus the number of individuals stored in the shared memory is shown.

5 Conclusion

Main contribution of the paper is seen as proposing and implementing an approach based on a team of agents to training feed forward ANN. The resulting

Table 1: PLANN-Team versus other approaches

	PLANN	parallel-PLANN	Cascade-PLA	PLANN-Team	E-PLANN-Team
			Accuracy (%)		
Credit	82.6 ±1.2	86.6 ±1	85.1 ±1	84.1 ±1	85.6 ± 0.6
Heart	81.3 ±1.4	86.5 ±1.4	87.6 ±1.1	84.4 ±1.1	86.7 ± 0.6
Cancer	96.4 ± 1	96.6 ±0.8	-	96.0 ± 1	97.2 ± 0.4
			Training time (sec.)		
Credit	150	34	-	61	47
Heart	90	27	-	44	40
Cancer	90	25	-	64	47

Table 2: ATANN versus the reported accuracy of training algorithms (source for the best reported: http://www.phys.uni.torun.pl/kmk/projects/datasets.html and http://www.phys.uni.torun.pl/kmk/projects/datasets-stat.html)

Problem	Approach	Literature reported accuracy (%)	Accuracy of E-PLANN-T (%)
Credit	MLP+BP	84.6	85.6
	RBF	85.5	
	C 4.5	85.5	
	kNN	86.4	
Heart	MLP+BP	81.3	86.7
	FSM	84.0	
	C 4.5	77.8	
	kNN	85.1	
Cancer	MLP+BP	96.7	97.2
	RBF	95.9	
	C 4.5	94.7	
	kNN	97.1	

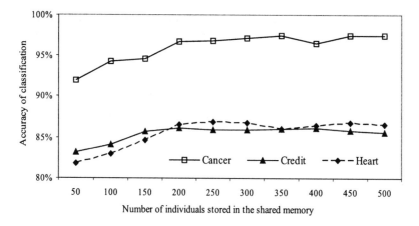

Figure 2: Accuracy of classification versus number of individuals stored in the shared memory

training tool seems to be a promising approach producing good or even competitive quality classifiers in a reasonable time. The proposed approach seems to be a worthy and flexible training tool, which application to ANN training should be further investigated. It has been also demonstrated that increasing the size of the population of solutions stored in the shared memory as well as increasing the number of agents could result in improving the classifier performance.

Future research should concentrate on searching for a more effective agents, establishing sound theoretical ground for agent's configuration and fine-tuning and investigating possibility of introducing negotiating agents. Another area for potential improvements is the management of the shared memory where various strategies for the selection, removal and replacement of individuals should be considered.

Acknowledgements
The research has been supported by the KBN, grant no. 3T11C05928

References

[1] W. Duch & J. Korczak. Optimization and Global Minimization Methods Suitable for Neural Network. Neural Computing Surveys 2, 1998, http://www.icsi.berkeley.edu/ jagopta/CNS.

[2] I. Czarnowski, P. Jędrzejowicz, E. Ratajczak. Population Learning Algorithm - Example Implementations and Experiments. Proceedings of the Fourth Metaheuristics International Conference, Porto, 2001, 607-612.

[3] I. Czarnowski & P. Jędrzejowicz. Population Learning Metaheuristic for Neural Network Training. Proceedings of the Sixth International Conference on Neural Networks and Soft Computing (ICNNSC), Zakopane, Poland, 2002.

[4] I. Czarnowski & P. Jędrzejowicz. Application of the Parallel Population Learning Algorithm to Training Feed-forward ANN. Proceedings of the Euro-International Symposium on Computational Intelligence (E-ISCI), Kosice, 2002.

[5] I. Czarnowski & P. Jędrzejowicz. An Agent-Based PLA for the Cascade Correlation Learning Architecture. Springer-Verlag, Lecture Notes in Computer Science (to appear in 2005)

[6] S.E. Fahlman & C. Lebiere. The Cascade-Corelation Learning Architecture. Advances in Neural Information Processing Systems 2, Morgan Kaufmann, 1990.

[7] J. Hertz, A. Krogh, R.G. Palmer. Introduction to the Theory of Neural Computation. WNT, Warsaw, 1995 (in Polish).

[8] P. Jędrzejowicz. Social Learning Algorithm as a Tool for Solving Some Difficult Scheduling Problems. Foundation of Computing and Decision Sciences, 1999, 24:51-66.

[9] O.L. Mangasarian & W.H. Wolberg. Cancer Diagnosis via Linear Programming. SIAM News, 1990, 23 (5):1-18.

[10] C.J. Merz & M. Murphy. UCI Repository of machine learning databases. [http://www.ics.uci.edu/~ mlearn/MLRepository.html]. Irvine, CA: University of California, Department of Information and Computer Science, 1998.

[11] Z. Michalewicz. Genetic Algorithms + Data Structures = Evolution Programs. Springer, Berlin, 1996.

[12] H.V.D. Parunak. Agents in Overalls: Experiences and Issues in the Development and Deployment of Industrial Agent-Based Systems. International Journal of Cooperative Information Systems, 2000, 9(3):209-228.

[13] Yi Shang & B.W. Wah. A Global Optimization Method for Neural Network Training. Conference of Neural Networks. IEEE Computer, 1996, 29: 45-54.

[14] B.W. Wah & Minglun Qian. Constrained Formulations for Neural Network Training and Their Applications to Solve the Two-Spiral Problem. Proceedings of the Fifth International Conference on Computer Science and Informatics, 2000, 1:598-601.

[15] D. Whitley. Genetic Algorithms and Neural Networks. Genetic Algorithms in Enginering and Computer Science, G.Winter, J.Perianx, M.Galan and P.Cuesta (eds.), John Wiley 1995, 203-216.

[16] S. Talukdar, L. Baerentzen, A. Gove, P. de Souza. Asynchronous Teams: Co-operation Schemes for Autonomous, Computer-Based Agents, Technical Report EDRC 18-59-96, Carnegie Mellon University, Pittsburgh, 1996.

[17] Xiao-Feng Xie and Wen-Jun Zhang. SWAF: Swarm Algorithm Framework for Numerical Optimization. In: Kalyanmoy Deb et al (eds.), Proceedings of the Genetic and Evolutionary Computation Conference (GECCO'2004), Heidelberg, Germany, June 2004. Seattle, WA, Springer Verlag, Lecture Notes in Computer Science, 2004, 3102:238-250.

SESSION 4:

CASE-BASED REASONING

Collaborative Recommending using Formal Concept Analysis[*]

Patrick du Boucher-Ryan and Derek Bridge

Department of Computer Science,

University College Cork,

Ireland

Abstract

We show how Formal Concept Analysis (FCA) can be applied to Collaborative Recommenders. FCA is a mathematical method for analysing binary relations. Here we apply it to the relation between users and items in a collaborative recommender system. FCA groups the users and items into concepts, ordered by a concept lattice. We present two new algorithms for finding neighbours in a collaborative recommender. Both use the concept lattice as an index to the recommender's ratings matrix. Our experimental results show a major decrease in the amount of work needed to find neighbours, while guaranteeing no loss of accuracy or coverage.

1 Introduction

Recommender systems act as experts who draw the attention of their users to items (products, services or information sources) that they predict will be of interest. *Collaborative recommender systems* achieve this by maintaining a pool of user opinions.

In a collaborative recommender, given n users, $U = \{u : 1 \ldots n\}$, and m items, $I = \{i : 1 \ldots m\}$, preferences are represented using a $n \times m$ matrix of ratings $r_{u,i}$. Note that it is possible and common that $r_{u,i} = \bot$, signalling that the user has not yet rated that item. An example of a ratings matrix for movies is shown as Table 1.

There are many ways of building collaborative recommenders. Here we describe just one, which we refer to as an Exhaustive Recommender (EX-CR); for more details, see [7]:

- The similarity $w_{u_a,u}$ between the active user u_a and each other user, $u \neq u_a$, is computed using Pearson correlation over their co-rated items, devalued in the case of users who have co-rated fewer than 50 items by a significance weight.

- Next, the *nearest neighbours* of u_a are selected, i.e. the N (in our case, 20) other users u for whom $w_{u_a,u}$ is highest.

---

[*]This work is supported by the Boole Centre for Research in Informatics, University College Cork under the HEA-PRTLI scheme.

	Wild One	X-Men	Yentl	Zorro
Ann	5	⊥	⊥	2
Bob	⊥	⊥	3	4
Col	2	5	⊥	2
Deb	2	5	4	2
Edd	⊥	4	⊥	2
Flo	4	3	4	⊥
Guy	4	5	⊥	3

Figure 1: A ratings matrix

- *Prediction:* Given an item i that has not been rated by u_a but that has been rated by at least one of the neighbours, u_a's rating for i can be predicted, $p_{u_a,i}$, essentially as a weighted average of the neighbours' ratings for item i.

- *Recommendation:* By predicting a rating for each item i that has not been rated by u_a but which has been rated by at least one neighbour, items can be sorted into descending order of $p_{u_a,i}$. This is the order in which they can be recommended.

Collaborative recommenders are the target of active research. The research aims to investigate and overcome problems such as latency [3], sparsity [15] and vulnerability to attack [9]. But the problem that we address here is the high dimensionality of the ratings data: in fielded systems the numbers of users and items can be very high. The challenges are efficiency and scalability: how to provide fast on-line predictions and recommendations without sacrificing accuracy and coverage, and how to continue to do this over time as ratings data grows and usage increases.

The key to tackling the dimensionality problem is to do some work *off-line*, in advance of making predictions and recommendations, to reduce the amount of work that needs to be done *on-line*. In *model-based* collaborative recommenders, *most* of the work is done off-line. A model is built from the ratings matrix: the matrix is mined for association rules or Bayesian networks to capture regularities [1, 8] or to remove redundancy [10]. Efficient predictions are made on-line from the model.

In *memory-based* collaborative recommenders, little, if any, work is done off-line; predictions are made directly from the matrix. An example of a purely memory-based system is the Exhaustive Recommender (EX-CR) that we described in the opening paragraphs of this section.

There are many ways of *combining* model-based and memory-based approaches. The simplest, which we adopt in our own implementation of the Exhaustive Recommender (EX-CR), is to pre-compute a matrix of all user-user correlations. This gives EX-CR a simple model that speeds up the process of finding neighbours. Further speed up may be obtained by building an index to the ratings matrix so that it is no longer necessary to perform an exhaustive on-line search through all the users. The common approach to this is to use some form of heuristic-based clustering algorithm, e.g. [2, 6, 13]. In the rest of this paper, we investigate an alternative, which builds an index using the technique of Formal Concept Analysis.

Sect. 2 explains those aspects of FCA that are relevant to this research. Then, in Sect. 3 we explain how we have applied FCA to collaborative recommenders. An empirical evaluation is presented in Sect. 4.

2 Formal Concept Analysis

Formal Concept Analysis (FCA) is a mathematical method for analysing binary relations. It was first introduced in [14]; see [4] for a concise textbook treatment. In FCA, data is structured into formal abstractions, called *concepts*, which form a *concept lattice*, ordered by a subconcept-superconcept relation. The last two decades have seen numerous applications of FCA in computer science. These have included applications in knowledge discovery [11], software engineering [12] and case-based reasoning [5].

2.1 Contexts and concepts

In FCA, a *context* (E, F, R) is a binary relation between a set of entities E and a set of features F, $R \subseteq E \times F$. When the sets are finite, the context can be specified by means of a cross-table. A simple example is shown as Fig. 2a.

Given a set of entities $E' \subseteq E$, we can define the *common features* CF of the members of E':

$$CF(E') =_{def} \{f \in F \mid \forall e \in E' \ (e, f) \in R\} \tag{1}$$

Similarly, given a set of features $F' \subseteq F$, we can define the *common entities* CE of the members of F':

$$CE(F') =_{def} \{e \in E \mid \forall f \in F' \ (e, f) \in R\} \tag{2}$$

For example, in Fig. 2a, $CF(\{e_1, e_3\}) = \{f_1\}$ and $CE(\{f_3\}) = \{e_2, e_4\}$.

Hence, we define a *concept* of a context (E, F, R) as a pair (E', F') where $CF(E') = F'$ and $CE(F') = E'$. In other words, in a concept (E', F') the set of entities that the members of F' have in common is E' and the set of features that the members of E' have in common is F'. In a concept (E', F'), E' (the set of entities) is called the concept's *extent* and F' (the set of features) is called the concept's *intent*. For example, $(\{e_1, e_3\}, \{f_1\})$ is a concept of the context shown in Fig. 2a. e_1 and e_3 are the members of the extent; f_1 is the sole member of the intent. $(\{e_1\}, \{f_1, f_2\})$ is another concept of this context.

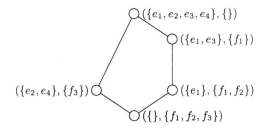

($\{e_1, e_2, e_3, e_4\}, \{\}$)

($\{e_1, e_3\}, \{f_1\}$)

($\{e_2, e_4\}, \{f_3\}$)

($\{e_1\}, \{f_1, f_2\}$)

($\{\}, \{f_1, f_2, f_3\}$)

	f_1	f_2	f_3
e_1	×	×	
e_2			×
e_3	×		
e_4			×

Fig. 2a. A context.

Fig. 2b. A concept lattice.

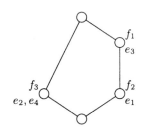

f_1
e_3

f_3
e_2, e_4

f_2
e_1

Fig. 2c. A concept lattice.

Figure 2: A context and its concept lattice.

2.2 Concept lattices

A partial ordering can be defined over the concepts of a context. Specifically,

$$(E_i, F_i) \leq (E_j, F_j) \Leftrightarrow E_i \subseteq E_j \qquad (3)$$

Equivalently,

$$(E_i, F_i) \leq (E_j, F_j) \Leftrightarrow F_i \supseteq F_j \qquad (4)$$

In the example, $(\{e_1\}, \{f_1, f_2\}) \leq (\{e_1, e_3\}, \{f_1\})$. This can be thought of as a subconcept-superconcept relation.

The ordering defines a complete lattice over the concepts of a context, and this is referred to as the *concept lattice*. Fig. 2b is a Hasse diagram depicting the concept lattice for the context of Fig. 2a. This helps us to visualise various properties. The supremum (the topmost node) is the concept whose extent is the set of all entities. In this example, there is no feature shared by all entities, so this concept's intent is the empty set. The infimum (the lowermost node) is the concept whose intent is the set of all features. In this example, no entity possesses all three features, so the extent of this concept is empty. Lower nodes in the diagram denote concepts with more features in their intent; higher nodes denote concepts with more entities in their extent.

2.3 Entry-level concepts

Given the set of all concepts of a context, we define the *entry-level concept* for an entity. The entry-level concept of entity e is the unique concept for which e is a member of the extent and e is not a member of the extent of any subconcept. For example, the concept $(\{e_1, e_3\}, \{f_1\})$ is the entry-level concept for entity e_3. In Fig. 2b, the entry-level concept of an entity is the lowest node labelled by that entity.

Similarly, the entry-level concept of feature f is the unique concept for which f is a member of the intent and f is not a member of the intent of any superconcept. So, for example, $(\{e_1\}, \{f_1, f_2\})$ is the entry-level concept of feature f_2. In Fig. 2b, it is the highest node labelled by that feature.

In Fig. 2b, we wrote concepts alongside nodes. Fig. 2c shows the same information but more concisely. We write alongside nodes just entry-level entities and features. This is the more conventional way of showing a concept lattice. It is easy to recover the information shown in Fig. 2b: the full extent at a node in Fig. 2c contains the entities that label this node and all descendant nodes; the full intent at a node in Fig. 2c contains the features that label this node and all ancestor nodes. This reduces clutter in diagrams. However, we stress that the data structures of our implementations store complete concepts as in Fig. 2b.

3 Applying FCA to Collaborative Recommending

We apply Formal Concept Analysis to a collaborative recommender's ratings matrix. The concept lattice can then act as an index to the ratings matrix to speed up the search for neighbours. This section explains the details.

3.1 Obtaining a concept lattice

FCA requires a context, i.e. a binary relation between entities and features. We take users to be entities and items (movies, TV programmes, etc.) to be features. We produce a cross-table from the ratings matrix: a cell contains $\times$ if and only if $r_{u,i} \neq \perp$. The context that corresponds to Fig. 1's ratings matrix is shown as a cross-table in Fig. 3. The corresponding concept lattice is shown in Fig. 4 (using the concise format illustrated in Fig. 2c).

Concepts group users and items in ways that are meaningful in collaborative recommending. For example, the node labelled by Col and Guy denotes the concept $(\{Col, Deb, Guy\}, \{WildOne, XMen, Zorro\})$. (Remember in diagrams such as Fig. 4 the extent is read from the descendants; the intent is read from the ancestors.) It shows that users Col, Deb and Guy have co-rated items Wild One, X-Men and Zorro. Of course, this does not mean their actual ratings (the numeric values) are the same. However, this brings us to a hypothesis: that the structure revealed by FCA will be positively co-related with the similarity values computed from the numeric ratings. We state this hypothesis as follows:

	WildOne	XMen	Yentl	Zorro
Ann	×			×
Bob			×	×
Col	×	×		×
Deb	×	×	×	×
Edd		×		×
Flo	×	×	×	
Guy	×	×		×

Figure 3: The context that corresponds to the ratings matrix in Fig. 1.

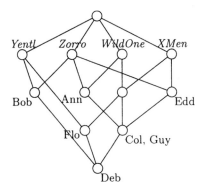

Figure 4: The concept lattice that corresponds to the context in Fig. 3.

Hypothesis. *Users who rate the same items tend to rate items the same.*

The more two people tend to watch (and rate) the same movies, for example, the more they will tend to have similar tastes in movies and tend to rate these movies with approximately the same scores.

We report the results of testing this hypothesis empirically in Sect. 4. For the moment, we remark that the truth of this hypothesis is not necessary for attaining speed up when using the concept lattice to search for neighbours. This speed-up will happen anyway. But, if the hypothesis is true, there is additional potential to improve performance.

We now describe two new alternative algorithms that use the lattice in the search for neighbours. We focus on the task of prediction. In other words, we are given active user u_a and item i and we want to predict u_a's rating for i. Predicting Col's rating for Yentl will be a running example.

3.2 Feature-Based Collaborative Recommender

Our feature-based algorithm (FE-CR) uses the entry-level concept of the *target item*. The extent of this concept is the set of users who have rated this item (entities that have this feature). Clearly, these are the only users who can contribute anything to a predicted rating for this item. In Fig. 4, for example, we would access the node labelled Yentl, as this denotes the entry-level concept for this movie. The extent of this concept can be read off the node's descendants, i.e. {Bob, Deb, Flo}. These are indeed the only users who have rated Yentl. (Remember, in the implementation the extent itself is stored explicitly; it does not have to be collected by walking the descendants.)

However, if there are more than N users in this concept's extent, then we need to find the N who are most similar to the target user. The FE-CR algorithm processes the members of the extent in the same way that the exhaustive algorithm processes the entire ratings matrix. Far fewer users will be visited by FE-CR than by the exhaustive algorithm, the actual efficiency depending on the size of the concept's extent. However, FE-CR guarantees that every user visited has rated the target item and that every user who has rated the target item is visited.

3.3 Entity-Based Collaborative Recommender

Our entity-based algorithm (EN-CR) walks the lattice, starting from the entry-level concept for the *target user*. Before we describe the algorithm, we make a few observations about the lattice depicted in Fig. 4 to show which nodes are important and which are not. We continue to use the example of predicting Col's rating for Yentl.

Consider Col's entry-level concept. In Fig. 4, it is labelled by Col and Guy. But the corresponding concept (reading the extent from descendants and the intent from ancestors) is ({Col, Deb, Guy}, { *WildOne, XMen, Zorro*}).

- Not only is this the entry-level concept for Col, it is also the entry-level concept for Guy. This shows that Guy is useless as a predictor. Because this is the entry-level concept for both of them, they have co-rated the same set of movies; Guy has no additional ratings and so cannot be used to make predictions for Col.

- Ann and Edd are not members of the extent of Col's entry-level concept; their entry-level concepts are superconcepts of Col's entry-level concept. But, they too are useless as predictors. Each of them has rated a proper subset of the movies that Col has rated. In particular, Ann has rated Wild One and Zorro; Edd has rated X-Men and Zorro. They have no additional ratings and so cannot be used to make predictions for Col.

- Deb, like Guy, belongs to the extent of Col's entry-level concept but her entry-level concept, unlike Guy's, is a subconcept of Col's entry-level concept. The movies she has rated are therefore a proper superset of Col's: she has rated all the movies he has, plus some. In particular, she has additionally rated Yentl. She can make predictions for Col. Furthermore, she has a lot of movies in common with Col and, to the degree that our hypothesis is true, is likely to be similar to Col.

- Flo's entry-level concept is neither a subconcept not a superconcept of Col's entry-level concept. But Flo's and Col's entry-level concepts have a common ancestor other than the supremum. In this case, this common ancestor is the unlabelled node near the centre of the diagram. This shows that they do have at least one co-rated movie (in fact, they have two, Wild One and X-Men) and it shows that Flo brings something new (her rating of Yentl). She has fewer movies in common with Col than Deb has and so, to the degree that our hypothesis is true, is likely to be less similar to Col (although this will depend on the actual ratings).

- Finally, Bob's entry-level concept, like Flo's, is neither a subconcept nor a superconcept of Col's, but Bob's and Col's entry-level concepts have a common ancestor other than the supremum, in this case the node labelled Zorro. So he has movies in common with Col but also additional movies. Because this common ancestor is at a higher level than the one that Flo shares with Col, Bob has fewer co-rated items than Flo and is likely to be less similar (again depending on the actual numeric ratings).

The above discussion of the example lattice should give a strong intuition about the operation of the EN-CR algorithm. It can use the lattice to visit users in a most-likely-neighbour-first order. Specifically then, it starts its traversal at the target user's entry-level concept. It ignores other users for whom this is also their entry-level concept (Guy in the example). It does not need to visit the subconcepts because users from these subconcepts (such as Deb in the example) are members of the extent of the target user's entry-level concept. These members of the entry-level concept are the first users whose correlation with the target user is computed and who may be added to the set of neighbours. Then the algorithm walks up the lattice, level by level, until it reaches the supremum. At each concept, it ignores users for whom the concept is their entry-level (Ann and Edd in the example). Other users are candidate neighbours and they will be encountered in order of the number of items they have in common with the target user. (In the example, Flo is encountered at the unlabelled node; Bob is encountered later, at the node labelled Zorro.)

4 Experimental Evaluation

4.1 Datasets

We tested our new algorithms on two datasets. The 100K MovieLens Dataset consists of 100000 ratings by 943 users for 1682 movies; the PTV Dataset contains 60000 ratings by 2341 users for 8164 TV programmes.[1] To model the

---

[1] We are grateful to the GroupLens project team, www.movielens.org, for the MovieLens data and to ChangingWorlds, www.changingworlds.com, for the PTV data.

	Number of ratings		
	10000	20000	30000
MovieLens	16224	169030	1047321
PTV	4448	25827	133897

Figure 5: Number of concepts.

growth of a recommender system over time, we use three subsets of the datasets containing increasing numbers of ratings (10000, 20000 and 30000 ratings).

Datasets are split into a training set from which the lattice is built and a test set of 5000 withheld ratings. The performance of the system at predicting each withheld rating is measured. Results are subject to five-fold cross-validation with different random training and test sets in each fold.

4.2   Concept lattices

The space requirements of our new approach are considerable. We must store the ratings matrix (of size $n \times m$) and, if it has been pre-computed, the user-user similarity matrix (of size n^2), as well as the lattice. In the worst case, the number of concepts in a concept lattice is exponential in the size of the context. It is important that in practice our lattices are of a manageable size.

The table in Fig. 5 shows the number of concepts in the lattices built from differently-sized datasets. While the number of concepts is manageable, we see that it grows faster than the ratings grow. This may cause problems for larger datasets. However, we have suggestions for future work (Sect. 5) that may control this. We also see that MovieLens lattices have four to eight times more concepts than PTV ones. The MovieLens datasets are less sparse than the PTV ones. There is thus a greater chance of commonalities between pairs of users and pairs of movies, which results in more concepts.

Fig. 6 shows the distribution of concepts of different sizes in a lattice that was constructed from 20000 MovieLens and PTV ratings; similar-shaped profiles apply in the case of lattices created from differently-sized datasets. In the figure, the x-axis is the size of a concept's intent (the number of movies it pertains to); the y-axis records how many concepts are of those sizes.

Concepts towards the top of a lattice are more general: extents are large and intents are small. Concepts lower down are more specific: extents are small and intents are large. What Fig. 6 shows is that the bulk of the concepts in the lattices are towards the top. For example, approximately 165000 MovieLens concepts have only two to four items in their intent. The number of concepts whose intent contains more than three items falls off very rapidly and they form only a tiny proportion of the lattice. We should point out that we have truncated the x-axis in Fig. 6 at 14. This does not mean that there are no concepts with intent sizes greater than 14. Excluding the infimum, for MovieLens there are a further 120 or so distinct intent sizes in the lattice, the largest intent size

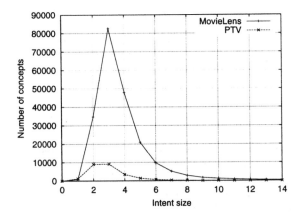

Figure 6: Number of concepts for intents of different sizes for datasets with 20000 ratings.

being 1353, but rarely do more than a couple of concepts have intents of these sizes. The story is similar for PTV, where the largest intent size is 4083 TV programmes.

A final comment concerns the lattice build time. While our code was not optimised in any significant way, we found that, given enough main memory, smaller lattices were built in minutes and the largest MovieLens lattice was built in approximately 2.5 days. In practice, lattices can be updated incrementally at no great cost when new users, items and ratings arrive.

4.3   Concept membership

We hypothesised that users who rate the same items would rate the items the same. Figure 7 gives some insight into whether our hypothesis holds true. It shows information about a lattice that was constructed from 20000 MovieLens ratings; similar findings apply to the lattices created from other datasets.

In the figure, the x-axis is again the size of a concept's intent; the y-axis measures average all-pairs user similarity. We plot the following:

Average similarity of all users: The average all-pairs user-user similarity over all users in the dataset. This is a flat line because it is independent of properties of the lattice.

Average non-zero similarity of all users: Here only non-zero values are averaged. In other words, this considers pairs of users who have at least one co-rated item. Again this is independent of properties of the lattice.

Average similarity of concept extents: For each concept, we took the extent and averaged the all-pairs user-user similarities. We then took the

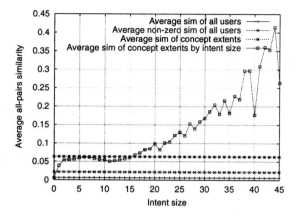

Figure 7: All-pairs similarities in a lattice for 20000 MovieLens ratings.

average of all these values. While this depends on the lattice, the plot is flat because it does not depend on intent sizes.

Average similarity of concept extents by intent size: For each concept, we took the extent and averaged the all-pairs user-user similarities. We then grouped and averaged these by the size of the concept's intent.

Figure 7 shows two things that support our hypothesis. First, the average similarity of concept extents is higher than the figures that are independent of the lattice. This suggests that similar users are indeed grouped together. Second, from the average similarity of concept intents by intent size, we see that users who belong to the same concept are more similar to each other the further down the lattice the concept is situated (i.e. the bigger its intent). This would imply that the more co-rated items, the more similar the users are.

4.4   Prediction efficiency

The predictions made by collaborative recommenders are conventionally evaluated for accuracy (e.g. mean absolute error) and coverage (the percentage of requests which the system is able to fulfil). However, by design, FE-CR and EN-CR are *guaranteed* to find the same set of N neighbours and therefore make the same predictions as EX-CR. The lattice simply speeds up the search for neighbours. We will therefore not show accuracy or coverage plots. Modulo minor differences (e.g. due to the random selection of members of the training and test sets), they are the same as plots to be found in the literature, e.g. [8].

   Our main concern in evaluating FE-CR and EN-CR, then, is their efficiency. Since execution times are difficult to measure reliably, we use instead two operation counts. (We do have timing figures and they tell a similar story.)

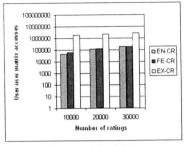

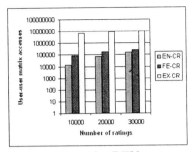

Fig. 8a. MovieLens   **Fig. 8b.** PTV

Figure 8: Number of user-user matrix accesses.

4.4.1 Number of user-user matrix accesses

Each time two users need to be compared, the user-user similarity matrix is consulted. We count the total number of accesses made to this matrix. The lattice enables FE-CR and EN-CR to ignore many users who cannot be predictors. This count will enable us to see how big the saving is compared with EX-CR's exhaustive approach.

The results are shown in Fig. 8. In both the MovieLens and PTV datasets, EX-CR requires by far the greatest number of matrix accesses — note the logarithmic scale. This is expected as, for each prediction, this algorithm will visit every user in the system. In particular, FE-CR and EN-CR make only 0.2-7.0% as many accesses as EX-CR. FE-CR and EN-CR are closer to each other, although EN-CR does fewer accesses.

4.4.2 Number of concepts visited

This count, of concepts visited, meaningfully applies only to the EN-CR algorithm, which walks the lattice, level-by-level, up from the target user's entry-level concept to the supremum. Obviously, the bigger the concept lattice the more concepts will be visited per prediction. (The plot for FE-CR will be flat: for each prediction request, it visits just the entry-level concept for the target item.) The results are shown in Figs. 9. Again the scale is logarithmic.

5 Conclusions

In this paper, we have shown how Formal Concept Analysis can be applied to collaborative recommenders. We build a concept lattice from a cross-table that is derived from the original ratings matrix and use this as an index to the ratings matrix when finding neighbours.

We proposed two new algorithms that use the lattice, FE-CR and EN-CR. Both do considerably less work than a conventional exhaustive algorithm, EX-

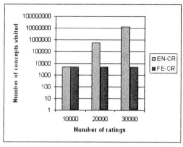
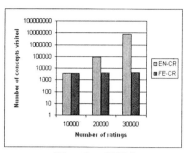

Fig. 9a. MovieLens   **Fig. 9a.** PTV

Figure 9: Number of concepts visited.

CR, but both guarantee accuracy and coverage results equal to those of the exhaustive system. Of the two, FE-CR is of lower practical use. It can only be used to make predictions: its inputs are both the target user and, crucially, the item for which a prediction is sought. It uses the latter to key into the concept lattice. Suppose instead we want to compute recommendations, in which case no target item will be available at the outset. FE-CR has nothing with which to key into the lattice.

By contrast, EN-CR can be used both to make predictions and recommendations. Given the target user, it walks the lattice to find the user's neighbours. The neighbours' ratings can then be used either to make predictions in the case where a target item is also supplied, or to recommend items rated by the neighbours but not yet rated by the target user. In future work we would like to test EN-CR on recommendation tasks and see whether properties of the lattice (and our hypothesis in particular) can give any further advantages.

Another avenue of future work, which might help to constrain the sizes of the lattices, is pruning concepts towards the bottom of the lattice. This would not lose any users or items. Users, for example, who are members of the extent of the pruned concepts are also members of the extents of their superconcepts. It would mean, however, that if two users share an entry-level concept in a pruned lattice, they would no longer necessarily have co-rated exactly the same items. There would be savings in space; some savings in time due to there being fewer concepts; but also some costs in time due to the need to process larger extents. The trade-offs between these could be investigated.

References

[1] J.S. Breese, D. Heckerman and C. Kadie, Empirical Analysis of Predictive Algorithms for Collaborative Filtering, *Procs. of the 14th Annual Conference on Uncertainty in Artificial Intelligence*, pp.43–52, 1998.

218

[2] D. Bridge and J. Kelleher, Experiments in Sparsity Reduction: Using Clustering in Collaborative Recommenders, *Procs. of the 13th Irish Conference on Artificial Intelligence and Cognitive Science*, pp.144–149, 2002.

[3] G. Carenini, J. Smith and D. Poole, Towards More Conversational and Collaborative Recommender Systems, *Procs. of the 8th International Conference on Intelligent User Interfaces*, pp.12–18, 2003.

[4] B.A. Davey and H.A. Priestley, *Introduction to Lattices and Order*, 2nd edn., Cambridge University Press, 2002.

[5] B. Díaz-Agudo and P.A. González-Calero, Classification-Based Retrieval using Formal Concept Analysis, *Procs. 4th International Conference on Case-Based Reasoning*, pp.173–188, 2001.

[6] D. Fisher, K. Hildrum, J. Hong, M. Newman, M. Thomas and R. Vuduc, SWAMI: A Framework for Collaborative Filtering Algorithm Development and Evaluation, *Procs. of SIGIR*, pp.366–368, 2000.

[7] J.L. Herlocker, *Understanding and Improving Automated Collaborative Filtering Systems*, Ph.D. thesis, University of Minnesota, 2000.

[8] J. Kelleher and D. Bridge, An Accurate and Scalable Collaborative Recommender, *Artificial Intelligence Review*, 21(3-4), pp.193–213, 2004.

[9] M.P. O'Mahony, N.J. Hurley and G.C.M. Silvestre, Efficient and Secure Collaborative Filtering through Intelligent Neighbour Selection, *Procs. ECAI*, pp.383–387, 2004.

[10] B.M. Sarwar, G. Karypis, J.A. Konstan, and J. Riedl, Application of Dimensionality Reduction in Recommender System – A Case Study, *Procs. of the Workshop on Web Mining for E-Commerce*, ACM WebKDD, 2000.

[11] G. Stumme, R. Wille and U. Wille, Conceptual Knowledge Discovery in Databases using Formal Concept Analysis Methods, *Procs. of the 2nd European Symposium on Principles of Data Mining and Knowledge Discovery*, pp.450–458, 1998.

[12] T. Tilley, R. Cole, P. Becker and P. Eklund, A Survey of Formal Concept Analysis Support for Software Engineering Activities, *Procs. of the First International Conference on Formal Concept Analysis*, 2003.

[13] L.H. Ungar and D.P. Foster, Clustering Methods for Collaborative Filtering, *AAAI Workshop on Recommendation Systems*, pp.112–125, 1998.

[14] R. Wille, Restructuring Lattice Theory: An Approach Based on Hierarchies of Concepts, in I. Rival (ed.), *Ordered Sets*, Reidel, pp.445–470, 1982.

[15] D.C. Wilson, B. Smyth and D. O'Sullivan, Sparsity Reduction in Collaborative Recommendation: A Case-Based Approach, *International Journal of Pattern Recognition and Artificial Intelligence*, 17(2), pp.863–883, 2004.

Using Case Differences for Regression in CBR Systems

Neil McDonnell, Pádraig Cunningham

Department of Computer Science, Trinity College Dublin, Ireland

neil.mcdonnell, padraig.cunningham@cs.tcd.ie

Abstract

Most case-based reasoning systems in operation today do not adapt the solutions of retrieved cases to solve new problems. This reflects the difficulty of acquiring and maintaining the knowledge needed to perform adaptation successfully. This paper describes a technique for performing numeric prediction (i.e. regression) in which adaptation knowledge is mined from the case-base itself. Experimental evidence suggests that the technique provides robust performance in real-world domains.

1. Introduction

Case-based reasoning (CBR) systems solve new problems by retrieving similar past problems and re-using their solutions. This re-use may involve copying the solution from a past problem, or *adapting* it to fit the precise needs of the new problem. Of the steps in the CBR problem-solving cycle [1], this adaptation step has proved most problematic. CBR is now in widespread commercial use in applications such as customer support and recommender systems. The purpose of these systems, however, is to *find* information in an efficient and user-friendly manner. They are 'retrieval only' systems in that they make no attempt to adapt the solutions that they find.

Adapting a retrieved solution to solve a new problem generally requires detailed knowledge of both the task and domain at hand. The adaptation 'problem' can therefore be summarized as follows:

- How can the knowledge required to perform adaptation be acquired?

- How can adaptation knowledge be represented so that it integrates seamlessly into a CBR system?

The acquisition of adaptation knowledge subjects CBR to the same knowledge engineering problem that has impeded the adoption of other knowledge-based techniques, e.g. expert systems. CBR's primary advantage as a technology has been its simplicity. Adaptation mechanisms that rely on the collection and maintenance of expert knowledge lessen or negate this advantage.

Representation of adaptation knowledge also presents a challenge. Ideally, the knowledge used for adaptation should be easy to store and manipulate within a CBR framework. More commonly, however, it has been stored in the form of rules

[2]. In situations where CBR has been applied to planning and design tasks, the adaptation process often employs external reasoning systems to manipulate domain-specific rule-sets [3]. In contrast to this 'knowledge-intensive' approach, CBR systems that have achieved most success have attempted to minimise the need for explicit domain knowledge. Such systems are sometimes referred to as 'knowledge-light' [4].

This paper describes a knowledge-light technique for applying CBR to the problem of numeric prediction (i.e. regression). Accurate and robust prediction of numeric values requires knowledge about how to alter the solutions of retrieved cases. This adaptation knowledge is mined directly from the case base. In dividing the knowledge in any CBR system into four containers (vocabulary, similarity measure, case base, and solution transformation), Richter also noted that knowledge may be moved between containers [5]. The technique described here uses knowledge from the first three containers to populate the fourth, thereby easing construction and maintenance of the overall system.

Section 2 describes an earlier regression technique that mined adaptation knowledge from the case base [6]. It also examines some limitations of this approach. Section 3 describes a new technique that seeks to address these limitations while also integrating the adaptation process more closely into the CBR cycle. An experimental evaluation of this technique is presented in Section 4.

2. Mining the Case Base for Adaptation Knowledge

The principal component of every CBR system is the case base (CB), a collection of previously encountered problem descriptions together with their solutions. As new problems are solved and stored, the knowledge contained in the CB increases and the system's problem-solving ability improves.

Problem-solving in CBR is both *lazy* and *local*; *lazy* because the process of finding a solution for a query case only occurs when the query is actually received, and *local* because the solution is calculated using only those prior cases most similar to the query (these are known as the query's 'nearest neighbours' or NNs). The contribution from each neighbour to the solution is often weighted by its distance from the query, typically using a Gaussian or other distance-weighting function.

When CBR is used for regression, the most common approach is to take a weighted average of solutions from a query's NNs. This presents two problems:

1. The predicted solution will always be bounded by the highest and lowest values among the NNs. This ignores the relative positions of the query and its NNs in domain space, and may not always give an accurate result. E.g. suppose we have a simple housing domain where *housePrice = f(numBedrooms)*. If a query is received with *numBedrooms=5* and its two NNs have *numBedrooms=4* and *3*, the predicted *housePrice* will be between those of the NNs when it should in fact be higher.

   Ideally, we would like to take the relative positions of the query and its NNs into account when making predictions.

2. Only those cases most similar to a query have some input into the predicted solution. In CBR systems, however, the CB contains a lot of implicit adaptation knowledge that is potentially useful. Ideally, we would like to extract and apply this knowledge to supplement local problem-solving techniques.

A regression technique addressing these problems was proposed by Hanney & Keane [6]. Sections 2.1 and 2.2 review this approach in some detail.

2.1 Using Adaptation Rules for Regression

It was stated above that adaptation knowledge is implicitly stored in the CB. So where precisely is it? The answer is that useful adaptation knowledge can be learnt by looking at how differences between cases are reflected in their solutions.

The following discussion will use examples from a simplified housing domain:

housePrice = f(numBedrooms, location)

where *numBedrooms* has range [1-6] and *location* has range [1-5], 1 being least desirable. *numBedrooms* and *location* are referred to as the problem attributes and *housePrice* as the solution. Each stored case has structure:

(numBedrooms, location, housePrice)

Let us assume the existence of a CB containing multiple (e.g. 20) such cases.

Consider removing a case from the CB and comparing it to all other cases. Since we know the solution to this case (call it Case A), case comparisons can be used to construct a set of rules as follows:

IF (problem changes from Case_1_problem → Case_A_problem) THEN
(solution changes from Case_1_solution → Case_A_solution)

IF (problem changes from Case_2_problem → Case_A_problem) THEN
(solution changes from Case_2_solution → Case_A_solution)

...

For example:

Rule 1
IF (numBedrooms changes from 1→2 and location from 3→4) THEN
(housePrice changes from €200,000 → €400,000)

Rule 2
IF (numBedrooms changes from 3→4 and location from 4→4) THEN
(housePrice changes from €550,000 → €680,000)

Each rule contains the difference between two cases and the consequent change in solution. Note that both problem attributes change value in Rule 1, while only one changes in Rule 2. In general, those attributes whose values change constitute the *differences* covered by the rule; those that are unchanged provide the rule's *context*.

It would be possible to generate a full set of rules for each case in the CB. For a CB of size *n*, this would produce *n* x *(n-1)* rules. To reduce storage requirements, each case may be compared with only a limited number of other cases. E.g. comparing each case with its 10 NNs produces a rule-set with size *n* x *10*.

When a query case is received, its solution is predicted as follows:

1. Retrieve the query's NN.

2. Calculate the differences between the two cases' problem parts.

3. Search for one or more rules matching the set of differences – these rules give the change in solution resulting from the case differences.

4. Make a prediction by adding together the solution from the NN and the solution changes in the matching rules.

This process can be explained more easily with an example. Suppose the following query is received: Q = *(numBedrooms=5, location=1)*. Then *housePrice* is predicted as follows:

1. Query's NN: *(numBedrooms=3, location=2, housePrice=€350,000)*

2. Differences between NN and Q: *(numBedrooms: 3→5, location: 2→1)*

3. Rules found to account for these differences:

   IF (numBedrooms changes from 3→5) THEN
   (housePrice changes from €300,000 → €450,000)

   IF (location changes from 2→1) THEN
   (housePrice changes from €300,000 → €270,000)

4. Predicted *housePrice* for Q: *€350,000 + €150,000 – €30,000 = €470,000*

Here, two rules bridge the gap between the query and its NN. They indicate what effect the differences in *numBedrooms* and *location* have on *housePrice*. Note that the context of each rule (i.e. the values of unchanging attributes) is not shown – the reason that context is sometimes omitted is explained below.

2.2 Problem-solving Capability of Adaptation Rules

Adaptation rules specify the impact that particular differences between cases have on the solution value, thereby codifying the adaptation knowledge contained in the CB. This knowledge is highly specific, however, depending as it does on the precise set of cases stored in the CB.

The limited scope of the knowledge contained in adaptation rules can be seen by considering a domain with 5 numeric problem attributes, each with 100 possible values. This domain has 100^5 (= 10^{10}) possible combinations of attribute values; a relatively well-stocked CB of 1000 cases will still contain only 0.000001 of all possible cases. Problem solving remains possible in domains such as this because cases tend to be clustered in those areas of domain space where query cases typically occur. Even allowing for this, however, it is highly unlikely that a rule-base will contain rules to cover the differences between a particular query case and its NN while also respecting the query's context.

The technique of using adaptation rules to solve new cases needs a problem-solving *bias* that allows it to broaden the range of problems it can tackle. Hanney & Keane introduce this bias in two ways. The first extends the set of attribute differences handled by a rule, while the second extends the context in which a rule may be applied. Both increase the applicability of individual rules to give them greater problem-solving potential.

Strategy 1: Combine adaptation rules to create generalised rules that cover a range of values for a problem attribute.

E.g. combine rules:

> *IF (numBedrooms changes from 2→3 and location from 4→4) THEN (housePrice changes from €400,000 → €500,000)*

> *IF (numBedrooms changes from 5→6 and location from 4→4) THEN (housePrice changes from €800,000 → €900,000)*

to create a generalised rule:

> *IF (numBedrooms changes by 1 in range 2→6 and location from 4→4) THEN (housePrice increases by €100,000)*

Strategy 2: Relax the context in which adaptation rules may be applied.

E.g. replace rule:

> *IF (numBedrooms changes from 1→2 and location from 4→4) THEN (housePrice changes from €250,000 → €380,000)*

with

> *IF (numBedrooms changes from 1→2) THEN (housePrice changes from €250,000 → €380,000)*

In the final example of Section 2.1, Strategy 2 was applied to create rules that depend only on attribute differences and not on context.

We have now looked at how adaptation rules are created and used to solve regression problems. We have noted that adaptation rules based on raw differences between cases have insufficient problem-solving bias to be really useful, and have looked at strategies to address this issue. Although the idea of mining adaptation knowledge from the CB is a good one, the problem-solving system described above has a number of serious limitations:

1. *Interacting attributes.*
   Section 2.1 showed a simple example of adaptation rules in action. Two rules bridged the gap between a query and its NN, each dealing with one of two attribute differences. Where two or more attributes interact with one another, however, this approach will not work. E.g. the effect of increasing *numBedrooms* by 2 and decreasing *location* by 1 may be less than the impact of these changes individually. One can also imagine domains in which combining attribute differences *increases* their influence. In short, using a combination of simple rules to handle multiple

attribute differences is only valid when there is no interaction between the attributes. Hanney & Keane propose using expert knowledge to edit the rule-base so that these interactions are avoided. But there may be interactions between several attributes, and their strength may vary in different parts of the attributes' ranges. In these circumstances, editing the rule-base manually becomes an impossible task.

2. *Variable attribute relevance.*
   Generalised rules created using Strategy 1 are not always valid because the strong assumption is made that the solution's response to changes in the problem attribute is *linear*. With the Strategy 1 example above, the assumption is made that changes in *numBedrooms* from 2→3, 3→4, 4→5 and 5→6 will result in the same change to *housePrice*. Clearly this may not be the case, e.g. changing *numBedrooms* from 1→2 may have a greater impact on *housePrice* than changing from 3→4. Strategy 1 cannot be applied where attributes have variable *relevance* through their range. Again, Hanney & Keane suggest using expert knowledge to take attribute relevance into account during rule-base construction.

   A related problem is that when matching rules to case differences, Hanney & Keane prefer those rules that cover the highest number of attribute differences. In situations where some attributes are more important (relevant) that others, results might be improved by matching differences in those attributes first.

3. *Contextual Dependencies.*
   Strategy 2 relaxes the context in which rules may be applied. Although the resulting rules have wider applicability than their predecessors, it is often the case that a rule's correctness is inextricably linked to its context; ignoring the context invalidates the rule. E.g. the effect of changing *numBedrooms* from 1→2 will very probably be different in *location* 1 than in *location* 4. Where there are *contextual dependencies* of this type, Strategy 2 cannot be applied. Hanney & Keane suggest using expert knowledge to manually identify and account for these dependencies.

4. *Additive solution errors.*
   In noisy domains, solutions to cases in the CB will not always be accurate. Let us suppose that solutions have mean error ε, and that errors are distributed symmetrically about the true values. When two cases are used to construct an adaptation rule, the rule's solution difference will have error limits equal to $2 \times \varepsilon$ (indeterminate errors are added together under subtraction). If k adaptation rules are used to cover the differences between a query and its NN, the predicted solution is calculated by adding the solution difference in each rule to the NN's solution. This gives error limits of $\varepsilon + k \times (2 \times \varepsilon)$ (the initial ε is the error in the NN's solution). Where predictions are made using 'adaptation paths' made up of several adaptation rules, results will exhibit a high mean absolute error. This will result in poor performance in noisy real-world domains where ε is high.

Faced with these problems, can adaptation knowledge mined from the CB be used to construct an accurate, robust regression system that minimizes the need for explicit expert knowledge? The next section proposes a novel technique to address these problems by combining adaptation knowledge with locally-weighted learning.

3. Using Case Differences for Regression

Before describing our technique for performing regression using CBR, it will help to re-state our objectives. We would like to use adaptation knowledge mined automatically from the CB, since this simplifies system design and maintenance. We would like to *generalise* this knowledge so that it applies beyond the specific cases used to generate it. And in so doing, we would like to avoid the problems listed in Section 2.2.

Let us begin by re-examining the example from the end of Section 2.1. We can now see that the prediction is unsound for several reasons. First, the differences between Q and its NN are bridged using two separate rules. If problem attributes *numBedrooms* and *location* are interacting, this will not give the correct result. Second, both rules improperly ignore context. In the first rule, for example, the effect of changing *numBedrooms* for a house *should* depend on *location*. Third, the prediction is not robust because its accuracy depends on the correctness of the NN and on two adaptation rules, each constructed using two cases. If any of these five cases has an inaccurate result, the prediction will also be wrong. The fundamental difficulty is that *adaptation knowledge (stored in the form of adaptation rules) is being applied in circumstances where it is not valid.*

Let us examine the knowledge stored in adaptation rules in more detail. Here is a rule previously shown in Section 2.1:

IF (numBedrooms changes from 3→4 and location from 4→4) THEN
(housePrice changes from €550,000 → €680,000)

This rule codifies the precise changes in attribute values between two particular cases. It also contains the context in which these changes occur (i.e. unchanging attribute values). How can this highly specific knowledge be generalised so that it applies to new cases with different attribute values? We propose dividing the adaptation knowledge mined from the CB into two types. *Difference cases* contain the knowledge needed to solve new problems, while *local linear models* restrict the application of this knowledge to circumstances where it is appropriate. Between them, they contain enough knowledge for successful adaptation.

3.1 Difference Cases

Difference cases are simpler than adaptation rules – they simply store the differences between pairs of cases. E.g. given cases:

Case 1: (numBedrooms=4, location=3, housePrice=550000)

Case 2: (numBedrooms=2, location=4, housePrice=500000)

a difference case can be constructed from the differences between them:

Difference Case 1: (2, -1, 50000)

Difference cases can be stored in a CB of their own called a *Difference CB*. To limit storage requirements, each case is compared with a limited number of other cases, e.g. if the CB size is *n*, comparing each case with its 10 NNs generates a Difference CB with *n* x *10* difference cases.

3.2 Local Linear Models

Local linear models are used to restrict the application of difference cases in two ways. First, they indicate where adaptation knowledge stored in difference cases can be reused. Second, they improve the robustness of predictions by helping to avoid noisy cases.

3.2.1 Using Local Linear Models to Guide Application of Difference Cases

Suppose the differences between a query and its NN are *(2, -1)*, i.e. *numBedrooms* increases by 2, *location* decreases by 1. The question is whether Difference Case 1 from above can be used to solve this query. The answer is that it can, but *only if the impact on housePrice of increasing numBedrooms by 2 and decreasing location by 1 is the same for the query as for Difference Case 1*. To decide whether Difference Case 1 can be applied, then, we would like to measure the effect that changing *numBedrooms* and *location* has on *housePrice*, both for the query and for Difference Case 1. That is, we would like to measure the *rate of change* of *housePrice* with respect to *numBedrooms* and *location*.

In the domain used in our examples, *housePrice = f(numBedrooms, location)*. More generally, if adaptation function *f* maps a set of problem attributes $a_1, a_2, ..., a_n$ to a solution *y*, i.e. $y = f(a_1, a_2, ..., a_n)$, then

$$grad\ f = \left(\frac{\partial y}{\partial a_1}, \frac{\partial y}{\partial a_2}, ..., \frac{\partial y}{\partial a_n} \right).$$

In other words, the *gradient* of *f* at any point is the rate of change of the solution with respect to each of its problem attributes. This is precisely what we need to help decide where difference cases can be applied – if we can calculate the gradient for each difference case and query case, we can search for difference cases whose gradients match the query and use (one of) them to make a prediction.

A difference case can be used to bridge the gap between a query and its NN if the gradient around the query is similar to the gradient around the difference case. This is because the impact of problem attribute differences on the solution will be similar in both areas of domain space. If the attribute differences match, the solution difference should also be correct.

Calculating case gradients is quite straightforward. Each case occupies a particular point in domain space given by its vector of attribute and solution values. E.g. the case *(numBedrooms=3, location=2, housePrice=€350,000)* can be represented as *(3, 2, 350000)*. Domain space is then a multi-dimensional Euclidean space with one dimension representing each problem attribute and the solution. The gradient at any point is equivalent to the *slope* of adaptation function *f* in each direction. Although function *f* is unknown, it can be approximated at any point by constructing a *local linear model*.

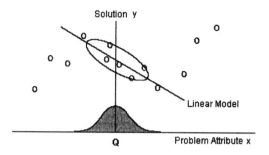

Figure 1 – Local Linear Model

Figure 1 illustrates the basics of local linear modelling. It shows a simple domain where the solution is a function of a single problem attribute. When a query Q is received, a local linear model can be constructed and used to predict its solution (see [7] for an introduction to local linear modelling). Neighbouring points are weighted by their distance from the query – Gaussian weighting is used in Figure 1 above – so that the model provides the best fit for points closest to Q. Note that the slope of the local linear model gives the rate of change of the solution with respect to the problem attribute in the area around Q. With a slope of roughly -0.5, an increase of 2 in the problem attribute results in a decrease of 1 in the solution. This linear model can be represented as $y = -0.5x + c$ (where c is a constant). The slope of problem attribute x is given by the attribute's parameter in the model equation.

In multi-dimensional domains, the gradient is a vector of slopes giving the rate of change of the solution with respect to each problem attribute. For our housing example *(3, 2, 350000)*, the gradient might be *(50000, 70000)*; at this point in domain space, increasing *numBedrooms* and *location* by 1 results in a *housePrice* increase of €50,000 and €70,000 respectively.

Summing up, *the gradient for each case in the CB can be calculated by constructing a local linear model at that point and taking its slope in each direction.* Each gradient can be stored with the corresponding case to make it easy to find. Recall, however, that we need the gradient of each difference case. A difference case constructed using two cases *(Case 1 – Case 2)* is assigned the gradient of the domain space around Case 2.

3.2.2 Using Local Linear Models to Avoid Noisy Cases

Difference cases and case gradients can be used to make a prediction as follows: retrieve a NN to the query, then account for the differences between them using a difference case whose gradient is similar to that around the query.

This procedure makes direct use of three specific cases: the NN and the two cases used to form the difference case. (These cases are referred to as an 'estimation triple' in [8].) If any of the three has an inaccurate solution, the prediction will also be inaccurate. Robustness can be improved by using local linear models to judge the *quality* of the three cases involved.

A high quality case is one whose stored solution is close to the true value. Since the true solution to each case is unknown, case quality can only be estimated. In

Section 3.2.1, a local linear model was constructed around each case in the CB. This can be used to estimate case quality: *a case is considered high quality if its stored solution is close to the value predicted by the linear model around it.* Conversely, a case is of low quality if its solution deviates significantly from the linear model constructed around it.

The predicted solution for a query Q is calculated using the formula:

$$solution_Q = solution_{NN} + (solution_{C1} - solution_{C2})$$

where cases C_1 and C_2 are used to construct a difference case matching *diff(NN, Q)*. Low quality cases are avoided by applying a penalty to those giving low values for *residual(NN)* and *(residual(C_1) – residual(C_2))*. *(residual(C_i)* is the difference between the stored value for case C_i and the value predicted using the linear model constructed around it.) Note that if C_1 and C_2 deviate from their linear model in the same direction and to the same degree, this will not affect their predictive quality.

Using linear models to judge the quality of cases is consistent with the underlying assumption of our regression technique, namely, that the unknown function generating the solution is continuous and can be approximated locally by a linear model. Linear models are *not* used to make predictions. Instead, they help find the 'best' difference cases by providing case gradients and identifying noisy cases.

3.3 Making Predictions using Difference Cases

CBR systems using difference cases for adaptation must undergo an initial training phase. All case attributes must have numeric values, so non-numeric attributes are converted to numeric and missing values are replaced. Difference cases are assembled into a Difference CB. The gradient at each case is calculated and stored.

When a new query case is received, its solution is predicted as follows:

1. Estimate the gradient around the query by building a local linear model.

2. Retrieve several (e.g. 10) of the query's NNs.

3. Construct difference cases by calculating the differences between the query and each of its NNs – call them *diff(NN_1, Q)*, *diff(NN_2, Q)*, etc.

4. Search the Difference CB for the best *n* difference cases matching any of *diff(NN_i, Q)*. (Note that some NNs may have several matching difference cases among the best *n*, while other NNs may have none.)

5. Make *k* predictions by adding the solution differences in the retrieved difference cases to the solutions from the corresponding NNs. Make a final prediction by taking the weighted average of the *k* predictions.

In Step 4, each difference case in the Difference CB is given a score based on how similar it is to *diff(NN, Q)*, and how similar its gradient is to the query's. The quality of the cases used in each difference case is also taken into account. In Step 5, robustness is improved by taking the weighted average of a number of predictions. (The optimal value for *k* can be found using cross validation.)

Note that only one difference case is used for each prediction. Experiments have shown that chaining together several difference cases to bridge a large gap between a query and its neighbour does not improve accuracy – the accumulated error from combining several difference case solutions offsets the benefit of bridging the gap more precisely.

We can illustrate this procedure by re-using the example from Section 2.1. For simplicity, suppose $n=1$ and $k=1$ – only a single NN is retrieved and only a single prediction made. With query $Q = (numBedrooms=5, location=1)$, $housePrice$ is predicted as follows:

1. Gradient at Q: $(50000, 70000)$

2. Query's NN: $(numBedrooms=3, location=2, housePrice=€350,000)$

3. Difference case for NN and Q: $diff(NN, Q) = (2, -1)$

4. Best-matching difference case: $(2, -1, 50000)$ with gradient $(40000, 65000)$

5. Predicted $housePrice$ for Q: $€350,000 + €50,000 = €400,000$

3.4 Advantages of Using Difference Cases for Regression

The advantages of using difference cases for regression are as follows:

- Adaptation knowledge is mined automatically from the CB, with no additional expert knowledge needed.

- All problems (listed in Section 2.2) associated with regression rules are avoided. Simple difference cases are used to solve new cases, with local linear models indicating when they can be applied.

- The adaptation process itself uses CBR to store and retrieve difference cases. Adaptation therefore integrates neatly into the CBR system, with the same case representation and retrieval mechanisms used for both.

- The key advantage of using difference cases is that *users can be provided with an intelligible explanation for each prediction*, allowing them to judge the quality of the result for themselves. All predictions are made using actual stored cases. Given a query Q, the following explanation can accompany the predicted solution:
  "Case A is very similar to Q and has solution x. The differences between the two cases are $(d_1, d_2, ...)$. A similar pair of cases, B and C, have (almost) the same differences between them. The difference between their solutions is d_s, therefore the predicted solution for Q is $x + d_s$."

4. Experimental Analysis

The performance of difference cases on a regression task was evaluated using the Boston Housing dataset from the UCI repository [9]. This dataset contains 506 instances, each with 13 numeric problem attributes and a numeric solution (house price). All attributes were normalised to the range 0-1.

Two sets of experiments were performed. The first evaluated the performance of the algorithm with different parameter settings. The second compared the performance of difference cases against that of standard machine learning algorithms. All experiments used 10 x 10-fold cross-validation.

4.1 Experiment 1: Regression using Difference Cases

Three versions of the difference case regression algorithm were compared.

1. Difference cases only. The differences between a query and its NN were bridged using the closest-matching difference case.

2. Difference cases + context information guiding their application:

   a) Difference cases in close proximity to the query were preferred. This is a simple approach to deciding where adaptation knowledge can be reused – adaptation knowledge from the neighbourhood of the query is always relevant.

   b) Local linear models were used to choose the 'best' difference cases (see Section 3).

3. Difference cases + context + weighted average. The weighted average of predictions made by the best 5 difference cases was taken, where problem solving context was provided by proximity to the query and by local linear models.

Performance can be seen to improve as context is used to guide the application of difference cases. Using linear models to guide the selection of difference cases can also be seen to produce better results than using proximity to the query.

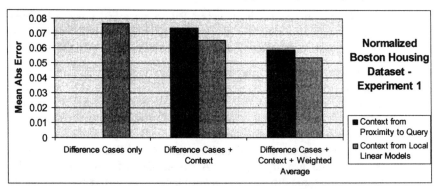

4.2 Experiment 2: Difference Cases vs. Standard Algorithms

The full difference case algorithm was compared with several standard regression techniques. As can be seen, performance is comparable with the state-of-the-art (represented by local linear modelling). As well as cutting-edge performance, the difference case algorithm offers the advantage that predictions can be accompanied by useful explanations (see Section 3.4). This makes it particularly suitable for use in those domains where explanations are essential, e.g. the medical domain.

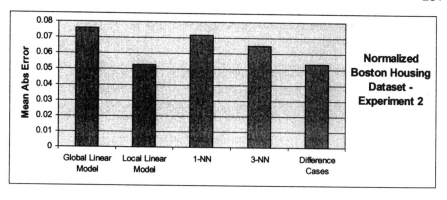

5. Related Work

Knowledge-light approaches to learning adaptation knowledge are constrained by the limited amount of knowledge contained in any case base, and by the fact that adaptation often takes very different forms in different domains. Nevertheless, a number of approaches to the introspective learning of adaptation knowledge have been proposed.

Hanney & Keane [6] and McSherry [8] consider the problem of learning adaptation knowledge for regression. Hanney and Keane's approach is outlined in Section 2 in some detail. Differences between pairs of cases are captured in adaptation rules which are then used to solve new cases. McSherry proposes using case differences for adaptation in linear domains, a technique referred to as the 'difference heuristic'. Both approaches suggest that the problem of interacting attributes could be addressed by adding expert domain knowledge to the adaptation process.

Jarmulak et al. [10] and Wiratunga et al. [11] look at the introspective learning of adaptation knowledge for a design task (tablet formulation). Case differences are stored together with contextual information in 'adaptation cases' that contain similar information to Hanney & Keane's adaptation rules. When solving new problems, adaptation cases in close proximity to the query are preferred. Attribute interactions and constraints are also mined automatically from the case base.

Previous research has recognised that case differences alone are often insufficient for effective problem-solving; what is lacking is some way to determine where this knowledge can usefully be applied. This paper proposes using local linear models to guide the application of case differences.

6. Conclusion

Automatic generation of adaptation knowledge simplifies the construction and maintenance of CBR systems. Learning adaptation knowledge from a case base is problematic because it is often unclear whether adaptation knowledge from one part of domain space can validly be used in another. This is a particular difficulty in domains where attribute relevance varies throughout domain space.

We have described a novel knowledge-light technique for performing regression using CBR. No explicit expert knowledge is needed; all adaptation knowledge is mined directly from the case base. This knowledge takes two forms: *difference cases* that contain the differences between pairs of cases, and *local linear models* that determine where difference cases may be applied. Early experiments suggest that the technique performs well in real-world domains.

References

1. Aamodt A. and Plaza E. Case-based reasoning: foundational issues, methodological variations, and system approaches. AI Communications 1994, 7(i):39-59
2. Leake D., Kinley A., and Wilson D. Learning to Improve Case Adaptation by Introspective Reasoning and CBR. In: Proceedings of the First International Conference on Case-Based Reasoning. Springer Verlag, 1995
3. Bartsch-Spörl B., Lenz M., and Hübner A. Case-Based Reasoning: Survey and Future Directions. In: Proceedings of XPS-99, volume 1570 of LNCS, pp. 67-89. Springer, 1999
4. Wilke W., Vollrath I., Althoff K.-D, and Bergmann R. A framework for learning adaptation knowledge based on knowledge light approaches. In Proceedings of the 5th German Workshop on Case-Based Reasoning, 1997
5. Richter M. Introduction. In: Wess S., Lenz M., Bartsch-Spörl B., and H.D. Burkhard H. D. (Eds.) Case-Based Reasoning Technology: From Foundations to Applications, LNAI 1400. Springer, 1998
6. Hanney K. and Keane M. Learning Adaptation Rules from a Case-Base. In: Proceedings of the Third European Workshop on Case-based Reasoning. Springer Verlag, 1996
7. Atkeson C., Moore A., and Schaal S. Locally weighted learning. AI Review, 1996
8. McSherry D. An adaptation heuristic for case-based estimation. In: Proceedings of the 4th European Workshop on Case-Based Reasoning. Springer, 1998
9. Hettich S., Blake C.L., and Merz C.J. UCI Repository of machine learning databases. University of California, Irvine, CA, 1998
10. Jarmulak J., Craw S., and Rowe R. Using Case-Base Data to Learn Adaptation Knowledge for Design. In: Proceedings of the 17th International Conference on Artificial Intelligence. Morgan Kaufmann, 2001
11. Wiratunga N., Craw S., Rowe R. Learning to Adapt for Case-Based Design. In: Proceedings of the 6th European Conference on Case-Based Reasoning. Springer, 2002

Formal Concept Analysis for Knowledge Refinement in Case Based Reasoning *

Belén Díaz-Agudo, Marco A. Gómez-Martín,
Pedro P. Gómez-Martín and Pedro A. González-Calero
Dep. Sistemas Informáticos y Programación
Universidad Complutense de Madrid
Madrid, Spain
email: {belend,marcoa,pedrop,pedro}@sip.ucm.es

June 6, 2005

Abstract

Case-based Reasoning (CBR) is a problem solving paradigm that uses past experiences to solve new problems. Although CBR is supposed to alleviate the problem of knowledge acquisition, knowledge is still required to obtain the initial case base and to develop the processes of retrieving, reusing, revising and retaining cases. In this paper we propose the use of Formal Concept Analysis (FCA) to acquire and refine the knowledge available in a CBR system. In particular, we show how FCA can help to acquire indexing knowledge that supports the retrieval process, and also the use of FCA to improve the quality of the case base by identifying lack of coverage and biased combinations of case attributes.

1   Introduction

Case Based Reasoning (CBR) is a knowledge-light approach for building intelligent systems where, instead of explicit models of the domain, past experiences are used to solve new problems. Although CBR is supposed to alleviate the problem of knowledge acquisition, knowledge is still required to obtain the cases and to develop the processes of retrieving, reusing, revising and retaining cases.

Formal Concept Analysis (FCA) is a method for data analysis, knowledge representation and information management. It was invented by Rudolf Wille [12] and applied in different domains, like psychology, medicine, linguistics and computer sciences among others.

Our previous work has shown the use of Galois lattices and Formal Concept Analysis to support CBR application designers in the task of *organizing* and *retrieving* cases that are similar to the current query [3, 2]. In this paper we

---

*Supported by the Spanish Committee of Science & Technology (TIC2002-01961)

propose the use of FCA as a *maintenance technique* to acquire and refine the knowledge available in a CBR system. In particular, we are using FCA to find coverage gaps in the case base, i.e., cases that are not currently available in the case base but will be needed for future reasoning processes.

In Section 2 we briefly describe our previously described use of Galois lattices as structures to classify and retrieve cases. Section 3 describes the use of FCA to improve the quality of the case base by identifying lack of coverage and biased combinations of case attributes. After describing our proposal, in Section 4 we exemplify it by a problem that we solve using CBR: an intelligent tutoring system call JV^2M to teach the compilation of object-oriented languages. Finally, Section 5 concludes the paper.

2 FCA for Discovery Case Indexing Knowledge

Case Based Reasoning is a well known AI technique that is applied to the development of knowledge based systems. CBR attempts to simulate the human act of identifying and solving problems using analogy and remembering previously solved cases. For example, an expert with several years of experience on a given domain eventually gathers a great amount of known cases. Hence, for a given situation, the expert knows possible solutions to be applied [8].

FCA is a mathematical approach to data analysis based on the lattice theory of Garret Birkhoff [1]. We claim that Galois lattices and Formal Concept Analysis are very adequate techniques to organize the case base and to support CBR application designers in the task of discovering knowledge embedded in the cases. FCA applied on a case library provides an internal sight of the conceptual structure and allows finding patterns, regularities and exceptions among the cases.

Our first approach was organizing the set of cases –case base– using a knowledge base of domain terminology. However, it is not an optimized structure to effectively classify and retrieve cases. Instead, we get a linearly organized case base that is travelled through whenever we need to retrieve a case. We compute a numeric similarity measure to compare a new problem with every case stored in the case base.

If we want to improve the efficiency of the retrieval process, we could use the domain knowledge concepts together with certain appropriate *index concepts*. These index concepts aggregate characteristics and organize the case base. If we use a good index structure, that is predictive enough, we could substitute the *computational retrieval approach*, based on numeric similarity computation, by a *representational retrieval approach*, based on classifying the query on the index structure to get the set of cases that are classified near it in the index structure. Typically, index concepts are manually added by a domain expert (this is the approach used for example in [11]). Instead we have used FCA as an inductive technique that elicits knowledge embedded in a concrete case library.

```
public void f() {            public void f(int b) {
    int a;                       int a;
    a = 3 + 5;                   a = 3 + b;
}                            }
```

a) Case 1   b) Case 2

```
public void f(int b) {
    int a;
    if (b == 0) a = 4;
}
```

c) Case 3

Figure 1: Case Base Example

FCA provides a way to identify groupings of objects with shared properties. FCA is especially well suited when we have to deal with a collection of items described by properties. This is a clear characteristic of the case libraries where there are cases described by features. Moreover the concept lattice resultant from FCA application, can be used as a case organization structure. Then, we propose the use of *classification based retrieval* over the conceptual structure obtained applying FCA over the case base. Our approach to case organization and classification based retrieval over the FCA concept lattice was first described in [3].

Formal Concepts resulting from FCA represent maximal groupings of cases with shared properties, and for a given query, we can access all the cases that share properties with the query at the same time so that they are grouped under the same concept. The order between concepts allows structuring the library according to the attributes describing the cases. The lower in the graph, the more characteristics can be said about the cases; i.e. more general concepts are higher up than more specific ones.

The dependency knowledge implicitly contained in the case base is also captured during the FCA process in the form of dependency rules among the attributes describing the cases. We propose the application of FCA as an automatic technique to elicit the attribute co-appearance knowledge inside a case library. Our approach is specially well suited in structured domains, that are characterized by the fact that there is an intrinsic dependency between certain elements in the domain. Considering these dependencies leads to better performance of CBR systems and it is an important factor for determining the relevance of the cases stored in a case base [10].

Case retrieval begins with an incremental query description process, where the user provides with certain descriptors, while the system proposes other properties by using the dependence rules captured during the FCA. When completing the query by using the dependence rules, intuitively, what we are

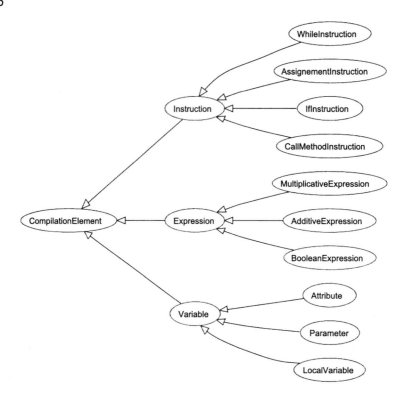

Figure 2: Java compilation elements

doing is to guide the user towards more specific and defined concepts in the lattice. Note, this kind of retrieval over the lattice finds all the cases where all the query descriptors appear, i.e. the cases retrieved as similar are those with the greater number of characteristics shared with the query. After that, we construct an individual with the query description, classify it in the lattice, and retrieves individuals placed near it. We use a Description Logic system whose recognition module automatically classifies the new individual in its corresponding place in the lattice. All instances classified under the most specific concept the query instance belongs to, are retrieved as similar.

The first retrieval step can be complemented with other knowledge intensive CBR processes, including more sophisticated retrieval processes with numeric similarity measures taking other attributes into account[1].

Let's see a simple example of the use of FCA to organize a case base.

2.1 A simple example of case indexing using FCA

Let's suppose a problem typically solved by teachers of future computer scientists: use CBR to generate a computer program using a case base of previously

---

[1] Note that FCA could be applied over a subset of the case descriptors

	Variable	LocalVariable	Parameter	Instruction	AssignmentInstr	IfInstruction	Expression	AdditiveExpr	BooleanExpr
Case 1	■	■		■	■		■	■	
Case 2	■	■	■	■	■		■	■	
Case 3	■	■	■	■	■	■	■		■

Table 1: Incidence Table

existing programs in the same programming language. To do that, we first retrieve a similar case and then modify it according to the new requirements.

Just to illustrate the use of FCA for case indexing, let's start with the simple case base having only three Java programs, listed in Figure 1. The domain knowledge contains the terminology about structures of the Java language in form of an ontology depicted in Figure 2. For example, Case 1 includes *Local-Variable*, *AssignmentInstruction* and *AdditiveExpression* elements. As it can be extracted from the hierarchy showed in Figure 2, the case also includes the internal concepts *Variable*, *Instruction* and *Expression* besides *CompilationElement*. For simplicity, we will not consider this last element (*CompilationElement*) in the rest of the paper.

To apply FCA, we interpret the case base as a *formal context* that is defined as a triple $\langle G, M, I \rangle$ where there are two sets G (of cases) and M (of attributes or characteristics), and a binary (incidence) relation $I \subseteq G \times M$, expressing which attributes describe each case (or which cases are described using a characteristic). Graphically, a context is usually described by a cross-table (Table 1). The application of FCA generates a *lattice* (Figure 3), that captures formal concepts representing the co-appearance of characteristics shared by the concrete cases. Each node in the Hasse diagram of Figure 3 represents a formal concept of the context, and the ascending paths of line segments represent the subconcept-superconcept relation.

Besides the hierarchical conceptual clustering of the cases, the concept lattice provides with a set of implications between attributes known as *dependence rules* [3]. A dependence rule between two attribute sets (written $M1 \rightarrow M2$, where $M1, M2 \subseteq M$) means that any object having all attributes in $M1$ has also all attributes in $M2$. We can read the dependence rules in the graph as follows:

- Each line between nodes labelled with attributes means a dependence rule between the attributes from the lower node to the upper one. For example, from Figure 3 we extract, among others, rules {*AdditiveExpr* → *Variable*} and {*AdditiveExpr* → *Expression*}.

- When there are several attributes in the same label it means that there is a co-appearance of all these attributes for all the cases in the sam-

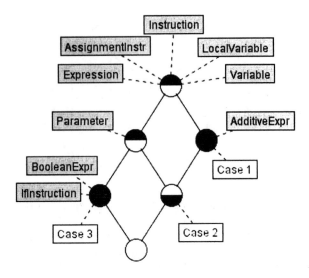

Figure 3: Lattice extracted from the formal context in Table 1

ple. For example, rules $\{IfInstruction \rightarrow Boolean\}$ and $\{Boolean \rightarrow IfInstruction\}$.

Dependency knowledge is present in our daily life and it is specially interesting and useful in structured domains. Note that FCA is an inductive technique and the dependency rules extracted are specific of a certain case base. It means that we can not assure we have captured general domain dependencies, like functional dependencies appearing during the design of a relational database. Next section describes our approach about using the coappearance of attribute values in the cases to help enriching the case base itself.

3 FCA for Knowledge Refinement in CBR

The main source of knowledge of a CBR system is located in the case base itself. Previous section explains two knowledge resources that we obtain if we analyze a certain case base using Formal Concept Analysis: an index lattice structure, that is used to organize the case base and improve the efficiency of the retrieval process, and a set of dependency implications, that we use to complement the query representing a new problem that will be solved by the CBR system.

CBR is regarded to be a more appealing approach to Knowledge Based System (KBS) development than the traditional rule based approach mainly due to the more intuitive nature of cases as a knowledge representation and reasoning formalism. For a long time the case base approach to KBS development was seen as a possible solution to the knowledge acquisition and maintenance problems associated with rule based systems. As the field of CBR has matured, support has grown for the view that CBR has not alleviated these problems as hoped, but in many ways compounded them. It has become apparent that as opposed to just the need to acquire domain (case) knowledge there is also a need to acquire vocabulary knowledge, retrieval (similarity / indexing) knowledge, adaptation knowledge, and maintenance knowledge before a CBR system can be regarded as fully operational. Domain experts are one resource for the knowledge required for these containers; automated learning methods is another.

In this paper, we propose a semi-automatic technique based on a complementary use of FCA and domain expert supervision. Our approach facilitates the initial acquisition of knowledge as well as its long-term maintenance as the CBR system evolves within its environment.

Due to the fact that the case base constitutes the knowledge core of the CBR system, it is extremely important to be able to assure its quality. We measure the quality of a case base in terms of the number of cases, the coverage of the problem domain. Quality also requires that the case base does not allow the inference of implications that, being true for all the cases in the case base, are not true in general.

In this section we explain a complementary use of FCA to refine a given case base. Once the domain expert has created the system case base, FCA can be used to refine it and to assure its quality. That is possible because FCA has the capability of finding implication between attributes in the formal context.

Using the analysis of all these implications the author can check if they are also valid in the universe of the problem domain. If the case base allows the inference of implications that are not valid in the domain universe, then the case base is biased, it has not enough quality and must be extended. Otherwise, we will find the same bias in the kind of problems that this case base is able to solve, or the kind of solutions it generates.

As an intuitive example suppose we are using a CBR system in a travel agency to store all the travels it is offering. Previously we have used FCA to automatically create *index concepts* such as "educative travel in summer" or "travel with snorkel and riding activities" that can be used in *computational retrieval approach* to improve the efficiency. This paper proposes a new use of FCA. Lets assume the manager is interested in knowing if her catalogue is complete enough. She could analise by herself all the travels in order to look for carencies (in other words, lack of coverage in the case base). Instead of that, we suggest the use of FCA to automatically infer implications in the case base. For example, the system could indicate that all the travels where clients can ski are in winter. Our manager would admit this implication. But if the system infers that all the trips to Miami are in spring the manager could consider trying to expand her catalogue.

The underlying process starts with a case base created by an expert. The case base is converted to a formal context as is described in the previous section. Using FCA we extract the dependency rules from the lattice. The domain expert establishes whether these rules are correct in the universe or not. When a dependency rule is incorrect, it means that additional cases has to be included because there are attributes that appear somehow linked together in all the

```
public void auxf() {
    System.out.
        print("In auxf()");
}
public void f() {
    auxf();
}
```

a) Case 4

```
public void f(int a) {
    if (a > 0)
        System.out.
            print("Positive");
}
```

b) Case 5

```
public void f() {
    if (this.age > 18)
        System.out.
            print("Big boy");
}
```

c) Case 6

```
public void birthday() {
    age = age + 1;
}
```

d) Case 7

Figure 4: New cases created to eliminate wrong dependencies

cases even though that is not imposed by the domain.

If the expert decides that this invalid implication is not admissible in the context of the CBR system, she must add a counterexample that breaks the implication. Usually, this new case will be created by the expert, though it is also possible to generate it using the mechanism of adaptation included in the CBR system when it is available.

The process finishes when all the dependency rules inferred from the formal context are considered valid in the domain by the expert.

3.1 A simple example of case base refinement using FCA

To exemplify the process, we will describe the evolution of the simple case base sketched in Section 2.1. In a real example the initial case base would have many more cases, and FCA would not report so many invalid dependencies. We have used the Java-based open source FCA Tool *ConExp*[2], that is able to calculate the *Duquenne-Guigues* base of implications [6].

Analysing the initial formal context from Table 1, *ConExp* infers that all the cases contain *Variable*, *LocalVariable*, *Instruction*, *AssignmentInstr* and *Expression*. Obviously this is not true in our domain. The expert is asked about including a new case with no local variables (see Figure 4.a).

The new case includes *Instruction* and *CallMethodInstr*. However, as it has no *Variable* attribute, the next invalid implication that *ConExp* reports is the dependency between *LocalVariable* and *Variable*. So the expert also has to create a program where the unique procedure to be execute has a parameter (see Figure 4.b), and that has *Instruction*, *CallMethodInstr*, *IfInstruction*, *Expression* and *BooleanExpr* attributes.

---

[2]See http://sourceforge.net/projects/conexp

From the new lattice, *ConExpr* extracts (among other things) the following dependence rules: {*BooleanExpr → Variable*; *BooleanExpr → Parameter*; *BooleanExpr → LocalVariable*; *BooleanExpr → Instruction*; *BooleanExpr → AssignmentInstr*; *BooleanExpr → IfInstruction*; *BooleanExpr → Expression*}.

Beginning with the first rule {*BooleanExpr → Variable*}, the expert confirms it as true (as it is not very common to find boolean expressions without variables as in "3 > 5"). However, the expert wants to eliminate the dependence between *BooleanExpr* and *Parameter*. It stands because all cases with parameters have also boolean expressions.

We introduce Case 6 (see Figure 4.c) to eliminate this dependency, adding to the formal context the attribute *Attribute* that represents a field access in the Java program (`this.age`). As *ConExp* infers that this new concept always appears with *IfInstruction*, the expert creates Case 7 (in Figure 4.d) to indicate that the new concept can appear without it.

At this point, FCA induces that every case including *Attribute* also includes *Variable*, *Instruction* and *Expression*. That is true in the domain, because:

- We consider that *Attribute* as a kind of *Variable*'s (also *LocalVble* is a *Variable*), as shown in Figure 2.

- All the cases have at least one instruction.

- All the field access are done through an expression.

The next incorrect dependency is {BooleanExpr → IfInstruction}, because all the boolean expressions appear attached to `if` instructions. Nevertheless, we will stop here, only sketching out the next step. The expert should break the new relation adding a new program including, for example, a `while` instruction (and its needed boolean expression). The old dependency would be substituted for two new ones ({*IfInstruction → BooleanExpr*} and {*WhileInstruction → BooleanExpr*}) that will be confirmed as correct.

The formal context with Cases 1–7 appears in Table 2 and the associated lattice is shown in Figure 5.

4   JV²M: a case study

The examples used throughout the paper about Java source code are, actually, cases used in JV²M [5], an Intelligent Tutoring System (ITS) that teaches the compilation of object-oriented languages. Concretely, students must learn to translate Java source code into object code, in other words, into code understood by the Java Virtual Machine (JVM).

The exercises of JV²M are stored in a case base, and are related to those *compilation concepts* they teach. Exercises are created only with pedagogical purposes, so most of them do not perform any concrete algorithm.

Instead of using a text-based user interface, the system provides with a 3D virtual environment that creates a metaphorical simulation of the JVM. The student is immersed in that learning environment and, instead of just write down the resulting object code, she *executes it* in the simulated JVM where she is enclosed. The learning environment is complemented with a pedagogical

	Variable	LocalVariable	Parameter	Instruction	AssignmentInstr	IfInstruction	Expression	AdditiveExpr	BooleanExpr	CallMethodInstr	Attribute
Case 1	■	■		■	■		■	■			
Case 2	■	■	■	■	■		■	■			
Case 3	■	■	■	■	■	■	■		■		
Case 4				■						■	
Case 5	■		■	■		■	■		■	■	
Case 6	■		■			■	■		■	■	■
Case 7	■			■	■		■	■			■

Table 2: Last formal context

agent [7, 9] called JAVY, a human-like figure that assists the student in the learning process. Interaction is similar to a 3D-graphical adventure game that tries to guarantee student motivation.

Each exercise is a complete Java program with a primary class that contains the proper `main` function. Students have to execute the Java code starting in a point marked by the author of the exercise. Using this approach, we allow the system to teach basic concepts without forcing it to present advanced aspects, for example a student learns how to use parameters of a function without using the no so intuitive `main` parameters, or the method call instruction.

As can be deduced, JV^2M uses the learning-by-doing approach of teaching. Students are faced with more and more complex exercises. The system selects the next exercise to practise depending on the user knowledge and tries to reach a balance to avoid both boring and frustrating the student.

Exercises are authored by tutors (aka. "domain experts"), and recovered from a case base. Each exercise is classified using concepts referring to Java language structures as described in Section 2.1. Instead of having a "plain" list of concepts, we have arranged them in a conceptual hierarchy, partially sketched in Figure 2.

The learning-by-doing cycle starts with the pedagogical module. Using a concrete pedagogical strategy, it decides which concepts the student should practice next and the set of concepts she should not practice because she has not the needed knowledge to understand them.

CBR retrieval uses these two set of concepts to get the most similar exercise. In [4] we have described this CBR approach including an adaptation phase that may change the exercise to make it teach a different set of concepts.

In this paper we have described two uses of FCA in CBR that can be applied to the JV^2M system: discovering case indexing knowledge (for optimizing the recover phase) in Section 2; and case base refinement in Section 3.

Concerning the JV^2M ITS exercises, FCA discovers two kinds of dependence rules. The first group refers to the relation between the compilation concepts

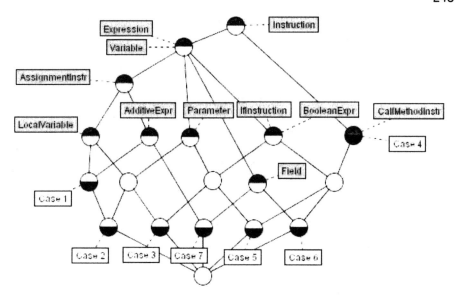

Figure 5: Lattice extracted from the formal context in Table 2

that we had, in fact, manually created in the ontology shown in Figure 2.

The second group if exemplified by a dependence rule such as {*IfInstruction* → *BooleanExpr*}. It shows us that when an exercises has an if instruction, a boolean expression always appears. This information should be used to teach how to compile boolean expressions *before* teaching to compile if instructions. Through this fact can be quite obvious for a human tutor, the important point here is that this knowledge has been automatically extracted from the case base (and, obviously, confirmed by an expert domain), so, in some way, FCA is being used to extract a *partial* order that should be incorporated into the the system to guide the pedagogical strategy which chooses the exercises. We are remarking *partial* because there are concepts that cannot be order by FCA (for example *IfInstruction* and *WhileInstruction*) and must be sort by an expert.

5 Conclusions and Future Work

CBR is a reasoning and learning paradigm that uses past experiences to solve new problems. CBR is supposed to alleviate the problem of knowledge acquisition due to the more intuitive nature of cases as a knowledge representation and reasoning formalism. However as the field of CBR has matured, it has been claimed that it has not alleviated these problems as hoped, but in many ways compounded them. It has become apparent that as opposed to just the need to acquire domain (case) knowledge there is also a need to acquire vocabulary knowledge, retrieval (similarity / indexing) knowledge, adaptation knowledge, and maintenance knowledge before a CBR system can be regarded as fully operational. Domain experts are one resource for the knowledge required for these containers automated learning methods another.

In this paper we go a bit further, and we have proposed a semi-automatic technique based on a complementary use of FCA and domain expert supervision. Our approach facilitates the initial acquisition of knowledge as well as its long-term maintenance as the CBR system evolves within its environment.

Due to the fact that the case base constitutes the knowledge core of the CBR system, it is extremely important to be able to assure its quality. We measure the quality of a case base in terms of the number of cases, the coverage of the problem domain. Quality also requires that the case base does not allow the inference of implications that, being true for all the cases in the case base, are not true in general.

If we analyze a certain case base using Formal Concept Analysis we obtain two useful knowledge resources: an index lattice structure, that is used to organize the case base and improve the efficiency of the retrieval process, and a set of dependency implications, that we use to complement the query representing a new problem that will be solved by the CBR system.

We have used FCA to acquire and refine the knowledge available in a CBR system. FCA has been useful to acquire indexing knowledge that supports the retrieval process, and to improve the quality of the case base by identifying lack of coverage and biased combinations of case attributes.

Both uses have been exemplified in JV^2M, an Intelligent Tutoring System where students must learn to translate Java source code into object code, i.e. into code understood by the Java Virtual Machine. As an additional benefit, FCA has proven to be useful during the design of the pedagogical strategy of an ITS. It extracts a *partial* order that should be incorporated into the the system to guide the pedagogical strategy which chooses the exercises.

In [4] we described the CBR module of JV^2M that receives a query with a set of concepts C_i that the user needs to learn (or practise), and a set of concepts N_k that should not be practised. The CBR system retrieves and adapts the most similar exercise to satisfy the query requirements.

We would like to integrate –and compare– the approach described in this paper, where there is an expert who is in charge of including new cases, with the approach that we described in [4]. Instead of asking the expert to include a new exercise because a certain dependency rule (for example, A → B) is not satisfied, we could generate the query *"practise A but not B"*, and let the automatic adaptation do the job.

As the next future work we aim to give tool support to FCA in jCOLIBRI[3] an object-oriented framework in Java to build CBR systems.

References

[1] G. Birkhoff. *Lattice Theory, third editon.* American Math. Society Coll. Publ. 25, Providence, R.I, 1973.

---

[3]http://sourceforge.net/projects/jcolibri-cbr/

[2] B. Díaz-Agudo and P. A. González-Calero. Classification based retrieval using formal concept analysis. In *Procs. of the of 4th International Conference on Case-Based Reasoning (ICCBR)*. Springer-Verlag, 2001.

[3] B. Díaz-Agudo and P. A. González-Calero. Formal concept analysis as a support technique for CBR. In *Knowledge-Based Systems, 14 (3-4), June.* Elsevier. (ISSN:0950-7051), pp. 163-172., 2001.

[4] P. P. Gómez-Martín, M. A. Gómez-Martín, B. Díaz-Agudo, and P. A. González-Calero. Opportunities for CBR in learning by doing. In *Proceedings of 6th International Conference on Case-Based Reasoning (ICCBR)*. Springer-Verlag, 2005.

[5] P. P. Gómez-Martín, M. A. Gómez-Martín, and P. A. González-Calero. Javy: Virtual environment for Case-Based Teaching of Java Virtual Machine. In V. Palade, R. J. Howlett, and L. C. Jain, editors, *KES*, volume 2773 of *Lecture Notes in Computer Science*, pages 906–913. Springer, 2003.

[6] J.-L. Guigues and V. Duquenne. Familles minimales d'implications informatives resultant d'un tableau de donnes binaires. *Math. Sci. Humanies 95, 1986, 5-18.*

[7] W. L. Johnson, J. Rickel, R. Stiles, and A. Munro. Integrating pedagogical agents into virtual environments. *Presence: Teleoperators & Virtual Environments*, 7(6):523–546, December 1998.

[8] D. Leake. *Case-Based Reasoning: Experiences, Lessons, & Future Directions.* AAAI Press / The MIT Press. ISBN 0-262-62110-X, 1996.

[9] J. C. Lester, S. A. Converse, S. E. Kahler, S. T. Barlow, B. A. Stone, and R. Bhogal. The persona effect: affective impact of animated pedagogical agents. In *Proceedings Human Factors in Computing Systems (CHI'97)*, pages 359–366, 1997.

[10] H. Muñoz-Avila and J. Hullen. Retrieving cases in structured domains by using goal dependencies. In *CBR Research and development(ICCBR'95).* Springer-Verlag, 1995.

[11] A. Napoli, J. Lieber, and R. Courien. Classification-based problem solving in CBR. In I. Smith and B. Faltings, editors, *Advances in Case-Based Reasoning – (EWCBR'96).* Springer-Verlag, Berlin Heidelberg New York, 1996.

[12] R. Wille. *Restructuring Lattice Theory: an approach based on hierarchies of concepts.* Rival, I., (ed.), Ordered Sets, 1982.

Recommendation Knowledge Discovery

David McSherry and Christopher Stretch

School of Computing and Information Engineering, University of
Ulster, Coleraine BT52 1SA, Northern Ireland

Abstract

Recently we presented a novel approach to the discovery of
recommendation rules from a product case base that take account
of *all* features of a recommended product, including those with
respect to which the user's preferences are unknown. In this
paper, we investigate the potential role of *default* preferences in
the discovery of recommendation rules. As we show in the
domain of digital cameras, the potential benefits include a
dramatic reduction in the effective length of the discovered rules
and increased coverage of queries representing the user's
personal preferences. Another important finding of the research
presented is that in a recommender system that takes account of
default preferences, many of the products in the case base may
never be recommended.

1 Introduction

In case-based reasoning (CBR) approaches to product recommendation, product
descriptions are stored in a case base and retrieved in response to a query
representing the user's preferences. An advantage of NN retrieval, the standard
CBR approach, is the ability to recommend the product that is *most similar* to the
user's query if there is no product that exactly matches her requirements [1]. In
common with other approaches, however, NN retrieval is potentially unreliable
when applied to incomplete queries because of its failure to take account of *all*
features of a recommended product that may affect its acceptability [2]. For
example, a property recommended to a user looking for a four bedroom, detached
property may exactly match the user's *known* requirements but not be acceptable
because of its location. Of course, one might argue that the user should have
specified a preferred location. However, incomplete queries are common in
practice, and the reliability of recommendations that simply ignore any features
that are not mentioned in the user's query is open to question.

Aiming to improve the reliability of recommendations based on incomplete
queries, we recently presented an algorithm for the discovery of recommendation
rules that take account of all features of a recommended product, including those

with respect to which the user's preferences are *unknown* [2]. We will refer to the rules discovered by our algorithm as *dominance* rules. In the following definition, *most-similar*(Q) is the set of cases that are most similar to a given query Q. We say that a given query Q^* is an *extension* of another query Q, or that Q is a *sub-query* of Q^*, if Q^* includes all the preferences in Q. We denote this by writing $Q \subseteq Q^*$.

Definition 1. *For any case C and query Q, we say that $Q \rightarrow C$ is a dominance rule if most-similar(Q^*) = {C} for all extensions Q^* of Q.*

Dominance rules are more reliable than decision-tree approaches and NN retrieval when applied to incomplete queries in that no competing case can equal the similarity of a recommended case regardless of the user's *unknown* preferences. The output produced by our algorithm is a set of dominance rules that require minimal information for their application in *Rubric*, an algorithm for rule-based retrieval of recommended cases [2]. Given a target query, *Rubric* checks through the available rules and retrieves the case recommended by the first rule that *covers* the target query. A dominance rule $Q \rightarrow C$ covers any query Q^* such that $Q \subseteq Q^*$. In the absence of a rule that covers the target query, *Rubric* may be forced to *abstain* from making a recommendation. However, our rule-based approach is intended to complement rather than replace existing approaches to retrieval in CBR recommender systems. For example, it can be combined with NN retrieval of a less strongly recommended case if none of the available dominance rules covers the user's known requirements.

In other recent work, we have argued that CBR recommender systems stand to benefit in terms of recommendation efficiency by taking account of *default* preferences in the recommendation process [3]. In a recommender system for personal computers (PCs), for example, it is reasonable to assume that most users would prefer to maximise processor speed, memory, and hard disk size, while minimising price. It should therefore be necessary to ask the user only about her *personal* preferences with respect to attributes such as make, PC type (e.g., laptop) and screen size. Avoiding unnecessary questions may also be beneficial in terms of solution quality, as providing preferred values for attributes like processor speed may require technical knowledge that the user is lacking.

In this paper, we investigate the potential role of default preferences in recommendation knowledge discovery. As we demonstrate in the domain of digital cameras, the potential benefits include a dramatic reduction in the effective length of the discovered rules and increased coverage of queries representing the user's personal preferences. Another important finding of the research presented is that when account is taken of default preferences in NN retrieval, many of the cases in a product case base may *never* be recommended.

In Section 2, we use a well-known case base in the digital camera domain to demonstrate our approach to the discovery of dominance rules. In Section 3, we present our approach to incorporating default preferences in NN retrieval and examine the effects on the *recommendability* of cases in a product case base. In Section 4, we show how our algorithm for dominance rule discovery can be modified to take account of default preferences and investigate the potential benefits in terms of rule length and coverage. Related work is discussed in Section 5, and our conclusions are presented in Section 6.

2 Rule Discovery in Cognisance

The recommendation rules targeted by *Cognisance*, our algorithm for recommendation knowledge discovery, are dominance rules of the form $Q \rightarrow C$, where Q is a query representing a list of preferred product features, and C is the case that will be retrieved in response to Q. Following a brief discussion of the roles of similarity and *case dominance* in the discovery process, we examine the results produced by our algorithm when applied to a well-known case base in the domain of digital cameras.

2.1 Similarity Measures

Given a query Q over a subset A_Q of the case attributes A, we define the similarity of any case C to Q to be:

$$Sim(C, Q) = \sum_{a \in A_Q} w_a sim_a(C, Q) \tag{1}$$

where for each $a \in A$, w_a is the importance weight assigned to a, and $sim_a(C, Q)$ is a *local* measure of the similarity of $\pi_a(C)$, the value of a in C, to $\pi_a(Q)$, the preferred value of a. When showing actual similarity scores, we will divide $Sim(C, Q)$ by the sum of all the importance weights to give a *normalised* similarity score. As usual in practice, we assume that for all $a \in A$, $0 \leq sim_a(x, y) \leq 1$ and $sim_a(x, y) = 1$ if and only if $x = y$. We also assume that for all $a \in A$, the distance measure $1 - sim_a$ satisfies the triangle inequality.

As often in practice, we define the similarity of a given case C to a query Q with respect to a numeric attribute a to be:

$$sim_a(C, Q) = 1 - \frac{|\pi_a(C) - \pi_a(Q)|}{\max(a) - \min(a)} \tag{2}$$

where, for example, $\max(a)$ is the maximum value of a in the case base.

2.2 Case Dominance

An important role in our approach to the discovery of dominance rules is played by the concept of *case dominance* [4]. It can be seen from the following definition that $Q \rightarrow C$ is a dominance rule if and only if C dominates all other cases with respect to Q.

Definition 2. *A given case C_1 dominates another case C_2 with respect to a query Q if $Sim(C_1, Q^*) > Sim(C_2, Q^*)$ for all extensions Q^* of Q.*

McSherry [4] uses the triangle inequality to show that a given case C_1 dominates another case C_2 with respect to a query Q if and only if:

$$Sim(C_1, Q) - Sim(C_2, Q) > \sum_{a \in A - A_Q} w_a(1 - sim_a(C_1, C_2)) \tag{3}$$

The cases dominated by a given case with respect to an incomplete query can thus be determined with a computational effort that increases only linearly with the size of the case base.

2.3 Discovery Algorithm

Given a target case C, our algorithm for dominance rule discovery (Figure 1) focuses on the discovery of all *maximally general* dominance rules $Q \rightarrow C$ such that $Q \subseteq description(C)$; that is, Q is a subset of the features that describe the product represented by C. A dominance rule $Q \rightarrow C$ is maximally general (MG) if there is no proper sub-query Q° of Q such that $Q^\circ \rightarrow C$ is also a dominance rule. Given a query Q over a subset A_Q of the case attributes A, we refer to $|A_Q|$ as the *length* of the query. The length of a dominance rule is the length of the query on its left-hand side (LHS).

By focusing on MG dominance rules, we aim to maximise coverage of the product space provided by the discovered rules. Restricting our attention to dominance rules $Q \rightarrow C$ such that $Q \subseteq description(C)$ greatly reduces the complexity of the discovery process. As we have shown in previous work, this cannot result in failure to discover dominance rules of the shortest possible length for a given target case [2].

```
algorithm Cognisance(C, Candidates)
begin
  Rules ← φ
  while |Candidates| > 0 do
  begin
      Q₁ ← first(Candidates)
      Deletions ← {Q₁}
      if C dominates all other cases with respect to Q₁
      then begin
              Rules ← Rules ∪ {Q₁ → C}
              for all Q₂ ∈ rest(Candidates) do
              begin
                  if Q₁ ⊆ Q₂
                  then Deletions ← Deletions ∪ {Q₂}
              end
          end
      Candidates ← Candidates - Deletions
  end
  return Rules
end
```

Figure 1. Algorithm for the discovery of all MG dominance rules $Q \rightarrow C$
for a target case C such that $Q \subseteq description(C)$

In Figure 1, C is the target case and *Candidates* is a list of all queries Q, in order of increasing length, such that $Q \subseteq description(C)$. Each such query is a candidate to appear on the LHS of a discovered dominance rule for C. For any candidate query Q_1 such that C dominates all other cases with respect to Q_1, *Cognisance* adds $Q_1 \rightarrow C$ to the list of discovered rules and eliminates all candidate queries Q_2 such that $Q_1 \subseteq Q_2$ from the remaining list of candidate queries.

It is worth noting that a dominance rule $Q_2 \rightarrow C$ is excluded by *Cognisance* only if it has already discovered a dominance rule $Q_1 \rightarrow C$ such that $Q_1 \subseteq Q_2$. As any query covered by $Q_2 \rightarrow C$ is also covered by $Q_1 \rightarrow C$, the exclusion of $Q_2 \rightarrow C$ causes no loss of coverage in *Rubric*. The worst-case complexity of applying *Cognisance* to all n cases in a product case library with k attributes is $O(k \times n^2 \times 2^k)$ if $n \geq 2^k$. If $n < 2^k$, the worst-case complexity is $O(k \times n \times 2^{2k})$.

2.4 The Digital Camera Case Base

The example case base that we use to demonstrate the discovery process in *Cognisance* is McCarthy *et al.*'s [5] digital camera (DC) case base, which contains the descriptions of over 200 digital cameras. Case attributes and weights assigned to them in our experiments are make (9), price (8), format (7), resolution (6), optical zoom (5), digital zoom (1), weight (4), storage type (2), and memory (3).

One of the dominance rules discovered by *Cognisance* in the DC case base is:

Rule 1: **if** make = toshiba **and** format = ultra compact **and** optical zoom = 3 **then** Case 201

The description of Case 201 in terms of make, price, format, resolution, optical zoom, digital zoom, weight, storage type, and memory is:

Case 201: toshiba, 219, ultra compact, 3.14, 3, 2, 205, SD/MMC Card, 8 (0.47)

Its similarity to the query on the LHS of Rule 1, shown in brackets, is 0.47. Note that normalisation by the sum of all the importance weights means that the maximum similarity of 1.0 is achievable only by a *full-length* query involving all the attributes in the case base.

The next most similar case to the query on the LHS of Rule 1 is:

Case 202: toshiba, 144, ultra compact, 1.92, 0, 4, 180, SD/MMC Card, 8 (0.43)

Given that Case 202 is considerably cheaper and lighter than Case 201, and has more digital zoom, it might be considered that if the user's preferences with respect to these attributes were known then Case 202 could prove to be a better match for the user's requirements than Case 201. However, as Rule 1 is a dominance rule, Case 202 can never equal the similarity of Case 201 to a query that includes the preferences make = toshiba, format = ultra compact, and optical zoom = 3 regardless of the user's preferences with respect to price, resolution, digital zoom, weight, storage type, or memory.

For example, suppose the query on the LHS of Rule 1 is extended to include the additional preferences:

price = 144, digital zoom = 4, weight = 180

Although Case 202 exactly matches these additional preferences, its similarity to the extended query is only 0.72, while the similarity of Case 201 to the extended query is 0.75.

We now examine the overall behaviour of our rule discovery algorithm on the DC case base. Of particular interest is the length of the discovered rules, as the length of a discovered dominance rule determines the coverage it provides and the number of attributes for which the user's preferences must be known for a reliable recommendation to be made. Also of interest is the number of dominance rules discovered for each case, as this may have an important bearing on the effectiveness of rule-based retrieval of recommended cases in terms of coverage, memory requirements and computational efficiency.

A total of 753 dominance rules, ranging in length from 3 to 8, were discovered by *Cognisance* in the DC case base. The average length of the discovered rules was 5.3. Figure 2 shows the cumulative relative frequencies of the discovered rule lengths. For each rule length from 1 to 9, it shows the percentage of discovered rules with less than or equal to that number of conditions. Rule lengths in the range from 3 to 5 can be seen to account for more than 50% of the discovered rules. The maximum *observed* rule length of 8 occurred in less than 2% of the discovered rules.

The discovered dominance rules provide clear benefits in terms of reducing the number of attributes whose preferred values must be known for a reliable recommendation to be made, with reductions in query length of up to 67%, and 41% on average, relative to full-length queries involving all 9 attributes in the case base.

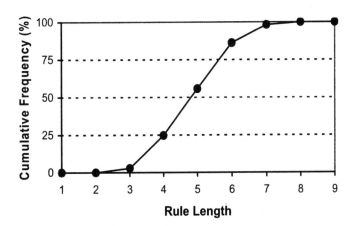

Figure 2. Cumulative relative frequencies of discovered rule lengths in the DC case base

Figure 3 shows the relative frequency of each rule-set size among the 210 cases in the DC case base. We have shown in previous work [2] that the size of the discovered rule set for any case in a case base with k attributes can never be more than $^k C_{\lfloor k/2 \rfloor}$, where $\lfloor k/2 \rfloor$ is the integer part of $k/2$. For a case base with 9 attributes like the DC case base, the maximum possible rule-set size is $^9C_4 = 126$. However, the discovered rule-set sizes are much smaller than this for all cases in the DC case base. The rule-set sizes that occur most frequently are 1, 2, and 3 while the average rule-set size over all cases is 3.6. The maximum rule-set size of 13 was observed for only one of the 210 cases in the case base.

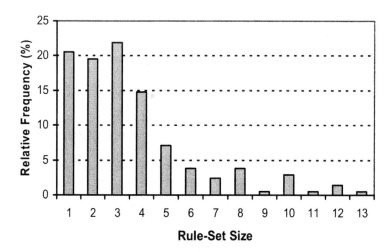

Figure 3. Numbers of discovered dominance rules for cases in the DC case base

2.5 Discussion

Our results on the DC case base clearly show the benefits of recommendation knowledge discovery in terms of enabling reliable recommendations to be made in the absence of complete information about the user's preferences. For example, a reliable recommendation may be possible even when the user's preferences are known for as few as 3 attributes as shown by the discovered rule:

Rule 1: **if** make = toshiba **and** format = ultra compact **and** optical zoom = 3 **then** Case 201

However, the fact that most of the attributes in the DC case base are numeric limits the coverage that the discovered rules can provide. Though greatly reducing the complexity of the discovery process, our focus on dominance rules $Q \rightarrow C$ such that $Q \subseteq description(C)$ means that the preferred value of each attribute in a discovered rule must be its value in the recommended case. While this makes good sense for nominal and discrete attributes, preferences expressed in terms of exact values of numeric attributes (e.g., price = 245) make the discovered rules seem unnatural as well as limiting the coverage they can provide. In the following section, we examine the potential role of default preferences with respect to numeric attributes in addressing this issue.

3 Default Preferences for Numeric Attributes

In CBR recommender systems, a common approach to assessing the similarity of a retrieved case with respect to a numeric attribute is one in which (a) the user is asked to specify a preferred value and (b) values that are closest to the preferred value receive the highest similarity scores (as in Equation 2). While this makes good sense for attributes such as *screen size* in the PC domain, the idea that a user who specifies £500 as an "ideal" price would prefer to pay £510 than £480 seems unrealistic.

Instead, attributes whose values most users would prefer to maximise or minimise are sometimes treated as *more-is-better* (MIB) or *less-is-better* (LIB) attributes in the retrieval process [1,6-7]. However, there may be no benefit in terms of recommendation efficiency; for example, it is typical for a preferred *minimum* to be elicited for a MIB attribute, and for the highest similarity score to be assigned to any value that is above the preferred minimum. In previous work, we have questioned whether it is realistic to treat all values of a MIB attribute that are above the preferred minimum as if they are equally preferred [7]. Another problem is that the attribute's discriminating power may be greatly reduced if the user chooses a "modest" value that is exceeded by most cases.

In more recent work, we presented an approach to retrieval based on default preferences in which there is no need for preferred values to be elicited for LIB or MIB attributes [3]. Instead, the preferred value of a LIB attribute is assumed to be the *lowest* value of the attribute in the case base, while the preferred value of a MIB attribute is assumed to be the *highest* value. The preferred values of any MIB and LIB attributes, together with default preferences for any nominal or discrete attributes with values most users can be assumed to prefer, are represented in a *default query* which we denote by Q_D.

In the DC case base, for example, it is reasonable to assume that most users would prefer to minimise price and weight while maximising memory, resolution, optical zoom, and digital zoom. So our default query includes default preferences for price (106 euro), memory (64 Mb), resolution (13.7 mega-pixels), optical zoom (10×), digital zoom (8×), and weight (100 gm). For example, 106 euro is the minimum price in the case base, while 64 Mb is the maximum memory. However, as no assumptions can reasonably be made about the preferred make, format, or storage type, these attributes do not appear in the default query.

In the case of a LIB or MIB attribute, there is now no need for a preferred value to be elicited from the user as a preferred value is provided in the default query. For example, it follows from Equation 2 that for any case C and LIB attribute a:

$$sim_a(C,Q_D) = 1 - \frac{\pi_a(C) - \min(a)}{\max(a) - \min(a)} = \frac{\max(a) - \pi_a(C)}{\max(a) - \min(a)} \qquad (4)$$

Our approach to retrieval based on default preferences can be used to complement existing recommendation strategies in various ways [3]. For example, initially presenting the case that is most similar to the default query may be beneficial in critiquing approaches to navigation of complex product spaces [5, 8-9], particularly when the user declines to enter an initial query. In NN retrieval, the default query can be combined with a query representing the user's personal preferences with respect to attributes for which default preferences are not defined.

In the latter approach, which we refer to as NN retrieval with default preferences, any query Q can be written in the form:

$$Q = Q_D \cup Q_E \tag{5}$$

where Q_D is the default query and Q_E is the query entered by the user. With default preferences for six of the nine attributes in the digital camera case base, an obvious benefit is a 67% reduction in query length relative to full-length queries in which the user is required to specify preferred values for all attributes in the case base.

In the following section, we investigate the potential benefits of default preferences in recommendation knowledge discovery. Before concluding this section, however, we examine an interesting phenomenon that arises from the use of default preferences in NN retrieval and also has important implications in the discovery of recommendation knowledge. As we now show, taking account of default preferences may mean that some of the cases in a product case base can *never* be recommended.

Proposition 1. *In NN retrieval with default preferences, a given case C_2 can never be recommended if there is another case C_1 such that C_1 dominates C_2 with respect to the default query Q_D.*

Proof. In NN retrieval with default preferences, every query Q is an extension of Q_D, the default query. It follows that if C_1 dominates C_2 with respect to Q_D, then $Sim(C_1, Q) > Sim(C_2, Q)$ for any query Q. Thus C_2 can never be recommended.

In general, the number of cases dominated by another case with respect to the default query is likely to depend on the size of the case base, the number of attributes for which default preferences are defined, and the importance weights assigned to them. However, as we now show in the digital camera domain, it is possible that only a minority of the cases in a product case base can ever be recommended when account is taken of default preferences.

In fact, only 56 of the 210 cases the DC case base can ever be recommended in NN retrieval with default preferences for 6 of the 9 attributes as represented in the default query:

$$Q_D = \{\text{price} = 106, \text{memory} = 64, \text{resolution} = 13.7, \text{optical zoom} = 10,$$
$$\text{digital zoom} = 8, \text{weight} = 100\}$$

One case that can never be recommended is:

Case 202: toshiba, 144, ultra compact, 1.92, 0, 4, 180, SD/MMC Card, 8 (0.29)

The reason is that Case 202 is dominated with respect to the default query by another camera of the same make:

Case 201: toshiba, 219, ultra compact, 3.14, 3, 2, 205, SD/MMC Card, 8 (0.33)

The similarities of the two cases to the default query are shown in brackets. That Case 202 is dominated by Case 201 can be seen from the fact that it is less similar to the default query than Case 201, and has the same make, format and storage type as Case 201. As the two cases must benefit equally in terms of similarity from any extension of the default query, Case 202 can never equal the similarity of Case 201 regardless of the user's personal preferences with respect to make, format, or storage type.

Of course, it is possible that Case 202 may be more acceptable to the user than Case 201, for example because of its lower price. The fact that the most similar case may not be the one that is most acceptable to the user is recognised, for example, in the k-NN strategy of recommending the k cases that are most similar to the user's query. This is an issue we will return to in our discussion of related work in Section 5.

4 Default Preferences in Cognisance

In this section, we examine the potential benefits of default preferences in the discovery of recommendation knowledge. Again we use the DC case base [5] to illustrate the approach, with default preferences as represented in the default query:

$$Q_D = \{price = 106, memory = 64, resolution = 13.7, optical\ zoom = 10,$$
$$digital\ zoom = 8, weight = 100\}$$

Only a minor change in the input to our discovery algorithm (Figure 1) is needed to ensure that account is taken of default preferences in the discovery process. In the dominance rules $Q \rightarrow C$ now targeted by our algorithm, Q includes the default preferences in Q_D as *assumptions* rather than conditions that may or may not be satisfied. Although it no longer makes sense to insist that $Q \subseteq description(C)$, we can ensure that $Q - Q_D \subseteq description(C)$.

Thus given a target case C, the set of candidate queries in *Cognisance* now consists of all queries $Q = Q_D \cup Q_E$ such that $Q_E \subseteq description(C)$. An important point to note is that the number of candidate queries is reduced from $2^{|A|}$ to $2^{|A|-|A_D|}$, where A is the set of all case attributes and A_D is the set of attributes for which default preferences are defined. With default preferences for 6 of the 9 attributes in the DC case base, the number of candidate queries is reduced from 512 to 8, which amounts to a dramatic reduction in the complexity of the discovery process.

Another important benefit is a reduction in the *effective* length of the discovered rules. As all the discovered rules include the default preferences, they need not be explicitly stated in a discovered rule. With default preferences omitted, the maximum possible length of a discovered rule is reduced to $|A| - |A_D|$. In the DC case base, the maximum rule length is $9 - 6 = 3$.

As before, the list of candidate queries is processed by *Cognisance* in order of increasing length, thus ensuring that the discovered dominance rules are maximally general with respect to the attributes in $A - A_D$. Figure 4 shows the candidate queries in *Cognisance* with the following case from the DC case library as the target case:

Case 29: scny, 336, compact, 5, 3, 4, 236, memory stick, 32

256

As might be expected, Case 29 cannot be reliably recommended without knowing the preferred *make* and *format*. The first (and only) dominance rule for Case 29 discovered by *Cognisance* is therefore:

Rule 2: **if** make = sony **and** format = compact **then** Case 29

Following the elimination of the underlined query in Figure 4, no further dominance rules are discovered for Case 29.

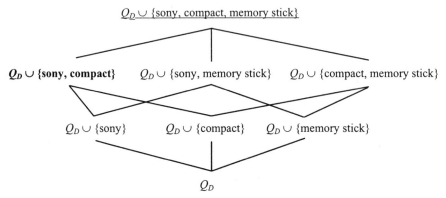

Figure 4. Dominance rule discovery for Case 29 in the DC case base

As we saw in Section 3, a case that is dominated with respect to the default query can never be recommended in NN retrieval with default preferences. As we now show, no rules can be discovered for such a case in our approach to dominance rule discovery.

Proposition 2. *If a given case C_2 is dominated by another case C_1 with respect to the default query Q_D, there can be no dominance rule $Q \rightarrow C_2$ such that $Q_D \subseteq Q$.*

Proof. If C_1 dominates C_2 with respect to Q_D, then $Sim(C_1, Q) > Sim(C_2, Q)$ for any query Q such that $Q_D \subseteq Q$. Thus $Q \rightarrow C_2$ cannot be a dominance rule, as this would imply that $Sim(C_2, Q) > Sim(C_1, Q)$.

As noted in Section 3, all but 56 of the 210 cases in the DC case base are dominated with respect to the default query. As confirmed by the results obtained when *Cognisance* is applied to the DC case base with each case in turn as the target case, this means that dominance rules can be discovered for only 56 cases when account is taken of default preferences. Another interesting feature of the results is that for all but one of the 56 non-dominated cases, only a single rule dominance rule was discovered. The only exception was a case for which two rules were discovered.

One of the 57 discovered rules is:

Rule 3: **if** make = toshiba **and** format = ultra compact **then** Case 201

According to Rule 3, Case 201 can be recommended to any user seeking an ultra-compact Toshiba camera. It is interesting to compare Rule 3 with a rule discovered by *Cognisance* without the benefit of default preferences:

Rule 1: **if** make = toshiba **and** format = ultra compact **and** optical zoom = 3 **then** Case 201

In Rule 3, there is no need for a preferred optical zoom to be specified as the preferred optical zoom is assumed to be 10×, the highest available in the case base.

Figure 5 shows the *lengths* of the dominance rules discovered by *Cognisance* with and without default preferences in the DC case base. Average rule length with default preferences is only 2.5 compared to 5.3 without default preferences. Also, the smallest rule length of 3 without default preferences is the maximum rule length with default preferences. On the other hand, none of the discovered rules has fewer than two conditions even when account is taken of default preferences. Interestingly, all but one of the 57 discovered rules include a preferred *make* and *format* in their conditions. This is perhaps not surprising, as it seems unlikely that a reliable recommendation could be made in practice without knowing the user's personal preferences with respect to make and format.

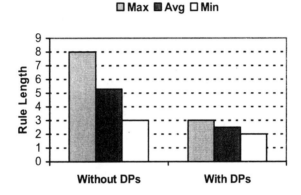

Figure 5. Lengths of discovered dominance rules with and without default preferences (DPs) in the DC case library

We now examine the effects of default preferences on coverage of queries representing the user's personal preferences. As there are 15 different makes, 6 possible formats, and 7 storage types in the DC case base, the number of possible queries involving one or more of these attributes (and no other attributes), is:

$$(15 + 1) \times (6 + 1) \times (7 + 1) - 1 = 895$$

Of course, many of the possible queries may be unrealistic, for example because a given storage type is not available for a given make of camera. Nevertheless, the 57 rules discovered by *Cognisance* cover 29% of the 895 possible queries. In contrast, the 753 rules discovered by *Cognisance* without the benefit of default preferences cover only 2 of the 895 possible queries representing the user's personal preferences with respect to make, format, and storage type.

5 Related Work

In any approach to the retrieval of recommended cases, more than a single recommendation cycle may be necessary to identify a case that is acceptable to the user. In future work, we plan to investigate the potential benefits of combining rule-based retrieval with techniques for extending recommendation dialogues beyond an initially unsuccessful recommendation such as critiquing [5,7-9] or referral of the user's query to other recommender agents [10].

Recent work by McSherry [11] provides a different perspective on recommendation rule discovery in which the discovered rules are used to describe the *behaviour* of an existing recommender system in localised areas of the product space. For example, the discovered rules can be used to identify conditions in which a given product will be recommended by the system, or regions of the product space that are sparsely represented. However, there is no discussion of their possible use for rule-based retrieval of recommended products.

One example of the use of default preferences to reduce the length of recommendation dialogues is Linden *et al.*'s [9] *Automated Travel Assistant*, a flight recommender that interactively builds flight itineraries from real-time airline information. However, retrieval is not based on similarity, and there is no evaluation of the impact of default preferences on recommendation efficiency. Default preferences can also play an important role in enabling recommender systems to explain their recommendations. In Shimazu's *ExpertClerk* [12], explanations of why the system is proposing two contrasting products are based on assumed preferences with respect to attributes not mentioned in the user's query. Similarly, McSherry's [7] *First Case* can explain why one case is more strongly recommended than another by highlighting the benefits it offers.

6 Conclusions

Improving the reliability of CBR recommendations based on incomplete queries is the goal that motivates our approach to the discovery of recommendation rules that take account of *all* features of a recommended case, including those with respect to which the user's preferences are unknown. The discovered *dominance* rules are provably reliable and non-conflicting while requiring minimal information for their application in a rule-based approach to the retrieval of recommended cases [2]. We have focused in this paper on the role of *default* preferences in dominance rule discovery. As we have shown in the domain of digital cameras, the potential benefits include a dramatic reduction in the length of the discovered rules and increased coverage of queries representing the user's *personal* preferences.

Another potential benefit is a reduction in the complexity of the rule discovery process that is likely to be of particular importance in product case bases with large numbers of attributes and/or cases. We have also shown that many of the cases in a product case base may *never* be recommended when account is taken of default preferences, a result that applies equally to rule-based and NN retrieval. In future research, we propose to investigate the wider implications of this important result, for example in the context of case-base maintenance.

Acknowledgement. Thanks to Kevin McCarthy and his co-authors for providing the digital camera case base [5] used to illustrate the ideas presented in this paper.

References

1. Wilke, W., Lenz, M., Wess, S.: Intelligent Sales Support with CBR. In: Lenz, M., Bartsch-Spörl, B., Burkhard, H.-D., Wess, S. (eds.) Case-Based Reasoning Technology. Springer-Verlag, Berlin Heidelberg New York (1998) 91-113
2. McSherry, D., Stretch, C.: Automating the Discovery of Recommendation Knowledge. Proceedings of the Nineteenth International Joint Conference on Artificial Intelligence (2005) 9-14
3. McSherry, D.: Incremental Nearest Neighbour with Default Preferences. Proceedings of the Sixteenth Irish Conference on Artificial Intelligence and Cognitive Science (2005) 9-18
4. McSherry, D.: Increasing Dialogue Efficiency in Case-Based Reasoning Without Loss of Solution Quality. Proceedings of the Eighteenth International Joint Conference on Artificial Intelligence (2003) 121-12
5. McCarthy, K., Reilly, J., McGinty, L., Smyth, B.: Experiments in Dynamic Critiquing. Proceedings of the International Conference on Intelligent User Interfaces (2005) 175-182
6. Bergmann, R., Breen, S., Göker, M., Manago, M., Wess, S.: Developing Industrial Case-Based Reasoning Applications: The INRECA Methodology. Springer-Verlag, Berlin Heidelberg New York (1999)
7. McSherry, D.: Similarity and Compromise. In: Ashley, K.D., Bridge, D.G. (eds.) Case-Based Reasoning Research and Development. LNAI, Vol. 2689. Springer-Verlag, Berlin Heidelberg New York (2003) 291-305
8. Burke, R.: Interactive Critiquing for Catalog Navigation in E-Commerce. Artificial Intelligence Review, **18** (2002) 245-267
9. Linden, G., Hanks, S., Lesh, N.: Interactive Assessment of User Preference Models: The Automated Travel Assistant. Proceedings of the Sixth International Conference on User Modeling (1997) 67-78
10. McSherry, D.: Conversational CBR in Multi-Agent Recommendation. IJCAI-05 Workshop on Multi-Agent Information Retrieval and Recommender Systems (2005) 33-40
11. McSherry, D.: Automating the Discovery of Recommendation Rules. In: Bramer, M., Coenen, F., Allen, T. (eds.) Research and Development in Intelligent Systems XXI. Springer-Verlag, London (2004) 87-100
12. Shimazu, H.: ExpertClerk: A Conversational Case-Based Reasoning Tool for Developing Salesclerk Agents in E-Commerce Webshops. Artificial Intelligence Review **18** (2002) 223-244

SESSION 5a:

KNOWLEDGE DISCOVERY IN DATA

Improved Methods for Extracting Frequent Itemsets from Interim-Support Trees

Frans Coenen

Department of Computer Science, University of Liverpool

Chadwick Building, Peach Street, Liverpool L69 7ZF, UK

frans@csc.liv.ac.uk

Paul Leng

Department of Computer Science, University of Liverpool

Chadwick Building, Peach Street, Liverpool L69 7ZF, UK

phl@csc.liv.ac.uk

Aris Pagourtzis*

Department of Computer Science, National Technical University of Athens

15780 Zografou, Athens, Greece

pagour@cs.ntua.gr

Wojciech Rytter†

Institute of Informatics, Warsaw University, Poland and

Department of Computer Science, New Jersey Institute of Technology, US

rytter@oak.njit.edu

Dora Souliou*

Department of Computer Science, National Technical University of Athens

15780 Zografou, Athens, Greece

dsouliou@cslab.ece.ntua.gr

Abstract

Mining association rules in relational databases is a significant computational task with lots of applications. A fundamental ingredient of this task is the discovery of sets of attributes (*itemsets*) whose frequency in the data exceeds some threshold value. In previous work [9] we have introduced an approach to this problem which begins by carrying out an efficient *partial* computation of the necessary totals, storing these interim results in a set-enumeration tree. This work demonstrated that making

*Aris Pagourtzis and Dora Souliou were partially supported for this research by "Pythagoras" grant of the Hellenic Ministry of Education, co-funded by the European Social Fund (75%) and National Resources (25%) under Operational Programme "Education and Initial Vocational Training" (EPEAEK II).

†Wojciech Rytter was supported for this research by grants 4T11C04425 and CCR-0313219.

use of this structure can significantly reduce the cost of determining the frequent sets.

In this paper we describe two algorithms for completing the calculation of frequent sets using an interim-support tree. These algorithms are improved versions of earlier algorithms described in the above mentioned work and in a consequent paper [7]. The first of our new algorithms (TTF) differs from its ancestor in that it uses a novel tree pruning technique, based on the notion of *(fixed-prefix) potential inclusion*, which is specially designed for trees that are implemented using only two pointers per node. This allows to implement the interim-support tree in a space efficient manner. The second algorithm (PTF) explores the idea of storing the frequent itemsets in a second tree structure, called the *total support tree* (*T*-tree); the improvement lies in the use of multiple pointers per node which provides rapid access to the nodes of the *T*-tree and makes it possible to design a new, usually faster, method for updating them.

Experimental comparison shows that these improvements result in considerable speedup for both algorithms. Further comparison between the two improved algorithms, shows that PTF is generally faster on instances with a large number of frequent itemsets, while TTF is more appropriate whenever this number is small; in addition, TTF behaves quite well on instances in which the densities of the items of the database have a high variance.

1 Introduction

An important data mining task initiated in [2] is the discovery of association rules over huge listings of sales data, also known as *basket data*. This task initially involves the extraction of *frequent* sets of items from a database of transactions, i.e. from a collection of sets of such items. The number of times that an itemset appears in transactions of the database is called its *support*. The minimum support an itemset must have in order to be considered as frequent is called the *support threshold*, a nonnegative integer denoted by t. The support of an association rule $A \implies B$, where A and B are sets of items, is the support of the set $A \cup B$. The *confidence* of rule $A \implies B$ is equal to $support(A \cup B)/support(A)$ and represents the fraction of transactions that contain B among transactions that contain A.

Association Rule Mining, in general, involves the extraction from a database of all rules that reach some required thresholds of support and confidence. The major part of this task is the discovery of the frequent itemsets; once the support of all these sets has been counted, determining the confidence of possible rules is trivial. Of course, there is no polynomial-time algorithm for this problem since the number of possible itemsets is exponential in the number of items. This problem has motivated a continuing search for effective heuristics for finding frequent itemsets and their support.

The best-known algorithm, from which most others are derived, is *Apriori* [4]. Apriori performs repeated passes of the database, successively counting the support for single items, pairs, triples, etc.. At the end of each pass, itemsets that fail to reach the support threshold are eliminated, and *candidate* itemsets for the next pass are constructed as supersets of the remaining frequent sets. As no frequent set can have an infrequent subset, this heuristic ensures that all sets that may be frequent are considered. The algorithm terminates when no further candidates can be constructed.

Apriori remains potentially very costly because of its multiple database passes and, especially, the possible large number of candidates in some passes. Attempts to reduce the scale of the problem include methods that begin by partitioning [11] or sampling [12] the data, and those that attempt to identify *maximal* frequent sets [5] or *closed* frequent sets [13] from which all others can be derived. A number of researchers have made use of *set-enumeration tree* structures to organise candidates for more efficient counting. The *FP-growth* algorithm of Han et al. [10] counts frequent sets using a structure, the *FP-tree*, in which tree nodes represent individual items and branches represent itemsets. FP-growth reduces the cost of support-counting because branches of the tree that are subsets of more than one itemset need only be counted once. In contemporaneous work, we have also employed set-enumeration tree structures to exploit this property. Our approach begins by constructing a tree, the *P*-tree, [9, 8], which contains an incomplete summation of the support of sets found in the data. The *P*-tree, described in more detail below, shares the same performance advantage of the FP-tree but is a more compact structure. Results presented in [7] demonstrate that algorithms employing the *P*-tree can achieve comparable or superior speed to FP-growth, with lower memory requirements.

Unlike the FP-tree, which was developed specifically to facilitate the FP-growth algorithm, the *P*-tree is a generic structure which can be the basis of many possible algorithms for completing the summation of frequent sets. In this paper we describe and compare two algorithms for this purpose, namely:

1. The *T-Tree-First (TTF)* algorithm.

2. The *P-Tree-First (PTF)* algorithm.

Both algorithms make use of the incomplete summation contained in the *P*-tree to construct a second set-enumeration tree, the *T*-tree, which finally contains frequent itemsets together with their total support. The algorithms differ in the way they compute the total support: algorithm *T*-Tree-First iterates over the nodes of *T*-tree, and for each of them it traverses the *P*-tree; algorithm *P*-Tree-First starts by traversing the *P*-tree and for each node that it visits, it updates all relevant nodes at the current level of the *T*-tree.

TTF and PTF are improved versions of known algorithms, described in [9] and [7] respectively. Here we will refer to them as TTF-old and PTF-old respectively (note however that PTF-old was called Apriori-TFP in [7]).

The contribution of this work lies in the introduction of techniques that can considerably accelerate the process of computing frequent itemsets. In particular, the main improvement in the first of our algorithms (TTF) is a novel tree pruning technique, based on the notion of *fixed-prefix potential inclusion*, which is specially designed for trees that are implemented using only two pointers per node. This allows to implement the interim-support tree in a space efficient manner. The second algorithm (PTF) differs from its predecessor in that it uses multiple pointers per node in the T-tree; this accelerates the access of the nodes of the T-tree and makes it possible to find and update appropriate T-tree nodes following a new, usually faster, strategy.

We perform experimental comparison of the two algorithms against their predecessors and show that in most cases the speedup is considerable. We also compare the two new algorithms to each other and discuss the merits of each. Our results show that PTF is faster than TTF if there are a lot of frequent itemsets in the database (small support threshold). On the other hand TTF gains ground as the support threshold increases and behaves even better for instances of variable item density which have been pre-sorted according to these densities.

2 Notation and Preliminaries

A database $\mathcal{D}$ is represented by an $m \times n$ binary matrix. The columns of D correspond to items (attributes), and the rows correspond to the transactions (records). The columns are indexed by consecutive letters a, b, ... of the alphabet. The set of columns (items) is denoted by $\mathcal{C}$. An *itemset I* is a set of items $I \subseteq \mathcal{C}$. For an itemset I we define:

- $E(I)$ (*E*-value of I) is the number of transactions that are exactly equal to I. This value is also called *exact support of I*.

- $P(I)$ (*P*-value of I) is the number of transactions that have I as a prefix. Also called *interim support of I*.

- $T(I)$ (*T*-value of I) is the number of transactions that contain I. Also called *total support* or, simply, *support of I*.

In this paper we consider the problem of finding all itemsets I with $T(I) \geq t$, for a given database $\mathcal{D}$ and threshold t.

For an item x we define the *density of x in $\mathcal{D}$* to be the fraction of transactions of $\mathcal{D}$ that contain x, that is $T(\{x\})/m$. We also define the *density of a database $\mathcal{D}$* to be the average density of the items of $\mathcal{D}$; note that the density of $\mathcal{D}$ is equal to the fraction of the total number of items appearing in the transactions of $\mathcal{D}$ over the size of $\mathcal{D}$ $(= nm)$.

We will make use of the following order relations:

- *Inclusion order:* $I \subseteq J$, the usual set inclusion relation,

- *Lexicographic order:* $I \leq J$, I is lexicographically smaller or equal to J if seen as strings,

- *Prefix order:* $I \sqsubseteq J$, I is a prefix of J if seen as strings. Note that $I \sqsubseteq J \Leftrightarrow I \subseteq J$ & $I \leq J$.

We will also use the corresponding operators without equality: $I \subset J$, $I \sqsubset J$ and $I < J$.

Notice that for any itemset I:

$$T(I) = \sum_{I \subseteq J} E(J)$$

and therefore:

$$T(I) = \sum_{I \subseteq J \ \& \ I \leq J} E(J) + \sum_{I \subseteq J \ \& \ J < I} E(J) = P(I) + \sum_{I \subseteq J \ \& \ J < I} E(J) \qquad (1)$$

This property will play an important role in our algorithms.

3   The Interim-Support Tree

Both new algorithms TTF and PTF (as well as their predecessors TTF-old and PTF-old) have a common first part which is a pre-processing of the database that results in the storage of the whole information into a structure called the P-tree or *interim-support tree*. The P-tree is a set-enumeration tree the nodes of which are distinct itemsets of the database as well as some common prefixes of these itemsets. For each node, the interim support (P-value) of the corresponding itemset is also stored.

The notion of interim-support trees was introduced in [9], where details of the construction of the P-tree were given, and more fully in [8]. The tree is constructed in a single pass of $\mathcal{D}$. As each transaction is examined, the tree is traversed in a top-down (preorder) manner until either a node with identical itemset is found or a new node is created to represent the new itemset at an appropriate place in the tree. During this traversal, the support of all ancestors (preceding subsets) of the itemset is incremented. When a new itemset is inserted which shares a common prefix with an existing itemset, this prefix is created, if not already present, as a parent node, and inherits the support of its children.

The significance of the P-tree is that it performs a large part of the counting of support totals very efficiently in a single database pass. The size of the P-tree is linearly related to the original database, from which all relevant information is preserved, and will be smaller in cases where the data includes many duplicated itemsets. In results presented in [7], both the memory requirements and construction time for the P-tree were less than for a corresponding FP-tree [10].

For the sake of memory efficiency the P-tree is implemented using two pointers per node: *down* and *right*. For a node v, its down pointer links v to one of its children — the lexicographically smaller. This child's right pointer points to another child of v, and so on. For example, in the implementation of a P-tree containing itemsets 'a', 'ab', 'ac', and 'abc' node 'a' points down to 'ab' which in turn points down to 'abc' and right to 'ac'.

Note that, for simplicity, we often identify nodes of the P-tree with the itemsets they contain. This should cause no confusion since itemsets in the P-tree are unique.

4   The T-Tree-First (TTF) algorithm

TTF is an improved version of the algorithm in [9] (which we call TTF-old here). In this section we give a detailed description of the new algorithm.

The algorithm first scans the database and creates the P-tree, as explained in the previous section.

It then starts building the T-tree (recall that the T-tree will finally contain all frequent itemsets together with their total supports). Each level of the T-tree is implemented as a linear list, where itemsets appear in lexicographic order; nodes of such a list neither point to nor are pointed from nodes that are in the list of another level. In the beginning, the algorithm builds level 1 of the T-tree, which contains all frequent singletons; to this end it counts their support traversing the P-tree. It then builds the remaining T-tree level by level using procedure **Iteration**(k).

The algorithm is presented below. A fundamental ingredient of TTF is function **CountSupport** which is described separately.

Algorithm T-Tree-First (TTF)

Input: Database $\mathcal{D}$, threshold t.
Output: The family $\mathcal{F}$ of frequent itemsets.

Build P-tree from database $\mathcal{D}$;

(* Build the 1-st level of T-tree *)
for $i = 1$ **to** n **do**
    if CountSupport(P-tree, $\{i\}$) $\geq t$ **then** add $\{i\}$ to $\mathcal{F}_1$;
(* Build the remaining levels of T-tree *)
for $k = 2$ **to** n **do**
    Iteration(k);
    if $\mathcal{F}_k = \emptyset$ **then exit**
    else $\mathcal{F} = \mathcal{F} \cup \mathcal{F}_k$;
return $\mathcal{F}$;

Some details of procedure **Iteration**(k) need to be clarified. Its goal is to build $\mathcal{F}_k$, that is, the k-th level of the T-tree. Itemsets in $\mathcal{F}_k$ must have all their $(k-1)$-size subsets in $\mathcal{F}_{k-1}$. Therefore, one can start from existing itemsets in $\mathcal{F}_{k-1}$ and try to augment them with one more item in order to create all potentially frequent itemsets. To avoid duplications the algorithm may proceed by considering for each frequent itemset X_{k-1} in $\mathcal{F}_{k-1}$ all X_{k-1}'s supersets $X_k = \{x\} \cup X_{k-1}$ for items x that are greater than any item of X_{k-1}.

Careful observation reveals that only if X_{k-1} and the node following it, denoted X'_{k-1}, differ at the last item it makes sense to consider such supersets.

The candidate superset X_k is then the union of X_{k-1} and X'_{k-1}. Then it is checked whether all the ($k - 2$ many) remaining ($k - 1$)-subsets of X_k are frequent; this is carried out by a special function called **ExistSubsets**, which we will not describe in detail here. If some of the examined subsets of X_k is not present in $\mathcal{F}_{k-1}$, X_k is not added to $\mathcal{F}_k$.

Procedure Iteration(k) (* *Building the k-th level of T-tree* *)

for each itemset $X_{k-1} \in \mathcal{F}_{k-1}$ **do**
    $X'_{k-1} := next(X_{k-1})$;
    while $X'_{k-1} \neq$ NULL **do**
        if X_{k-1} and X'_{k-1} differ only at the last item **then**
            $X_k := X_{k-1} \cup X'_{k-1}$;
            if ExistSubsets($X_k, \mathcal{F}_{k-1}$) **then**
                $T(X_k) :=$ **CountSupport**(P-tree, X_k);
                if $T(X_k) \geq t$ **then** add X_k to $\mathcal{F}_k$;
            $X'_{k-1} := next(X'_{k-1})$;
        else exit while;

In order to complete the description of TTF it remains to describe its most critical part, that is, function **CountSupport**, which counts the total support of an itemset X in the P-tree in a recursive manner. An essential ingredient of **CountSupport** is the notion of *fixed-prefix potential inclusion*:

Fixed-Prefix Potential Inclusion. $I \overset{pot}{\subseteq}_K J$: $\exists J'$, $common prefix(J, J') = K$ & $I \subseteq J'$.

    Examples: 'bdf' $\overset{pot}{\subseteq}_{`ab'}$ 'abc', 'bdf' $\overset{pot}{\not\subseteq}_{`ab'}$ 'abd'.

    In words, $I \overset{pot}{\subseteq}_K J$ means that there is an itemset greater than J, sharing with J a common prefix K, that contains I.

    A second interesting inclusion relation can be defined in terms of $\overset{pot}{\subseteq}_K$:

Potential Inclusion. $I \overset{pot}{\subseteq} J \overset{def}{=} I \overset{pot}{\subseteq}_J J$, i.e. $\exists J'$, $J \sqsubseteq J'$ & $I \subseteq J'$.

    Examples: 'bdf' $\overset{pot}{\subseteq}$ 'abde', 'bdf' $\overset{pot}{\not\subseteq}$ 'abdg'.

    In words, $I \overset{pot}{\subseteq} J$ means that there is an extension of J that contains I.

    The use of the above inclusion relations can significantly reduce the number of moves needed to count the support of an itemset in trees with two pointers per node. Suppose that we are looking for appearances (i.e. supersets) of an itemset I in the P-tree and we are currently visiting a node that contains itemset J:

- Nodes that are below the current node contain itemsets J' which have J as prefix. Therefore, if $I \overset{pot}{\not\subseteq} J$ there is no point visiting the subtree rooted at the current node.

- Nodes that are to the right of the current node (siblings) contain itemsets that have $par(J)$ (parent of J) as prefix — and so does J — and are greater than J. If $I \stackrel{pot}{\not\subseteq}_{par(J)} J$ there is no point visiting the subtrees rooted at these nodes.

These two tests result in much better tree pruning comparing to the one applied by the TTF-old algorithm. As an example, suppose that we are trying to find the support of itemset $X=$'bd' in a P-tree in which there is a node 'ab' with children 'abde' and 'abefg'. Then, once the tree traversal reaches node 'abde' it adds its support to $T(X)$ and does not move to the right, that is, it avoids visiting 'abefg'. On the other hand, TTF-old [9] would also examine 'abefg' (and other siblings if such existed) because it only terminates its search whenever it finds itemsets lexicographically equal or greater than X.

Function CountSupport(*pnode*, X): integer
(* Counts the total support of itemset X
in the subtree of P-tree rooted at pnode *)

$T := 0$;

if *pnode* $\neq NULL$ **then**
    $J := pnode \rightarrow itemset$;
    if $X \stackrel{pot}{\subseteq} J$ **then** *(* makes sense to search children *)*
        if $X \subseteq J$ **then** $T := T + P(J)$
            (* inclusion is a special case of potential inclusion *)
        else $T := T+$ **CountSupport**(*pnode* $\rightarrow$ *down*, X);
    if $X \stackrel{pot}{\subseteq}_{par(J)} J$ **then** *(* makes sense to search right siblings *)*
        $T := T+$ **CountSupport**(*pnode* $\rightarrow$ *right*, X);

return T;

Finally, let us explain how to check potential inclusion and fixed prefix potential inclusion. It can be shown that the following tests suffice. The proof is omitted.

- $X \stackrel{pot}{\subseteq} J$: if $X \subseteq J$ then $X \stackrel{pot}{\subseteq} J$ is true. Otherwise let x be the lexicographically smaller item of X that is not item of J (such x exists). If for all items j of J are lexicographically smaller than x then $X \stackrel{pot}{\subseteq} J$ is true otherwise it is false.

- $X \stackrel{pot}{\subseteq}_K J$: assume $K \sqsubseteq J$ (otherwise the inclusion $X \stackrel{pot}{\subseteq}_K J$ is obviously false). Let x be the first item of $X \setminus K$ and J be the first item of $J \setminus K$. If $x > j$ the inclusion $X \stackrel{pot}{\subseteq}_K J$ holds otherwise it is false.

5   The P-Tree-First (PTF) Algorithm

PTF is an improved version of the algorithm Apriori-TFP [7] (which we call PTF-old here). PTF also begins by constructing the P-tree exactly as TTF, but then it follows an inverse approach in order to update the T-tree. In particular, during the processing of level-k of the T-tree, each node of the P-tree is visited once. Let I be the itemset of a visited node; the algorithm updates all nodes of level-k that are subsets of I, except for those that are also subsets of $par(I)$ (parent of I) — the latter have already been updated while visiting $par(I)$.

Following again the a-priori strategy [4], level-k itemsets of the T-tree are constructed from the itemsets of level-$(k-1)$, by adding single items to each of them. Then, the P-tree is traversed as described above in order to compute support for all nodes of level-k. Nodes with support smaller than the threshold are removed before the generation of level-$(k+1)$.

Algorithm P-Tree-First (PTF)

Input: Database $\mathcal{D}$, threshold t.
Output: The family $\mathcal{F}$ of frequent itemsets.

Build P-tree from database $\mathcal{D}$;

add $\emptyset$ to $\mathcal{F}_0$; *(* create a dummy level with one empty itemset *)*
(* Build level-k of the T-tree *)
for $k = 1$ **to** n **do**
    Iteration(k);
    if $\mathcal{F}_k = \emptyset$ **then exit for**
    else $\mathcal{F} = \mathcal{F} \cup \mathcal{F}_k$;
return $\mathcal{F}$;

Our innovation here is the use of multiple pointers at each node of the T-tree in contrast to PTF-old where two pointers per node are used. This provides rapid access to the nodes of the T-tree which allows for a new strategy for T-tree update. In particular, while building level k, once a node I of the P-tree is visited, all its k-subsets (subsets of size k) are generated; once such a k-subset is generated, it is sought in the T-tree and, if present, its support is updated accordingly. Whenever such an itemset J has a subset J' which is not frequent (hence neither J can be frequent) the algorithm discovers this quite early and the update process terminates. For example, if the algorithm visits a node of the P-tree with itemset 'acdfghk' and the current level of the T-tree is level-6 the algorithm should update all size-6 subsets of 'acdfghk'. Consider 'acdfgh'; the algorithm will try to find this node starting from 'a' in level-1, continuing to 'ac' in level-2, and then to 'acd', 'acdf' and 'acdfg'. If 'acd' is non-frequent, i.e. does not exist in level-3, the algorithm stops and considers the lexicographically next size-6 subset of 'acdfghk'. In fact, it saves even more comparisons by considering 'acfghk' as next subset because there is no need to check any subset that contains 'acd'. On the other hand, PTF-old traverses a potentially large list of candidate itemsets in order to check whether any of them is a k-subset of I. This could be much slower than the above described procedure, especially if I has few k-subsets in that list. A detailed description of the update of level-k of the T-tree is given below.

Procedure Iteration(k) *(* Building k-th level of T-tree *)*
for each itemset $X_{k-1} \in \mathcal{F}_{k-1}$ **do**
    for each item x greater than all items of X_{k-1} **do**
        add $X_k := X_{k-1} \cup \{x\}$ to $\mathcal{F}_k$;
        let the x-th down pointer of X_{k-1} point to X_k;
(* Update total supports of nodes in $\mathcal{F}_k$ *)
for each node I of the P-tree **do**
    $non\text{-}frequent := \{dummy\}$;
    for each itemset $J \subseteq I$ with $|J| = k$ **do**
        if $J \subseteq par(I)$ or $non\text{-}frequent \subseteq J$ **then**
            proceed to the lex. next $J \subseteq I$ such that
                J is not subset of $par(I)$ and does not contain $non\text{-}$
$frequent$
        else
            descend the T-tree following prefixes of J
                until J is found or some $J' \sqsubseteq J$ is missing;
            if J is found **then** $T(J) := T(J) + P(I)$
            else $non\text{-}frequent := J'$; *(* J' is not in the T-tree *)*
remove from $\mathcal{F}_k$ all nodes with support $< t$ (threshold);

---

6   Experimental Comparison

We implemented four algorithms in ANSI-C: TTF, TTF-old, PTF and PTF-old. We run several experiments using a Pentium 1.6 GHz PC. We first experimented with datasets created by using the IBM Quest Market-Basket Synthetic Data Generator (described in [4]). We follow a standard notation according to which a dataset is described by four parameters: T represents the average transaction length (roughly equal to the database density times the number of items), I represents the average length of maximal frequent itemsets, N represents the number of items, and D represents the number of transactions in the database. We generated datasets T10.I4.N50.D10K and T10.I4.N20.D100K and run experiments with all four algorithms. The execution time of each algorithm for these two datasets and threshold varying from 5% to 1% is shown in Figure 1.

These results show that both algorithms TTF and PTF are faster than their predecessors, except for rather large thresholds. As regards TTF and TTF-old, the reason for this behaviour is that TTF-old performs fewer tests at each P-tree node that it visits; thus, whenever a contiguous part of the tree is traversed by both TTF and TTF-old, it is TTF-old the one which does it faster. Now, whenever the frequent itemsets are few, they are also (most probably) of small size; a small itemset has higher chances to appear in a contiguous part of the P-tree which therefore cannot be pruned by TTF. PTF-old can also be faster than PTF if there are only few frequent itemsets because in such a case it can be faster to traverse the list of candidate itemsets than generating all subsets of a node.

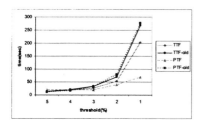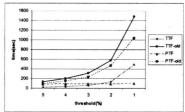

Figure 1: Results for datasets T10.I4.N50.D10K (left) and T10.I4.N20.D100K (right).

Comparing now the two new algorithms, we observe that PTF is faster than TTF for small thresholds ($\leq$ 2%). This is due to the fact that whenever the number of frequent itemsets is large, TTF performs a lot of P-tree traversals, while PTF performs only one full P-tree traversal per T-tree level. Since the size of the P-tree can be rather large (even comparable to the size of the database) its traversal is quite slow; hence, whenever TTF performs many traversals, even partial, the overall slowdown is considerable. On the other hand, PTF performs several T-tree traversals at each level but these are fast thanks to the use of multiple pointers. The two algorithms have comparable running time for thresholds above 2%. This is because for relatively sparse T-tree the P-tree traversals performed by TTF are few; in this case the economizing techniques of TTF balance, or even beat the advantages of PTF.

To further compare TTF and PTF we implemented a probabilistic generator in order to create datasets of *variable item density* (each item has a different expected density). This generator fills the i-th item of a row with probability $p_f - (i-1)p_s$, i.e., the probability decreases linearly as we move from the first to the last item of a row; p_f represents the probability of appearance of the first item and p_s is the decrement step. The expected density of the database is equal to $p_f - \frac{(n-1)}{2}p_s = \frac{p_f - p_l}{2}$, where p_l is the probability of appearance of the last item and n is the number of items in each row.

We have generated four variable-density datasets, one for each of the following four types (where letter 'V' stand for 'variable-density'): V.T4.N20.D10K, V.T6.N20.D10K, V.T4.N20.D100K, and V.T6.N20.D100K; the corresponding first item selection probabilities and decrement steps (in parentheses) are 0.4 (0.02), 0.6 (0.03), 0.4 (0.02), and 0.6 (0.03) respectively.

We run experiments with support thresholds ranging from 5% to 0.5%. For each dataset type / threshold combination we have measured the execution time of PTF and TTF, averaging over ten experiments, one for each dataset of the type.

Results for the datasets with 10K transactions appear in Figure 2. Figure 3 shows results for the datasets with 100K transactions.

Comparison of the algorithms for Variable-Density Datasets. The compar-

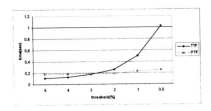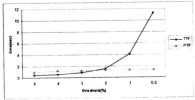

Figure 2: Results for datasets V.T4.N20.D10K (left) and V.T6.N20.D10K (right).

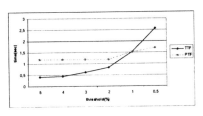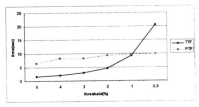

Figure 3: Results for datasets V.T4.N20.D100K (left) and V.T6.N20.D100K (right).

ison of the two algorithms is much more interesting when it comes to variable-density data sets. As before, PTF behaves better for small thresholds (roughly smaller than 2%) but TTF is faster for larger thresholds. Besides, PTF exhibits almost constant running time in most experiments. Now, whenever the T-tree is small and sparse, it happens that the few full P-tree traversals performed by PTF can take longer than the (more but not too many) partial P-tree traversals of TTF. The main reason is that potentially frequent itemsets consist mainly of lexicographically smaller items, hence the partial P-tree traversals of TTF are limited to a small part of the P-tree and are therefore much faster. On the other hand, TTF performs a full P-tree traversal at each level of the T-tree that contains potentially frequent itemsets, regardless of the number of these itemsets, hence it needs almost the same time as before, since it considers a similar number of levels.

Comparing the performance of the two algorithms with respect to uniformity of item densities one observes that while PTF exhibits roughly the same performance for both uniform and variable item densities, TTF is considerably faster on instances of variable item density; indeed, our results show that for variable-density datasets, TTF outperforms PTF for support thresholds above 3%, even above 2% or 1% in some cases. This is due to the fact that the performance of PTF is mainly determined by the rank of the higher level of frequent itemsets, while the performance of TTF depends heavily on the part of the P-tree that must be visited each time — which is much smaller for variable density instances, because frequent itemsets consist mainly of lexicographically smaller items.

Let us note here that for our experiments we built the variable-density datasets in such a way that the lexicographically greater items are of smaller density. This property is essential for the performance of TTF, since it guarantees that most frequent itemsets consist mainly of lexicographically small items which appear in a small part of the P-tree. Therefore, to make TTF work well for real datasets, a sorting of the items in order of decreasing density should be performed in a preprocessing step.

7 Conclusions

In this work we have developed and implemented two *Apriori*-style algorithms for the problem of frequent itemsets generation, called T-Tree-First (TTF) and P-Tree-First (PTF), that are based on the interim-support tree approach [9]. The two algorithms follow inverse approaches: TTF iterates over the itemsets of T-tree, and for each of them traverses the relevant part of the P-tree in order to count its total support; PTF starts by traversing the P-tree and for each visited node it updates all relevant nodes at the current level of the T-tree.

Our algorithms are improved versions of known algorithms, described in [9] and [7]. We have introduced several new techniques that result in faster algorithms comparing to these earlier attempts. The most important of them are the *fixed-prefix potential inclusion* technique, which is used in algorithm TTF, and the use of *multiple pointers* in the T-tree, employed by PTF. The former allows faster support counting for P-trees that are built using only two pointers per node, thus being particularly memory-efficient. The latter provides fast access to the T-tree and makes PTF a generally efficient algorithm. We show experimentally that our new algorithms achieve considerable speedup comparing to their predecessors.

The main difference between the two algorithms is that TTF performs a partial P-tree traversal for each potentially frequent itemset, while PTF performs only one, but full, P-tree traversal for each level of potentially frequent itemsets. As a result, PTF is considerably faster than TTF in instances where there are a lot of frequent itemsets, while TTF gains ground in instances where there are fewer potentially frequent itemsets, especially if for each of them it suffices to check only a small part of the P-tree. For example, the latter case may occur whenever item densities have a high variance.

In conclusion, each of the two heuristics has its own merits and deserves further exploration. As a suggestion for further research, it would be interesting to investigate possible combinations of the two inverse approaches of TTF and PTF. For example, it seems reasonable to use PTF as long as the current level of the T-tree contains a lot of frequent itemsets, while it may be wise to turn to TTF once the current level becomes sparse, especially if the majority of the

276

potentially frequent itemsets can be only found in a small part of the P-tree.

References

[1] F. Angiulli, G. Ianni, L. Palopoli. On the complexity of inducing categorical and quantitative association rules, arXiv:cs.CC/0111009 vol. 1, Nov. 2001

[2] R. Agrawal, T. Imielinski, and A. Swami. Mining Association Rules between Sets of Items in Large Databases. In *Proc. of ACM SIGMOD Conference on Management of Data*, Washington DC, May 1993.

[3] R. Agrawal, T. Imielinski, and A. Swami. Database mining: a performance perspective. *IEEE Transactions on Knowledge and Data Engineering*, 5(6):914–925, Dec 1993. Special Issue on Learning and Discovery in Knowledge-Based Databases.

[4] R. Agrawal and R. Srikant. Fast Algorithms for mining association rules. In *VLDB'94*, pp. 487–499.

[5] R. Agrawal, C. Aggarwal and V. Prasad. Depth First Generation of Long Patterns. In *KDD 2000*, ACM, pp. 108-118

[6] E. Boros, V. Gurvich, L. Khachiyan, K. Makino. On the complexity of generating maximal frequent and minimal infrequent sets, in *STACS* 2002.

[7] F. Coenen, G. Goulbourne, and P. Leng. Computing Association Rules using Partial Totals. In L. De Raedt and A. Siebes eds, *Principles of Data Mining and Knowledge Discovery* (Proc 5th European Conference, PKDD 2001, Freiburg, Sept 2001), Lecture Notes in AI 2168, Springer-Verlag, Berlin, Heidelberg: pp. 54–66.

[8] F. Coenen, G. Goulbourne and P. Leng. Tree Structures for Mining Association Rules. *Data Mining and Knowledge Discovery*, 8 (2004), pp. 25-51

[9] G. Goulbourne, F. Coenen and P. Leng. Algorithms for Computing Association Rules using a Partial-Support Tree. *Journal of Knowledge-Based Systems* 13 (2000), pp. 141–149.

[10] J. Han, J. Pei, Y.Yin and R. Mao. Mining Frequent Patterns without Candidate Generation: A Frequent-Pattern Tree Approach. *Data Mining and Knowledge Discovery*, 8 (2004), pp. 53-87

[11] A. Savasere, E. Omiecinski and S. Navathe. An Efficient Algorithm for Mining Association Rules in Large Databases. In *VLDB 1995*, pp. 432-444

[12] H. Toivonen. Sampling Large Databases for Association Rules. In *VLDB 1996*, pp. 1-12.

[13] M. J. Zaki. Generating Non-Redundant Association Rules. In *Proc. SIGKDD-2000*, pp. 34-43, 2000.

The Impact of Rule Ranking on the Quality of Associative Classifiers

Fadi Thabtah[1], Peter Cowling[2] and Yonghong Peng[3]

[1]Department of Computing and Engineering, University of Huddersfield
Huddersfield, UK
F.Thabtah@hud.ac.uk

[2] MOSAIC Research Centre, [3]Department of Computing, University of Bradford
Bradford, UK
{P.I.Cowling, Y.H.Peng}@bradford.ac.uk

Abstract

Associative classification is a promising approach that utilises association rule mining to build classifiers. Associative classification techniques such as CBA and CMAR rank rules mainly in terms of their confidence, support and cardinality. We propose a rule sorting method that adds more tie breaking conditions than existing methods in order to reduce rule random selection. In particular, our method looks at the class distribution frequency associated with the tied rules and favours those that are associated with the majority class. We compare the impact of the proposed rule ranking method and two other methods presented in associative classification against 12 highly dense classification data sets. Our results indicate the effectiveness of the proposed rule ranking method on the quality of the resulting classifiers for the majority of the benchmark problems, which we consider. In particular, our method improved the accuracy on average +0.62% and +0.40% for the 12 benchmark problems if compared with (support, confidence) and (support, confidence, lower cardinality) rule ranking approaches, respectively. This provides evidence that adding more appropriate constraints to break ties between rules positively affects the predictive power of the resulting associative classifiers.

1. INTRODUCTION

Association rule discovery and classification are analogous tasks in data mining, with the exception that the ultimate goal for classification is the prediction of classes, while association rule discovery describes associations between attribute values in a database. In recent years, association rule mining has been successfully used to build accurate classification models (classifiers), which resulted in a new approach coming to life, known as associative classification (AC) [1 & 2]. Several studies [2, 3, 4 5 & 13] show that the AC approach is able to extract more accurate classifiers than traditional classification techniques, such as decision trees [6], rule induction [7 & 8] and probabilistic approaches [9]. In contrast to rule induction techniques, which greedily and locally derive rules, AC explores the complete training data set and aims to construct a global classifier that can cover as many instances as possible.

Generally, to build an associative classifier, the complete sort of class association rules (CARs) is first extracted from the training data set and one subset is chosen to form the classifier. The selection of such a subset can be accomplished in many ways, for instance in the CBA [2] and L^3 [10] algorithms, the selection of the classifier is done by evaluating the complete set of CARs on the training data and considering rules that cover at least one training data object. On the other hand, the CPAR algorithm [5] uses a greedy method to choose the classifier. Once the classifier is created, its predictive power is then evaluated on test data objects.

Rule preference is known to be an important concept in classification [11]. Given a set of training data objects, the number of potential classification rules that imply these objects is relatively large, and consequently classification algorithms must have a basis for favouring one rule over another. In the AC approach, rule preference during the ranking process of the rules is important since higher ranked rules are often applied more than lower ranked rules in the prediction step. Thus, it is vital to use appropriate conditions to decide which rule is better.

Many AC techniques have been proposed in recent years, such as CMAR [4], CPAR [5], L^3 [10], Negative-Rules [12] and MCAR [13]. These techniques use several different approaches to discover rules, extract rules, rank rules, store rules, prune redundant or "harmful" rules (Those that lead to incorrect classification) and classify new test objects. The goal of this paper is to study the different approaches used by the state-of-the-art AC techniques for rule ranking and compare their effect on the quality of the resulting classifiers. Particularly, we study the effect of rule ranking procedures proposed in two popular AC algorithms (CBA, CMAR) on the accuracy of the derived classifiers. Furthermore, we present a new rule ranking method that adds upon previous approaches by considering the distribution frequencies of class labels in the training data for each rule in order to minimise randomisation.

The rest of the paper is organised as follows: AC and its main concepts are presented in Section 2. Different methods used to discriminate between rules and our proposed rule ranking method, are given in Section 3. Section 4 is devoted to experimental results and finally, conclusions are presented in Section 5.

2. ASSOCIATIVE CLASSIFICATION

2.1 The PROBLEM

AC is a special case of association rule mining in which only the class attribute is considered in the rule's consequent, for example in a rule such as $X \rightarrow Y$, Y must be the class attribute. Let us define the classification problem in an association rule framework. The training data set T has m distinct attributes $A_1, A_2, \ldots, A_m$ and C is a list of class labels. Attributes could be categorical (meaning they take a value from a finite set of possible values) or continuous (where they are real or integer). In the case of categorical attributes, all possible values may be mapped to a set of positive integers. For continuous attributes, any discretisation method can be used.

Definition 1: A row or a training object in T can be described as a combination of attribute names A_i and values a_{ij}, plus a class denoted by c_j.

Definition 2: An item can be described as an attribute name A_i and a value a_{ij}.

Definition 3: An itemset can be described as a set of items contained in a training object.

Definition 4: A rule r is of the form <itemset, c>, where $c \in C$ is the class.

Definition 5: The actual occurrence (*actoccr*) of a rule r in T is the number of rows in T that match the itemset defined in r.

Definition 6: The support count (*suppcount*) of a rule r is the number of rows in T that match r's itemset, and belong to r's class.

Definition 7: a rule r passes the *minsupp* threshold if $(suppcount(r)/|T|) \geq minsupp$, where $|T|$ is the number of instances in T.

Definition 8: a rule r passes *minconf* threshold if $(suppcount(r)/actoccr(r)) \geq minconf$.

Definition 9: An itemset i that passes the *minsupp* threshold is said to be a frequent itemset.

Definition 10: An actual class association rule is represented in the form: $(A_i, i_1, a_i, i_1) \wedge \ldots \wedge (A_i, i_k, a_i, i_k) \rightarrow c_i$, where the antecedent of the rule is an itemset and the consequent is a class.

A classifier is of the form $H : I \rightarrow Y$, where I is a set of itemsets and Y is the class. The main task of AC is to construct a set of rules (a model) that is able to predict the classes of previously unseen data, known as the test data set, as accurately as possible. In other words, the goal is to find a classifier $h \in H$ that maximises the probability that $h(a) = y$ for each test instance (a, y).

2.2 SOLUTION STRATEGY

Figure 1 shows the general steps used in an AC approach, in which the generation of the CARs is relatively computational expensive because it is similar to the discovery of frequent itemsets in association rule mining, which is a challenging problem [14, 15, 16 & 17]. Methods that find the complete set of frequent itemsets generally find itemsets that are potentially frequent and then work out their frequencies with classes in the training data. Once all frequent itemsets are identified, for each one of them that passes the *minconf* threshold, a rule such as $X \rightarrow C$ is generated, where C is the largest frequency class associated with itemset X in the training data (Step 2).

The problem of generating classification rules is straightforward, given that all frequent itemsets are already identified as no support counting or scanning of the training data are required. In step 3, a selection of an effective subset of rules is accomplished using various methods and finally the quality of the selected subset of rules (the classifier) is measured on an independent test data set to find the accuracy.

Let us explain the discovery of frequent itemsets and the construction of the classifier in AC using an example. Consider the training data shown in Table 1, which represents three attributes A_1 (a_1, b_1, c_1), A_2 (a_2, b_2, c_2) and A_3 (a_3, b_3, c_3) and two class labels (y_1, y_2). Assuming *minsupp* = 20% and *minconf* = 80%, the frequent one, two and three itemsets for Table 1 are shown in Table 2, along with the relevant supports and confidences. In cases where an itemset is associated with multiple classes, only the class with the largest frequency is considered by AC methods. All frequent itemsets in bold in Table 2 pass the *minconf* threshold, and will be converted into

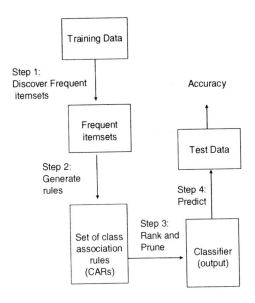

Figure 1 Associative classification steps

Table 1 Training data set

rowids	A_1	A_2	A_3	class
1	a_1	a_2	b_3	y_1
2	a_1	a_2	c_3	y_2
3	a_1	b_2	b_3	y_1
4	a_1	b_2	b_3	y_2
5	b_1	b_2	a_3	y_2
6	b_1	a_2	b_3	y_1
7	a_1	b_2	b_3	y_1
8	a_1	a_2	b_3	y_1
9	c_1	c_2	c_3	y_2
10	a_1	a_2	b_3	y_1

potential rules in the classifier.

There are many AC algorithms proposed in the literature [2, 3, 4, 10 & 12] where most of which are based on the CBA algorithm [2]. The CBA algorithm uses Apriori candidate generation step [14] to find the rules, where only the subset that leads to the lowest error rate against the training data set is selected to from the classifier. The selection of the subset is accomplished using the database coverage heuristic [2], where each rule is evaluated against the training data in order to determine rules, which cover at least one training data object. The selection of which rule is evaluated first is based on the rule ranking parameters, and therefore, highest order rules are normally evaluated before other potential rules, which give them the opportunity to be used more frequently in predicting test data objects.

Table 2 Potential classifier for Table 1

Frequent *Ruleitems*		Supp	Conf
Antecedent	Consequent / class		
<a_2, b_3>	y_1	4/10	4/4
<a_1, a_2, b_3>	y_1	3/10	3/3
<b_3>	y_1	6/10	6/7
<a_1,b_3>	y_1	5/10	5/6
<a_2>	y_1	4/10	4/5
<a_1,a_2>	y_1	3/10	3/4
<a_1>	y_1	5/10	5/7

3. COMMON ASSOCIATIVE CLASSIFICATION RULE RANKING METHODS

Rule ranking before building the classifier plays an important role in the classification process since the majority of AC algorithms such as [2, 4 & 10] utilise rule ranking procedures as the basis for selecting the classifier during pruning. In particular, CBA and CMAR algorithms for example use the database coverage pruning to build their classifiers, where using this pruning, rules are tested according to their ranks. The precedence of the rules is normally determined according to several parameters, including, support, confidence and rule antecedent cardinality. This section highlights the different constraints considered by current algorithms to discriminate between rules in the rule ordering process and also discusses the impact they have on the quality of the resulting classifiers.

3.1 SUPPORT, CONFIDENCE And CARDINALITY METHOD

One of the common rule ranking techniques, which favours rules with large support and confidence values, was introduced in [2], and is shown in Figure 2. The ranking technique employed by CBA considers principally confidence and support to order

282

Given two rules, r_a and r_b, r_a precedes $r_b (r_a \succ r_b)$ if

1. The confidence of r_a is greater than that of r_b.
2. The confidence values of r_a and r_b are the same, but the support of r_a is greater than that of r_b.
3. Confidence and support values of r_a and r_b are the same, but r_a was generated earlier than r_b.

Figure 2 CBA rule ranking method

rules, and when two rules have identical support and confidence, the choice is based on the one generated earlier. This means, CBA selects rules with lower cardinality first since it employs the Apriori step-wise algorithm [14] in its rule generation step. The Apriori algorithm generates rules starting from those that have length 1, then 2 and so on.

The CBA sorting method fails to break many ties for highly correlated classification data sets, where the expected number of the produced rules is relatively large. For example, for the "vote" data set downloaded from [18] and using *minsupp* of 2% and *minconf* of 40%, there are 7755 potential rules with identical confidence, of which 6802 have the same support. Also, from the 6802 potential rules with identical confidence and support, there are 5126 that have the same cardinality and only 1113 potential rules from which have different cardinality. These numbers of potential rules have been produced without using any pruning. The remaining rules are ranked randomly if we use the CBA rule sorting method, where many rule ranking decisions may be sub-optimal, reducing the quality of the resulting classifier. Additional tie breaking conditions have the potential to improve classification accuracy over the (support, confidence, cardinality) method.

Another similar rule ranking method to CBA one, which favours specific rules (those with higher antecedent cardinality), was developed in [10]. The main reason for giving specific rules higher ranking than others is to reduce the chance of misclassification and to try specific rules first in the prediction step, then if they fail to cover a test instance, rules with a smaller number of attributes are considered.

Given two rules, r_a and r_b, r_a precedes $r_b (r_a \rangle r_b)$ if:

1. The confidence of r_a is greater than that of r_b.
2. The confidence values of r_a and r_b are the same, but the support of r_a is greater than that of r_b.
3. Confidence and support of r_a and r_b are the same, but r_a has fewer conditions in its left hand side than of r_b.
4. Confidence, support and cardinality of r_a and r_b are the same, but r_a is associated with a a class that occurs more frequently in the training data than that of r_b.
5. All above criteria are identical for r_a and r_b, but r_a generated from rows that occur earlier in the training data than that of r_b.

Figure 3 The proposed rule ranking method

The majority of AC algorithms developed after the introduction of CBA, including, [3, 4 & 10] have used the (support, confidence, lower cardinality) ranking method. These algorithms tend to prefer general rules (those with very small numbers of attribute values in their antecedent) since they occur more frequently in the training data. However, such rules may suffer from large error rates. Generally speaking, specific rules (rules with a high cardinality) are supersets of some general rules and cover smaller numbers of training instances. Thus, their chance of misclassification on the training data is usually smaller than that of general rules.

3.2 The PROPOSED RULE RANKING METHOD

Selecting appropriate parameters to favour one rule on another in rule ordering is crucial task since most AC algorithms use rule ranking as the basis to select rules while constructing the classifier. The CBA and CMAR algorithms favour rules principally with reference to confidence, support and lower cardinality. When several rules have identical confidence, support and cardinality, these methods randomly choose one of the rules, which in some cases may degrade accuracy. Since AC approach generates normally large sized classifiers, where rules can be in the order of thousands, so that, there may be several rules with the same support, confidence and cardinality.

Consider for instance the "glass" data set from [18], if it is mined with *minsupp* of 2% and *minconf* of 40% using the CBA algorithm and without using any pruning, there are 759 potential rules that have identical confidence, 624 of these have identical support as well. Also, there are 409 of the 624 potential rules have the same cardinality, leaving no way for CBA or CMAR rule ranking methods to discriminate between them. A more serious case is the "autos" data set, if we mine it using the same support and confidence, there are 2660 potential rules with the same confidence and 2494 of them have identical support too. When the support is lowered further, there may be huge numbers of potential rules with identical support and confidence.

We propose the rule ranking method shown in Figure 3, which adds two tie breaking conditions to the existing methods. Beside confidence, support and cardinality, our method considers the class distribution frequency associated with each rule and favours rules that are associated with the most representative class. For example, if two rules, r_1 and r_2, have the same support, confidence and cardinality, but r_2 is associated with a class label, which has been occurred more frequently in the training data than that of r_1, our method favours r_2 on r_1 in the rule ranking process. In cases where two or more rules have also the same class frequencies, then we select one randomly. Our rule random selection considers the rule's items row ordering in the training data set and prefer rules that have a higher order. We will show in Section 4 the effectiveness of the proposed rule ranking method on the quality of the produced classifiers.

3.3 IMPACT Of RULE RANKING ON CLASSIFIERS

Every rule-based AC technique performs global sorting on the rules in the process of building the classifier. This sorting can be considered a first step toward pruning noisy and redundant rules and explains the reason why these algorithms sort rules before pruning. Sorting aims to give good quality classification rules the chance to be selected first in the process of predicting test data objects, and thus rule ranking can be seen as an important step, which may influence the quality of the resulting classifier. Presented previously in this section, the measures used to discriminate between rules are confidence, support and cardinality. But the question still remains, which rule ranking method is the most effective?

It is the firm belief of the authors that if more effective conditions can be imposed to break ties, random selection will be minimised and better quality classifiers will result. This is because pruning heuristics such as database coverage [2] and lazy pruning [10] consider rules based on their rank when constructing the classifier. Examples demonstrated in Section 3.3 indicate that there is a potential for additional measures to break ties between rules beside support, confidence and cardinality due to the large number of rules extracted using AC approaches. In the next section, we show by experimental results the effectiveness of adding new parameters to discriminate between tied rules on the classification accuracy.

4. EXPERIMENTAL RESULTS

We conducted a number of experiments on 12 highly dense classification data sets from [18] using stratified ten-fold cross validation [19]. The impact of three rule ranking methods: (confidence, support), (confidence, support, lower cardinality) [2 & 4] and our proposed method on the quality of the resulting classifiers from the 12 benchmark problems have been compared. The choice of such rule ranking methods is based on their wide use in AC. We have implemented the three methods in Java within a recent proposed AC algorithm, MCAR [13]. Following experiments conducted in [2, 12 & 13] the *minsupp* was set to 2%. The confidence threshold, on the other hand, has a smaller impact on the behaviour of any AC method, and it has been set in our experiments to 40%. All experiments were conducted on Pentium IV 1.7 Ghz, 256 MB RAM machine using Java under Windows XP.

To investigate the behaviour of the rule ranking methods, Table 3 shows the number of times each condition does not break tie between rules for the 12 classification problems. Column 2 indicates the number of potential rules with similar confidence, column 3 represents the number of potential rules with the same confidence and support. Column 4 shows the number of potential rules that have identical confidence, support and cardinality and column 5 represents rules from column 4 that share the same class frequency. Column "RowOrd " indicates the number of times the rule's items row ordering condition has been used after trying (support, confidence, cardinality, class frequency). We have used a *minsupp* of 2% and a *minconf* of 40% to produce the potential rules in Table 3.

Values shown in Table 3 represent the potential rules tested by the MCAR algorithm during the ranking process and before building the classifier or performing any pruning and this explains their large numbers. Table 3 shows that support and confidence are not effective in distinguishing between rules in most benchmark problems, we consider. For the "Cleve" data set for instance, there are 17092 potential rules with the same confidence as some other rule, with 16289 rules having identical confidence and support. There are 14647 with the same confidence, support and cardinality as some other rule, where 12942 from the 14647 are associated with classes that have the same frequency in the training data set. The frequent use of the additional conditions in the process of the rule ranking especially class frequency parameter suggests that more discrimination between potential rules positively increases the accuracy of the classifiers.

To show the effectiveness of the rule sorting method on the quality of the classifiers, we conduct a number of experiments to compare the impact on accuracy of the proposed rule ranking method and two other methods, which are (support, confidence) and (support, confidence, lower cardinality). Each value shown in Table 4 represents an overage over ten cross validation runs each using a different random seed when partitioning the training data set.

The figures show a slight improvement of our rule ranking method over that of (support, confidence) and (support, confidence, lower cardinality). In particular, our method achieved on average +0.62% and +0.40% improvements with regards to accuracy on the 12 benchmark problems over (support, confidence) and (support, confidence, lower cardinality) rule ranking

Table 3 Number of times each condition in the proposed rule ranking method does not break tie between potential rules

Data	No. of Rules with the same Conf.	No. of Rules with the same Conf. & Supp.	No. of Rules with the same Conf., Supp. & Cardinality	No. of Rules with the same Conf., Supp., Cardinality &Class Freq.	RowOrd
Autos	2660	2492	2117	1683	181
Glass	759	624	409	245	7
Lymph	11019	10775	10217	9595	2381
Cleve	17092	16289	14647	12942	469
Tic-tac	2297	2047	1796	1541	278
Diabetes	252	91	15	3	0
Breast	3471	2980	2217	1643	75
Vote	7755	6802	5126	4013	207
Heart	4791	4267	3383	2562	145
wine	31012	30486	29730	4500	0
weather	96	85	75	61	37
Pima	252	91	15	3	0

approaches, respectively. It appears that the additional constraints imposed to break ties slightly improve the predictive power of the resulting classifiers over the test data sets.

Table 4 Impact of the three rule ranking methods on the accuracy

Data	(Supp, Conf)	(Supp, Conf, Lower cardinality)	The proposed method
Cleve	**82.44**	82.16	81.35
Breast-w	94.61	95.11	**96.32**
Diabetes	76.90	77.05	**77.18**
Glass	67.76	68.79	**69.97**
Pima	77.16	**77.34**	77.11
Tic-Tac	99.76	99.77	**100.00**
Led7	70.95	**71.07**	71.00
Heart-s	81.30	81.87	**82.14**
Lymph	**79.10**	77.13	78.57
Vote	**88.86**	88.17	87.70
zoo	95.38	97.73	**97.78**
Contact-lenses	72.93	73.54	**75.54**
Average	82.26	82.48	**82.88**

5. CONCLUSIONS

In this paper, the problem of rule ranking in associative classification has been investigated. Particularly, we propose a rule ranking technique, which expands previous rule ranking methods by looking at the class distribution frequencies to discriminate between tied rules. In addition, we use a rule random selection that looks at the rule items ordering in the training data and favour rules that are associated with a higher order. These tie breaking conditions together with existing support, confidence and cardinality approaches have been used to minimise the need for random selection. Empirical Evaluations using 12 highly correlated classification data sets from *Weka* data collection revealed that adding more constraints to discriminate between rules improved the accuracy of the resulting classifiers. Our proposed rule ranking method improved the accuracy for the 12 classification data sets on average +0.62% and +0.40% over (support, confidence) and (support, confidence, lower cardinality) rule ranking approaches, respectively. Moreover, the results show that our additional parameters for breaking ties are used often.

Reference

1. Agrawal, R. & Srikant, R. Fast algorithms for mining association rule. *Proceedings of the 20th International Conference on Very Large Data Bases* (pp. 487-499), 1994.
2. Ali, K., Manganaris, S. & Srikant, R. Partial classification using association rules. In Heckerman, D., Mannila, H., Pregibon, D., and Uthurusamy, R., (eds.). *Proceedings of the Third International Conference on Knowledge Discovery and Data Mining*, (pp. 115-118.), 1997.
3. Antonie, M. & Zaïane, O. An associative classifier based on positive and negative rules. *Proceedings of the 9th ACM SIGMOD workshop on Research issues in data mining and knowledge discovery* (pp. 64 - 69). Paris, France, 2004.
4. Baralis, E. & Torino, P. A lazy approach to pruning classification rules. *Proceedings of the ICDM'02*, (pp. 35), 2000.
5. Cendrowska, J. PRISM: An algorithm for inducing modular rules. *International Journal of Man-Machine Studies*. Vol.27, No.4, pp.349-370, 1987.
6. Cohen, W. Fast effective rule induction. *Proceedings of the 12th International Conference on Machine Learning* (pp. 115-123). Morgan Kaufmann, CA, 1995.
7. Duda, R. & Hart, P. Pattern classification and scene analysis, John Wiley & son, 1973.
8. Li, W., Han, J. & Pei, J. CMAR: Accurate and efficient classification based on multiple-class association rule. *Proceedings of the ICDM'01* (pp. 369-376). San Jose, CA 2001.
9. Lim, T., Loh, W. & Shih, Y. A comparison of prediction accuracy, complexity and training time of thirty-three old and new classification algorithms. *Machine Learning*, 40(3): 203--228, 2000.
10. Lin, J. & Dunham, M. Mining Association Rules: Anti-Skew Algorithms, *Proceedings of the Fourteenth International Conference on Data Engineering*, (pp. 486-493), 1998.
11. Liu, B., Hsu, W. & Ma, Y. Integrating Classification and association rule mining. *Proceedings of the KDD* (pp. 80-86). New York, NY, 1998.
12. Michaliski, R. A theory and methodology of inductive learning. Artificial Intelligence 20, 1983, 111-161, 1983.
13. Park, J., Chen, M., and Yu, P. An Effective Hash-Based Algorithm for Mining Association Rules. *Proceedings of the ACM SIGMOD*, (pp. 175-186). San Jose, CA, 1995.
14. Quinlan, J. C4.5: *Programs for Machine Learning*. San Mateo, CA: Morgan Kaufmann, 1993.
15. Thabtah, F., Cowling, P. & Peng, Y. MCAR: Multi-class Classification based on Association Rule Approach. *Proceeding of the 3rd IEEE International Conference on Computer Systems and Applications* (pp. 1-7). Cairo, Egypt, 2005.
16. Witten, I. & Frank, E. *Data mining: practical Machine learning tools and techniques with Java implementations*. San Francisco: Morgan Kaufmann, 2000.
17. Yin, X. & Han, J. CPAR: Classification based on predictive association rule. *Proceedings of the SDM* (pp. 369-376). San Francisco, CA, 2003.
18. Wang, K., Zhou, S. & He, Y. *Growing Decision Tree on Support-less Association Rules.* Proceedings *of the sixth ACM SIGKDD international conference on Knowledge discovery and data mining*, Boston, Massachusetts, pp. (265 – 269), 2000.
19. WEKA : Data Mining Software in Java: http://www.cs.waikato.ac.nz/ml/weka.

Reliable Instance Classification with Version Spaces

E.N. Smirnov, I.G. Sprinkhuizen-Kuyper

Department of Computer Science, Universiteit Maastricht
Maastricht 6200 MD, The Netherlands
{smirnov, kuyper}@cs.unimaas.nl

G.I. Nalbantov

ERIM, Erasmus University Rotterdam
Rotterdam 3000 DR, The Netherlands
nalbantov@few.eur.nl

Abstract

This paper proposes considering version spaces as an approach to reliable instance classification. The key idea is to construct version spaces containing the hypotheses of the target concept or its close approximations. So, the unanimous-voting classification rule of version spaces does not misclassify; i.e., instance classifications become reliable.

We implement version spaces by testing them for collapse. We show that testing can be done by any learning algorithm and use support vector machines. The resulting combination is called version space support vector machines. Experiments show 100% accuracy and good coverage.

1 Introduction

In the last decade machine-learning classifiers were applied to various classification problems [6]. Nevertheless, only few classifiers were employed in real applications, especially in critical domains. The main reason is that it is difficult to determine if a classification assigned to a particular instance is reliable.

There are several approaches to reliable instance classification [1, 6, 7, 9, 11]. Most of them output confidence values for each classification. If these values are above a certain threshold, the instance classifications are considered as reliable.

The two most prominent approaches to reliable instance classification are the Bayesian framework [9] and the typicalness framework [6, 7, 11] (see section 8). The Bayesian framework is a natural approach to reliable classification but it is often misleading. The typicalness framework partially overcomes this problem but it depends heavily on the learning algorithm used.

To overcome these problems of the presented frameworks we propose to consider version spaces [8, 9, 13] as an approach to reliable instance classification. The key idea is to construct version spaces containing hypotheses of the target concepts to be learned or their close approximations. In this way the unanimous-voting rule does not misclassify instances; i.e., instance classifications are reliable.

We analyze the instance classification of version spaces for the case when data are non-noisy and hypothesis space is expressive as well as for the opposite three cases. For the latter instance classification can be unreliable and we propose a volume-extension approach. The approach is to grow the volumes of version spaces s.t. instance misclassifications are blocked.

To demonstrate version spaces for reliable classification we implement the unanimous-voting rule by testing version spaces for collapse [4, 13]. We show that testing can be done by any learning algorithm and use support vector machines (SVM) [3, 16]. The resulting combination is called version space support vector machines (VSSVM). We combine VSSVM with the volume-extension approach. VSSVM experiments show 100% accuracy and good coverage.

The paper is organized as follows. The task of reliable instance classification is formalized in section 2. Section 3 considers version spaces and reliable instance classification, and then introduces the volume-extension approach. SVM are described in section 4. Section 5 introduces VSSVM. The volume-extension approach for VSSVM is in section 6. Section 7 presents experiments with VSSVM. A comparison is given in section 8. Finally, section 9 concludes the paper.

2   Task of Reliable Instance Classification

Assume that we have l different training instances $\mathbf{x}_i$ in $\mathbb{R}^n$. Each $\mathbf{x}_i$ has a class label $y_i \in Y$ with respect to a binary target concept, i.e., $Y = \{-1, +1\}$. The class labels separate the instances into two sets I^+ and I^- ($\mathbf{x}_i \in I^+$ iff $y_i = +1$; $\mathbf{x}_i \in I^-$ iff $y_i = -1$). Given a space H of hypotheses h ($h : \mathbb{R}^n \rightarrow Y \cup \{0\}$), the task of reliable instance classification is to find a hypothesis h that correctly classifies future, unseen instances. When correct classification is not possible, h outputs 0.

3   Version Spaces

This section considers version spaces for reliable instance classification.

3.1   Definition and Classification Rule

Version spaces are sets of hypotheses consistent with training data [8, 9, 13].

Definition 1. *Given a hypothesis space H and training data $\langle I^+, I^- \rangle$, the version space $VS(I^+, I^-)$ is defined as follows:*

$$VS(I^+, I^-) = \{h \in H | cons(h, \langle I^+, I^- \rangle)\}$$

where $cons(h, \langle I^+, I^- \rangle) \leftrightarrow (\forall \mathbf{x}_i \in I^+ \cup I^-)(y_i = h(\mathbf{x}_i))$.

The version-space classification rule is the unanimous voting. Given a version space $VS(I^+, I^-)$, an instance $\mathbf{x}$ receives a classification $y \in Y \cup \{0\}$ as follows:

$$y = \begin{cases} +1 \text{ if } (VS(I^+, I^-) \neq \emptyset) \wedge (\forall h \in VS(I^+, I^-))(h(\mathbf{x}) = +1) \\ -1 \text{ if } (VS(I^+, I^-) \neq \emptyset) \wedge (\forall h \in VS(I^+, I^-))(h(\mathbf{x}) = -1) \\ 0 \quad \text{otherwise.} \end{cases}$$

Definition 2. *The volume $V(VS(I^+, I^-))$ of a version space $VS(I^+, I^-)$ is the set of all instances that cannot be classified by $VS(I^+, I^-)$.*

By theorem 1 below, the unanimous-voting rule can be implemented if version spaces can be tested for collapse [4, 13]. If $VS(I^+, I^-)$ is nonempty and an instance $\mathbf{x}$ is to be classified, theorem 1 states that all the hypotheses in $VS(I^+, I^-)$ assign class $+1$ (-1) to $\mathbf{x}$ iff $VS(I^+, I^- \cup \{\mathbf{x}\})$ $(VS(I^+ \cup \{\mathbf{x}\}, I^-))$ is empty.

Theorem 1. *If $VS(I^+, I^-)$ is nonempty, then*

$$(\forall \mathbf{x})((\forall h \in VS(I^+, I^-))(h(\mathbf{x}) = +1) \leftrightarrow VS(I^+, I^- \cup \{\mathbf{x}\}) = \emptyset), \text{ and}$$

$$(\forall \mathbf{x})((\forall h \in VS(I^+, I^-))(h(\mathbf{x}) = -1) \leftrightarrow VS(I^+ \cup \{\mathbf{x}\}, I^-) = \emptyset).$$

The problem to test version spaces for collapse is equivalent to the consistency problem. The consistency problem is to determine the existence of a hypothesis consistent with training data. Hence, the unanimous-voting rule of version spaces can be implemented by any consistency algorithm [4, 13].

In practice the algorithms used are not always perfect consistency algorithms. An algorithm is not a perfect consistency algorithm if it is not able to find always a consistent hypothesis when the hypothesis belongs to the hypothesis space. If the algorithm used is not a perfect consistency algorithm, version spaces are defined such that they are non-empty iff the algorithm finds a consistent hypothesis. The algorithm parameters P influence when version spaces are empty.

3.2 Analysis of Reliable Instance Classification

Version spaces are sensitive with respect to class noise in training data and expressiveness of hypothesis space [8, 9, 13]. Class noise indicates that the class labels of some instances are incorrect. Expressiveness of a hypothesis space H indicates if the hypothesis h_t of the target concept is in H.

Below we study the reliability of instance classification with version spaces.

Case 1: Non-noisy Training Data and Expressive Hypothesis Space. Since the hypothesis space H is expressive, $h_t \in H$. Since the training data $\langle I^+, I^- \rangle$ are non-noisy, h_t is consistent with $\langle I^+, I^- \rangle$. Thus, according to definition 1 $h_t \in VS(I^+, I^-)$ [8, 9, 13]. In this way, if an instance $\mathbf{x}$ is classified by $VS(I^+, I^-)$, $\mathbf{x}$ is classified by h_t; i.e., $\mathbf{x}$ is classified correctly. Thus, for case 1 version spaces outputs only reliable instance classifications.

Case 2: Noisy Training Data. If there is noise, the set I^+ (I^-) is a union of a noise-free set I_f^+ (I_f^-) and a noisy set I_n^+ (I_n^-). The noisy data $\langle I_n^+, I_n^- \rangle$

cause removal of the set $NVS = \{h \in VS(I_f^+, I_f^-)|\neg cons(h, \langle I_n^+, I_n^- \rangle)\}$ from $VSSVM(I_f^+, I_f^-)$. Thus, the resulting version space $VS(I^+, I^-)$ classifies instances classified by $VS(I_f^+, I_f^-)$, but it errs on all instances in the volume of NVS.

Case 3: Inexpressive Hypothesis Space. If the hypothesis space H is inexpressive ($h_t \notin H$), it is possible that the hypotheses in $VS(I^+, I^-)$ do not approximate the target concept well.; i.e., there may exist an instance $\mathbf{x}$ that is misclassified by all the hypotheses in $VS(I^+, I^-)$. Thus, $VS(I^+, I^-)$ can result in instance misclassifications.

Case 4: Noisy Training Data and Inexpressive Hypothesis Space. This case comprises cases 2 and 3, and can be derived from their descriptions.

3.3 Volume-Extension Approach

The volume-extension approach is a new approach to overcome simultaneously the problems with noisy training data and inexpressive hypothesis spaces. Assume a hypothesis space H and an implementation of the unanimous-voting rule based on an imperfect consistency algorithm with parameters P. Then, if a version space $VS(I^+, I^-)$ misclassifies instances, the approach redefines the hypothesis space H and/or the parameters P s.t. the volume of the new version space $VS'(I^+, I^-)$ grows and blocks instance misclassifications. Below we consider this approach for all the three problematic cases in subsection 3.2.

Case 2: since the volume of NVS is the error region for $VS(I^+, I^-)$, we redefine H/P s.t. the volume of $VS'(I^+, I^-)$ comprises maximally the volume of NVS;

Case 3: since the causes of misclassification for $VS(I^+, I^-)$ are the hypotheses in $VS(I^+, I^-)$ not approximating the target concept well, we redefine H/P s.t. $VS'(I^+, I^-)$ includes more hypotheses approximating better the target concept. This means that if we have an instance $\mathbf{x}$ misclassified by $VS(I^+, I^-)$, we redefine H (P) s.t. $VS'(I^+, I^-)$ includes a hypothesis classifying $\mathbf{x}$ as the target concept. Thus, $\mathbf{x}$ will not be classified, so the misclassification is blocked.

Case 4: case 4 comprises cases 2 and 3, and the previous explanations hold here.

To apply the volume-extension approach we have to guarantee that the volumes of new version spaces $VS'(I^+, I^-)$ comprise those of version spaces $VS(I^+, I^-)$. When we redefine a hypothesis space H to a new one H' this is guaranteed by theorem 2 below when for each $\langle I^+, I^- \rangle$ if there is a consistent hypothesis $h \in H$, then there is a consistent hypothesis $h' \in H'$.

Theorem 2. *Consider hypothesis spaces H and H' s.t. for each $\langle I^+, I^- \rangle$ if there is $h \in H$ consistent with $\langle I^+, I^- \rangle$, then there is $h' \in H'$ consistent with $\langle I^+, I^- \rangle$ as well. Then, for each $\langle I^+, I^- \rangle$ we have $V(VS(I^+, I^-)) \subseteq V(VS'(I^+, I^-))$.*

To apply the volume-extension approach we have to guarantee that by re-defining the parameters P of the imperfect consistency algorithm in the unanimous-voting-rule implementation we have to find dependencies checking for each two parameter sets P and P' if the volumes of version spaces VS' comprise those of version spaces VS.

We conclude that the volume extension approach can cause blocking instance misclassification for cases 2, 3, and 4. This result and case 1 allow us to state that *version spaces are an approach to reliable instance classification.*

4 Support Vector Machines

Support Vector Machines (SVM) [3, 16] were proposed for the classification task. The hypothesis space of SVM is the set of all oriented hyperplanes in a Euclidian space $\mathbb{R}^n$ or in a higher dimensional feature space F obtained by a mapping $\phi(\mathbf{x})$ on the instances $\mathbf{x}$ from $\mathbb{R}^n$. The parameters of the SVM hyperplane are derived from the solution of the following optimization problem:

$$\max_\alpha \; \sum_{i=1}^l \alpha_i - \tfrac{1}{2} \sum_{i,j=1}^l \alpha_i \alpha_j y_i y_j k(\mathbf{x}_i, \mathbf{x}_j) \tag{1}$$

$$\text{subject to } 0 \le \alpha_i \le C, \; i = 1, 2, \cdots, l, \text{ and } \sum_{i=1}^l y_i \alpha_i = 0,$$

where $k(\mathbf{x}_i, \mathbf{x}_j) = \phi(\mathbf{x}_i)' \phi(\mathbf{x}_j)$ is a kernel function that calculates inner products of instances $\mathbf{x}_i$ and $\mathbf{x}_j$ in feature space F. One kernel is the Radial Basis Function (RBF) defined as $k(\mathbf{x}_i, \mathbf{x}_j) = e^{-\gamma \|\mathbf{x}_i - \mathbf{x}_j\|^2}$ where γ is a parameter. When a kernel is used, instead of the original hypothesis space H of SVM we have a hypothesis space of hyperplanes in a higher dimensional feature space F. We denote this space as $H(p)$ where p is the kernel parameter.

Maximizing the term $-\sum_{i,j=1}^l \alpha_i \alpha_j y_i y_j k(\mathbf{x}_i, \mathbf{x}_j)$ in (1) corresponds to maximizing the margin between the two classes. The constant C determines the trade-off between the margin and the amount of training errors. The alphas are the weights associated with the training instances. All instances with nonzero weights are called "support vectors", and only they determine the position of the SVM hyperplane $h(p, C, \langle I^+, I^- \rangle)$. This hyperplane consists of all points $\mathbf{x}$ which satisfy $\sum_{i=1}^l y_i \alpha_i k(\mathbf{x}_i, \mathbf{x}) + b = 0$. The b parameter is found from the so-called Kuhn-Tucker conditions associated with (1). The classification of a new instance $\mathbf{x}$ is found by: $h(p, C, \langle I^+, I^- \rangle)(\mathbf{x}) = \mathrm{sgn}(\sum_{i=1}^l y_i \alpha_i k(\mathbf{x}_i, \mathbf{x}) + b)$.

In this paper we are interested in the asymptotic behaviors of SVM with the RBF kernel w.r.t. the parameter γ of RBF and the constant C [5].

The γ parameter determines the level of proximity between any two points in the feature space F. If γ increases, any two points become more dissimilar. Thus, it becomes easier to separate them by the SVM hyperplane with the same C parameter. Thus, we assume for arbitrary data $\langle I^+, I^- \rangle$ that γ is monotonic with the probability that $h(\gamma, C, \langle I^+, I^- \rangle)$ is consistent with $\langle I^+, I^- \rangle$.

For the constant C the things are similarly, when C increases, the sum of training errors increases, while other things stay equal. Consequently, the SVM algorithm will try to find a new balance between the margin width and amount of training errors. In particular, the margin will decrease and, simultaneously with that, the amount of classification errors will generally go down. Therefore, we assume for arbitrary data $\langle I^+, I^- \rangle$ that the parameter C is monotonic with the probability that $h(\gamma, C, \langle I^+, I^- \rangle)$ is consistent with $\langle I^+, I^- \rangle$.

5 Version Space Support Vector Machines

This section introduces version space support vector machines (VSSVM). In subsection 5.1 we define VSSVM. In subsections 5.2 and 5.3 we provide the classification algorithm of VSSVM and an example.

5.1 Definition

VSSVM are version spaces that can be tested for collapse with SVM.

Since SVM are imperfect consistency algorithms if $C < \infty$, we define the VSSVM to be empty when the hypothesis $h(p, C, \langle I^+, I^- \rangle)$ generated by the SVM is not consistent with the training data $\langle I^+, I^- \rangle$ (cf. section 3.1).

Definition 3. *Given a hypothesis space $H(p)$, a constant C, and training data $\langle I^+, I^- \rangle$, the version space support vector machine $VS_C^p(I^+, I^-)$ is:*

$$VS_C^p(I^+, I^-) =$$
$$\begin{cases} \{h \in H(p) | cons(h, \langle I^+, I^- \rangle)\} & \text{if } cons(h(p, C, \langle I^+, I^- \rangle), \langle I^+, I^- \rangle) \\ \emptyset & \text{otherwise.} \end{cases}$$

According to definition 3 to test whether VSSVM are empty we need to apply SVM. To apply SVM we need only the training data $\langle I^+, I^- \rangle$. Hence, the training sets are the version-space representation of VSSVM.

VSSVM are version spaces. Hence, the inductive bias of VSSVM is the restriction bias [9, 13]. The kernel parameter p defines the hypothesis space $H(p)$ of VSSVM and the parameter C determines when VSSVM are empty in $H(p)$. Hence, the restriction bias of VSSVM is controlled by these two parameters.

5.2 Classification Algorithm

The classification algorithm of VSSVM implements the unanimous-voting rule. It is based on theorem 1. To test version spaces for collapse SVM are employed.

The classification algorithm is given in figure 1. Assume that an instance $\mathbf{x}$ is to be classified. Then, the algorithm builds a hyperplane $h(p, C, \langle I^+, I^- \rangle)$. If $h(p, C, \langle I^+, I^- \rangle)$ is inconsistent with $\langle I^+, I^- \rangle$, according to definition 3, the version space $VS_C^p(I^+, I^-)$ is empty. Thus, according to the unanimous-voting rule the algorithm returns 0; i.e., the classification of $\mathbf{x}$ is unknown. If the hyperplane $h(p, C, \langle I^+, I^- \rangle)$ is consistent with $\langle I^+, I^- \rangle$, $VS_C^p(I^+, I^-)$ is nonempty. In this case the algorithm builds hyperplanes $h(p, C, \langle I^+, I^- \cup \{\mathbf{x}\} \rangle)$ and $h(p, C, \langle I^+ \cup \{\mathbf{x}\}, I^- \rangle)$. If $h(p, C, \langle I^+, I^- \cup \{\mathbf{x}\} \rangle)$ is inconsistent with $\langle I^+, I^- \cup \{\mathbf{x}\} \rangle$ and $h(p, C, \langle I^+ \cup \{\mathbf{x}\}, I^- \rangle)$ is consistent with $\langle I^+ \cup \{\mathbf{x}\}, I^- \rangle$, $VS_C^p(I^+, I^- \cup \{\mathbf{x}\})$ is empty and $VS_C^p(I^+ \cup \{\mathbf{x}\}, I^-)$ is nonempty. Thus, by theorem 1 the algorithm

---

Input: An instance **x** to be classified;
      Training data sets I^+ and I^-;
      Kernel and its parameter p; (optional)
      The parameter C of SVM;
Output: classification of **x**;
      Build a hyperplane $h(p, C, \langle I^+, I^- \rangle)$;
      if $\neg cons(h(p, C, \langle I^+, I^- \rangle), \langle I^+, I^- \rangle)$ **then return** 0;
      Build hyperplanes $h(p, C, \langle I^+, I^- \cup \{\mathbf{x}\} \rangle)$ and $h(p, C, \langle I^+ \cup \{\mathbf{x}\}, I^- \rangle)$;
      if $\neg cons(h(p, C, \langle I^+, I^- \cup \{\mathbf{x}\} \rangle), \langle I^+, I^- \cup \{\mathbf{x}\} \rangle)$ and
        $cons(h(p, C, \langle I^+ \cup \{\mathbf{x}\}, I^- \rangle), \langle I^+ \cup \{\mathbf{x}\}, I^- \rangle)$ **then return** +1;
      if $cons(h(p, C, \langle I^+, I^- \cup \{\mathbf{x}\} \rangle), \langle I^+, I^- \cup \{\mathbf{x}\} \rangle)$ and
        $\neg cons(h(p, C, \langle I^+ \cup \{\mathbf{x}\}, I^- \rangle), \langle I^+ \cup \{\mathbf{x}\}, I^- \rangle)$ **then return** -1;
      return 0.

Fig. 1. The Classification Algorithm of VSSVM.

assigns class $+1$ to **x**. If not, the algorithm checks analogously if it can assign class -1. If both classes cannot be assigned, 0 is returned; i.e., the classification of **x** is unknown.

5.3 Example

We illustrate our classification algorithm for the space H of all oriented lines in $\mathbb{R}^2$ and training data: $I^+ = \{(1,0), (2,0), (1,1), (2,1)\}$ and $I^- = \{(-1,0), (-2,0), (-1,1), (-2,1)\}$ (see figure 2). For large C ($C = +\infty$) only the points to the right of the three line segments through the training points $(1,0)$ and $(1,1)$ will be classified as positive and the corresponding region to the left of the three line segments through the training points $(-1,0)$ and $(-1,1)$ will be classified as negative. Running our algorithm with $C = 30$ results in the classifications in figure 2: positively classified: $+$, negatively classified: $*$, and not classified: $\square$. It is clear from the figure that for $C = 30$ the volume of VSSVM is smaller and thus the coverage is larger, than for $C = +\infty$.

6 The Volume-Extension Approach for VSSVM

To overcome the problems of noisy training data and inexpressive hypothesis spaces for VSSVMs we apply our volume-extension approach for the RBF kernel without re-defining the hypothesis space $H(p)$. Below we show that increasing the parameters C and γ increases the volume of VSSVM.

In section 4 we assumed that the parameters γ and C are monotonic with the probability that the SVM hyperplane $h(\gamma, C, \langle I^+, I^- \rangle)$ is consistent with data $\langle I^+, I^- \rangle$. This implies that for two values γ_1 and γ_2 of the parameter γ s.t. $\gamma_1 < \gamma_2$ and arbitrary $\langle I^+, I^- \rangle$ the probability that $h(\gamma_2, C, \langle I^+, I^- \rangle)$ is consistent with $\langle I^+, I^- \rangle$ is higher than the probability that $h(\gamma_1, C, \langle I^+, I^- \rangle)$ is consistent with $\langle I^+, I^- \rangle$. This implies by theorem 3 below that the volume of $VS_C^{\gamma_1}(I^+, I^-)$

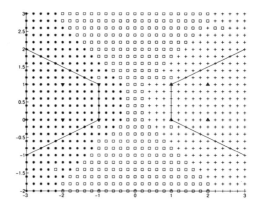

Fig. 2. Illustration of the volume of VSSVM for $C = +\infty$ (bounded by the lines) and $C = 30$ (I^+ marked by $\triangle$, I^- marked by ∇, positively classified: $+$, negatively classified: $*$, and not classified: $\square$).

is a subset of the volume of $VS_C^{\gamma_2}(I^+, I^-)$ if $\gamma_1 < \gamma_2$. Thus, our initial assumption (γ is monotonic with the probability of $cons(h(\gamma, C, \langle I^+, I^- \rangle), \langle I^+, I^- \rangle)$), implies that (A1) the volume of VSSVM is monotonic with the parameter γ. Analogously, we can show that (A2) the volume of VSSVM is monotonic with the parameter C using theorem 4 below. We note that (A1) and (A2) are our key assumptions which are additionally supported by our experiments.

Theorem 3. *Let γ_1 and γ_2 be values of the parameter γ such that for each $\langle I^+, I^- \rangle$ if $h(\gamma_1, C, \langle I^+, I^- \rangle)$ is consistent with $\langle I^+, I^- \rangle$, $h(\gamma_2, C, \langle I^+, I^- \rangle)$ is consistent with $\langle I^+, I^- \rangle$. Then, for each $\langle I^+, I^- \rangle$ we have $V(VS_C^{\gamma_1}(I^+, I^-)) \subseteq V(VS_C^{\gamma_2}(I^+, I^-))$.*

Theorem 4. *Let C_1 and C_2 be values of the parameter C such that for each $\langle I^+, I^- \rangle$ if $h(\gamma, C_1, \langle I^+, I^- \rangle)$ is consistent with $\langle I^+, I^- \rangle$, $h(\gamma, C_2, \langle I^+, I^- \rangle)$ is consistent with $\langle I^+, I^- \rangle$. Then, for each $\langle I^+, I^- \rangle$ we have $V(VS_{C_1}^{\gamma}(I^+, I^-)) \subseteq V(VS_{C_2}^{\gamma}(I^+, I^-))$.*

Applying the volume-extension approach means to find C and γ in order to (re)define hypothesis spaces and VSSVM such that instances are classified reliably. Using the assumptions that the volume of VSSVM is monotonic with C and γ we can find minimal values for C and γ using binary search such that instances are classified reliably and the volume of VSSVM is minimized.

7 Experiments

We experimented with VSSVM using the RBF kernel. We conducted two types of experiments. The first one assumed that the training data are noise free and the hypothesis spaces are expressive. The second type had the opposite assumption. The method for evaluation was the leave-one-out method.

With the leave-one-out method one instance is left out from the training set and this instance is used for testing the classifier obtained by training on the training set without that instance. This process is repeated for all instances in the original training set. So all instances are used as a test instance for a training set not containing the instance.

We measure our results in terms of coverage and accuracy. The coverage is the percentage classified test instances in the leave-one-out process with respect to all instances. The accuracy is the percentage correctly classified test instances with respect to all the classified test instances (the covered instances).

7.1 Experiments: Non-noisy Data and Expressive Hypothesis Space

These experiments were done for VSSVM. When training data are noise free and the hypothesis space $H(\gamma)$ is expressive we have case 1; i.e., instances classified by VSSVM are classified correctly. To guarantee this property in the leave-one-out experiments, we had to guarantee for each instance $\mathbf{x} \in I^+$ that if $\mathbf{x}$ is classified by $VS_C^\gamma(I^+ \setminus \{\mathbf{x}\}, I^-)$ (the version space if $\mathbf{x}$ is left out), then $\mathbf{x}$ is classified correctly. For this purpose in our experiments we required two conditions:

(a) $VS_C^\gamma(I^+ \setminus \{\mathbf{x}\}, I^-) \neq \emptyset$ if $\mathbf{x} \in I^+$ and $VS_C^\gamma(I^+, I^- \setminus \{\mathbf{x}\}) \neq \emptyset$ if $\mathbf{x} \in I^-$;
(b) $VS_C^\gamma(I^+, I^-) \neq \emptyset$.

If condition (a) holds, we have three possible cases for an instance $\mathbf{x} \in I^+$: (a1) $\mathbf{x}$ is classified correctly as $+1$ by $VS_C^\gamma(I^+ \setminus \{\mathbf{x}\}, I^-)$; (a2) $\mathbf{x}$ is classified incorrectly as -1 by $VS_C^\gamma(I^+\setminus\{\mathbf{x}\}, I^-)$; and (a3) $\mathbf{x}$ is not classified: some hyperplanes in $VS_C^\gamma(I^+ \setminus \{\mathbf{x}\}, I^-)$ classify $\mathbf{x}$ as $+1$ and the remaining hyperplanes as -1. To block case (a2) we used condition (b): since $VS_C^\gamma(I^+, I^-)$ is non-empty, there is at least one hyperplane in $VS_C^\gamma(I^+ \setminus \{\mathbf{x}\}, I^-)$ that classifies $\mathbf{x}$ as $+1$. Thus, each instance $\mathbf{x} \in I^+$ classified by $VS_C^\gamma(I^+\setminus\{\mathbf{x}\}, I^-)$ is classified correctly. The same conclusion holds for each instance $\mathbf{x} \in I^-$ and $VS_C^\gamma(I^+, I^- \setminus \{\mathbf{x}\})$.

Due to the assumptions that γ and C are monotonic with the volume of VSSVM, the volumes of $VS_C^\gamma(I^+, I^-)$, $VS_C^\gamma(I^+ \setminus \{\mathbf{x}\}, I^-)$, and $VS_C^\gamma(I^+, I^- \setminus \{\mathbf{x}\})$ are minimal for the minimal values γ_{min} and C_{min} for which these VSSVMs are still nonempty. To find γ_{min} and C_{min} for each of these VSSVMs we used binary search. Since the minimal values γ_{min} and C_{min} differ for $VS_C^\gamma(I^+, I^-)$ and $VS_C^\gamma(I^+ \setminus \{\mathbf{x}\}, I^-)$, and $VS_C^\gamma(I^+, I^- \setminus \{\mathbf{x}\})$, we found common values γ_{min}^c and C_{min}^c as maximal over all minimal values. γ_{min}^c and C_{min}^c were used in our experiments. Hence, we guaranteed that the volumes of $VS_C^\gamma(I^+, I^-)$, $VS_C^\gamma(I^+ \setminus \{\mathbf{x}\}, I^-)$, and $VS_C^\gamma(I^+, I^- \setminus \{\mathbf{x}\})$ are minimized s.t. conditions (a) and (b) hold.

Table 1 provides the results of our experiments with VSSVM for 8 binary datasets [2]. The accuracy of VSSVM is 100%, and the coverage is maximized.

Data Set	Parameters		VSSVM	
	γ	C	$C_{VS_C^{\gamma}}$	$A_{VS_C^{\gamma}}$
Breast Cancer	0.16	28.4	33.3%	100%
Heart Cleveland	0.04	6839.0	55.1%	100%
Hepatitis	0.02	2140.0	69.7%	100%
Horse Colic	0.015	12030.0	54.9%	100%
Ionosphere	0.05	4030.0	77.2%	100%
Labor	0.02	61.0	84.2%	100%
Sonar	0.65	0.664	62.5%	100%
W. Breast Cancer	0.8	70.9	82.5%	100%

Table 1. VSSVM Experiments: Non-noisy Training Data and Expressive Hypothesis Spaces. $C_{VS_C^{\gamma}}$ is the coverage of VSSVM. $A_{VS_C^{\gamma}}$ is the accuracy of VSSVM.

7.2 Experiments: Noisy Data and/or Inexpressive Hypothesis Space

VSSVM Experiments. When training data are noisy and/or the hypothesis space $H(\gamma)$ is inexpressive we have one of cases 2, 3, and 4; i.e., VSSVM can misclassify instances. Therefore, in the leave-one-out experiments, we had to provide the possibility that an instance $\mathbf{x} \in I^+$ ($\mathbf{x} \in I^-$) is misclassified by $VS_C^{\gamma}(I^+ \setminus \{\mathbf{x}\}, I^-)$ ($VS_C^{\gamma}(I^+, I^- \setminus \{\mathbf{x}\})$). For this purpose in our experiments we required only condition (a) from the previous subsection to hold.

To find values of the parameters γ and C we used the approach from the previous subsection. The only difference is that in these experiments we used values γ_{min} and C_{min} specific for different $VS_C^{\gamma}(I^+ \setminus \{\mathbf{x}\}, I^-)$ and $VS_C^{\gamma}(I^+, I^- \setminus \{\mathbf{x}\})$ that were not related to $VS_C^{\gamma}(I^+, I^-)$ (see column *Parameters* in table 2). Hence, condition (a) held and the volumes of VSSVMs were minimized.

Table 2 provides the results of the experiments with VSSVM. The accuracy is decreased.

Experiments with VSSVM and the Volume-Extension Approach. The columns *VSSVM* of tables 1 and 2 show that the problems with noisy training data and inexpressive hypothesis spaces decrease the accuracy of VSSVM. Therefore, we applied our volume-extension approach for VSSVM. We run two sets of experiments. In the first one we applied the volume-extension approach by sequentially increasing the parameter C, given γ, to the point when the accuracy of VSSVM reached 100%. The setup of the experiments coincides with that of the experiments for VSSVM when only condition (a) holds. The only difference is that we added sequentially a growing increase I_C to the found minimal value C_{min} for each $VS_C^{\gamma}(I^+ \setminus \{\mathbf{x}\}, I^-)$ and each $VS_C^{\gamma}(I^+, I^- \setminus \{\mathbf{x}\})$ (see sub-column I_C of table 3). In the second set of experiments we applied the volume-extension approach for the parameter γ using an analogous experimental setup.

In figure 3 we show the coverage and accuracy of VSSVM when we used the volume-extension approach for the parameters γ and C for the sonar data [2].

Data Set	Parameters		VSSVM	
	γ	C	$C_{VS_C^\gamma}$	$A_{VS_C^\gamma}$
Breast-Cancer	0.078	$103.9 \cdots 147.5$	53.4%	70.5%
Heart Cleveland	0.078	$1201.3 \cdots 2453.2$	56.4%	95.9%
Hepatitis	0.078	$75.4 \cdots 313.4$	78.7%	89.3%
Horse Colic	0.078	$719.2 \cdots 956.2$	34.0%	80.8%
Ionosphere	0.078	$1670.2 \cdots 1744.8$	86.9%	91.1%
Labor	0.078	$3.0 \cdots 17.4$	63.2%	91.7%
Sonar	0.078	$20.7 \cdots 41.8$	69.2%	68.1%
W. Breast Cancer	0.156	$3367.0 \cdots 3789.1$	93.7%	96.5%

Table 2. VSSVM experiments: Noisy Training Data and/or Inexpressive Hypothesis Space. Column *Parameters* presents the ranges of the parameters γ and C. Column *VSSVM* presents the results for VSSVM. $C_{VS_C^\gamma}$ is the coverage of VSSVM. $A_{VS_C^\gamma}$ is the accuracy of VSSVM.

The figure shows that the coverage and the accuracy of VSSVM are monotonic with γ and C. This confirms the applicability of our assumptions about the monotonicity of the volume of VSSVM with respect to γ and C. Note that the monotonicity for the coverage does not hold strictly: In our experiments we found sometimes nonmonotonic behavior close to γ_{min}^c, C_{min}^c.

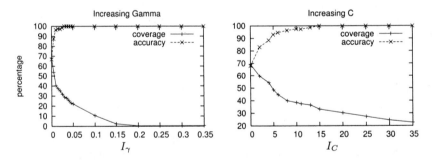

Fig. 3. The coverage and accuracy of VSSVM in functions of parameters γ and C for sonar data. I_γ is the increase of parameter γ. I_C is the increase of parameter C.

The results of our experiments with VSSVM and the volume-extension approach are given in columns *Vol.Extenstion:C* and *Vol.Extenstion:γ* of table 3. They show that by applying the volume-extension approach the accuracy is again 100%. This means that the volume-extension approach is capable of solving the problems with noisy training data and inexpressive hypothesis spaces.

Data Set	Parameters		Vol. Extension: C			Vol. Extension: γ		
	γ	C	I_C	$C_{VS_C^\gamma}$	$A_{VS_C^\gamma}$	I_γ	$C_{VS_C^\gamma}$	$A_{VS_C^\gamma}$
Breast-Cancer	0.078	103.9 $\cdots$ 147.5	35	9.32%	100%	0.06	9.32%	100%
Heart Cleveland	0.078	1201.3 $\cdots$ 2453.2	500	15.8%	100%	0.035	6.60%	100%
Hepatitis	0.078	75.4 $\cdots$ 313.4	95	41.3%	100%	0.10	14.2%	100%
Horse Colic	0.078	719.2 $\cdots$ 956.2	1000	6.80%	100%	1.6	5.98%	100%
Ionosphere	0.078	1670.2 $\cdots$ 1744.8	1200	28.5%	100%	0.08	14.8%	100%
Labor	0.078	3.0 $\cdots$ 17.4	13	40.4%	100%	0.16	26.3%	100%
Sonar	0.078	20.7 $\cdots$ 41.8	15	33.7%	100%	0.03	28.8%	100%
W. Breast Cancer	0.156	3367.0 $\cdots$ 3789.1	700	79.5%	100%	0.02	71.8%	100%

Table 3. Volume-extension experiments: Noisy Training Data and/or Inexpressive Hypothesis Space. Column *Parameters* presents the ranges of the parameters γ and C. Column *Vol.Extenstion:C* presents the results of VSSVM when the Volume Extension Approach is applied for parameter C. Here I_C is the minimal increase of C for which the accuracy of 100% for VSSVM is found. Column *Vol.Extenstion:γ* presents the results of VSSVM when the Volume Extension Approach is applied for parameter γ. Here I_γ is the minimal increase of γ for which the accuracy of 100% for VSSVM is found. $C_{VS_C^\gamma}$ is the coverage of VSSVM. $A_{VS_C^\gamma}$ is the accuracy of VSSVM.

8 Comparison with Relevant Work

8.1 Version Spaces

We compare VSSVM with the relevant work in version spaces in the context of the problems of inexpressive hypothesis spaces and noisy training data.

Inexpressive Hypothesis Spaces. To overcome the problem of inexpressive hypothesis spaces the inductive bias of version spaces, the restriction bias, was proposed to be relaxed by extending hypothesis spaces. The static approaches assumed that hypothesis spaces are rich and extended in advance [8, 10, 12, 13]. Hence, the learning process was guided by restriction and search biases. The dynamic approaches extended dynamically hypothesis spaces [15] w.r.t. classification problems. These spaces were assumed to be correct. Hence, the learning process was guided by restriction bias. VSSVM and the volume-extension approach correspond to the dynamic approaches. The main advantage of VSSVM is that the hypothesis spaces can be much easier extended using C and γ.

Noisy Training Data. To overcome the problem of noisy training data restriction bias is combined with search bias. For example, the extended version-space approach [8] maintained in parallel a set of version spaces consistent with different subsets of training data determined by parameters introducing the search bias. Other approaches implemented search biases on version-space representations [12–14]. VSSVM correspond best to the approaches based on extended version spaces. The key difference is that the inductive bias of VSSVM is the restriction bias only. Hence, VSSVM prove that the restriction bias is useful.

8.2 Reliable Instance Classification

Bayesian Framework. The Bayesian framework [8] is one of the first approaches used for reliable instance classification. This is due to the fact that the posterior class probabilities are natural estimates of the reliability of instance classification. These probabilities are computed from prior probabilities. Since it is difficult to estimate correctly the prior probabilities, the Bayesian framework is often misleading [7]. VSSVM can be also misleading but they can be corrected by the volume-extension approach (see table 2).

Meta Learning. An approach that learns a meta classifier to predict the correctness of instance classifications was given in [1]. Its main problem was that the meta classifier is never correct; i.e., the approach can misclassify. VSSVM can also misclassify but they can be corrected by the volume-extension approach.

Typicalness Framework. The typicalness framework is introduced in [6, 7, 11]. To compare VSSVM and the typicalness framework we need a strangeness function. Consider instance $\mathbf{x}_i$ with a label y_i in a sequence S of labelled instances. When VSSVM classifies $\mathbf{x}_i$ based on the other instances in S, we have three possibilities: (1) $\mathbf{x}_i$ gets label y_i; (2) $\mathbf{x}_i$ is not classified; (3) $\mathbf{x}_i$ gets label $-y_i$. We consider these three cases as cases of increasing strangeness of $\mathbf{x}_i$ with a given label y_i in S. Therefore, we define our VSSVM strangeness function as:

$$f(S, i) = \begin{cases} 0 & \text{if the instance } \mathbf{x}_i \text{ is classified as } y_i \\ 0.5 & \text{if the instance } \mathbf{x}_i \text{ is not covered} \\ 1 & \text{if the instance } \mathbf{x}_i \text{ is classified as } -y_i \end{cases}$$

This strangeness function results in a typicalness of 1 if the instance $\mathbf{x}_i$ is classified by VSSVM with the class y_i. The typicalness of the classification $-y_i$ is about $1/(l+1)$ where l is the number of training instances. If the typicalness of a classification y_i is close to 1 and that of the opposite classification $-y_i$ is almost 0, then the classification y_i is reliable. Thus, instance classifications by VSSVM are reliable in the sense of the typicalness framework.

9 Conclusion

In this paper we showed that version spaces and VSSVM can provide reliable instance classifications for the case when training data are non-noisy and hypothesis spaces are expressive as well as for the opposite three cases. This is due to the nature of version spaces and the volume-extension approach proposed.

We foresee two future research directions. The first one is to extend version spaces and VSSVM for non-binary classification tasks. The second direction is to extend VSSVM for problems for which no consistent hypotheses exist.

References

1. S. Bay and M. Pazzani. Characterizing model errors and differences. In *Proceedings of the Seventeenth International Conference on Machine Learning (ICML-2000)*, pages 196–201, 2000.
2. C. Blake and C. Merz. UCI repository of machine learning databases, 1998.
3. C. Burges. A tutorial on support vector machines for pattern recognition. *Data Mining and Knowledge Discovery*, 2(2):121–167, 1998.
4. H. Hirsh, N. Mishra, and L. Pitt. Version spaces and the consistency problem. *Artificial Intelligence*, 156(2):115–138, 2004.
5. S. Keerthi and C.-J. Lin. Asymptotic behaviors of support vector machines with gaussian kernel. *Neural Computation*, 15:1667–1689, 2003.
6. M. Kukar. Transduction and typicalness for quality assessment of individual classifications in machine learning and data mining. In *Proceedings of the 4th IEEE International Conference on Data Mining (ICDM-2004)*, pages 146–153, 2004.
7. T. Melluish, C. Saunders, I. Nouretdinov, and V. Vovk. Comparing the Bayes and typicalness frameworks. In *Proceedings of the 12th European Conference on Machine Learning (ECML-2001)*, pages 360–371. Springer, 2001.
8. T. Mitchell. *Version spaces: an approach to concept learning*. PhD thesis, Electrical Engineering Dept., Stanford University, Stanford, CA, 1978.
9. T. Mitchell. *Machine learning*. McGraw-Hill, New York, NY, 1997.
10. K. Murray. Multiple convergence: an approach to disjunctive concept acquisition. In *Proceedings of the Tenth International Joint Conference on Artificial Intelligence (IJCAI-87)*, pages 297–300, Los Altos, CA, 1987. Morgan Kaufmann.
11. I. Nouretdinov, V. Vovk, V. V'yugin, and A. Gammerman. Transductive confidence machine is universal. Technical report, Department of Computer Science, Royal Holloway, University of London, 2002.
12. M. Sebag and C. Rouveirol. Resource-bounded relational reasoning: induction and deduction through stochastic matching. *Machine Learning*, 38(1-2):41–62, 2000.
13. E. Smirnov. *Conjunctive and disjunctive version spaces with instance-based boundary sets*. PhD thesis, Department of Computer Science, Maastricht University, Maastricht, The Netherlands, 2001.
14. E. Smirnov and H. van den Herik. Applying preference biases to conjunctive and disjunctive version spaces. In *Proceedings of the Ninth International Conference on Artificial Intelligence: Methodology, Systems, and Applications (AIMSA-2000)*, LNAI 1904, pages 321–330, Berlin, Germany, 2000. Springer.
15. P. Utgoff. *Shift of bias for inductive concept learning*. PhD thesis, Computer Science Department, Rutgers University, New Brunswick, NJ, 1984.
16. V. Vapnik. *Statistical Learning Theory*. John Wiley, NY, 1998.

SESSION 5b:

REASONING AND DECISION MAKING

Acting Irrationally to Improve Performance in Stochastic Worlds

Roman V. Belavkin

School of Computing Science, Middlesex University

London, NW4 4BT, United Kingdom

Abstract

Despite many theories and algorithms for decision–making, after estimating the utility function the choice is usually made by maximising
its expected value (the *max EU* principle). This traditional and 'rational' conclusion of the decision–making process is compared in this paper
with several 'irrational' techniques that make choice in Monte–Carlo fashion. The comparison is made by evaluating the performance of simple
decision–theoretic agents in stochastic environments. It is shown that
not only the random choice strategies can achieve performance comparable to the max EU method, but under certain conditions the Monte–
Carlo choice methods perform almost two times better than the max EU.
The paper concludes by quoting evidence from recent cognitive modelling
works as well as the famous decision–making paradoxes.

1 Introduction

During the last several decades, the theory of decision–making under uncertainty has received an extensive treatment by scientists. The most prominent
contributions have been made by von Neumann and Morgenstern (1944), Savage (1954), Anscombe and Aumann (1963). Despite the differences in their
approach to uncertainty (i.e. objective or subjective), the notion of *utility* has
been successfully used to compute the preferences of a decision–maker. Theories such as the dynamic programming by Bellman (1957) and the reinforcement
learning partly due to Sutton and Barto (1981) have enabled us to compute
the utilities necessary for optimal decision–making. Combined with probabilistic inference (e.g. the Bayes' conditional probability rule), these theories have
been used successfully in decision–theoretic agents and robots that can learn
autonomously and find solutions to various problems.

Despite these successes, however, soon after its emergence the theory of rational decision–making has been strongly criticised by some psychologists and
economists. One simple counter example is the so–called *rational donkey* paradox, when a donkey is placed between two identical haystacks. If the donkey is
perfectly rational (i.e. chooses according to the max EU principle), then it will
not be able to choose between alternatives with equal EUs. Therefore, some
additional mechanism must be involved in choosing, such as a roulette wheel.
Moreover, it has been noticed experimentally that human subjects always express some degree of randomness in their choice behaviour even in situations

when the choice they make seems irrational according to their previous experience (Myers, Fort, Katz, & Suydam, 1963). The latest cognitive architectures, such as ACT–R (Anderson & Lebiere, 1998), use noise in the utility in order to model the 'imperfect' choice behaviour of humans or animals. Several studies have demonstrated recently that this noisy and 'irrational' component of decision–making may in fact play an important function optimising the behaviour in stochastic environments (Belavkin & Ritter, 2003).

Another famous and powerful counter example to the theory of rational choice has been suggested by Allais (1953) (also known as the Allais paradox) that showed how the theory failed to compute a preference between decisions, which on the other hand was obvious to most of the human subjects. One version of this problem is as follows. Consider a choice between two lotteries:

1. 1/3 chance of winning £300 or 2/3 of not winning anything;

2. A sure win of £100.

One can easily check that two lotteries have equal expected utilities (£100 exactly). Thus, there should be no preference according to the max EU principle. However, most of us (about 70%) would prefer the second lottery demonstrating risk–averse behaviour. Interestingly, when the problem is presented with gains replaced by losses (i.e. loosing money instead of winning), then the preferences of subjects also revert, and a risk–taking behaviour is observed. This paradox has been observed in many experiments using different interpretations. One of the most famous is the study by Tversky and Kahneman (1974), and several theories, such as the *framing* and *prospect* theories (Tversky & Kahneman, 1981), have been proposed to explain these observations. However, most of the theories do not explain the uncertainty that is always present in preferences and choice behaviour of subjects.

In this paper, agents that do not use the max EU principle will be considered. Instead, a Monte–Carlo technique will be used to make decisions randomly (i.e. by drawing samples from probability distributions). These methods will be compared with the more traditional choice strategy by maximising the EUs of decisions. The performance will be analysed using both direct measures of performance as well as information theoretic concepts. Thus, the main focus of this work is the effectiveness of different choice methods, especially in stochastic environments.

A simple decision–theoretic agent architecture and the experimental setup will be described in the first two sections. The results of the tests will be reported in the third section. It will be shown experimentally that although the random methods may lead sometimes to irrational decisions, on average they perform as good as the rational ones, and often significantly outperform them.

The concluding section will discuss the results in the view of psychological evidence as well as the cognitive modelling research. Although resolving the paradoxes of decision–making, mentioned above, was not the goal of this study, some interesting observations will be made that may explain the results observed experimentally.

2   A Simple Decision–Theoretic Architecture

In this section, the design of a very simple decision–theoretic agent will be outlined. This agent will be able to explore its environment, learn and improve its performance according to some criteria. First, let us introduce some notation.

Let $X = \{x_1, \ldots, x_m\}$ be a set of states that an agent can occupy in the world, and let $Z = \{z_1, \ldots, z_n\}$ be a set of actions that the agent can execute. Each action can transfer the agent from one state to another: $x_j = z_k(x_i)$. For convenience of notation, let us denote the set of new states as $Y = \{y_1, \ldots, y_m\}$. Thus, the agent implements a mapping $Z : X \rightarrow Y$. In stochastic environments, this mapping is not deterministic and can be described by the probability distribution

$$\boldsymbol{P}(X, Y, Z) = \begin{pmatrix} p_{11}^1 & \cdots & p_{1m}^1 \\ \vdots & \ddots & \vdots \\ p_{m1}^1 & \cdots & p_{mm}^1 \end{pmatrix} \cdots \begin{pmatrix} p_{11}^n & \cdots & p_{1m}^n \\ \vdots & \ddots & \vdots \\ p_{m1}^n & \cdots & p_{mm}^n \end{pmatrix} ,$$

where $p_{ij}^k = P(x_i, y_j, z_k)$ is the joint probability of transition from x_i to y_j by executing z_k. In Markov decision problems, matrix (p_{ij}^k) is called the *transition model*. If the agent has no preference between states of the world or actions, then a transition to any state is allowed, and distribution $\boldsymbol{P}(X, Y, Z)$ may be uniform. Let us assume that the agent prefers some states to the others. For example, an agent may loose energy in state i faster than in j, and therefore $i \succ j$ (where $\succ$ denotes binary preference relation). Thus, agent's actions should make transitions to the more preferable states more often.

Traditionally, preferences are expressed by a *utility*, which is a map from states to real numbers $U : X \rightarrow \mathbf{R}$. Note, however, that the real numbers are, in fact, not necessary, as only countable sets of states can be ordered by utility. In this paper, we shall consider the uncertainty about utility to be both due to the stochastic nature of the world (i.e. objective uncertainty) and due to the lack of information about its distribution (i.e subjective uncertainty). Thus, we follow the Anscombe and Aumann theory.

Because perception is not in the scope of this paper, let us assume that an agent can ideally recognise the states of the world and which actions it performs. We also assume that the agent can assess correctly the utility of the current state.

The associations between states and actions are recorded by the agent's memory M_{ji}^k, which is a matrix with elements simply counting each transition. The reader should be able to check that after normalisation, the memory M_{ji}^k represents the transition model $\boldsymbol{P}(X, Y, Z)$. Initially, the memory of an agent contains no information. In information theoretic terms, this corresponds to the maximum of entropy $H(X, Y, Z) = E\{-\ln \boldsymbol{P}(X, Y, Z)\}$. The maximum is achieved when $\boldsymbol{P}(X, Y, Z)$ is uniform, and the reader can check that $\max H(X, Y, Z) = \ln(m \times m \times n)$. Note that this information theoretic approach allows us to avoid the argument of objective and subjective probabilities: The prior distribution is defined through the absence of information.

The agent also has a memory for utilities $U(X)$ of the states it has visited. This memory also has no information initially (i.e. utilities of all states are equal). Because no states are preferred, and all transition probabilities are equal initially, the agent starts acting completely randomly. By exploring the world in such a manner, the agent can assess and learn its preferences $U(X)$ (i.e. which states have been 'better' in the past). Consequently, some transitions should become more probable than others, and the entropy $H(X,Y,Z)$ should decrease as a result of changes in probabilities. This change can be evaluated by computing mutual information between variables X, Y and Z:

$$I(X,Y,Z) = H(X) + H(Y) + H(Z) - H(X,Y,Z) ,$$

where $H(X)$, $H(Y)$ and $H(Z)$ are marginal entropies (i.e. for $P(X)$, $P(Y)$ and $P(Z)$), while $H(X,Y,Z)$ is the entropy of joint distribution $P(X,Y,Z)$. If X, Y and Z are statistically independent, then $P(X,Y,Z) = P(X)P(Y)P(Z)$, and $I(X,Y,Z) = 0$. Positive values of $I(X,Y,Z)$ mean that an agent has developed preferences.

Finally, let us consider how the memory of an agent can be optimised in terms of storage requirements. Suppose that there are several states with exactly the same utility: $\exists x_1, x_2 \in X : U(x_1) = U(x_2)$. This means that the agent has no preference between these states. We can reduce the size of the transition model M_{ji}^k by considering states only with different utilities: $Y \subseteq X : y_1 \neq y_2 \Rightarrow U(y_1) \neq U(y_2) \; \forall y_1, y_2 \in Y$. The cardinality of set Y should be the same as of set U, and it is smaller than cardinality of X. By ordering elements of Y according to U the separate storage for utilities becomes redundant. In this notation, the transitional model implements the Savage approach (i.e. actions map from states to utilities).

In this paper, we shall consider an extreme case when utility divides the world into two subsets of states: S (successes) and F (failures). Thus, $Y = \{S, F\}$. Although this is a crude approximation, it is useful to understand the difference in performance of agents with reduced sets of future states. Note, that such a binary approach has been already successfully used to model human and animal behaviour. The ACT–R cognitive architecture (Anderson & Lebiere, 1998), mentioned earlier, uses the notion of successes and failures to reinforce probabilities of production rules. Many unsupervised and reinforcement learning algorithms also employ binary reward functions.

In the next section, three methods for choosing an action will be presented. These methods are the only architectural difference between the three types of agents tested in this paper.

3   Rational and Irrational Choice

One of the greatest results of probability theory is the relation between conditional probability and joint distribution (known as the Bayes formula)

$$P(X \mid Y, Z) = \alpha P(X, Y, Z) , \tag{1}$$

where α is the normalising constant. As has been mentioned earlier, the associative memory M_{ij}^k of an agent after normalisation represents the joint distribution $\boldsymbol{P}(X, Y, Z)$, which can be used for inference. Indeed, given a transitional model, we can estimate the probability of future outcomes y_j conditional to the current state x_i and actions taken z_k.

3.1 The Maximum Expected Utility

The traditional approach to decision–making is to maximise the expected utility of future states

$$z_k = \arg\max_{z_k \in Z} E\{U\}\,, \text{ where } E\{U\} = \sum_{y_j \in Y} P(y_j \mid x_i, z_k) U(y_j)$$

Agents using this approach behave 'rationally' always choosing what seems to be the best action. The first criticism of this method is that there is no way of choosing an action if expected utilities are equal (and they are at the beginning when no information is available). This problem has been mentioned earlier as the rational donkey paradox. To overcome this limitation, some Gaussian noise of relatively small variance is usually introduced which corrupts the expected utilities by some random values. This approach is used by the ACT–R cognitive architecture (Anderson & Lebiere, 1998), and the noise has allowed for modelling many experiments on human and animals' choice behaviour. The max EU agent, described in the experiments below, used randomness only when the expected utilities were equal. This is equivalent to adding noise of a very small variance.

Another potential drawback we can notice in this method is that only the first moments of utility distributions are used (i.e. the expected values of utilities). The variance and all other potentially useful characteristics of utility distributions are ignored. This may explain the lack of exploration in behaviour of agents using this principle. Indeed, immediately after experiencing the first success, the agent switches to using only the successful action.

3.2 Random Utility

Although small noise can help agents to resolve some problems, it is not clear how large should be the variance of noise corrupting the utilities. Moreover, studies in cognitive modelling of choice behaviour have suggested recently that noise variance should be dynamic. It has been proposed by Belavkin and Ritter (2004) that noise variance should be proportional to the variance of the utility distributions (i.e. the second moments of their distributions). This can be implemented in the following way: Given current state x_i and particular action z_k, the future state y_j can be drawn randomly from its probability distribution, which is inferred using the Bayes formula (1). The utility map U can be used to asses the utility $u_j = U(y_j)$ of such a random state. An action z_k can be chosen by maximising u_j for all actions in Z

$$z_k = \arg\max_{z_k \in Z} u(y_j)\,, \text{ where } y_j \leftarrow \boldsymbol{P}(Y \mid x_i, z_k)$$

This method implements choice by random utilities drawn from their probability distributions, and this allows the agent to act randomly when there is little knowledge about the environment. Indeed, when distributions are close to uniform, their variances are large and there is no clear preference between states. On the contrary, when the agent forms strong preferences, the variance also reduces. Interestingly, this implements a search strategy somewhat similar to the simulated annealing algorithm (Kirkpatrick, Gelatt, & Vecchi, 1983), because the variance is reducing on average, but it also may increase if the agent finds itself in a local maxima.

3.3 Random Action

In this third variation, instead of maximising the utility of future states, the actions are selected directly from their probability distributions. Indeed, we can consider the following conditional probability:

$$P(Z \mid X, Y) = \alpha P(X, Y, Z)$$

Given the utility map U, we can always select future state $y_j \in Y$ maximising the utility (in fact, in our notation Y is a partially ordered set). The action can be drawn from the probability distribution conditional to the current state x_i and the maximum utility state $y_{\max}$

$$z_k \leftarrow P(Z \mid x_i, y_{\max}) \ , \text{ where } y_{\max} = \arg \max_{y_j \in Y} U(y_j)$$

Again, the agent will choose actions randomly if the joint distribution is uniform. If, however, some actions lead to the maximum utility state more often, then after some training the behaviour should become more 'rational'.

Although there is an obvious difference between the max EU and the random choice strategies, it is not so clear how different are the last two methods. One may notice that cardinalities of sets Y and Z are quite different. Thus, the probability distributions of Y and Z also have different properties and possibly different rates of convergence.

4 Experiment Description

For the purpose of simplicity, the experiments were conducted with environments of small number of discrete states each of which can have a reward (e.g. food) or not. Thus, reward of each state is either 0 or 1. In the experiments, described below, a one–dimensional world of only five states has been used. The agent can also perform only three actions: Stay in the same place, move left or move right.

In this paper, the utility function does not take into account the length of sequence, and therefore we do not consider environmental histories. Again, this is done for simplicity, but the results can be generalised later for utilities that take into account the length of sequence or time. In fact, such a setup is an extreme case of decaying utility with zero decay time.

On each step, the agent records the following information into its memory: The transition m_{ij}^k from state x_i to a new state y_j (or utility) using action z_k. If the agent moves to the state with a reward, then the reward is collected. The rewards can re–appear at different places of the world either randomly or according to some pattern. Three different patterns have been used in the tests:

Random : rewards can occur in any place of the world with equal probability.

Poor : the number of places in the world, where rewards can occur, is smaller than the number of places without rewards.

Rich : the number of places with rewards is larger than the number of places without.

The rates, at which the rewards regenerate in the world, can also be changed. The experiments have been run using several rates of rewards changing from very low to very high rates.

Two main criteria have been used to measure the performance of the agents:

1. The proportion of rewards collected (i.e. a percentage of rewards collected out of all rewards that have appeared).

2. The increase of mutual information between states and actions.

In the next section, the results of tests are reported.

5   Results of the Experiments

Figure 1 compares the performance of three decision theoretic agents in completely random (top), poor (middle) and rich (bottom) worlds. The ordinates on the charts show the percentage of rewards collected by the agents out of all rewards appearing in identical environments and during the same period of time. One can see that very similar performance is achieved by all three agents. For the random pattern (top graph of Figure 1), because the probability of any place containing a reward was the same, all agents have collected similar number of rewards. There seems to be a small variation in the performance when the rate of rewards is the lowest, but this can be explained by the small number of rewards. For all other rates, the performance of all agents is almost identical. For the poor (middle) and the rich (bottom) patterns, the number of rewards collected is greater than for the random world, which indicates that all agents were able to learn where to expect the rewards.

Interestingly, although the number of rewards collected is very similar, the behaviour of agents is very different: The max EU agent most of the time 'preferred' to stay in the same place, and therefore collected only those rewards that appeared in the same place. On the contrary, both random agents have explored the world more and collected the rewards from different places.

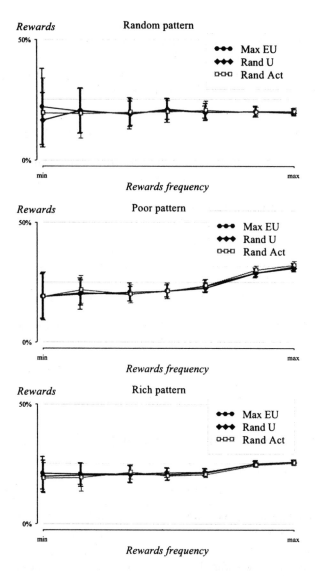

Figure 1: Proportion of rewards collected as a function of rewards frequency for random (top), poor (middle) and rich (bottom) patterns.

One can see that although agents use different tactics for action selection, their performance in terms of number of rewards is very similar. This is an interesting result because two of the agents are not using the traditional max EU principle, and one would expect them to have a disadvantage.

Figure 2 illustrates results of agents with binary representation of future states (i.e. $Y = \{S, F\}$). One can see the dramatic change in performance: Agents collected twice as many rewards as the agents with a full set of future

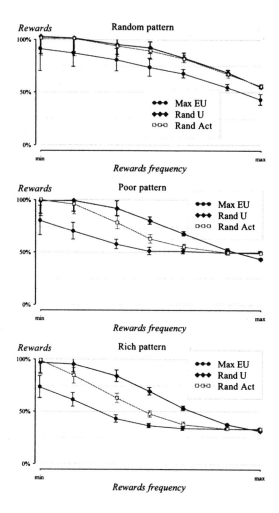

Figure 2: Proportion of rewards collected as a function of rewards frequency for random (top), poor (middle) and rich (bottom) patterns.

states. Perhaps, this result can be explained by the smaller size of the transition model, and hence its ability to learn and re–learn faster.

Furthermore, the charts demonstrate that randomly acting agents have performed better than the max EU agent: At low and medium rates of rewards and rewards occurring according to some regular patterns, the randomly acting agents have collected almost two times more rewards. This result is due to a more explorative behaviour of random agents as opposed to the max EU agent that tends to over–exploit some options. Perhaps, in stochastic worlds with scarce resources, exploration is a more beneficial strategy.

Finally, one may notice that the best performance was demonstrated by the random utility agent. It is not clear exactly why such a result is observed, but

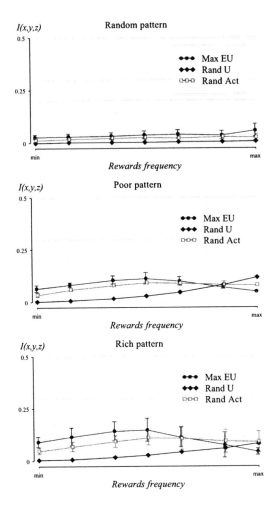

Figure 3: Mutual information acquired as a function of rewards frequency for random (top), poor (middle) and rich (bottom) patterns.

one reason that may be considered is that these agents used three actions (stay, move left and right) and two possible utilities (success and failure). Perhaps, a smaller cardinality of a set contributes to a faster learning of the probability distribution over this set. However, this hypothesis is yet to be tested.

Figure 3 shows the amount of mutual information $I(X, Y, Z)$ accumulated in these tests. One can see that the random utility agent (the one that has the best performance) has acquired the least amount of information in almost all cases. Moreover, the charts show that too much mutual information hinders the performance. Indeed, as was mentioned earlier, positive mutual information reflects the amount of preferences formed by the agent. However, excessive preference to particular states or actions may lead to over–exploitation and not sufficient exploration, which is not a beneficial strategy in stochastic worlds. This is particularly well illustrated by the top graphs of Figures 2 and 3 comparing the performance and mutual information for a completely random world: The max EU agent has the worst performance, but accumulated more information than the 'irrational' agents. This result, however, does not reflect the reality of the world: There is no regular pattern of rewards, and therefore a preference for a particular state is unnecessary.

6 Discussion

In this paper, methods for choosing actions alternative to the traditional maximum expected utility have been tested. The simulations, described here, demonstrated that Monte–Carlo techniques can achieve better performance in stochastic environments because they facilitate a more explorative strategy. Moreover, the balance between exploitation and exploration is maintained due to the characteristics of probability distributions other than the expected values (i.e. moments of higher order than one, such as variance). In addition, the simulations showed that the performance can be improved by reducing the size of the transitional model. This is achieved by considering the set of utilities instead of the set of future states as in traditional Markov decision models.

The idea of dynamic randomness in decision–making proportional to the variance of probability distributions has been discussed recently in the cognitive modelling society: Models that used adaptive dynamic noise in the utilities of production rules matched better the data from studies on animal learning (see Belavkin & Ritter, 2003). The dynamics of noise variance was shown to be proportional to the entropy associated with the success in the task as well as the variance of utilities of the rules. The simulations with such a dynamic control over the uncertainty in decision–making have also achieved better learning and adaptation of behaviour. These results correspond well to the outcomes of the simulations reported in this paper.

An interesting question is whether the random utility theory can also explain why people demonstrate clear preferences in situations when the expected utility theory suggests no preference between decisions, as in the Allais paradox described in the Introduction. Recall that subjects were asked to choose between two alternative lotteries (one with only 1/3 chance of winning £300 and another with a sure win of £100). Although both alternatives had equal expected utilities of £100, the majority of subjects (about 70%) preferred the second lottery. This behaviour can be explained by the random utility choice method, described earlier in this paper. Note that in the first lottery, we should win nothing two out of three times, while in the second lottery we always win £100. Thus, according to the random utility method, two out of three times the random utility of the first option is smaller than that of the second. Remarkably, this proportion also reflects the fact that only about 70% of subjects choose the second lottery, but not all (see Tversky & Kahneman, 1974). The reader may check that the risk–taking behaviour for the reversed version of this problem (i.e. loosing money instead of winning) can also be explained in this fashion.

Although explaining the decision–making paradoxes was not among the main intentions of this research, it is an interesting outcome. It seems that the random decision–making, as opposed to the expected utility theory, promises not only a better performance for agent architectures, but also a better theory for cognitive scientists.

Acknowledgements

I thank both reviewers for very useful comments and suggestions. I also thank Frank Ritter for additional comments and proof–reading of the draft.

References

Allais, M. (1953). Le comportement de l'homme rationnel devant le risque: Critique des postulats et axiomes de l'École americaine. *Econometrica, 21*, 503–546.

Anderson, J. R., & Lebiere, C. (1998). *The atomic components of thought.* Mahwah, NJ: Lawrence Erlbaum.

Anscombe, F. J., & Aumann, R. J. (1963). A definition of subjective probability. *Annals of Mathematical Statistics, 34*, 199–205.

Belavkin, R. V., & Ritter, F. E. (2003, April). The use of entropy for analysis and control of cognitive models. In F. Detje, D. Dörner, & H. Schaub (Eds.), *Proceedings of the Fifth International Conference on Cognitive Modelling* (pp. 21–26). Bamberg, Germany: Universitäts–Verlag Bamberg.

Belavkin, R. V., & Ritter, F. E. (2004). Optimist: A new conflict resolution algorithm for ACT–R. In *Proceedings of the Sixth International Conference on Cognitive Modelling* (pp. 40–45). Mahwah, NJ: Lawrence Erlbaum.

Bellman, R. E. (1957). *Dynamic programming.* Princeton, NJ: Princeton University Press.

Kirkpatrick, S., Gelatt, C. D., & Vecchi, J. M. P. (1983, May). Optimization by simulated annealing. *Science, 220*(4598), 671–680.

Myers, J. L., Fort, J. G., Katz, L., & Suydam, M. M. (1963). Differential monetary gains and losses and event probability in a two–choice situation. *Journal of Experimental Psychology, 77*, 453–359.

Neumann, J. von, & Morgenstern, O. (1944). *Theory of games and economic behavior* (first ed.). Princeton, NJ: Princeton University Press.

Savage, L. (1954). *The foundations of statistics.* NY: John Wiley & Sons.

Sutton, R. S., & Barto, A. G. (1981). Toward a modern theory of adaptive networks: Expectation and prediction. *Psychological Review, 88*(2), 135–170.

Tversky, A., & Kahneman, D. (1974). Judgment under uncertainty: Heuristics and biases. *Science, 185*, 1124–1131.

Tversky, A., & Kahneman, D. (1981). The framing of decisions and the psychology of choice. *Science, 211*, 453–458.

On the Use of OBDDs in Model Based Diagnosis: an Approach Based on the Partition of the Model

Gianluca Torta, Pietro Torasso

Dipartimento di Informatica, Università di Torino (Italy)

{torta, torasso}@di.unito.it

Abstract

In this paper we discuss how OBDDs (Ordered Binary Decision Diagrams) can be exploited for the computation of consistency-based diagnoses in Model-Based Diagnosis. Since it is not always possible to efficiently encode the whole system model within a single OBDD, we propose to build a set of OBDDs, each one encoding a portion of the original model. For each portion of the model, we compute an OBDD encoding the set of local diagnoses; the OBDD encoding global diagnoses is then obtained by merging all the local-diagnoses OBDDs. Finally, minimal-cardinality diagnoses can be efficiently computed and extracted.

The paper reports formal results about soundness, completeness and computational complexity of the proposed algorithm. Thanks to the fact that encoding diagnoses is in general much simpler than encoding the whole system model, this approach allows for the successful computation of global diagnoses even if the system model could not be compiled into a single OBDD. This is exemplified referring to a challenging combinatorial digital circuit taken from the ISCAS85 benchmark.

1 Introduction

In order to handle the computational complexity of the MBD task and the potentially exponential number of solutions to diagnostic problems two main approaches have been followed. The first one aims at reducing the computational burden by limiting the cost of the search for the solutions; examples of this approach include the use of hierarchical models (e.g. [4]), structure-based approaches (e.g. [5]) and computation of just the leading diagnoses according to some preference criteria (e.g. [14]).

Another approach that has recently received attention involves forms of off-line compilation of the system model that make the run-time search for diagnostic solutions a computationally inexpensive task. So far most of the attention has been drawn by the symbolic representation of the search and solution spaces of diagnostic problems. In particular, there has been a growing interest in the MBD community for representing both the search and solution spaces symbolically through OBDDs ([11], [12], [10], [13]). OBDDs [8] are a well-known mathematical tool used in several areas of computing (including AI, see e.g.

[3]) for efficiently representing and manipulating large state spaces. However, the adoption of OBDDs is not a *per se* panacea for the MBD task as pointed out e.g. in [12]; in particular, the effectiveness of the encoding of the system model strongly depends on the variable order and in some cases it is hard or even impossible to avoid the explosion of the OBDD size.

In the present paper we address the problem of computing consistency-based diagnoses of a complex system when it is not possible or convenient to compile the system model with a single OBDD, and therefore the system has to be partitioned into a set of subsystems. The approach we have taken is based on the use of OBDDs both for representing the portions of the system model and for encoding the sets of local and global diagnoses. In particular, for each portion of the model, we compute an OBDD encoding the set of local diagnoses; the OBDD encoding global diagnoses is then obtained by merging all the local-diagnoses OBDDs. Finally, minimal-cardinality diagnoses can be efficiently computed and extracted.

The idea of decomposing a complex problem into simpler sub-problems has a long tradition in AI; solving a problem by decomposition is particularly easy when the problem can be partitioned into independent (or loosely dependent) sub-problems so that the global solutions can be (almost) immediately built from local solutions. Unfortunately, in diagnostic problem solving, it is often impossible to partition the system model so that the diagnostic sub-problems do not interact with each other. For this reason, the assembly of global diagnoses from the (possibly very large) sets of local diagnoses is a non-trivial task. However, thanks to the constraints imposed by the observations on the system, the OBDD encoding global diagnoses is in general much smaller than the OBDD encoding the whole system model. By computing the OBDD encoding global diagnoses without the need of constructing the OBDD for the global system model, our technique can allow for the successful computation of global diagnoses even if the system model could not be compiled into a single OBDD. We shall see that this strongly depends on the quantity and location of the observations provided with the diagnostic problems.

In this paper we have taken a principled approach by reporting formal results on soundness, completeness and computational complexity of the proposed algorithm. Moreover, we present some heuristics which are able to control (to some extent) the complexity of encoding the portions of the system model and of the process of assemblying the global diagnoses.

The effectiveness of the approach is illustrated by applying it to a simplified model of the propulsion sub-system of a spacecraft as well as to the model of a combinatorial digital circuit from the ISCAS85 benchmark which is considered extremely hard to be dealt with OBDDs.

2 Basic Definitions

Short Summary on OBDDs. (see [8] for more details) An OBDD is a formalism for compactly representing a Boolean function $\mathcal{F}(x_1, \ldots, x_n)$. Given a total ordering of the Boolean variables $x_1, \ldots, x_n$, an OBDD is a rooted DAG whose nodes include two terminal nodes labelled **0** and **1** and non-terminal nodes each labelled with one of the x_i variables. Every internal node x_i has exactly two successors *low* and *high* (if x_j is successor of x_i in the DAG then x_j must follow x_i in the ordering). Every path $\mathcal{P}$ from the root to node **1** can be viewed as an assignment to the variables involved in $\mathcal{P}$ ($x_i = 1$ if $high(x_i)$ is in $\mathcal{P}$ and $x_i = 0$ if $low(x_i)$ is in $\mathcal{P}$) which guarantees that the value of $\mathcal{F}$ is 1. The *size* of an OBDD is defined as the number of its nodes.

It is known that the OBDD of minimal size is unique for a given function $\mathcal{F}$ and a fixed variable order $\mathcal{VO}$; we denote with *build* the operator that, when applied to $\mathcal{F}$ and $\mathcal{VO}$, returns the canonical OBDD representing $\mathcal{F}$ according to order $\mathcal{VO}$. While the complexity of the *build* operator is in the worst case exponential in the number of variables n, in many cases the size of the OBDD representing $\mathcal{F}$ is much smaller than 2^n.

Manipulations of Boolean functions can be mapped to operations on the OBDDs which represent them. In particular, binary logical operations can be performed on OBDDs $\mathcal{O}_1$ and $\mathcal{O}_2$ with the *apply* operator whose complexity is $O(|\mathcal{O}_1| \cdot |\mathcal{O}_2|)$; moreover the *restrict* operator substitutes a constant (i.e. either 0 or 1) to a variable in time linear on the size of the OBDD.

Formal Characterization of Diagnostic Problem. The concepts of system description, diagnostic problem and diagnosis are formalized as follows.

Definition 1 *A* System Description *(SD) is a pair* $\langle SV, DT \rangle$ *where:*
- *SV is a set of discrete system variables partitioned in a subset SV_{exo} of exogenous variables and a subset SV_{end} of endogenous variables. Set SV_{exo} is further partitioned in subsets* INPUTS *(system inputs and commands) and* COMPS *(components), while SV_{end} is further partitioned into* OBS *(observables) and* INTVARS *(non-observables);* DOM(V) *is the finite domain of variable $V \in SV$. In particular, for each $C \in COMPS$,* DOM(C) *contains a set of behavioural modes, one corresponding to the nominal mode (OK) and the others to faulty behaviours*
- *DT (Domain Theory) is a set of propositional logical formulas defined over SV representing the behaviour of the system (under normal and/or abnormal conditions)*

Definition 2 *A diagnostic problem is a 3-tuple $DP = \langle$ SD, **OBS**, **INPUTS** $\rangle$ where SD is the System Description,* **OBS** *is an instantiation of* OBS *variables and* **INPUTS** *is an instantiation of* INPUTS *variables.*

Definition 3 *Let $DP = \langle$ SD, **OBS**, **INPUTS** $\rangle$ be a diagnostic problem. We say that an instantiation* $\mathbf{D} = \{C_1(bm_1), \ldots, C_n(bm_n)\}$ *of COMPS is a* consistency-based diagnosis *for DP iff:*
$$DT \cup \mathbf{INPUTS} \cup \mathbf{OBS} \cup \mathbf{D} \not\vdash \bot$$

3 Encoding the System Description

While OBDDs are a formalism for encoding Boolean functions over Boolean variables, a System Description is a set of logical formulas over multi-valued variables.

As shown in [12], [13], it is possible to map a System Description into an OBDD by performing the following steps:
- mapping each multi-valued variable V in $\mathcal{SV}$ into a set of Boolean variables V_B
- translating each logical formula occurring in DT to the corresponding Boolean formula involving just Boolean variables
- building the OBDD $\mathcal{O}_{DT}$ which represents the Domain Theory DT as the conjunction of the OBDDs representing each of the Boolean formulas obtained in the previous step

As shown in [13], from $\mathcal{O}_{DT}$ it is possible to enumerate all the logical models of DT (i.e. assignments to the $\mathcal{SV}$ variables) through a simple function $instset()$ in time linear to the number of such logical models.

It is well known from the OBDD literature that a major issue in encoding a Boolean function with an OBDD concerns the choice of the variable order; indeed such a choice can have a huge impact on the size of the resulting OBDD [8]. Moreover it has been shown that the problem of finding an optimal variable order is NP-hard [2] and for this reason a number of tractable heuristics have been proposed for selecting a suitable order (e.g. [1]).

In [13] some heuristics have been proposed for dealing with the variable order problem for encoding System Descriptions with OBDDs. Such heuristics are based on a System Causal Network $\mathcal{N}$ that captures the topology of the system (in case of component-based models) and the causal relationships (e.g. input/output) among system variables.

Heuristic **S2** from [13] is basically a depth-first search on the System Causal Network $\mathcal{N}$ which orders causes before effects. In the present paper we have adopted **S2** to order the system variables; however, the approach discussed in this paper could be coupled with other variable order heuristics as well.

Since there is no a-priori guarantee that a System Description can be efficiently encoded with an OBDD, it is important to consider different domains exhibiting different characteristics in terms of number of components, sizes of the variables domains, system topology.

Example. A first example system model that we consider in this paper consists in a simplified version of the model of the propulsion system of the Cassini spacecraft presented in [9] (figure 1).

The model involves 90 multi-valued variables (33 of which represent components). In particular, we have modelled a pressurizer helium tank (T_1), an oxidizer tank (T_2), a fuel tank (T_3), a set of valves (V_T and $V_{11}, \ldots, V_{28}$), two engines (E_1 and E_2), pipe join points ($J_{11}, \ldots, J_{22}$) and pipe split points ($S_1, S_2, S_3, S_{11}, \ldots, S_{22}$).

Apart from pipe join and split points that cannot fail, all other components have fault behavioural modes; in particular we have taken into consideration 1

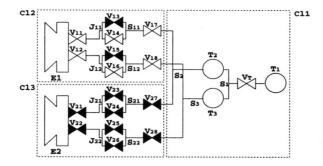

Figure 1: Propulsion system.

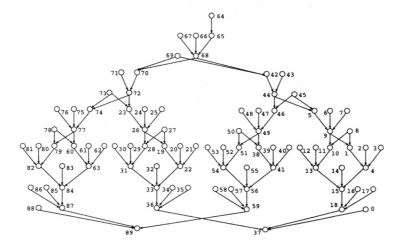

Figure 2: System Causal Network for the Propulsion system.

fault mode for engines and tanks and 5 fault modes for valves. Valves can be commanded to be open or closed (depicted in white and black respectively in figure 1). The Domain Theory for the system contains **740** logical formulas.

Figure 2 shows the System Causal Network $\mathcal{N}$ of the propulsion sub-system and the indexes assigned to its nodes by **S2**. The graph has a *cycle base* of 13 cycles, involving up to 18 nodes [1]. Translating the model of the propulsion system according to the steps above, yields a compact OBDD involving **277** Boolean variables with a size of **4,727** nodes (note that the full truth table for representing the propulsion system would then require 2^{277} rows). □

In [13] we have encoded the model of an industrial plant that is more complex than the model of the propulsion system both in terms of number of multi-valued variables (250 variables, 31 of which represent components) and, more important, of the topology of the Causal Network (cycle base of 48 cycles

---

[1]The size of the cycle base is given by $m - (n - 1)$ where m and n are respectively the number of edges and the number of nodes in $\mathcal{N}$.

322

involving up to 14 nodes). The direct application of the approach yields an OBDD whose size is about **375,500** nodes; such a size is still manageable with state-of-the-art OBDD tools, but obviously has a significant impact on the cost of computing diagnoses.

If we move to the domain of combinatorial digital circuits (in particular, the ISCAS85 benchmark), it is well known that some of them are so complex that they have resisted so far to be encoded into a single OBDD [6]. In section 7 we will consider one of such circuits (namely, c499) and we will show that it can be successfully diagnosed by applying the partitioning techniques described in the following sections.

4 Partitioning the Domain Theory

As noted at the end of the previous section, building $\mathcal{O}_{DT}$ can be practically inefficient or even impossible for some complex domains. In this section we discuss how to partition DT into a set of *clusters* $\mathcal{CL}_1$, ..., $\mathcal{CL}_k$ so that each $\mathcal{CL}_i$ is easier to encode than DT. In the following sections we will then show how the global system diagnoses can be obtained by combining the local diagnoses computed for each cluster.

Definition 4 *Given a System Description* $SD = \langle SV, DT \rangle$, *a partitioning* Π_{DT} *of* DT *is a set* $\{\mathcal{CL}_1, \ldots, \mathcal{CL}_k\}$ *s.t.:*
$DT = \bigcup_{i=1,\ldots,k} \mathcal{CL}_i$ *and* $\forall i \neq j : \mathcal{CL}_i \cap \mathcal{CL}_j = \emptyset$

We denote with $\mathcal{SV}_i$ the subset of System Variables that appear in formulas in $\mathcal{CL}_i$; similarly, for any subset $\mathcal{SS}$ of $\mathcal{SV}$ (e.g. *COMPS*), we denote with $\mathcal{SS}_i$ its restriction to the variables that appear in formulas in $\mathcal{CL}_i$.
We require that the sets of components $COMPS_i$ and $COMPS_j$ are disjoint for $i \neq j$; however in general $\mathcal{SV}_i$ and $\mathcal{SV}_j$, $i \neq j$ are not disjoint. We denote with $\mathcal{SH}_{\Pi_{DT}}$ the set of variables in $\mathcal{SV}$ that are shared by at least two clusters defined by Π_{DT}.

Given SD $= \langle SV, DT \rangle$ and a partitioning $\Pi_{DT} = \{\mathcal{CL}_1, \ldots, \mathcal{CL}_k\}$, it is possible to encode DT as a set $\mathcal{P}_{DT} = \{\mathcal{O}_{\mathcal{CL}_1}, \ldots, \mathcal{O}_{\mathcal{CL}_k}\}$ (where $\mathcal{O}_{\mathcal{CL}_i}$ is an OBDD encoding $\mathcal{CL}_i$) so that the following property holds:
$\mathcal{O}_{DT} = apply(\wedge, \mathcal{O}_{\mathcal{CL}_k}, apply(\ldots apply(\wedge, \mathcal{O}_{\mathcal{CL}_2}, \mathcal{O}_{\mathcal{CL}_1})))$
It is easy to see that the endogenous system variables that are not observable and are not shared by two or more clusters can be safely forgotten from each $\mathcal{O}_{\mathcal{CL}_i}$ by existential quantification[2]:
$\mathcal{O}^R_{\mathcal{CL}_i} = \text{ForgetVars}(\mathcal{O}_{\mathcal{CL}_i}, \mathcal{SV}_{end,i} \backslash (\mathcal{SH}_{\Pi_{DT}} \cup OBS_i))$
In the following, we refer to $\mathcal{O}^R_{\mathcal{CL}_i}$ as reduced OBDD of $\mathcal{CL}_i$ because of the cancellation of variables local to the cluster.

Under appropriate conditions, we have a guarantee about the size of $\mathcal{O}^R_{\mathcal{CL}_i}$, as stated by the following property.

---
[2]Existential quantification of variable B in OBDD $\mathcal{O}$ consists in computing the restrictions $\mathcal{O}_1$ and $\mathcal{O}_0$ of $\mathcal{O}$ with $B = 1$ and $B = 0$ respectively and then applying the $\vee$ operator between $\mathcal{O}_1$ and $\mathcal{O}_0$.

```
1 Function ComputeDiagnoses(P_{DT}^R, OBS, INPUTS)
2    For i=1 To |P_{DT}^R|
3       O_{DIAG,i} := O_{CL_i}^R
4       ForEach I(val) ∈ INPUTS
5          O_{DIAG,i} := restrict(O_{DIAG,i}, I_{val}))
6       ForEach O(val) ∈ OBS
7          O_{DIAG,i} := restrict(O_{DIAG,i}, O_{val}))
8    O_{temp} := 1
9    For i=1 To |P_{DT}^R|
10      O_{temp} := apply(∧, O_{temp}, O_{DIAG,i})
11   O_{DIAG} := ForgetVars(O_{temp}, SH_{Π_{DT}})
12   Return O_{DIAG}
13 EndFunction
```

Figure 3: Computation of Diagnoses

Property 1 *If the value of each endogenous variable V is determined by a subset $SV_{exo,V}$ of the exogenous variables and the variable order is such that V follows all the variables in $SV_{exo,V}$, the call to* ForgetVars() *leads to an OBDD $O_{CL_i}^R$ smaller than O_{CL_i}.*

Example (continued). A possible way of partitioning the model of the propulsion system is illustrated in figure 1, where three clusters CL_1, CL_2 and CL_3 have been identified. The set of shared variables $SH_{Π_{DT}}$ consists in just 4 variables, namely the outputs of pipe split points S_2 and S_3.

The sizes of the OBDDs O_{CL_1}, O_{CL_2} and O_{CL_3} are respectively **220**, **1,189** and **1,189**[3]. The sum of the sizes of O_{CL_i} is well below the size of the OBDD O_{DT} encoding the whole system (**2,598** versus **4,727** nodes).□

5 Computing Diagnoses

Computing the Complete Set of Diagnoses as an OBDD. Figure 3 reports a sketch of the diagnostic algorithm; the algorithm receives as inputs the set of reduced OBDDs $P_{DT}^R = \{O_{CL_1}^R, \ldots, O_{CL_k}^R\}$, an assignment **INPUTS** of the system inputs and an assignment **OBS** of the system observables.

Each OBDD $O_{CL_i}^R$ encoding cluster CL_i is incrementally constrained with variable assignments in **INPUTS** and **OBS** by using the standard OBDD operator *restrict*.

The resulting OBDDs $O_{DIAG,i}$ are merged through the *apply* operator (they are ANDed together) and finally, since diagnoses are defined just in terms of assignments to $COMPS$ variables, the variables shared by two or more clusters are forgotten.

The following theorem states that the algorithm is both correct and complete w.r.t. the computation of consistency-based diagnoses [4].

---

[3]The sizes of the reduced OBDDs $O_{CL_i}^R$ are respectively **154**, **519** and **519**.

[4]The proofs of the properties and theorems stated in this paper are omitted because of lack of space

Theorem 1 *Let* $DP = \langle SD, \mathbf{OBS}, \mathbf{INPUTS} \rangle$ *be a diagnostic problem,* Π_{DT} *be a partitioning of the Domain Theory and* $\mathcal{P}_{DT}^R$ *the set of reduced OBDDs encoding* Π_{DT}.
Algorithm ComputeDiagnoses() *invoked with* $\mathcal{P}_{DT}^R$, **OBS** *and* **INPUTS** *as arguments computes an OBDD* $\mathcal{O}_{DIAG}$ *s.t. instset*($\mathcal{O}_{DIAG}$) *contains all and only the consistency based diagnoses for DP.*

As for the computational complexity of the diagnostic algorithm, the following results can be directly derived from the computational complexity of the standard OBDD operators.

Property 2 *The time complexity for computing* $\mathcal{O}_{DIAG,i}$, $i = 1, \dots, |\Pi_{DT}|$ *is* $O(|\mathcal{SV}_{end}| \cdot |\mathcal{O}_{CL_i}^R|)$. *Moreover,* $|\mathcal{O}_{DIAG,i}| \leq |\mathcal{O}_{CL_i}^R|$.

Property 3 *The time and space complexity for computing* $\mathcal{O}_{temp}$ *from* $\mathcal{O}_{DIAG,i}$, $i = 1, \dots, |\Pi_{DT}|$ *is* $O(\prod_{i=1}^{|\Pi_{DT}|} |\mathcal{O}_{DIAG,i}|)$.

Moreover, under the assumptions of property 1, $|\mathcal{O}_{DIAG}| \leq |\mathcal{O}_{temp}|$.

Computing Preferred Diagnoses. In most diagnostic systems, especially when the set of returned diagnoses can be very large, we are interested only in the preferred diagnoses, according to some particular preference criterion. Preferred diagnoses can be efficiently computed from $\mathcal{O}_{DIAG}$ when the selected preference criterion is to minimize the number of faults.
The basic idea consists in pre-compiling an OBDD *Filter[k]* representing the set of all assignments to *COMPS* involving k faults, for each $k = 0, \dots, n$; by filtering the set of all the diagnoses $\mathcal{O}_{DIAG}$ with such OBDDs we then determine the sets of diagnoses with k faults.
The set of minimum cardinality diagnoses can be computed by replacing statement (12) in function ComputeDiagnoses() (figure 3) with the following statements:

```
O_PREF = apply(∧, O_DIAG, Filter[0]); k=1
While (O_PREF = 0)
    O_PREF = apply(∧, O_DIAG, Filter[k]); k = k+1
Return O_PREF
```

The algorithm intersects $\mathcal{O}_{DIAG}$ with *Filter[k]* starting with $k = 0$ and stopping as soon as the result $\mathcal{O}_{PREF}$ is not empty.
Figure 4 shows the algorithm to be run offline for computing the complete set of *fault cardinality filters*. OBDD *Filter[k]* represents all and only the instantiations of *COMPS* variables containing exactly k faulty components. OBDD *Filter[0]* represents the situation with no fault, i.e. all the components are in the *OK* mode. Intuitively, for each instantiation of *COMPS* represented in *Filter[k − 1]*, *Filter[k]* substitutes the assignment of the *OK* mode to a component C_i with all the possible faulty behavioural modes of C_i.
The following result ensures that both the off-line computation of fault cardinality filters is tractable and that the size of any computed filter is limited.

```
1 Function ComputeFaultCardinalityFilters(COMPS)
2   n = |COMPS|
3   Filter[0] = build(C_{1,OK} ∧ ... ∧ C_{n,OK})
4   For k=1 To n
5     Filter[k] = build(0)
6     For i=1 To n
7       O_i = restrict(FILTER[k-1], C_{i,OK})
8       O_i = apply(∧, O_i, build(~ C_{i,OK}))
9       Filter[k] = apply(∨, Filter[k], O_i)
10  Return Filter[]
11 EndFunction
```

Figure 4: Computing the Fault Cardinality Filters

Property 4 *The time complexity for computing fault cardinality filters is polynomial in* $|COMPS|$. *The size of each filter* $Filter[k], k = 0, \ldots, |COMPS|$ *is* $O(|COMPS|^2)$.

Instead of representing all the assignments to *COMPS* with exactly k faults, it may be useful to represent all the assignments with *up to* k faults. This can be easily obtained by building an OBDD *FilterUpTo[k]* as the disjunction of OBDDs *Filter[0]*, ..., *Filter[k]*. Complexity results similar to the ones of property 4 hold for the times of computation and sizes of *FilterUpTo[k]*.

6 Controlling the Problem Size

From properties 2 and 3 it follows that the complexity of the ComputeDiagnoses() algorithm depends on the following main factors:
- the ability of encoding each cluster CL_i with an OBDD $O^R_{CL_i}$ of reasonable size
- the ability of reducing the size of each OBDD $O^R_{CL_i}$ with the *restrict* operations so that $|O_{DIAG,i}|$ is significantly smaller than $|O^R_{CL_i}|$
- the ability of limiting the size of O_{DIAG} w.r.t. the product of the sizes of $O_{DIAG,i}$ In the following we discuss strategies that aim at dealing with each of these factors.
Controlling the Sizes of $O^R_{CL_i}$ **and** $O_{DIAG,i}$. A way to control the sizes of $O^R_{CL_i}$ consists in duplicating some of the system variables so that the clusters become less connected with each other. In the extreme case where enough variables have been duplicated so that a cluster CL_i has become completely disconnected from the other ones, the variable order heuristic can index variables in CL_i by only considering their relationships within the cluster, and obtain in general a significantly better local order[5].
It is worth noting that, in order to compute the OBDD O_{DIAG} (representing

---

[5]In [13] the approach of duplicating a limited number of variables has been successfully applied to the model of the industrial plant described in section 3, with a significant improvement since the OBDD size has dropped from about **375,500** to about **59,000** nodes.

the global diagnoses) from the OBDDs $\mathcal{O}_{DIAG,i}$ (representing the local diagnoses for $\mathcal{CL}_i$), one must in general state the equivalence of the duplicated variables, and this can of course make the size of $\mathcal{O}_{DIAG}$ grow drastically.

The assertion of equivalence can be completely avoided in case the values of the duplicated variables are provided with the Diagnostic Problem at hand, i.e. when the duplicated variables are a subset of $INPUTS \cup OBS$. In such a case, all the copies of a duplicated variable V are restricted to their known value during the computation of local diagnoses, so that they disappear before the construction of $\mathcal{O}_{DIAG}$.

As concerns the sizes of OBDDs $\mathcal{O}_{DIAG,i}$, the reduction obtained w.r.t. the size of $\mathcal{O}_{\mathcal{CL}_i}^R$ is strongly influenced by the presence in cluster $\mathcal{CL}_i$ of variables belonging to $INPUTS$ and OBS. While in general an increase of the observability of the system to be diagnosed has a positive effect on the size of $\mathcal{O}_{DIAG,i}$, the partitioning criteria should prefer partitions where each cluster contains some inputs and/or observable variables; in general, the most effective observables are the ones that are shared by two or more clusters.

Controlling the Size of $\mathcal{O}_{DIAG}$. First of all, note that the upper bound expressed by property 3 is quite pessimistic since in most cases the merge of two clusters does not yield an OBDD whose size is the product of their sizes. However, especially when the degree of observability of the system is very limited (e.g. only system inputs and outputs are observable), it is possible that the size of $\mathcal{O}_{DIAG}$ becomes unmanageable.

In such a case, imposing a limit on the cardinality of the diagnoses we are interested in can help manage the complexity. If we denote with $CARD_{max}$ such a limit, this can be straightforwardly done by adding the following statement after line (10) within the second **For** loop in function **ComputeDiagnoses()** (figure 3):

$$\mathcal{O}_{temp} = \text{apply}(\wedge, \mathcal{O}_{temp}, \text{FilterUpTo}[CARD_{max}])$$

Thanks to the limited size of $FilterUpTo[CARD_{max}]$ this operation is guaranteed to be efficient w.r.t. the size of $\mathcal{O}_{temp}$. The rationale behind this heuristic is that the number of potential diagnoses drops from exponential to polynomial w.r.t. $|COMPS|$ (more precisely it becomes $O(|COMPS|^{CARD_{max}})$).

It is quite clear that a fine-grained partitioning of DT makes the task of computing the local diagnoses easier but it may make the computation of the global diagnoses through the merging of local diagnoses the bottleneck of the entire diagnostic process. For this reason, the number of clusters should be limited.

A natural choice consists in partitioning DT in such a way that the clusters correspond to macro-components/subsystems of the device that can be encoded with OBDDs of reasonable size. Such a choice usually leads to clusters that exhibit a high degree of internal connectivity and a more limited degree of connectivity with the other clusters so that the number of shared variables is not too high. This makes more practical the duplication of a significant portion of the shared variables; moreover, most of the endogenous variables can be removed off-line during the creation of OBDDs $\mathcal{O}_{\mathcal{CL}_i}^R$.

7 Testing the Approach

Very satisfying results have been obtained in diagnosing the propulsion sub-system according to the partition discussed in section 4: even in presence of 3 simultaneous faults, the computation of all the global diagnoses as well as the preferred ones took just a few milliseconds[6]. Such results are however only minor improvements w.r.t. the ones obtained by applying our approach without partitioning the model since the OBDD encoding the whole system is extremely compact as reported in section 4.

We have then tested the effectiveness of the approach on a very challenging problem by considering the model of a combinatorial digital circuit that is known to be extremely hard to be encoded with OBDDs [6], namely circuit c499 from the ISCAS85 benchmark. According to the specification provided by the benchmark in *netlist* format, we have modelled all the wires of c499 as components, so that the resulting model has 499 components, 41 system inputs, 32 system outputs and 467 internal variables. The total number of multi-valued system variables is then 1039.

All the logical gates have three possible behavioural modes: *ok*, *sa0* (stuck at 0) and *sa1* (stuck at 1), while the wires have either the same three behavioural modes or just *ok* and *sa1*.

As expected, the algorithm was unable to encode c499 with a single OBDD using variable order strategy **S2** (we stopped the computation after the OBDD size reached 3,000,000 nodes). We have then partitioned DT in 5 clusters, three of which constitute the first macro-component of c499 while the other two constitute the second macro-component; the total number of variables shared by the clusters is 96.

After the duplication of the System Inputs, the algorithm was able to encode the circuit: the total size of the OBDDs encoding the five clusters is just 82,795 nodes and the time needed to compute them is about 8 sec.

Since the model of c499 and strategy **S2** satisfy the requirements of property 1, the off-line elimination of non-shared endogenous variables is guaranteed to lead to OBDDs of even smaller sizes; after such process (which takes about 8 sec), the total size of the OBDDs drops to 52,267 nodes.

We first tested the ability of the proposed algorithm to actually compute global diagnoses by means of 10 test cases whose minimal-cardinality diagnoses involve two faults. In particular, we have run the 10 test cases under different degrees of observability of the circuit by defining OBS as the following sets[7]: **OUT** (only system outputs), **8SH** (system outputs plus 8 shared variables), **16SH** (system outputs plus 16 shared variables).

Table 1 reports the average time needed for computing $\mathcal{O}_{DIAG}$ and its size with different degrees of observability. In column **UpTo5** we report results concerning the case where diagnoses with up to 5 faults are represented. It is

---

[6]Our implementation of the diagnostic algorithm has been written in Java 2 (JDK 1.4.2) and run on a laptop machine equipped with Centrino CPU at 1.4GHz and 512MB RAM. The OBDD functions were provided by the *BuDDy* C++ package via the *JBDD* interface.

[7]In all cases the system inputs were known.

OBS	UpTo5		Complete	
	time	size	time	size
OUT	1,455	474,719	N/A	N/A
8SH	601	103,024	1,458	1,161,710
16SH	306	22,408	410	366,468

Table 1: Statistics for circuit c499 (times in msec).

easy to see that observability plays a major role in determining the efficiency both in space and time of the diagnostic process. However, it is worth noting that the diagnostic algorithm is able to successfully solve all the diagnostic cases even when the observability is set at the minimum (only system inputs and outputs are known); moreover in such a case the computation of $\mathcal{O}_{DIAG}$ is obtained in less than 1.5 sec.

Significant speed-ups (and reduction in the size of $\mathcal{O}_{DIAG}$) are obtained when we increase the observability to include 8 and then 16 shared variables[8].

A further test has been made by considering all possible diagnoses without putting any limit to the number of faults (see column **Complete**). It is clear that the number of possible global diagnoses is extremely large. For the case where the observability is reduced to just system inputs and outputs, the algorithm is unable to compute $\mathcal{O}_{DIAG}$ since its size is too large. However, a slight increase of observability is sufficient to make the diagnostic cases solvable: for 16 observable shared variables the size of $\mathcal{O}_{DIAG}$ is manageable and, more interesting, each diagnostic case can be solved in less than half a second.

The ability of the algorithm to deal with a large number of simultaneous faults has been proved by solving cases whose minimal diagnoses involved 5 faults. In some cases the number of minimal cardinality diagnoses exceeded 2,500 different diagnoses; even in such cases, the time needed to compute the OBDD representing all the minimal cardinality diagnoses was less than 10sec with observability **8SH**.

8   Conclusions

In order to handle the computational complexity of the MBD task and the potentially exponential number of solutions to diagnostic problems, an approach that has recently received attention involves the symbolic representation of the search and solution spaces of diagnostic problems; so far most of the attention has been drawn by OBDDs (see e.g. [11], [10]), because of the maturity of the theoretical analysis on OBDDs as well as the availability of efficient tools implementing the standard operators.

In the present paper we extend previous work on the diagnosis of static systems based on OBDDs ([12], [13]) by proposing an approach for dealing with complex system models through the partitioning of the model into a set of interacting subsystems. The rationale behind our approach is that, even

---

[8]Note that, even with observability **16SH**, the sub-problems corresponding to the diagnosis of the five clusters do not become independent.

when it is impossible or impractical to encode the system model with a single OBDD, it can be easier to encode the set of diagnoses, provided enough system observations are given with the diagnostic problems.

We report formal results on soundness, completeness and computational complexity of the proposed algorithm. A significant contribution of this analysis is the identification of some parameters, apart from variable order, which have a strong impact on the feasibility of solving diagnostic cases with OBDDs; in particular, we have shown that the degree of observability plays a major role in keeping under control the size of the OBDDs representing local diagnoses.

It is quite clear that the effectiveness of the proposed approach depends on the partitioning of the global system as discussed in section 6. An important source of information for guiding the partitioning is the hierarchical description of the system in terms of subsystems and components; in fact, this kind of knowledge allows the domain expert to subdivide the system into meaningful portions which share a limited number of variables. It is worth noting that in the domain of digital circuits as the ones in the ISCAS85 benchmark the knowledge about the hierarchical structure of a circuit is widely available, so that the partitioning process can take advantage of this knowledge.

Another relevant characteristic of our approach concerns the fact that the selection of the preferred diagnoses is imposed on global diagnoses, while no restriction is imposed on the fault cardinality of diagnoses local to each cluster. The computation of all the local diagnoses instead of just the leading ones has a strong advantage when we need to perform an incremental diagnosis by considering several test vectors. In such a case, indeed, the refinement process can be performed on OBDDs $\mathcal{O}_{DIAG,i}$ which represent the complete sets of local diagnoses, and the limit on the maximum allowed cardinality of global diagnoses can be imposed just at the end of the process, when OBDDs $\mathcal{O}_{DIAG,i}$ are merged into $\mathcal{O}_{DIAG}$. This result should be contrasted with the solutions based on direct computation of leading diagnoses, where efficiency is obtained by computing only a limited number of diagnoses (the preferred ones). A significant example of this approach is described in [14] where results concerning the diagnosis of several ISCAS85 circuits are reported; these results were obtained by limiting the number of computed leading diagnoses to 10. Since in this way it is possible to miss the correct solution, [9] has improved the approach by adding a backtracking mechanism that is triggered when the arrival of new observations leads to an empty set of solutions; however there is no guarantee about the number of time instants involved by such backtrackings and therefore they can potentially be very expensive.

Very recently, other approaches to the symbolic representation of the system models are emerging. A particularly promising proposal is the one reported in [7] for the compilation of propositional theories into d-DNNF: for example [7] reports that circuit c499 has been compiled into a d-DNNF of 2,214,814 edges (without resorting to model decomposition).

Finally, it would clearly be worth exploring the potential application of the proposed approach to distributed diagnosis, where several diagnostic agents compute local diagnoses and a distinguished agent (or supervisor) has the task of merging them into globally consistent diagnoses.

References

[1] F. Aloul, I. Markov, K. Sakallah, FORCE: a Fast and Easy-to-Implement Variable-Ordering Heuristic, Proc. Great Lakes Symposium on VLSI - GLSVLSI, 116-119, 2003

[2] B. Bollig, I. Wegener, Improving the Variable Ordering of OBDDs is NP-complete, IEEE Transactions on Computers 45(9), 932-1002, 1994

[3] P. Bertoli, A. Cimatti, M. Roveri, P. Traverso, Planning in Nondeterministic Domains under Partial Observability via Symbolic Model Checking, Proc. 17th Int. Joint Conf. on AI - IJCAI, 473-478, 2001

[4] L. Chittaro, R. Ranon, R.: Hierarchical Model-Based Diagnosis Based on Structural Abstraction. Artificial Intelligence 155(1–2) (2004) 147–182

[5] A. Darwiche: Model-Based Diagnosis using Structured System Descriptions. Journal of Artificial Intelligence Research 8 (1998) 165–222

[6] A. Darwiche, A Compiler for Deterministic, Decomposable Negation Normal Form, Proc. 18th National Conf. on AI - AAAI, 627-634, 2002

[7] A. Darwiche, New Advances in Compiling CNF to Decomposable Negation Normal Form, Proc. 16th European Conf. on AI - ECAI, 328-332, 2004

[8] R. Bryant, Symbolic Boolean manipulation with Ordered Binary-Decision Diagrams, ACM Computing Surveys 24, 293-318, 1992

[9] J. Kurien, P. P. Nayak, Back to the Future for Consistency-Based Trajectory Tracking, Proc. 17th National Conf. on Artificial Intelligence, 370-377, 2000

[10] A. Schumann, Y. Pencolé, S. Thiébaux, Diagnosis of Discrete-Event Systems using Binary Decision Diagrams, Proc. 15th Int. Workshop on Principles of Diagnosis, 197-202, 2004

[11] J. Sztipanovits, A. Misra, Diagnosis of discrete event systems using Ordered Binary Decision Diagrams, Proc. 7th Int. Workshop on Principles of Diagnosis, 1996

[12] P. Torasso, G. Torta Computing Minimum-Cardinality Diagnoses Using OBDDs, LNAI 2821, 224-238, 2003

[13] G. Torta, P. Torasso, The Role of OBDDs in Controlling the Complexity of Model Based Diagnosis, Proc. 15th Int. Work. on Principles of Diagnosis, 9-14, 2004

[14] B. C. Williams, P. P. Nayak, A Model-Based Approach to Reactive Self-Configuring Systems, Proc. AAAI96, 971-978, 1996

Issues in Designing Tutors for Games of Incomplete Information: a Bridge Case Study

Ray Kemp, Ben McKenzie, Elizabeth Kemp

Massey University

New Zealand

{r.kemp, b.mckenzie, e.kemp}@massey.ac.nz

Abstract

There are a number of commercial packages for playing the game of bridge, and even more papers on possible techniques for improving the quality of such systems. We examine some of the AI techniques that have proved successful for implementing bridge playing systems and discuss how they might be adapted for teaching the game. We pay particular attention to the issue of incomplete information and include some of our own research into the subject.

1.   Introduction

The world abounds with chess and *bridge*[1] packages which can play a game against a human opponent. In chess, whatever standard players are at, they can find a system that can play at their level or beyond if they wish to be extended. Bridge has not had the same success [1].

The question arises, to what extent these packages help new players learn the game, rather than just providing a means of practising the knowledge and skills that they have already acquired. A further question is whether games of incomplete information require special skills which can be developed in specific ways in order to improve performance, or, at least, to speed up the learning process. In this paper we address these issues using the game of bridge as an example.

Note that by 'incomplete information' we imply that there are some facts that will not be known for at least part of the game. Even if players accurately observe and remember everything that has happened, there is still some information that is hidden from them, and they need to take this into account when formulating strategies. In many card games, such as poker, the whole point of the exercise is that something is hidden, otherwise there would be no contest.

Interestingly, this is not quite the case in bridge, where a novice, and even a good club player could not guarantee to get an optimal result even if all the cards are seen. Newspapers and magazines often publish 'double dummy' quizzes which challenge the reader to achieve a particular result even when all the cards are in

---

[1] Terms with which readers who do not play bridge may not be familiar, are italicised when first used. They are defined in the glossary at the end of this paper.

view. Some such quizzes can be demanding even for experts. Solving such quizzes using enumeration techniques is quite beyond humans. Due to combinatorial explosion, only relatively recently has the solving of such problems become amenable to computers. Now there is a commercial package called Deep Finesse [2] which can analyse any double dummy problem.

In a normal game, players do not get the luxury of seeing all the *hands*. In the first phase (the *auction*) they only get to see their own hand of thirteen cards. During the second phase (the *play* of the cards), one hand (the *dummy*) is laid on the table so that the other three players each get to see this hand plus their own. Gradually, cards from each of the other hands are revealed.

To aid the process of determining the lie of unknown cards, players can signal to one another what they have by playing cards in a specific order or by discarding a particularly high or low card. Experts can manage quite well without even this degree of help. A famous player, Rixi Markus, once remarked when playing with another person for the first time, that he should not signal to her since she would know exactly what he had by the time only a few cards had been played anyway.

The issue of incomplete information is a crucial one. Novices may need to practice remembering what cards have been played in order to improve their performance. In the simplest case, as *declarer*, novices are taught to count how many *trumps* have been played, so that they know how many the opponents have left. Obviously a computer is able to remember exactly what cards have been played, so may be able to provide some simple help in that regard. However, novices are taught to reduce their cognitive load by abstracting this information (eg remembering that three low hearts have been played rather than that they are the 3, 5 and 6 of the *suit*, or that the jack of diamonds is the top diamond left rather than the equivalent information that the ace king and queen of diamonds have all been played). Occasionally, knowledge of exactly what low cards have been played is essential, but it is probably too much to ask novices to remember such information.

More advanced players try to mentally record inferences too. In this way, they build up a picture of opponents' hands which can help them make their own decisions. The opponents' play may indicate the presence or absence of key cards.

In section two, we consider possible ways in which the approaches used in intelligent tutoring systems (ITSs) [3] could be applied to bridge. We then look at what AI techniques have been used for designing and implementing bridge playing systems and assess how effective they would be in teaching situations.

2. ITS Methods Applied to Bridge

Intelligent tutoring systems take a variety of approaches to teaching by computer. We now look at some of these, and speculate what these would involve when teaching the game of bridge. Some of these approaches may be already incorporated into bridge systems, but many are not. We are not concerned at this point with how systems could be implemented to provide these features (or even whether they are feasible with today's technology), but how we might interpret these teaching methods in the bridge playing context.

2.1 Learning by Doing

Learning by doing has been a popular method used in teaching systems. Providing a realistic simulation of an activity with which the learner can interact is usually less fraught (and, in some cases, less dangerous) than trying the real thing. An early version of such an approach was taken by Hollan et al in STEAMER [4] which was used to train operators in the control of the steam propulsion plant of a large ship. Although the actual operation of the model contained no AI (it was a straight numerical simulation), expert knowledge of concepts was incorporated into the graphics. The inclusion of extra dials that, for example, showed the rate of change of variables, helped the user to understand what was happening. This is what Hollan et al referred to as 'conceptual fidelity': faithfulness to the expert's abstract conceptualization of the system rather than to its physical properties.

There are a large number of systems available that allow the user to learn by doing: by playing a game of bridge against the computer. Although the real thing is not inherently dangerous, bridge players are not noted for their patience, and a novice making a lot of mistakes would not be generally welcomed in many bridge circles. The simulated game on the computer offers a method of learning which is less frustrating. Generally, the systems present a straight forward depiction of the cards and the way they are played.

2.2 Coaching

Coaching systems can observe the learner carrying out activities and provide help and explanations. To be able to achieve this, the system would normally require some degree of transparency. A common approach in ITSs is to provide logical or cause-effect models of the domain. As with expert systems, such an approach enables 'why' or 'how' questions to be answered in a sensible way. See, for example, the work on qualitative modelling [5, 6].

In a bridge system, such coaching might involve observing the *bidding* and play of the novice and being available to provide advice either in an active or passive way. In either case, the system should be able to provide reasons for actions or bids that are recommended or otherwise. They are taking the place of a human spectator who might sit behind a player and whispers advice during or after the playing of a hand.

2.3 Cognitive Apprenticeship

A slightly different approach to learning is to use cognitive apprenticeship [7]. Here, it is the novice who is the observer, initially, at least. They learn by observing and then gradually take over aspects of the task. The expert can still perform some of the trickier parts, providing scaffolding [7]. The parts that the expert takes over might be ones that novices would not be able to do or might be parts that just reduce their cognitive load. Gradually, the expert allows users to take over more and more of the task (fading) until they are doing everything themselves.

In bridge playing terms, there are many opportunities for this teaching approach. Novices might attempt the bidding, leaving the expert to take care of the playing, for example. Later on, they may attempt to play the cards, too, but have their cognitive load reduced by having all the cards displayed of all hands (double dummy). Even leaving the cards that have been played turned upwards (they are normally turned over so cannot be seen) would be helpful for the beginner.

2.4 Metacognition

Metacognition [8,9] is concerned with 'thinking about one's own thoughts' [8] when carrying out a task. Associated activities include planning what to do, monitoring one's own activities, making any necessary adjustments, predicting outcomes and reflecting upon them, and making revisions after completing a task. A number of systems have incorporated metacognitive elements, including SICUN which provides assistance in clinical decision making [10] and Ecolab which helps primary school children learn about the environment [11,12].

In bridge, we might ask users what card they plan to *lead* to a *contract* when *defending*. During the play of a hand, users can be asked whether they think that they will make (or defeat) a contract. They can also be asked whether they are in an appropriate contract. Afterwards, the system might ask them if they could have played the contract better, or inquire whether they think they should be in a different one. They can replay *deals* or even get the computer to do so. They might be given a list of techniques that are typically used in playing a contract, and asked which of those they used, and which they might have used.

3. Game Playing Techniques for Teaching

3.1 Game Tree Search

As with many other games, the most effective methods developed so far for simulating bridge playing involve game tree searches. It is generally agreed that, even using this approach, the best programs currently only perform at the level of the average club player [13]. There is also a consensus that the main reason for this is the fact that bridge is a game of incomplete information. As noted earlier, if all the hands are known then Deep Finesse can play a perfect game.

Thus, if one wished to learn by doing then playing against an expert might seem a reasonable approach to take. This is not necessarily the case, however. Maybe a novice needs to learn with fellow novices, not just because they will be more forgiving, but because s/he may have occasional victories. These are the kind of successes that would only come infrequently against an expert.

There is another problem with Deep Finesse. It does not follow the rules of the game but can see all the hands and bases all its analyses on this information. Basically, it cheats. The main difficulty is that being able to see all hands will have the consequence that it will make decisions which are counter to what one might expect from other information that one has and from the laws of probability. An example is shown below[2]:

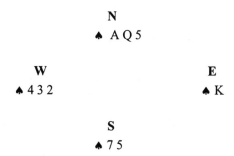

N

♠ A Q 5

W   **E**

♠ 4 3 2   ♠ K

S

♠ 7 5

Here, unless there was compelling evidence to suggest that East had the king of spades, South's best play is to lead a low card from hand and after West has played, insert the queen, hoping West has the missing *honour*. This gives a fifty percent chance of making most *tricks*. Deep Finesse however would go for what it knows is a 100% chance and play the ace straight away since it can see that East has the singleton king. This kind of play might puzzle and confuse novices, and could lead them into bad habits.

GIB [1,14] is one of the foremost bridge playing systems currently available and utilizes a game tree approach both in bidding and playing. Several modifications have been included to make it more efficient. Since it cannot see all the cards, it uses monte carlo methods to simulate hundreds of thousands of deals which conform to the information known about the hands. The play that works with the most hands is the one that is chosen.

Although GIB has not been designed to employ human strategies and tactics, as such, it finds good lines of play which often involve the use of techniques that the average player could clearly recognize. Such techniques usually have well-known names such as finesse, squeeze or end-play. However, GIB cannot identify them as such. They are just the best plays that its extensive search recommends.

Since the program would always give reasonable advice and would play and defend well then it would provide a good environment in which the learner could learn by doing. However, since, like most game tree systems, it is a black box approach, it could not be used directly for providing coaching. The novice could ask for advice part way through a hand and GIB could provide a tip – its own evaluation of the next play – but justification in terms of statistical payoff function values would not be helpful to a human.

A framework for apprenticeship learning in which the novice starts by observing and then gradually carries out some of the tasks (such as bidding or part of the play) could quite easily be set up using systems such as GIB. Other aids could be provided. For example, the cards might be left exposed after each trick is played in

---

[2] The four players are identified with the points of the compass. Each plays with the person opposite so North plays with South and East plays with West. They are usually abbreviated to N,S,E and W.

order to reduce the cognitive load. Obviously, hands could be replayed quite easily. A disconcerting feature of GIB, however, is that its play on a hand may vary due to the monte carlo approach. It can use different strategies and even win different numbers of tricks when deals are replayed. If, the user wants to have a second attempt at playing a deal then this could be confusing.

Again, metacognitive strategies such as those employed in SICUN and ECOLAB could be added to GIB. As noted previously, there are a number of different ways we could try to encourage learners to reflect on their play and strategies. It is a good idea to get students to anticipate what they going to do (planning), get them to work out part way through whether things are going as expected (monitoring) and check at the end whether things worked out (reflection). Obviously, these questions can be posed in any system but it may not be possible to get support from the system to get coherent answers.

3.2 Planning

In Tignum [13,15], Smith et al use the idea of a decision tree which is then evaluated to produce a plan for all or part of the game. It differs from the normal game tree in that branches correspond to recognisable bridge tactics or strategies for winning tricks. Which ones are investigated depends upon the conditions satisfied at the particular point in the game. So for example, in one tree there might be three branches with the labels 'set up hearts', 'take spade finesse' and 'cash all high cards'. In each sub-tree further sub-tasks are identified for achieving these goals.

At each stage, tasks are decomposed until primitive tasks that can be carried out directly are reached. This is based on classical planning schemes such as STRIPS [16] and NOAH [17] but modified to include multi-agents and uncertainty. The method had some success and was incorporated into Bridge Baron 8 [13], a popular commercial bridge playing system. It is a candidate, therefore, for learning by doing.

It also has strategies and tactics that are readily identifiable by humans. Smith et al list a number of techniques including finessing, ducking, and setting up *ruffs* that would be well-known to bridge players. Other plays such as end-plays and squeezes can be expressed in terms of the basic procedures. Because of its basic transparency, turning this into a teaching system would be relatively easy.

Variants of the STRIPS pre-conditions, add and delete operators are used to determine when strategies and tactics are applicable and what their effects will be. As described in Kemp and Smith [18] planning type scenarios such as these can readily be used to provide advice for learners, by telling them what they might do next, and what their intermediate goals should be. They can also be adapted to indicate to the user when something is going wrong.

Since Tignum works at the planning level, it should be relatively easy to incorporate metacognitive techniques: prompting users to encourage them to consider their plans, monitor their performance and reflect upon what they have achieved.

3.3 Logic-based methods

A number of groups have attempted to use a logic-based approach to modelling bidding and playing in bridge. One interesting approach, employed by Ando and Uehara [19], examines how an effective system for aiding bidding can be built using rules which can be both used to determine appropriate bids and to work out what one can expect from other players' bids.

This is done by expressing the rules in ECLiPSe, a constraint logic programming language which, unlike Prolog, can handle uninstantiated arithmetic expressions. This enables a rule to be used to determine what bid should be made, given a hand, or, alternatively, given a bid, to be able to store information indicating what the hand likely contains. This is very useful in bidding since one needs to be able to carry out both types of analysis. Whether it is an opponent or *partner* who makes a bid, one needs to be able to assess what values it will indicate.

For example Ando and Uehara give a rule for making an opening bid of one spade in a *bidding system* called Goren:

Opening_bid([1, spade], [[NS,NH,ND,NC], P, LT]) :-
  NS #>= 5,
  P #>= 13, P #< 21,
  LT #<= 7, LT #>= 5.

NS, NH, ND, NC denote the number of cards that a hand contains in each of the four suits, P is the total number of *high card points* and LT is the *losing trick count*. If the hand is known then each of the parameters can be instantiated and a check made to see if the rule succeeds, by evaluating the right hand side. Alternatively, if it is known that the bid is one spade then the system can store the right hand side as an expression that corresponds to the information known about the hand. Actual values can be determined later.

Bridge players generally use bidding systems, of which Goren is only one of many. These systems define rules and guidelines for what bids to make in what circumstances. This enables partnerships to communicate information efficiently and to set the scene for determining the final contract.

However, these systems are not detailed enough to deal with even a small proportion of different situations, particularly in a competitive auction where both *sides* are bidding. Here, it is often a case of trying to determine what the final contract might be that will maximize one's gains (or minimize one's losses). Often the bidding goes outside the scope of the bidding systems and a player has to base his/her actions on what the profits and losses might be for succeeding or failing in a contract, taking into account what is known about the partnership and opponent card holdings. Ando and Uehara have a separate set of rules for dealing with this kind of situation. They are called 'action rules' which select bids to make depending upon this knowledge.

The knowledge of the unseen hands comes from analysis of the earlier bidding rules, and of the later action rules as well, so the system has to build up a model of not only what it thinks the other players have, but also what the other players think it has. Depending upon which parameters are grounded, the action rules can either be used to determine an action, or to determine what other players possibly have.

This scheme provides an effective way of reaching a good contract but, because of its transparency, could quite easily form the basis of a coaching system for teaching bidding. Since the rules can be either used for determining bids or finding out what bids mean, this information could be conveyed to novices during the bidding to help them understand not only what the right bid is to make but also why. They can also be told what it is likely that the opponents have.

Ando and Uehara do not consider the repercussions of their approach to the playing phase but the two phases are very much interlinked. The more knowledge players have about the contents of other players' hands the better they can play or defend a contract. One classic text on defence [20] suggests in the introduction that any buyers who are not prepared to try to estimate what cards the opponents hold should take their copy of the book back to the retailer and try to get a refund.

Our work at Massey starts with the premise that an effective bridge tutoring system needs to be transparent and should be able to justify actions, and keep the student up-to-date with the current situation.

First of all, we needed to have an internal language for representing what is known. For this we adapted the specification system developed by Hans van Staveren [21]. He devised a method of describing features of bridge hands which could be input to a program which generates hands satisfying the criteria. This involves the use of a number of functions each of which specifies some aspect of the hand. Our version uses slightly different functions:

hcp(<hand>) - total number of high card points in the player's hand

hcp(<hand>, <suit>) - total number of hcps in a given suit in the hand

suitLength(<hand>, <suit>) - number of cards in that suit in the hand

hasCard(<hand>, <card>) - a predicate denoting that the given hand contains the specified card

Given certain pieces of information about a hand we can often infer further results. If for example, one piece of information tells us that North's hand has zero to fifteen points and another piece of information indicates that the hand contains ten to twenty then we can infer:

$$hcp\,(\,N\,) \in \{0..15\} \;\wedge\; hcp(\,N\,) \in \{10..20\} \rightarrow hcp(\,N\,) \in \{10..15\}$$

There are also various other facts that we know from the properties of the cards and the rules of the game. For example, all the points must add up to forty, so:

$$hcp\,(N\,) + hcp\,(\,S\,) + hcp\,(\,E\,) + hcp\,(\,W\,) = 40$$

From the two results above we can infer

$$hcp\,(\,S\,) + hcp\,(\,E\,) + hcp\,(\,W\,) \in \{25..30\}$$

If we look at the points in individual suits we can make similar kinds of inferences. For example, a *convention* called Ogust allows a player to effectively check whether their partner has at least two of the top three honours in a suit. If the answer is positive for the spade suit then we could assert:

hcp (N, ♠) ∈ {5..10}

and again this could be combined with other known facts, such as that there are only ten high card points in every suit, to make further assertions.

Another useful property of hands is the length of suits, particularly suits that are being considered as trumps. For example, a certain bidding system may require players to have at least five cards in a *major suit* before they can bid it. If North opens the bidding with spades then we could make the assumption:

suitLength (N, ♠) ≥ 5

Since there are only thirteen spades in the pack then we can infer that the other players' combined length in spades is less than 9.

Sometimes the hcp and suitLength functions can be used together. For example, if we know that South has, at most, two hearts, then South cannot have more than seven points in the suit (the ace, king). Thus, we can say:

suitLength(S, ♥) < 3 → hcp(S, ♥) ≤ 7

This can be generalized, of course, over all hands and over all suits:

∀h ∈ hands ∀s ∈ suits suitLength(h, s) < 3 → hcp(h, s) ≤ 7

Other results of a similar nature can be used, as well as complementary ones. For example, if we know that South has six or more points in a suit then South must have at least two cards in it.

The hasCard function similarly overlaps with the other functions and helps make valuable inferences. For example, if we know West has the queen of clubs and jack of clubs, then s/he has at least two clubs and has at least three high card points:

hasCard(W,Q,♣) ∧ hasCard(W,J,♣) → hcp(W,♣)≥3 ∧ suitLength(W,♣)≥2

Again, this and other similar results can be quantified over hands and suits. Good card players use all this kind of information all the time to help them 'read' the cards and even novices should start to think along these lines from an early stage.

Any observation can be justified in one of three ways:

A property of the visible hand(s)

An assumption based on a bid by an unseen hand

An inference made based on rules of arithmetic and of the game

What a teaching system can do is generate facts and inferences, storing them in a graph structure. Each of the 'facts' and inferences will be carefully labelled showing why they are believed to be correct. These facts can be used for making bids within the system, either directly via a set of rules, or by using some scheme of random generation of hands to work out the most likely bids.

Because of the incomplete information factor, we may have to store more than one alternative interpretation of an action or a bid. There is a well-known conventional bid in bridge which has a number of variations and is called 'the multi-two diamonds'. In one version of this convention, an opening bid of two diamonds has nothing to do with the diamond suit but shows a weak but long major suit. If East opens with this bid then we may make a note that:

$$\text{hcp}(E) \geq 6 \wedge \text{hcp}(E) \leq 10 \wedge (\text{suitLength}(E, \heartsuit) = 6 \vee \text{suitLength}(E, \spadesuit) = 6)$$

Simple inferencing, substitution and instantiating methods can be used to draw inferences from these kinds of observations. Alternatively, if we wish to check a conjecture then we can test whether our current knowledge can substantiate it, or what piece of information is missing.

Note that, since all quantified statements and functions are over finite domains they reduce to propositional logic form so theorem proving and checking are simple.

As observed earlier, the information gleaned during the bidding stage is invaluable for the actual playing. We have been looking particularly at the help that we can give novices in deciding upon an *opening lead*. The opening lead to a contract is made before dummy's cards are revealed and so the defender has only the contents of his/her own hand and the inferences from the bidding for guidance. In fact, it is one of the most crucial decisions a defender has to make, and can make or break a contract. Several books have been written on this aspect of the game alone. In our proposed system, learners see their own hand and the bidding that has taken place. Based on this, they have to decide a lead. First, they are required to think of a lead, and then they are asked what information they know about the other hands. They can check this against what the system has inferred from the bidding.

A further problem with incomplete information is that one of our 'facts' may turn out to be untrue. An opponent may make a bid or play that is inconsistent with their system, either in error or to deliberately confuse matters. There are whole books on the art of 'false carding', playing a card which is likely to mislead the opponents. Computer bridge programs are notoriously vulnerable to misinformation by the opponents or partner.

All we can do, is say that we can only be definite about the cards that we see in our hand and the ones that are revealed by other players. Only in special circumstances, often near the end of play of a hand can any player be absolutely certain about the positioning of every card. As noted earlier, however, even partial information can be vital for deciding upon the right bid or play.

For example, using defeasible logic [22] we might express the fact that South will normally have at least five cards in spades to bid the suit as:

$$\text{openingBid}(S, 1, \spadesuit) \Rightarrow \text{suitLength}(S, \spadesuit) \geq 5$$

We choose to believe this statement unless subsequent information contradicts it. It may be that other information based on this assumption will have to be reviewed as well. Schemes for updating networks of beliefs are well-known – see for example Martins' work [23].

As with the planning methods, the transparency of the logic techniques makes it relatively easy to consider a coaching approach where users can be given information on the likely current situation, why opponents have taken particular actions and what action they might take.

Metacognitive methods might also be employed in the logic approach. For example, in Ando and Uehara's system it might be used to keep a note via the action rules of what the goal contract might be. Also, we can monitor the behaviour during play, and assess the results at the end since we have a human-friendly trace of decisions and why they were made. We are working on the problem of providing scaffolding to show students what inferences they should be able to make. This will help them in their bidding and subsequent play.

4. Conclusion

We have considered various techniques that are used in attempting to get the computer to play a good game of bridge. Most of them have AI features that take into account the human player's state of incomplete knowledge. As a result, they all play games that a human player can follow and appreciate. However, many of them do not use strategies that a human would understand.

In bridge, as in many other activities, seeing the big picture and being able to relate to patterns which can be understood and utilized is important. The black box approach might be very effective for producing top-class bridge playing programs but has limited value in a teaching environment. Schemes which are perhaps less effective in real terms but have the transparency to be able to offer advice or support other teaching and learning approaches appear to have more potential in providing effective learning environments for those who wish to learn bridge using a computer.

References

1. Ginsberg, M., GIB: Imperfect Information in a Computationally Challenging Game. Journal of Artificial Intelligence Research, 2001. 14: pp. 303-358.
2. http://www.deepfinesse.com/dfentry.html accessed on 6 June 2005
3. Sleeman, D. and J.S. Brown, eds. Intelligent Tutoring Systems. 1982, Academic Press: London.
4. Hollan, J.D., E.L. Hutchins, and L.M. Weitzman, STEAMER: an interactive, inspectable, simulation-based training system. AI Magazine, 1984. 5: pp. 15-27.
5. de Kleer, J. and J.S. Brown, Mental models of physical mechanisms and their acquisition, in Cognitive Skills and their Acquisition, J.R. Anderson, Editor. 1981, Lawrence Erlbaum: Hillsdale, NJ. pp. 285-309.
6. Forbus, K., Qualitative Physics: Past, Present and Future, in Exploring Artificial Intelligence, H. Shrobe, Editor. 1988, Morgan Kaufmann: San Mateo, CA. pp. 239-296.
7. Collins, A., J.S. Brown, and S.E. Newman, Cognitive apprenticeship: teaching the crafts of reading, writing and mathematics, in Knowing, Learning and Instruction, L.B. Resnick, Editor. 1989, Lawrence Erlbaum Associates: Hillsdale, NJ. pp. 453-494.

8. Flavell, J.H., Cognitive Development., Englewood Cliffs, New Jersey: Prentice-Hall, 1977.

9. Hacker, D.J., Metacognition: Definition and Empirical Foundations. www.psyc.memphis.edu/trg/meta.htm accessed on 6 Jun 2005

10. Lajoie, S.P., R. Azevedo, and D.M. Fleiszer, Cognitive Tools for Assessment and Learning in a High Information Flow Environment. Journal of Educational Computing Research, 1998. 18(3): pp. 205 - 235.

11. Luckin, R. Ecolab: Exploring the construction of a Learning Assistant. in Intelligent Tutoring Systems: 4th International Conference, ITS'98. 1998: Springer. pp. 304 - 313.

12. Rebolledo-Mendez, G. Modelling the Motivational State of the Learner in a Vygotskyan Inspired ITS. in AIEd-2003 Proceedings of Young Researcher Track. 2003. Sydney: University of Sydney.

13. Smith, S.J.J., D.S. Nau, and T.A. Throop. Success in Spades: Using AI Planning Techniques to Win the World Championship of Computer Bridge. in IAAI-98/AAAI-98. 1998: AAAI. pp. 1079-1086.

14. Ginsberg, M.L. GIB: Steps Toward an Expert-Level Bridge-Playing Program. in Sixteenth International Joint Conference on Artificial Intelligence. 1999. Stockholm, Sweden: Morgan Kaufmann. pp. 584-593.

15. Smith, S.J.J., D.S. Nau, and T. Throop, A Planning Approach to Declarer Play in Contract Bridge. Computational Intelligence, 1996. 12(1): pp. 106-130.

16. Fikes, R.E. and N.J. Nilsson, STRIPS: a new approach to the application of theorem proving to problem solving. Artificial Intelligence, 1971. 2: pp. 189-208.

17. Sacerdoti, E.D., A Structure for Plans and Behaviour. Artificial Intelligence Series, ed. N.J. Nilsson. 1977, New York: Elsevier Computer Science Library.

18. Kemp, R.H. and S.P. Smith, Domain and task representation for tutorial process models. International Journal of Human-Computer Studies, 1994. 41: pp. 363-383.

19. Ando, T. and T. Uehara. Reasoning by Agents in Computer Bridge Bidding. in Second International Conference on Computers and Games. 2001: Springer Verlag. pp. 346 - 364.

20. Kelsey, H.W., Killing Defence at Bridge. 1966, London: Faber and Faber.

21. http://www.greatbridgelinks.com/gblSOFT/StaverensDealer-progr.html accessed on 6 Jun 2005

22. Nute, D., Defeasible logic, in Handbook of Logics in Artificial Intelligence and Logic Programming. 1994, Oxford University Press. pp. 353-395.

23. Martins, J.P., A Structure for Epistemic States, in New Directions for Intelligent Tutoring Systems, E. Costa, Editor. 1991, Springer-Verlag: Heidelberg. pp. 198-212.

24. http://www.ecatsbridge.org/Documents/files/Laws/1997%20Laws.pdf accessed on 26 August 2005

Glossary[3]

Auction – The first part of a deal, where bids are made in order to determine a contract.

Bid – An undertaking to win at least a specified number of odd tricks in a suit or with no trumps.

Bidding System – A scheme that a partnership employ to communicate information to each other about their hands. This is done by giving quite specific meanings to many of the bids, some of which may be conventional. Commonly used bidding systems include Acol and Goren.

Bridge – A card game for four players (two per side). Each deal has two phases, the auction and the play. In the auction, each side competes for the contract. In the second phase, one player (the declarer) from the side that has made the highest bid in the auction attempts to make the number of tricks specified in the contract. The opponents attempt to defeat the contract.

Call – Any bid or pass.

Contract – The undertaking by declarer's side to win, at the denomination named, the number of odd tricks specified in the final bid.

Convention – A call, that by partnership agreement, conveys a meaning other than willingness to play in the denomination named.

Deal - The hands distributed to each player and subsequent bidding and playing.

Declarer – The player who attempts to make the contract bid by his/her side.

Defender – An opponent of the declarer.

Denomination – Either a suit or no trumps.

Dummy – Declarer's partner during the playing part of the deal.

Hand – The cards originally dealt to a player, or the ones s/he has left.

High card points (hcps) – The Work Point Count of a hand.

Honour – Any Ace, King, Queen, Jack or Ten.

Lead – The first card played to a trick.

Losing Trick Count – An alternative method to the Work Point Count method of estimating the value of a hand. It takes into account the number of tricks the hand is likely to lose.

Major Suits – Hearts and spades.

Odd Trick – Each trick to be won by declarer's side in excess of six.

Opening Lead – The card that is led to the first trick.

---

[3] Based on [24]

Partner – The player with whom one plays as a side against the other two players (partners sit opposite one another).

Pass - A call specifying that a player does not, at that turn, elect to bid.

Play – The second part of a deal when players attempt to win tricks.

Ruff – The playing of a trump card when one does not have a card of the suit led.

Side – Two players who constitute a partnership against the other two players.

Suit – One of four groups of cards in the pack, each group comprising thirteen cards and having a characteristic symbol: spades (♠), hearts (♥), diamonds (♦), clubs (♣).

Trick – The unit by which the outcome of the contract is determined, consisting of four cards, one contributed by each player in rotation, beginning with the lead.

Trump – Each card of the suit (if any) named in the contract.

Work Point Count – the heuristic of evaluating a hand by counting each ace as 4 points, each king as three, each queen as two and each jack as one, and computing the sum.

Qualitative Representation and Reasoning with Uncertainty in Space and Time

Baher A. El-Geresy

School of Computing, University of Glamorgan

Treforest, Wales, UK

Alia I. Abdelmoty

Department of Computer Science

Cardiff University,

Cardiff, Wales, UK

Abstract

Imprecision, indeterminacy and vagueness are all terms which have been studied recently in studies of representations of entities in space and time. The interest has arisen from the fact that in many cases, precise information about objects in space are not available. In this paper a study of spatial uncertainty is presented and extended to temporal uncertainty. Different types and modes of uncertainty are identified. A unified framework is presented for the representation and reasoning over uncertain qualitative domains. The method addresses some of the main limitations of the current approaches. It is shown to apply to different types of entities with arbitrary complexity with total or partial uncertainty. The approach is part of a comprehensive research program aimed at developing a unified complete theory for qualitative spatial and temporal domains.

1   Introduction

The ability to handle a certain level of indeterminacy makes techniques of qualitative spatial reasoning (QSR) attractive to many application domains [Haa95, FM91, Liu69]. Precise information required in quantitative methods are sometimes neither available nor needed. For example, "vague" expressions of place names, locations and spatial relationships may be used in searches over large geographic databases, where in many cases exact positional information is not available or can't be expressed. Recently, the rapid development of wireless communication devices and sensor networks enabled the emergence of a wide variety of applications that require efficient access to and management of dynamic spatio-temporal data. In many such applications, data are generated at rapid rates and accepting " approximate" data is a strategy for reducing both data size and associated costs. Recently, there has been an upsurge on explicit representation of imprecise and indeterminate regions [CDF97]. Current approaches to representation and reasoning are mostly limited to handling simple entities in both the space and time dimensions. Proposals are generally extensions of existing approaches for representation in spatial and teporal domains and therefore tend to carry their limitations.

This paper starts with a study of the notion of qualitative uncertainty. Possible types and modes of uncertainty are identified. A uniform model of representation in uncertain spaces and time is then presented and examples are used to demonstrate its validity for random object types. A reasoning mechanism is proposed and applied for the composition of relations.

Types of Uncertainty Representation and reasoning formalisms for handling "crisp" objects have been proposed previously. In this work we introduce the different types of uncertainty that may exist in space and time. The 1d temporal domain is considered as a special case of the much richer 3D space. Hence, in what follows we provide a general view of uncertainty in space. Different spatial attributes can be associated with an object in 3D space to define, for example, its position, shape, configuration, orientation, etc. The accuracy of the representation of the object is directly dependent on the values of those attributes. To precisely define a spatial object, each of its associated properties must hold a unique value. However, this value may be one of a number of possible and correct values that can be associated with a spatial property. For example, Eiffel Tower as a place could be defined to be in Europe, in France, in Paris, or can be described exactly by its (x,y) map grid reference. Hence, spatial uncertainty of objects

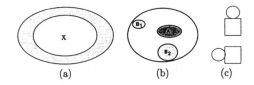

Figure 1: (a) Object extension uncertainty. (b) Configuration uncertainty. (c) Object orientation uncertainty

in space occurs when one or more spatial attribute associated with an object holds more than one of a set of possible values.

Different types of uncertainty can be defined as follows.

Positional uncertainty: where the precise location of an object or one of its constituting components is not certain. An example from the temporal domain is: "John came back from holiday last month".

Extension uncertainty: where the extent of the object's boundary or the boundary of one of its components is not certain, as shown in figure 1(a). The shaded ring in the figure represents the area within which the boundary may be found. This type of uncertainty is also applicable in the temporal domain.

Configuration uncertainty: where the specific components making up a composite spatial object and their number are not certain. Figure 1(b) shows a region with holes where it is not known whether the component holes are A and B_1 or A and B_2. An example of this type of uncertainty in the temporal domain is: Activity A should overlap or occur during activity B.

Orientation uncertainty: where the orientation of the object, or the orientation of one of its components is not certain as shown in figure 1(c). This type of uncertainty is not applicable in the 1D directed temporal domain.

Modes of Uncertainty

To illustrate the different modes of uncertainty, examples from the temporal domain are used, for the sake of simplicity of its one dimensional nature. Two modes of uncertainty can be distinguished, namely, discrete and range. An example of discrete uncertainty is stating that, "I will arrive at either 10 am or 11 am". An example of range uncertainty, is when the arrival time is defined by a range of ordered values, for example, "I will arrive between 10:00 am and 11:00 am". Examples of those modes in space are used later on in the paper. Note that all types of uncertainty listed above can exist in both the discrete and range modes.

2 Related work

Three possible models for representing uncertainty in space and time are fuzzy models, probabilistic models and exact models [ES97, BG00, BTM02, CM02, DFP96]. With exact models, "existing definitions, techniques, data stuctures, algorithms need not be redeveloped but modified or simply used .. " [ES97]. "Exact" approaches are generally based on one of two models of representation in space, namely, the Region-Connection-Calculus (RCC) [CG94, HC01, RS01, CDF97, CDF96b, CG94] and the Intersection-based approach [TN, Zha98, TJ, Sch01]. They deal mainly with simple convex regions and with range uncertainty over the boundary of those regions. In the temporal domain, most approaches are based on the work of Allen ??.

In the spatial domain the "egg and yolk" approach [CG96] uses an analogy for defining objects, where the difference between the egg and the yolk represents a range of uncertainty of the object's boundary. Different sets of relations have been identified for those objects; 46 relations in [CG96] using first order logic and 44 relations using the intersection-based approach [CDF96a]. Clementini et al [CDF97] added a further set of 12 relations for representing composite objects with indeterminate boundaries.

Other variations of the above methods have also been used to define the set of relations by considering the egg and yolk as crisp objects and then considering the combinatoric set of relations between them. In [HC01], the changes in the egg and yolk were considered for the purpose of defining a spatio-temporal interpretation of the method, for example, by noting the increase, decrease or the stability of the egg and yolk respectively.

In the fuzzy approaches, [TN] used an aggregate uncertainty with values of 1.0 and 0.5 concentric regions of core and support to define the set relations as above. In [Zha98], the fuzzy set was divided up into more than 2 concentric regions with values between 1 and 0. Some works have also addressed the definition of fuzzy complex regions [Sch01] and a degree of belief is assigned based on a ratio of representation of the characteristic feature, e.g. the area of overlap to the area of one of the objects. Applications of fuzzy relations has been demonstrated in [TJ] in the domain of guiding autonomous vehicle motion.

It is worth noting here that as far as known, no work in space has been reported on the other types of uncertainty, namely, orientation and spatial arrangements. Modes of uncertainty were mainly confined to range uncertainty and no work has addressed the discrete mode of uncertainty. Also, no methods have yet been proposed to the composition of relations in uncertain space.

3 Representation of Uncertainty of object Properties

An exact modelling approach is adopted here. In this section a representation scheme for the different types and modes of spatial and temporal uncertainty is presented. The method is based on and extends the approach proposed in [BA97] for representing crisp spatial and temporal objects. Figure 2(a) is an example of the representation of a simple object using this method. Objects of interest and their embedding space are divided into components according to a required resolution. The connectivity of those components is explicitly represented. In the decomposition strategy, the complement of the object in question is considered to be infinite, and the suffix 0, e.g. (x_0) is used to represent this component. Object x in figure 2(a) is composed of three components, namely, x_1; an areal component representing the object's interior, x_2; a linear component representing the object's boundary, and x_0, the rest of the embedding space. In what follows, examples of representation of objects with spatial uncertainty are given.

3.1 Representation of Object Location uncertainty

Discrete location uncertainty can be represented by placing a copy of the object in each of the possible values of the uncertain location, as shown in figure 2(b) for spatial and temporal objects respectively. In the figure, object x is represented by both copies x' and x''. Using the representation scheme as above, the space containing both copies is represented by the intersection of their respective components. The intersection of x' and x'' is a definite part of the component x_1. The rest of both x' and x'' can be either x_1 or x_0, and hence is labelled $(x_1 \vee x_0)$. Similarly, different parts of objects' boundaries can be labelled according to whether their comprising points are possibly part of either x_1 or x_2 or x_0 as shown in figure 2(c).

If the locations of x' and x'' represents the bounds of a range uncertainty as shown in figure 2(d), the representation changes to include the boundary as one of the possible components inside the two circles and between the circles and their tangents as shown. Also, the two points representing certain points on the boundary x_2 do not exist any longer.

3.2 Representation of object extension uncertainty

A decomposition scheme in the case of range uncertainty is shown in figure 3(a) where the boundary x_2 of x can exist anywhere between $(x_1 \vee x_2)$ and $(x_2 \vee x_0)$. It is interesting to note that all related work on uncertainty of space [] was concerned mainly with range uncertainty over simple convex regions. Note that if the boundaries of vagueness, i.e. $(x_1 \vee x_2)$ and $(x_0 \vee x_2)$ are not known (opensets) then uncertainty

348

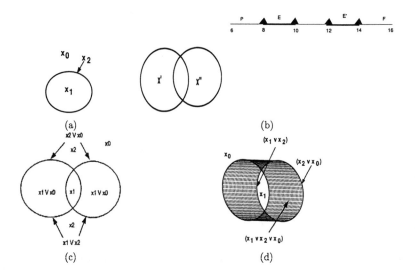

Figure 2: (a) Topology of objects represented by components. (b) and (c) Discrete location uncertainty. (d) Range uncertainty.

in this case is represented as in figure 3(b) where the limiting boundaries are omitted and the object is represented by two components, x_1 and x_0. This representation is used in [CG96, CDF96a].

An example of discrete uncertainty of object's extension is shown in figure 3(c) where the boundary can exist either at $(x_1 \vee x_2)$ or $(x_2 \vee x_0)$. The area in-between must be either x_1 or x_2.

In the case of a combined location and extension uncertainty the representation in figure 3(d) is used where there are no assigned regions for x_1 only.

Partial uncertainty in the case of convex region is represented as in figure 4(a) where part of the boundary is definite (x_2) and the rest is bounded between ($x_1 \vee x_2$) and ($x_2 \vee x_0$). A similar partial range uncertainty in case of concave object is shown in figure 4(b) where the mode is discrete partial uncertainty since it's only the boundary of concavity which is under uncertainty.

4   Temporal Uncertainty

The approach presented in this paper can be used to represent uncertainty in the temporal domain. In figure 8(a), a temporal interval is shown embedded in a directed on-dimensional space, with two semi-infinite lines representing the past P and future F of the interval. The interval itself is decomposed into three components, two points s and e, representing its start and end and an open line d representing its duration.

Different types of uncertainty can be represented in a similar fashion as before. For example, a temporal interval with uncertainty over its start and end states is shown in figure 8(b). An example of this case is: "the event will start between 9 and 10 and ends between 1 and 2". Similarly , figure 8(c) is an example of partial discrete uncertainty. Here, the case represented is: "the event will start between 9 and 10 and ends at 1".

The reasoning method proposed can therefore be extended homogeneously to the temporal dimension. Finding a common approach for the representation and reasoning over space and time provides an opportunity for integrating of the temporal dimension in the management of spatial data.

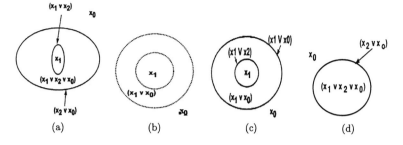

Figure 3: (a), (b), (c) Extent-Discrete uncertainty. (d) Combined location and extension uncertainty

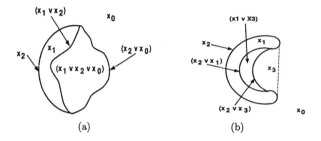

Figure 4: (a) Partial Extent uncertainty. (b) Partial Extent-Range uncertainty.

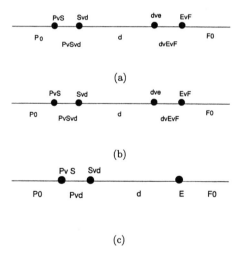

Figure 5: (a) A temporal interval. (b) and (c) Example of temporal intervals with uncertainty.

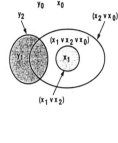

	y_1	y_2	y_0
x_1	0	0	1
$x_1 \vee x_2$	0	0	1
$x_1 \vee x_2 \vee x_0$	1	1	1
$x_2 \vee x_0$	1	1	1
x_0	1	1	1

(a)   (b)

Figure 6: (a) Relationship between a range-uncertain object x and a crisp object y (b) Corresponding intersection matrices.

5 Representation of Spatial Relations in Uncertain Spaces

In this section, the representation of the topological relations through the intersection of their components is adopted and generalized for objects with spatial uncertainty. The complete set of spatial relationships are identified by combinatorial intersection of the components of one space with those of the other space.

If $R(x, y)$ is a relation of interest between objects x and y, and X and Y are the spaces associated with the objects respectively such that m is the number of components in X and l is the number of components in Y, then a spatial relation $R(x, y)$ can be represented by one instance of the following equation:

$$
\begin{aligned}
R(x, y) &= X \cap Y \\
&= \left(\bigcup_{i=1}^{m} x_i \right) \cap \left(\bigcup_{j=1}^{l} y_j \right) \\
&= (x_1 \cap y_1, \cdots, x_1 \cap y_l, x_2 \cap y_1, \cdots, x_m \cap y_l)
\end{aligned}
$$

The intersection $x_i \cap y_j$ can be an empty or a non-empty intersection. The above set of intersections shall be represented by an intersection matrix, as follows,

$$
R(x, y) =
$$

	y_0	y_1	y_2	$\cdots$
x_0				
x_1				
x_2				
$\vdots$				

Different combinations in the intersection matrix can represent different qualitative relations. The set of valid or sound spatial relationships between objects is dependent on the particular domain studied.

Example: Range Extent Uncertainty Relations

Consider the relationship between objects x and y in figure 6(a). Object x is spatially vague, with range uncertainty mode. Object y is crisp. The intersection matrix representing the relationship is shown in 6(b). The intersection matrix can be rewritten by mapping the components uncertainty into intersections relation uncertainty between crisp objects in figure 7(a). On comparing the matrix with the set of of 8 relations between two simple crisp regions, a different representation of the relation in 6(a) can be described as a disjunctive set of relations {$disjoint \vee touch \vee overlap$} as shown in figure 7(b).

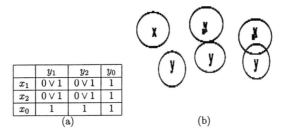

	y_1	y_2	y_0
x_1	$0 \vee 1$	$0 \vee 1$	1
x_2	$0 \vee 1$	$0 \vee 1$	1
x_0	1	1	1

(a)   (b)

Figure 7: (a) Mapped intersection relation. (b) Possible relations.

5.1 Representation of Temporal Relations in Uncertain Space

In the above section it was shown how range and discrete uncertainty can be represented using disjunctive sets of components. In this section, we consider the representation of relations between two uncertain events where the uncertainty is discrete and partial.

Consider the following scenario: "John arrived at the party between 7pm and 8pm and left at 11:00 pm. Alice arrived either before or after John and left at 10:30 pm.". Figure 8(a) depicts this scenario in graphical form and the intersection matrix of the temporal relations is shown in figure 8(b).

6 Reasoning with Uncertainty

The reasoning approach consists of: a) general constraints to govern the spatial relationships between objects in space, and b) general rules to propagate relationships between the objects.

6.0.1 General Reasoning Rules

Composition of spatial relations is the process through which the possible relationship(s) between two object x and z is derived given two relationships: R_1 between x and y and R_2 between y and z. Two general reasoning rules for the propagation of intersection constraints are presented. The rules are characterized by the ability to reason over spatial relationships between objects of arbitrary complexity in any space dimension. These rules allow for the automatic derivation of the composition (transitivity)tables between any spatial shapes.

Rule 1: Propagation of Non-Empty Intersections

Let $x' = \{x_1, x_2, \cdots, x_{m'}\}$ be a subset of the set of components of space X whose total number of components is m and $m' \leq m$; $x' \subseteq X$. Let $z' = \{z_1, z_2, \cdots, z_{n'}\}$ be a subset of the set of components of space Z whose total number of components is n and $n' \leq n$; $z' \subseteq Z$. If y_j is a component of space Y, the following is a governing rule of interaction for the three spaces X, Y and Z.

$$
\begin{aligned}
(x' \sqsupseteq y_j) \quad &\wedge \quad (y_j \sqsubseteq z') \\
&\rightarrow \quad (x' \cap z' \neq \phi) \\
&\equiv \quad (x_1 \cap z_1 \neq \phi \vee \cdots \vee x_1 \cap z_{n'} \neq \phi) \\
&\qquad \wedge (x_2 \cap z_1 \neq \phi \vee \cdots \vee x_2 \cap z_{n'} \neq \phi) \\
&\qquad \wedge \cdots \\
&\qquad \wedge (x_{m'} \cap z_1 \neq \phi \vee \cdots \vee x_{m'} \cap z_{n'} \neq \phi)
\end{aligned}
$$

The above rule states that if the component y_j in space Y has a positive intersection with every component from the sets x' and z', then each component of the set x' must intersect with at least one component of the set z' and vice versa.

352

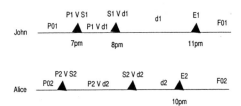

(a)

	P_{01}	$P_1 \vee S_1$	$P_1 \vee d_1$	$S_1 \vee d_1$	d_1	E_1	f_{01}
P_{01}	1	0	0	0	0	0	0
$P_2 \vee S_2$	1	0	0	0	0	0	0
$P_2 \vee d_2$	1	1	1	1	1	0	0
$s_2 \vee d_2$	0	0	0	0	1	0	0
d_2	0	0	0	0	1	0	0
E_2	0	0	0	0	1	0	0
f_{02}	0	0	0	0	1	1	1

(b)

Figure 8: (a) Graphical representation of sample uncertain temporal events. (b) Corresponding intersection matrix.

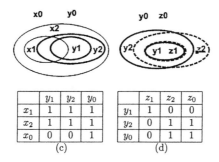

	y_1	y_2	y_0
x_1	1	1	1
x_2	1	1	1
x_0	0	0	1

	z_1	z_2	z_0
y_1	1	0	0
y_2	0	1	1
y_0	0	1	1

(c) (d)

Figure 9: (a) and (b) Spatial relationships between vague regions x, y and z. (c) and (d) Corresponding intersection matrices.

The constraint $x_i \cap z_1 \neq \phi \lor x_i \cap z_2 \neq \phi \cdots \lor x_i \cap z_{n'} \neq \phi$ can be expressed in the intersection matrix by a label, for example the label a_r ($r = 1$ or 2) in the following matrix indicates $x_1 \cap (z_2 \cup z_4) \neq \phi$ (x_1 has a positive intersection with z_2, or with z_4 or with both). A $-$ in the matrix indicates that the intersection is either positive or negative.

	z_1	z_2	z_3	z_4	$\cdots$	z_n
x_1	$-$	a_1	$-$	a_2	$-$	$-$

Rule 1 represents the propagation of non-empty intersections of components in space. A different version of the rule for the propagation of empty intersections can be stated as follows.

Rule 2: Propagation of Empty Intersections

Let $z' = \{z_1, z_2, \cdots, z_{n'}\}$ be a subset of the set of components of space Z whose total number of components is n and $n' < n$; $z' \subset Z$. Let $y' = \{y_1, y_2, \cdots, y_{l'}\}$ be a subset of the set of components of space Y whose total number of components is l and $l' < l$; $y' \subset Y$. Let x_i be a component of the space X. Then the following is a governing rule for the spaces X, Y and Z.

$$(x_i \sqsubseteq y') \land (y' \sqsubseteq z')$$
$$\rightarrow (x_i \cap (Z - z_1 - z_2 \cdots - z_{n'}) = \phi)$$

6.1 Example: Reasoning with Range Extent Uncertainty

In [CDF01], Clementini et al defined a set of 44 possible relations between objects with undetermined boundaries (range extension uncertainty). In this example, we use two of those relations, shown in figure 9, to demonstrate the composition of spatial relationships in uncertain spaces. In [CDF01] objects were represented using three components, of boundary, interior and exterior. Using the proposed representation methodology above, objects are represented by the three components: $\{x_1, (x_1 \lor x_0), x_0\}$ as shown in figure 3(b), where the broad boundary is represented by the disjunctive set of possible components. In this example, x_2 is used to represent $(x_1 \lor x_0)$.

The reasoning rules are used to propagate the intersections between the components of objects x and z as follows. From rule 1 we have,

- y_1 intersections:

$$\{x_1, x_2\} \sqsupseteq y_1 \quad \land \quad y_1 \sqsubseteq \{z_1\}$$
$$\rightarrow x_1 \cap z_1 \neq \phi \land x_2 \cap z_1 \neq \phi$$

- y_2 intersections:

$$\{x_1, x_2\} \sqsupseteq y_2 \quad \land \quad y_2 \sqsubseteq \{z_2, z_0\}$$
$$\rightarrow x_1 \cap (z_2 \cup z_0) \neq \phi \land x_2 \cap (z_2 \cup z_0) \neq \phi$$

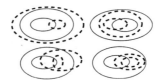

Figure 10: Possible configurations for the composition in figure 8.

- y_0 intersections:

$$\{x_1, x_2, x_0\} \sqsupseteq y_0 \quad \wedge \quad y_0 \sqsubseteq \{z_2, z_0\}$$
$$\rightarrow \quad x_1 \cap (z_2 \cup z_0) \neq \phi \wedge x_2 \cap (z_2 \cup z_0) \neq \phi$$
$$\wedge \quad x_0 \cap (z_2 \cup z_0) \neq \phi$$

Refining the above constraints, we get the following intersection matrix.

	z_1	z_2	z_0
x_1	1	a_1, c_1	a_2, d_1
x_2	1	b_1, c_2	b_2, d_2
x_0	0	?	1

Where a_1 and a_2 represent the constraint $x_1 \cap (z_2 \vee z_0) = 1$ and b_1 and b_2 represent the constraint $x_2 \cap (z_2 \vee z_0) = 1$, c_1 and c_2 represent the constraint $z_2 \cap (x_1 \vee x_2) = 1$ and d_1 and d_2 represent the constraint $z_0 \cap (x_1 \vee x_2) = 1$ and the ? represents $(1 \vee 0)$. The result matrix corresponds to one of four possible relationships between x and z, namely numbers 21, 22, 23 and 25, as shown in 10.

Reasoning with temporal uncertainty is handled in a similar way to reasoning in the spatial domain above, where spatial components are substituted with components in the temporal domain.

7 Conclusions

In this paper, uncertainty in space and time is studied. Four types of spatial uncertainty were identified, related to the different spatial properties of objects, namely, positional, extension, configuration and orientation. The first three types are applicable in the temporal domain. The concept of the "mode" of uncertainty was also introduced. Spatial and temporal uncertainty operates in two different modes, namely, discrete and range. Related approached have addressed the range uncertainty mode and were generally limited to handling simple object types, such as convex regions and intervals. No work has addressed the problem of reasoning with uncertainty. In this paper, an exact approach to the representation of uncertain space is proposed. The model is flexible and handles the different types and modes of uncertainty homogeneously. The approach can also be used is situations of partial uncertainty of objects and relations. The representation method is complemented with a general reasoning formalism to propagate different types of relations in uncertain spaces. Extending of the method to the temporal dimension has also been demonstrated. Work is in progress for further developing the methods and their realisation for spatio-temporal domains.

References

[BA97]   El-Geresy B.A. and Abdelmoty A.I. Order in Space: A General Formalism for Spatial Reasoning. *Int. J. on Artificial Intelligence Tools*, 6(4):423–450, 1997.

[BG00]   S. Badaloni and M. Giacomin. A fuzzy extension of allen's interval algebra. *LNAI*, 1792:155–165, 2000.

[BTM02] A. Bosch, M. Torres, and R. Marin. Reasoning with disjunctive fuzzy temporal constraint networks. In *Proc. of TIME 2002*, pages 36–43, UK, 2002.

[CDF96a] E. Clementini and P. Di Felice. An Algebraic Model for Spatial Objects with Indeterminate Boundaries. In P.A. Burrough and A.U. Frank, editors, *Geographic Objects with Indeterminate Boundaries*, GISDATA, pages 155–169. Taylor & Francis, 1996.

[CDF96b] E. Clementini and P. Di Felice. An Algebraic Model for Spatial Objects with Undetermined Boundaries. In *GISDATA Specialist Meeting: Spatial Conceptual Models for Geographic Objects with Undetermined Boundaries*. Taylor & Francis, 1996.

[CDF97]   E. Clementini and P. Di Felice. Approximate topological relations. *International Journal of Approximate Reasoning*, 16:173–204, 1997.

[CDF01]   E. Clementini and P. Di Felice. A spatial model for complex objects with a broad boundary supporting queries on uncertain data. *Data & Knowledge Engineering*, 37(3):285–305, 2001.

[CG94]   A.G. Cohn and N.M. Gotts. Expressing Spatial Vagueness in Terms of Connection. In *GISDATA Specialist Meeting: Spatial Conceptual Models for Geographic Objects with Undetermined Boundaries*. Taylor & Francis, 1994.

[CG96]   A.G. Cohn and N.M. Gotts. The "Egg-Yolk" Representation of Regions with Indeterminate Boundaries. In P.A. Burrough and A.U. Frank, editors, *Geographic Objects with Indeterminate Boundaries, GISDATA*, pages 171–187. Taylor & Francis, 1996.

[CG94]   A. Cohn and N. Gotts. A theory of spatial regions with indeterminate boundaries. In *Topological Foundations of Cognitive Science*, 94.

[CM02]   M.A. Cardenas and R. Marin. Syntax and semantics for a fuzzy temporal constraint logic. *Annals of Mathematics and Artificial Intelligence*, 36:357–380, 2002.

[DFP96]   D. Dubois, H. Fargier, and H. Prade. Possibility theory in constraint satisfaction problems: Handling priority, preference and uncertainty. *Applied Intelligence*, 6:287–309, 1996.

[ES97]   M. Erwig and M. Schneider. Vague Regions. In *Proc. of the 5th Int. Symposium on Large Spatial Databases, (SSD'97)*, pages 298–320. Springer Verlag LNCS-1262, 1997.

[FM91]   H. Fujihara and A. Mukerjee. Qualitative Reasoning about Document Design. Technical report, Texas University, 1991.

[IIaa95]   V. Haarslev. Formal Semantics of Visual Languages using Spatial Reasoning. In *Proceedings of the IEEE Symp. on Visual Languages*, pages 156–163, 1995.

[HC01]   S.M. Hazarika and A.G. Cohn. Taxonomy of spatio-temporal vagueness: An alternative egg-yolk interpretation. In *Joint COSIT-FOIS Workshop on Spatial Vagueness, Uncertainty and Granularity*, Maine, USA, 2001.

[Liu69]   J. Liu. Spatial Reasoning about Robot Complaint Movements and Optimal Paths in Qualitatively Modeled Environments. *International Journal of Robotics Research*, 15(2):181–210, 1969.

[RS01]   A.J.O. Roy and J.G. Stell. Spatial Relations between Indeterminate Regions. *International Journal of Approximate Reasoning*, 27(3):205–234, 2001.

[Sch01]   Markus Schneider. A design of topological predicates for complex crisp and fuzzy regions. *Lecture Notes in Computer Science*, 2224:103–116, 2001.

[TJ]   Eddie Tunstel and Mo Jamshidi. Fuzzy relational representation of uncertain spatial maps for autonomous vehicles.

[TN]   Erlend Tssebro and Mads Nygrd. An advanced discrete model for uncertain spatial data.

[Zha98]   F.B. Zhan. Approximate analysis of binary topological relations between geographic regions with indeterminate boundaries. *Soft Computing*, 2:28–34, 1998.

AUTHOR INDEX